Cindy L. Miller-Perrin & Robin D. Perrin

Child Maltreatment

An Introduction

SAGE Publications
International Educational and Professional Publisher
Thousand Oaks London New Delhi

For information:

SAGE Publications, Inc.
2455 Teller Road
Thousand Oaks, California 91320
E-mail: order@sagepub.com

SAGE Publications Ltd.
6 Bonhill Street
London EC2A 4PU
United Kingdom

SAGE Publications India Pvt. Ltd.
M-32 Market
Greater Kailash I
New Delhi 110 048 India

Printed in the United States of America

Library of Congress Cataloging-in-Publication Data

Miller-Perrin, Cindy L. (Cindy Lou), 1962-
Child maltreatment: An introduction / by Cindy L. Miller-Perrin and Robin D. Perrin.
p. cm.
Includes bibliographical references and index.
ISBN 0-7619-1577-X (cloth: alk. paper)
ISBN 0-7619-1578-8 (pbk: alk. paper)
1. Child abuse—United States. I. Perrin, Robin D. II. Title.
HV6626.52 .M545 1999
362.76'0973—dc21 99-6011

99 00 01 02 03 10 9 8 7 6 5 4 3 2 1

Acquiring Editor: C. Terry Hendrix
Editorial Assistant: Pat Mayer
Production Editor: Diana E. Axelsen
Editorial Assistant: Karen Wiley
Designer: Christina M. Hill
Typesetter: Marion Warren
Indexer: Virgil Diodato
Cover Designer: Ravi Balasuriya

Brief Contents

Detailed Contents

Preface

The history of childhood is a nightmare from which we have only recently begun to awaken. The further back in history one goes, the lower the level of child care, and the more likely children are to be killed, abandoned, beaten, terrorized, and sexually abused.

deMause, 1974, p. 1

Even a cursory examination of history reminds us that child maltreatment is not a new phenomenon. It has probably existed in families since the beginning of time. The mistreatment of children, however, did not receive serious attention as a social problem until the child-saving movement of the mid- to late 1800s. The research community essentially ignored the problem until the 1960s, when Colorado physician Dr. C. Henry Kempe first publicized his research on the multiple bone fractures appearing in the X rays of abused children.

Since the discovery of child maltreatment in the 1960s, progress in the field has been rapid, as many grassroots organizations, mental health professionals, university researchers, lawmakers, medical personnel, criminal justice workers, and the media have mobilized their efforts to understand the problem. The combined efforts of these groups have led to a growing national concern about child maltreatment. Today, with news coverage of highly publicized cases, cover stories in magazines, television programs, and movies, we are familiar with child maltreatment. Although the media exposure has helped make people more aware, much is still unknown about this complex and multifaceted problem.

It is our hope that this book, *Child Maltreatment: An Introduction,* will serve us all in our attempt to "discover" and understand this serious social problem. We, as authors, want to continue to bring the topic into the mainstream of public knowledge. To achieve these goals, we have drawn together a voluminous research literature that describes the magnitude, consequences, and explanations of child maltreatment. We also discuss the professional and social response to child maltreatment, in hopes of furthering our understanding of how to treat child maltreatment victims and how to prevent child maltreatment.

The information in this volume is organized to present a broad overview and summary of research findings. Throughout the book, we have attempted to keep our commitment to responsible scholarship and have made every attempt to control our own biases when presenting research on controversial topics. We have tried to cultivate the reader's interest by highlighting a number of current controversies within boxed inserts. Six chapters begin with an interview of a nationally or internationally known expert, providing an example of the variety of philosophies and training typical of the many professionals working in the field of child maltreatment. For readers who are interested in obtaining further details on specific topics, additional references and resources can be found in appendixes at the end of the book.

It is, perhaps, only fair to acknowledge that our ultimate goal is a lofty one: We hope that we have presented the content in such a way that readers can find their own personal roles in the struggle to end child maltreatment. Child maltreatment is a pervasive problem that affects families and communities all over the world. An effective response to the problem will require the commitment of many individuals from a variety of segments within society. We hope that this text will increase understanding about child maltreatment and motivate readers to join the effort to combat this problem.

We have many people to thank for their contributions to this text. First, we wish to acknowledge C. Terry Hendrix, senior editor at Sage Publications, as well as the other involved staff at Sage. This is our second opportunity to work with Sage, and through both the expected and the unexpected, Terry has always been encouraging and helpful. He is absolutely marvelous to work with and is a true leader in the battle to end child maltreatment. We also wish to thank Ann West for her support, guidance, and perceptive comments. The reviewers deserve everlasting praise for their careful reading of the text. We learned much from their insights. We are also indebted to the scholars who granted us permission to interview them, for their willingness to be involved in this project and for their contributions to the field.

Finally, we want to thank our friends, colleagues, and students at Pepperdine University. We are so fortunate to be able to work in a supportive environment and with such caring people. Special thanks go to Steve Monsma, the chair of our division, who continues to encourage us in our work, and to Melissa Houghton, who tackled many a cumbersome task for us, often on short notice.

1

History and Definitions of Child Maltreatment

CHAPTER OUTLINE

August 3, 1998: *St. Petersburg Times*

A 2-year-old girl died of massive brain injuries after her mother's 20-year-old boyfriend violently shook her. The boyfriend was baby-sitting at the time while the girl's mother attended parenting classes.

August 4, 1998: *Orlando Sentinel*

The stepmother of an 8-year-old girl was charged with aggravated child abuse and domestic violence after she scalded the child with boiling water. The girl had severe blistering from the burns on the forehead, face, and neck. The stepmother reportedly threw the hot water on the girl because she continued to lie after being punished.

August 5, 1998: *Pittsburgh Post-Gazette*

A mother (age 17) and father (age 20) were arrested on charges of child abuse and neglect after one of their 8-month-old twin sons died of malnutrition. The other twin was severely malnourished but survived and was placed in foster care.

August 6, 1998: *Los Angeles Times*

A 2-year-old boy was severely beaten in a North Hollywood apartment. The boy suffered severe physical injuries including a split liver, broken ribs, and massive internal bleeding. The boy's father is a key suspect in the beating.

August 7, 1998: *Pittsburgh Post-Gazette*

A man was sentenced to 10 years in prison and lifetime parole for sexually assaulting a 6-year-old girl repeatedly during a 1-year period. The perpetrator had a previous conviction for fondling a mentally disabled teenager during an 18-month period.

August 8, 1998: *Los Angeles Times*

A 40-year-old stepfather pleaded guilty to aggravated sexual abuse after raping his 11-year-old stepson and forcing him to pose for pornographic photographs and video. The stepfather reportedly threatened to hurt his stepson's mother if he did not comply with his sexual requests. The boy reported that he withstood the abuse in an attempt to protect his mother and younger sister.

August 9, 1998: *Sun-Sentinel*

An 18-year-old woman was charged for the murder of her 2-year-old daughter. The little girl died after being taken off life support following a severe blow to her head. The mother told authorities that her daughter was injured after falling from the roof of a car, but the sheriff's deputies did not believe the mother's story.

The newspaper excerpts above represent a sample of the stories that appeared across the United States for the week of August 3, 1998, through August 9, 1998. What do these accounts tell? First, they remind us that child maltreatment is a human tragedy. Reading about violence and abuse is often unsettling, but it is especially heart-wrenching when the victims are helpless, as children typically are. Child maltreatment is also tragic because more times than not, children are victimized by their own family members—the very people charged with providing the care and nurturance necessary for healthy development. In most of the cases above, the maltreatment was committed by a child's parents or caregiver, a pattern consistently supported by research evidence (e.g., Department of Health and Human Services [DHHS], 1996, 1998).

These newspaper stories also remind us that child maltreatment is a pervasive problem touching the lives of thousands of parents and children each year. The seven stories here represent only a fraction of the cases in U.S. papers the first week of August 1998. Furthermore, most child maltreatment occurring that week, especially in less serious form, was never reported in the nation's newspapers. Most child maltreatment remains hidden inside the home.

These news accounts also illustrate the diverse forms of child maltreatment. The story of the 8-year-old girl who was scalded by boiling water, for example, illustrates a case of physical child abuse by a caregiver. Child sexual abuse can include a variety of behaviors such as fondling (the August 7 story), rape, or child pornography (the August 8 story). Child neglect, the most common form of child maltreatment, is illustrated by the story of the twin boys who were not provided with adequate nutrition. Although not addressed in any of the newspaper stories, an additional form of child maltreatment will be a focus of this book—psychological maltreatment.

Newspaper accounts are limited, however, in how well they teach us all there is to know about child maltreatment. News media accounts of child maltreatment are not always representative of typical cases encountered by child protective services (CPS), social workers, law enforcement professionals, psychologists, and physicians. Nor can newspaper accounts provide the depth of understanding necessary to comprehend the complex nature of child maltreatment. If we hope to understand the causes, consequences, and solutions of child maltreatment, in its various forms, we must examine the topic more comprehensively.

In this book, we attempt to provide the reader with accurate, empirically based information. After completing the final chapter, the reader should have a good understanding of issues associated with defining child maltreatment, estimates of the problem, physical and psychological consequences of child maltreatment, various theories that attempt to explain child maltreatment, and methods for treating and preventing child maltreatment. We begin this first chapter by considering two important introductory questions: When (and how) did child maltreatment come to be recognized as a social problem? How is child maltreatment defined?

CHILDREN AS VICTIMS

We are the parents of two children, and we, like most parents, take extraordinary measures to protect our children from the problems of this world. We place restrictions on what they can and cannot watch on television, we talk to them about safety, and we protect them from high-risk situations. Research suggests, however, that despite the efforts of thousands upon thousands of parents such as ourselves, children often are victims in this world. For serious crimes such as rape, assault, and robbery, National Crime Victimization data suggest that victimization rates are two to three times higher for 12- to 19-year-olds than for adults (Finkelhor & Dziuba-Leatherman, 1994). Approximately one in five prison inmates reports having victimized a child (Greenfield, 1996).

No doubt these child victimization rates reflect that teens are especially likely to be the victims and perpetrators of crime (teens are the most criminal subpopulation of Americans), yet even for younger children, the victimization rates are shocking (Finkelhor & Dziuba-Leatherman, 1995). Approximately 16% of all rape victims, for example, are under the age of 12 (Langan & Harlow, 1994). Among violent child victimizers serving time in state prisons, more than half report committing crimes against children 12 or younger (Greenfield, 1996).

> Approximately 16% of all rape victims are under the age of 12.

Why are children so overrepresented in victimization data? One obvious reason is that children are physically dependent on adults. They cannot choose their associations, and they cannot retaliate when they are victimized (Finkelhor & Dziuba-Leatherman, 1994). This vulnerability is especially evident within the family. Research consistently suggests that children are more likely to be assaulted, or to witness assault, *in their own homes* than they are on the most violent of American streets (Bachman & Saltzman, 1996; Hotaling, Straus, & Lincoln, 1990; Straus, Gelles, & Steinmetz, 1980). Among prison inmates who have committed crimes against children, approximately one third indicate the victim was *their own child* (Greenfield, 1996). Overall, about 20% of all child murders are committed by a family member, and 50% of murders of young children (under the age of 10) are committed by family members. The Department of Health and Human Services (1998) estimated that in 1996, approximately 1,077 children died as a result of abuse or neglect. The overwhelming majority of these children (82%) were under the age of 5, and 43% were under the age of 1 at the time of death.

In many ways, these data reflect only the tip of the iceberg of the actual amount of child maltreatment. Only a small percentage of child abuse, of course, results in death, and most parents who abuse or neglect their children are not charged with crimes. Child maltreatment most commonly consists of less severe acts of violence and emotional abuse that affect hundreds of thousands of children each year. Current figures estimate that 3,195,000 reports of child maltreatment were received by social service agencies in 1997 (Wang & Daro, 1998). This figure includes *reports* (i.e., accusations) for physical and sexual abuse, neglect, and psychological maltreatment. Because many of these reports eventually go unsubstantiated, one might be tempted to conclude that 3.19 million is an overestimate. It is much more likely, however, that because most child maltreatment is never reported, these figures significantly underestimate the actual amount of maltreatment in society. Another factor that contributes to underestimation is that child maltreatment involves more than just violent interactions between a parent and a child, and nonviolent abusive interactions (e.g., verbal abuse) are especially unlikely to be reported to authorities. Indeed, anonymous surveys of parental disciplinary strategies report significantly higher rates of child maltreatment (Straus, Hamby, Finkelhor, Moore, & Runyan, 1998).

As child advocates, we argue that it is important to consider the victimization of children and to emphasize the need for societal intervention and protection of our most vulnerable citizens. As child advocates, we are strongly motivated by this purpose. For those who are not so motivated by this purpose, however, we offer a more practical rationale for studying the victimization of children. It is possible that child maltreatment, which clearly results from social ills, may also be a possible cause of these ills. We argue that rather than seeing family maltreatment and other social ills as separate entities, we need to view them as causally interconnected.

Some evidence for a causal connection between family violence and societal violence, for example, has arisen from studies showing that men who are violent in the home are especially likely to be violent outside the home (e.g., Hotaling et al., 1990; Shields, McCall, & Hanneke, 1988). In a 4-year longitudinal study of 1,000 adolescents conducted by the Office of Juvenile Justice and Delinquency Prevention (OJJDP, 1995), 38% of youths from nonviolent families reported perpetration of some type of violence; by contrast, 78% of youths exposed to maltreatment, violence by parents, and a general family climate of hostility reported perpetration of violent acts. When compared with children who are not victimized, children who are victims of assault within the family are more likely to be adult murderers, rapists, and assaulters outside the family (Hotaling et al., 1990). The greater the severity and frequency of the victimization, the greater the likelihood of severe and frequent violent offending outside the family (Straus, 1994a). Although the relationship between childhood victimization and adult perpetration is far from perfect, research evidence continues to point to the profound influence childhood victimization plays in producing the next generation of abusers (e.g., Burke, Stets, & Pirog-Good, 1989). Indeed, the adage "violence begets violence," although no doubt overly simplistic, seems generally true. According to OJJDP administrator Shay Bilchik (cited in "Violence in Families," 1995), the research seems clear: "If we can reduce family violence—not just abuse and neglect—we can prevent future violence by its young victims" (p. 6). Clearly, child maltreatment is worthy of our attention.

The adage "violence begets violence" seems to be generally true.

UNDERSTANDING THE SOCIAL CONSTRUCTION OF SOCIAL PROBLEMS

Given the magnitude of violence occurring within the family, few dispute that child maltreatment is a social problem. Academia has begun to include coverage of the topic in most social problems textbooks, and separate courses on child maltreatment emerged in the 1980s. Beginning in the mid-1980s, several new journals devoted specifically to family intimate violence and child maltreatment have appeared, including *Child Abuse & Neglect, Journal of Interpersonal Violence, Child Maltreatment,* and *Journal of Child Sexual Abuse.* In addition, a number of social movement organizations and federal agencies are devoted to child protection, including the International Society for Prevention of Child Abuse and Neglect (ISPCAN), the American Professional Society on Abuse of Children (APSAC), the Child Welfare League of America (CWLA), the Kempe National Center, Parents Anonymous, and the National Committee to Prevent Child Abuse (NCPCA). These organizations conduct studies, disseminate information, and advocate for children.

Through television and the print media, we are bombarded with disturbing stories of child abuse. Arguably, child protection sits higher on the American agenda list than at any other time in history. Nevertheless, it is important to recognize that child maltreatment was a *social condition* long before it was recognized as a *social problem.* Of course, child maltreatment is not the only contemporary social problem that has not always been defined as such. Imagine a social problems textbook written in 1899. What social problems would one expect to find listed in the table of contents? Racial and gender inequality? Environmental problems? Child sexual abuse? Certainly these conditions existed, and measured in absolute levels were "harmful," but it is unlikely that they would have been recognized as social problems.

Child protection sits higher on the American agenda list than at any other time in history.

Many sociologists point out that social problems are socially constructed (Spector & Kitsuse, 1977). From a social constructionist perspective, there is no objective way to identify "social problems." This perspective holds that *societal reactions* are central to the process of redefining a social *condition* as a social *problem.* Societal reactions can come from many sources: individual citizens, churches, social movement organizations, political interest groups, and the media, to name but a few. In their various reactions to particular social conditions, such institutions play the crucial role in transforming the condition into a problem.

These various interest groups, or *claims-makers,* are each actively engaged in the process of raising awareness about a particular social condition. Claims-making refers to the "activities of individuals or groups making assertions of grievances or claims with respect to some putative condition" (Spector & Kitsuse, 1977, p. 75). Generally speaking, the process begins when a claims-maker or interest group arouses concern about a particular condition that it sees as unacceptable (Best, 1989). Claims-makers may have a vested interest, or they may be "moral entrepreneurs" engaged in a purely moral crusade (Becker, 1963). As the cause of the particular complainant group comes to be recognized by society more generally, the social condition becomes a social problem. Social problems, then, are essentially "discovered" through this process of societal reactions and social definition. From this perspective, social problems come and go as societal reactions and responsive behaviors change (Studer, 1984).

The social constructionist perspective provides helpful insights into why violence is sometimes condemned as abuse in some cultures but not in others. The Sambia of Papua New Guinea, for example, believe that the only way a boy can grow into manhood is by ingesting semen orally from older boys and men. In other words, a boy becomes masculine, strong, and sexually attractive to women only if he performs fellatio (Herdt, 1987). This behavior is normative for the Sambia. Perhaps in 100 years, it will be defined as deviant behavior. For this social change to occur, however, claims-makers would have to successfully challenge the cultural practice.

The social constructionist perspective is also helpful in explaining how empirical generalizations come to be accepted as fact. Although one might hope that research findings could stand on their own, the reality is that the "facts" are often interpreted differently by competing claims-makers. Experts continue to debate, for example, how best to estimate child maltreatment (Chapter 2), the effectiveness of spanking (Chapter 7), the existence of repressed memories and satanic ritualistic abuse (Chapters 4 and 6), and whether child maltreatment is increasing or decreasing (Chapters 4 and 5). Each side is armed with its own set of empirical findings espoused as "the truth." From a social constructionist perspective, whoever wins the empirical battle earns the right to define the nature of the problem and the "facts" about the problem to the general public. The social constructionist perspective is also important because it gives us a theoretical framework within which to interpret the "discovery" of child maltreatment.

DISCOVERING CHILD MALTREATMENT: THE HISTORICAL CONTEXT

> This history of childhood is a nightmare from which we have only recently begun to awaken. The further back in history one goes, the lower the level of child care, and the more likely children are to be killed, abandoned, beaten, terrorized, and sexually abused. (deMause, 1974, p. 1)

We sometimes ask our students if human beings have instincts, that is, innate behavior patterns that are *not learned* and that appear in all normal humans. One common response is "Yes! The maternal instinct." Parents (and mothers in particular) are innately programmed, we are told, to love, protect, and nurture their children. Perhaps this is so. But if it is, then why is the history of child treatment so gruesome? If parents instinctually protect their children, why is history littered with abuse, abandonment, and infanticide?

Discovering Childhood

Before child maltreatment could be discovered, childhood had to be discovered. We argue that contemporary conceptions of children—they should be loved and nurtured and protected from the cruel world—have emerged only within the past few hundred years. Such conceptualizations are in many ways a human creation, a social construction. Human societies have constructed understandings of childhood as a special phase in life. In contemporary Western culture, for example, children are more than young human beings. Culturally defined norms dictate what children need and deserve. These norms differ dramatically from those in times past. Today, children are more valued, more nurtured, more fragile, and more protected than they ever have been before.

Empey and Stafford (1991) identify three periods in the history of childhood: *indifference to childhood* (pre-15th century), *discovery of childhood* (15th-18th centuries), and *preoccupation with childhood* (19th and 20th centuries). The historical indifference to children is well documented (Bakan, 1971; deMause, 1974; Pagelow, 1984; Piers, 1978). What today we call children were, in previous times, "regarded more as small or inadequate versions of their parents than as sacred beings in need of special protection" (Empey & Stafford, 1991, pp. 6-7). The harshness of life, the high rates of disease, and the visibility of death all contributed to a devaluation of life. It should come as no surprise, therefore, that the lives of children were less valued as well.

Children's lives were worth so little that many societies practiced infanticide (Piers, 1978). Some contemporary scholars maintain that infanticide was the most frequent crime in all of Europe and remained a relatively common practice until about 1800 (Piers, 1978; see Box 1.1, "Infanticide or Sudden Infant Death Syndrome?"). Another common practice, at least among women who could afford it, was to send their newborn to a wet nurse until it could be weaned. Unfortunately, because many wet nurses were poor and malnourished and sometimes nursed too many infants, mortality rates among wet-nursed infants were quite high (Empey & Stafford, 1991). Given modern conceptions of the importance of the mother-child bond, these practices seem unbelievable and remind us that this bond is, to some degree, culturally defined.

Children's lives were worth so little that many societies practiced infanticide.

The discovery of childhood, the recognition that childhood represents a distinct and important developmental period, occurred during several centuries. In 14th-century Italy, upper-class women still preferred to use wet nurses (they feared that nursing would stretch their breasts), although historical documents do show an emphasis on the need to select competent and healthy wet nurses (Empey & Stafford, 1991). During the 1600s, Protestant reformers in the New World offered mixed perceptions of children, suggesting that children were valued gifts of God but also "had 'wrong-doing' hearts and were altogether 'inclined to evil.' If that inclination was not to 'rage and burn,' it had to be controlled" (p. 36). During the last 200 years, society has witnessed a preoccupation with children, focusing on methods to control children as well as on nurturance and protection of children (Empey & Stafford, 1991; Rice, 1995; Wurtele & Miller-Perrin, 1992) The past 100 years, in particular, have been

(text continued on p. 11)

BOX 1.1 Infanticide or Sudden Infant Death Syndrome?

Historians tell us that most human societies have practiced and condoned infanticide in one form or another. Prior to the 4th century A.D. in Rome and Greece, infanticide was a legal and culturally approved solution to unwanted pregnancies. Children who were too big or too small, cried too much, had physical defects, were illegitimate, or were simply unwanted were often killed or abandoned. Female infanticide has been most commonly associated with patriarchal cultures, in which baby boys are prized because they are physically stronger and because only boys can carry on the family name (deMause, 1974). DeMause maintains that the killing of girl infants was common during the first century B.C., as illustrated by these instructions from a husband to his wife: "If, as may well happen, you give birth to a child, if it is a boy let it live; if it is a girl, expose it" (p. 26).

One of the ways historians estimate rates of infanticide is with sex ratios. Boy-to-girl ratios should be approximately 1:1. Certain human practices, however, can alter the ratios. Wars, for example, tend to produce low boy-to-girl ratios (because men are more likely to be killed), whereas infanticide tends to produce high boy-to-girl ratios (because girls are more likely to be killed). By the Middle Ages, the practice of infanticide was no longer culturally condoned, but with sex ratios of approximately 1.7 boys for every girl in Europe in A.D. 1400, it seems clear that it commonly existed. The practice continued there through the 19th century. In London, for example, dead babies lying in the streets were still a common sight as late as 1890 (deMause, 1974). In 19th-century China, boy-to-girl ratios were nearly 4:1 in some rural areas primarily dependent on farming (Ho, 1959). Even today in China, the cultural devaluation of girls, combined with a one-child policy that penalizes urban residents with more than one child and rural residents who have more than three, has led to speculation of widespread infanticide. Demographers estimate that approximately 12% of Chinese girl infants are "missing" each year (Riley, 1996).

Infanticide is a horrific act. It is difficult to imagine that humans are capable of killing their own flesh and blood. The act of infanticide is so shocking that it is easy for those of us living in North America to assume that such acts are committed only in other parts of the world or in previous times in history. In the United States, however, more than one thousand children are killed each year by their parents or caregiver (Wang & Daro, 1998). These figures are likely underestimates of infanticide rates because infant deaths can be easily misclassified as accidental or resulting from a medical condition (Ewigman, Kivlahan, & Land, 1993; McClain, Sacks, Froehlke, & Ewigman, 1993). Consider, for instance, the controversial issues surrounding sudden infant death syndrome (SIDS).

Wayneta Hoyt's first child, 3-month-old Eric, died in 1965. At the time, Hoyt explained to authorities that her son had inexplicably stopped breathing. Hoyt's misfortune continued, and she lost her next two children in September of 1968. Julie, 48 days old, choked to death while eating, and 2-year-old James stopped breathing. Although authorities were initially suspicious, they eventually came to accept Hoyt's claims of innocence and concluded that the three children had been victims of SIDS, a poorly understood medical syndrome that essentially describes a child who inexplicably stops breathing (Begley, 1997; Bergman, 1997).

In 1968, after the deaths of Julie and James, pediatrician Alfred Steinschneider, an expert in SIDS, became interested in the Hoyt case. Dr. Steinschneider knew that the probability of losing a single child to SIDS is low and that the probability of losing three is astronomical. Dr. Steinschneider surmised that SIDS must have a strong genetic component. He hypothesized that perhaps a genetic defect caused prolonged sleep apnea, a cessation of breathing for more than 15 seconds, and that apnea could be a predictor of SIDS (Toufexis, 1994).

Dr. Steinschneider continued an active personal and research interest in the Hoyt case when Wayneta Hoyt's final two children, Molly and Noah, were born. He had hoped to find support for his theory and, perhaps, prevent any more deaths. Despite the attention, however, 2-month-old Molly died in 1970, and 3-month-old Noah died in 1971 (Toufexis, 1994). The deaths of Molly and Noah further confirmed the apnea theory, at least in the eyes of Dr. Steinschneider. His 1972 article "Prolonged Apnea and the Sudden Infant Death Syndrome," based in large part on the Hoyt case, became the most commonly cited article in the SIDS field (Bergman, 1997). Dr. Steinschneider went on to further establish himself as an expert in the field and is currently president of the Sudden Infant Death Syndrome Institute in Atlanta (Toufexis, 1994).

In the mid-1980s, however, an assistant prosecutor doing research on SIDS came across the 1972 Steinschneider article. It seemed to William Fitzpatrick that the five Hoyt children were victims of infanticide rather than SIDS. Years later, in 1992, Fitzpatrick became the Onondaga County district attorney in Onondaga, New York, and decided to pursue the case. On April 25, 1995, a New York jury found Wayneta Hoyt guilty of murdering all five children.

In August 1998, a shockingly similar case made national headlines when Marie Noe, age 69, was charged with murdering her eight children between 1949 and 1968. Authorities at the time had been suspicious, but with no evidence of foul play, the cause of death had been left "undetermined." This was in many ways the easy conclusion to reach because as Philadelphia District Attorney Lynne Abraham told *Newsweek* magazine, during the 1950s and 1960s, "America was not prepared to admit that some parents might kill their children" (Underwood & Begley, 1998, p. 36). Today, however, we are.

The Hoyt and Noe cases, and others such as these in which homicides have been mistaken for SIDS, inevitably lead to this question: How many grieving parents have used SIDS as a cover for infanticide? In a scathing critique of medical claims-making, journalists Richard Firstman and Jamie Talan (1997) argue in their book *The Death of Innocents* that doctors have inadvertently covered up many infanticides with the SIDS diagnosis. Firstman and Talan contend that following the publication of Steinschneider's 1972 article, the medical community unquestioningly and blindly endorsed Steinschneider's argument claiming that prolonged apnea causes SIDS, that apnea runs in families, and that the SIDS risk can be reduced if high-risk infants are equipped with a monitor to alarm parents when infant breathing is sporadic. By 1990, 60,000 parents had their infants hooked up to apnea monitors, with sales exceeding $40 million (Wecht, 1998). Firstman and Talan maintain that with the apnea theory so thoroughly entrenched in the medical community, multiple infant deaths that should have been suspicious were instead seen as confirming the apnea theory.

Even those who are critical of the SIDS research, however, warn against returning to a time when parents of children who die inexplicably are approached with suspicion and accusations. It is clear that infants do sometimes inexplicably stop breathing and die. In the overwhelming majority of these cases, SIDS, not infanticide, is the cause (Bergman, 1997; Wecht, 1998). It is apparent, however, that the Hoyt case has forever changed the way authorities respond to potential SIDS deaths. Most states now require autopsies for all inexplicable infant deaths as well as an examination of the scene of death and medical history of the child (Toufexis, 1994). The Hoyt case has also drawn attention to the empirical uncertainties of SIDS. Most experts now agree that there is no demonstrated relationship between SIDS and apnea, no intrafamily patterns, and no evidence that apnea monitors reduce the risk of SIDS (Bergman, 1997). "We should never have published this article," *Pediatrics* editor Dr. Jerold Lucey recently wrote in reference to the 1972 Steinschneider manuscript. "Some physicians still believe SIDS runs in families. It doesn't—murder does" (quoted in Begley, 1997, p. 72).

marked by increased state interest in the welfare and control of children, through the passage of child labor laws, the creation of the juvenile court, mandatory education requirements, and child protection laws. This preoccupation with children is a likely result of the increasing value placed on children, but it no doubt also reflects the state's interest in protecting itself from troubled children and the troubled adults these children often become (Pfohl, 1977).

Discovering Physical Child Abuse

Before childhood was discovered, behavior that today we label child maltreatment was not necessarily seen as abusive. How could this be? First, as stated above, high rates of death and disease diminished the bond of affection and concern for one's children (Walker, Bonner, & Kaufman, 1988). Second, the political powerlessness of children, a group without independent status or rights, provided a basis for adults to establish rules and laws governing their treatment and care. Most societies thus regarded children as the property of their parents and subsequently allowed adults to treat their property as they saw fit. In some cases, parents probably also viewed their children as economic liabilities, one more mouth to feed and body to clothe (Walker et al., 1988; Wolfe, 1991). A final contributing factor is that the Puritan reformers who helped discover childhood in the 17th century also helped discover the incorrigible nature of children. Because children were naturally "inclined to evil" and "perverted," they required stern discipline.

Many trace the actual discovery of child abuse to the House of Refuge Movement of the early 1800s. In large part a reaction to the growing industrialization and urbanization of the United States, this movement was guided by the medieval principle of *parens patriae*—the state has the right and responsibility to protect those who cannot protect themselves (Pfohl, 1977). Children who were neglected, abused, or otherwise "on the road to ruin" were housed in one of the many state-supported institutions of the early and mid-1800s. Although some argue that the founders of the refuge movement were motivated more by preventive penology of poor and immigrant children than by child protection, they represent the first to intervene in neglect and abuse cases on behalf of the state (Empey & Stafford, 1991; Pfohl, 1977).

Probably the most famous court case involving child abuse was tried in 1874 (Bremner, 1971; Wiehe, 1996). Church social worker Etta Wheeler discovered that 8-year-old Mary Ellen Wilson was being beaten and starved by her stepmother. After unsuccessfully attempting to seek help from several other sources, she took the case to Henry Bergh, the founder of the Society for the Prevention of Cruelty to Animals. Mary Ellen was, after all, a member of the animal kingdom (Wiehe, 1996). A courtroom full of concerned New Yorkers, most of them upper-class women, heard the shocking details of Mary Ellen's life. She had been beaten almost daily and had not been allowed to play with friends or to leave the house. She had an unhealed gash on the left side of her face, a result of a blow to the head with a pair of scissors. The jury took only 20 minutes to find the stepmother guilty of assault and battery (Pleck, 1987).

The case of Mary Ellen attracted considerable attention, and the resulting public outcry eventually led to the 1874 founding of the Society for the Prevention of Cruelty to Children (SPCC; Pagelow, 1984). The SPCC, and the larger child-saving movement of which it was a part, advocated for a dramatic change in the way society deals with children. Increasingly, child protection advocates argued that children need to be loved and nurtured—and protected when they are not. Accordingly, they argued that parents did not have complete authority over children (Finkelhor, 1996).

Finkelhor (1996) states that two social changes during the 20th century directly contributed to the success of the child-saving movement. First, a large group of specialized professionals—nurses, social workers, schoolteachers and counselors, legal advocates, and family counselors—took on the task of protecting children. Second, as women gained more freedom in their personal lives and more power in the workplace, they "could afford to acknowledge and disclose some of the seamier realities of family life" (p. ix).

Largely as a result of the claims-making of women's groups, professional advocates, and social movement organizations such as the SPCC, state legislatures passed child protective statutes in the early 1900s, criminalizing abusive and neglectful behavior and specifying procedures for meeting the needs of abused and neglected children (Pleck, 1987). Although there was considerable movement toward child protection during this time, sociolegal reactions remained somewhat sporadic. Reporting of child abuse, for example, was not required, so most child abuse remained unacknowledged.

In 1962, Dr. C. Henry Kempe and his colleagues described the "battered child syndrome" and suggested that physicians should report abuse (Kempe, Silverman, Steele, Droegemueller, & Silver, 1962). Kempe defined child abuse as a clinical condition with diagnosable medical and physical symptoms resulting from deliberate physical assault. Kempe's work was important not simply because he identified and defined child abuse, because indeed, child abuse had been identified and defined before. The research was important because it identified child abuse as a serious problem, marking the initiation of medical claims-making about the child abuse problem. When medical doctors combined forces with other professionals and advocacy groups already fighting for child protection, the movement rapidly gained momentum. In 1974, Congress enacted the Child Abuse Prevention and Treatment Act to encourage reform, which provided federal funding to help states fight child abuse.

Discovering Child Sexual Abuse

Throughout history and in certain cultures, sexual interactions involving children have been commonplace. These interactions were often seen as appropriate and, in some cases, even healthy for children. In his disturbing review of literature and art, deMause (1974) indicates that the children of ancient Greece and Rome, especially the boys, were often sexually exploited. Aristotle believed that masturbation of boys by adult males hastened their manhood. Greek authors regularly depict "adults feeling the 'immature little tool' of boys" (p. 44).

Among the Romans, anal intercourse with boys was common and was said to be especially pleasurable if the boy had been castrated. Ancient documents even include directions for how to perform the castration:

> Since we are sometimes compelled against our will by persons of high rank to perform the operation . . . by compression it is thus performed; children, still of a tender age, are placed in a vessel of hot water, and then when the parts are softened in the bath, the testicles are to be squeezed with the fingers until they disappear. (deMause, 1974, p. 46)

Although it is not clear how commonly these practices occurred, their matter-of-fact depiction in the literature and art of the time suggests that they were not widely condemned.

Reactions against this type of behavior, and subsequent societal redefinitions, grew during several centuries. Despite dramatic changes through time, however, condemnation of sexual contact between adults and children is far from universal. As we mentioned earlier, among the Sambia of Papua New Guinea, young boys are still required to perform fellatio on older men (Herdt, 1987). Even in North America, there are those who believe that adult-child sexual interactions are appropriate and healthy. One extreme minority perspective is expressed by the North American Man-Boy Love Association (NAMBLA), an organization founded in 1978 (Hechler, 1988) that supports adult-child sexual interactions or "transgenerational sex." Robert Rhodes, a NAMBLA spokesperson, made the following comments when asked whether the organization views itself as an advocacy group for children:

> Yes. Considering the legitimacy of sexual relationships with children, there are two main theories that you can work from. One was the classical Greek theory—that is to say that the older partner in a sexual relationship served as initiator and tutor of the younger partner. You can also take a children's liberationist viewpoint—that is to say that children insofar as is possible—and it's far more possible than the current structure allows—should be given liberty to run their own lives as they choose, including the ability to determine how and with whom they should have sex. (cited in Hechler, 1988, pp. 193-194)

The views of NAMBLA effectively illustrate the role that claims-making groups play, and continue to play, in the discovery of child maltreatment. NAMBLA's sexual liberation perspective represents a minority view, of course. It also represents a criminal view. Yet from a historical perspective, its views are not that unusual.

Today, sexual exploitation statutes now offer children considerable protection (see Wurtele & Miller-Perrin, 1992). The 1978 Protection of Children Against Sexual Exploitation Act and the 1986 Child Sexual Abuse and Pornography Act make it a federal crime to exploit a child sexually or to permit a child to engage in child pornography.

Discovering Child Neglect and Psychological Maltreatment

Child neglect is sometimes referred to as the "most forgotten" form of maltreatment (Daro, 1988). The limited interest is surprising, especially considering that neglect is far more common than physical and sexual abuse. Psychological maltreatment is also pervasive, and experts argue that the emotional-psychological component of abuse is central to all maltreatment (Erickson & Egeland, 1996). Although physical wounds may heal, psychological wounds often run deep.

> Only in this century has the neglect of children's basic needs been defined as a social problem.

Why the lack of recognition of child neglect and psychological maltreatment? The most obvious reason is that physical abuse and, to a lesser degree, sexual abuse result in observable harm. Child physical abuse still tends to be defined only by the physical harm it causes. Sometimes, there are physical signs of neglect (e.g., malnutrition), but usually neglect and psychological maltreatment are elusive, the negative effects of which may never become fully apparent.

As is true of all forms of child maltreatment, child neglect is not new. Only in this century has the neglect of children's basic needs been acknowledged and defined as a social problem (Wolock & Horowitz, 1984). Psychological maltreatment has received even less recognition. Professionals have tended to view psychological maltreatment as a side effect of other forms of abuse and neglect, rather than as a unique form of maltreatment. Only in the past decade has psychological maltreatment been recognized as a form of child maltreatment existing in its own discrete form (see Hart & Brassard, 1993; Loring, 1994; Wiehe, 1990). Surveys suggest that Americans do consider psychological maltreatment a serious problem, with 75% indicating that "repeated yelling and swearing" is harmful to a child's well-being (Daro & Gelles, 1992).

DEFINING CHILD MALTREATMENT

The Social Construction of Deviance Definitions

The claims-making process is important not only in the discovery of a social problem. Indeed, "claims-makers do more than simply draw attention to particular social conditions. *Claims-makers shape our sense of just what the problem is*" (Best, 1989, p. xix; emphasis added). Various child advocates and professionals involved in the field of child maltreatment define the problem differently, depending, in large part, on their professional goals and purpose. Legal professionals focus on documentation of abuse and proof of existence of abusive acts by a perpetrator. In contrast, researchers employ a variety of definitions, depending on their particular theoretical perspective or research requirements. Mental health professionals might employ a broader definition, and one that focuses on the injury and suffering that result from child maltreatment. Child protection advocates may bring their unique assumptions and claims into discussions about child maltreatment. Clearly, because these competing claims-makers are rarely in agreement, there are no universal definitions in the field.

Imagine, for example, how a society might come to define a crime such as child rape. What is a child? What is rape? Legislators, with considerable input from a variety of interest groups, negotiate answers to such questions. The answers, seldom objectively determined, are social products of a particular time and place.

Defining child physical abuse is even more complex. The competing voices in this debate have produced a fascinating dialogue about what types of behaviors do or do not constitute abuse. Many social scientists, including prominent family violence researcher Murray Straus, believe that corporal punishment is a form of child maltreatment. Straus (e.g., 1994a) argues that in addition to being wrong, it is an ineffective form of discipline. He has even gone so far as to label corporal punishment child abuse (Straus, 1994b). Straus, along with many social scientists, child advocates, and child advocacy organizations that condemn corporal punishment, is a claims-maker attempting to influence societal definitions of maltreatment. If these voices are completely successful in their claims-making, then spanking could be criminalized, as it is in Scandinavia (Straus, 1994a).

Other formidable forces, with whom Straus and those opposed to corporal punishment compete, are also claims-makers engaged in their own moral campaign to preserve corporal punishment. At present, the prospanking forces are winning. In every state in the United States, hitting a child for the purpose of correction is exempt from the crime of assault, as long as the child is not injured (Straus & Mathur, 1996; see Box 1.2, "California Penal Code and Child Maltreatment," articles 11165.3 and 11165.4). The 1994 General Social Survey (Davis & Smith, 1994) found that three fourths of Americans agree or strongly agree with the following statement: "It is sometimes necessary to discipline a child with a good, hard spanking." Although this percentage is lower than it has been in past years (down from 84% in 1986), clearly, cultural norms continue to support the use of corporal punishment. This culture of acceptance exists apart from but is certainly influenced by a Christian voice that suggests spanking is endorsed by God (Ezzo, 1998): "He who spares his rod hates his son, but he who loves him disciplines him diligently" (Proverbs 13:24, New American Standard Version).

Each of these competing interest groups has a different conception of child maltreatment, and each is engaged in a moral campaign. The winner supposedly earns the right to define child maltreatment.

Because definitions are negotiated by competing claims-makers, there is inevitable ambiguity. This ambiguity presents several problems for those of us charged with the task of studying violence and controlling abuse in society.

(text continued on p. 17)

BOX 1.2 California Penal Code and Child Maltreatment

Reprinted below are several sections of the California Penal Code. These are the primary sections in the California Code relating to physical abuse, sexual abuse, and child neglect. Please note that the Penal Code is not divided specifically into "physical," "sexual," and "neglect" headings. These organizational categories have been created here for the convenience of the reader. The numbers listed represent the particular section of the code in which the law can be found. More information on the California Code can be obtained at www.leginfo.ca.gov/calaw.html

Purpose of the Laws

11164

(a) This article shall be known and may be cited as the Child Abuse and Neglect Reporting Act.

(b) The intent and purpose of this article is to protect children from abuse. In any investigation of suspected child abuse, all persons participating in the investigation of the case shall consider the needs of the child victim and shall do whatever is necessary to prevent psychological harm to the child victim.

Definition of Child

11165

As used in this article, "child" means a person under the age of 18 years.

Definitions of Child Physical Abuse

11165.3

As used in this article, "willful cruelty or unjustifiable punishment of a child" means a situation where any person willfully causes or permits any child to suffer, or inflicts thereon, unjustifiable physical pain or mental suffering, or having the care or custody of any child, willfully causes or permits the person or health of the child to be placed in a situation such that his or her person or health is endangered.

11165.4

As used in this article, "unlawful corporal punishment or injury" means a situation where any person willfully inflicts upon any child any cruel or inhuman corporal punishment or injury resulting in a traumatic condition. It does not include an amount of force that is reasonable and necessary for a person employed by or engaged in a public school to quell a disturbance threatening physical injury to person or damage to property, for purposes of self-defense, or to obtain possession of weapons or other dangerous objects within the control of the pupil, as authorized by Section 49001 of the Education Code. It also does not include the exercise of the degree of physical control authorized by Section 44807 of the Education Code. It also does not include an injury caused by reasonable and necessary force used by a peace officer acting within the course and scope of his or her employment as a peace officer.

11165.6

As used in this article, "child abuse" means a physical injury which is inflicted by other than accidental means on a child by another person. "Child abuse" also means the sexual abuse of a child or any act or omission proscribed by Section 273a (willful cruelty or unjustifiable punishment of a child) or 273d (unlawful corporal punishment or injury). "Child abuse" also means the neglect of a child or abuse in out-of-home care, as defined in this article. "Child abuse" does not mean a mutual affray between minors. "Child abuse" does not include an injury caused by reasonable and necessary force used by a peace officer acting within the course and scope of his or her employment as a peace officer.

Definitions of Child Sexual Abuse

11165.1

As used in this article, "sexual abuse" means sexual assault or sexual exploitation as defined by the following:

(a) "Sexual assault" means conduct in violation of one or more of the following sections: Section 261 (rape), subdivision (d) of Section 261.5 (statutory rape), 264.1 (rape in concert), 285 (incest), 286 (sodomy), subdivision (a) or (b), or paragraph (1) of subdivision (c) of

Section 288 (lewd or lascivious acts upon a child), 288a (oral copulation), 289 (penetration of a genital or anal opening by a foreign object), or 647.6 (child molestation).

(b) Conduct described as "sexual assault" includes, but is not limited to, all of the following:

1. Any penetration, however slight, of the vagina or anal opening of one person by the penis of another person, whether or not there is the emission of semen.
2. Any sexual contact between the genitals or anal opening of one person and the mouth or tongue of another person.
3. Any intrusion by one person into the genitals or anal opening of another person, including the use of any object for this purpose, except that, it does not include acts performed for a valid medical purpose.
4. The intentional touching of the genitals or intimate parts (including the breasts, genital area, groin, inner thighs, and buttocks) or the clothing covering them, of a child, or of the perpetrator by a child, for purposes of sexual arousal or gratification, except that, it does not include acts which may reasonably be construed to be normal caretaker responsibilities; interactions with, or demonstrations of affection for, the child; or acts performed for a valid medical purpose.
5. The intentional masturbation of the perpetrator's genitals in the presence of a child.

(c) "Sexual exploitation" refers to any of the following:

1. Conduct involving matter depicting a minor engaged in obscene acts in violation of Section 311.2 (preparing, selling, or distributing obscene matter) or subdivision (a) of Section 311.4 (employment of minor to perform obscene acts).
2. Any person who knowingly promotes, aids, or assists, employs, uses, persuades, induces, or coerces a child, or any person responsible for a child's welfare, who knowingly permits or encourages a child to engage in, or assists others to engage in, prostitution or a live performance involving obscene sexual conduct, or to either pose or model alone or with others for purposes of preparing a film, photograph, negative, slide, drawing, painting, or other pictorial depiction, involving obscene sexual conduct. For the purpose of this section, "person responsible for a child's welfare" means a parent, guardian, foster parent, or a licensed administrator or employee of a public or private residential home, residential school, or other residential institution.
3. Any person who depicts a child in, or who knowingly develops, duplicates, prints, or exchanges, any film, photograph, video tape, negative, or slide in which a child is engaged in an act of obscene sexual conduct, except for those activities by law enforcement and prosecution agencies and other persons described in subdivisions (c) and (e) of Section 311.3.

Definitions of Child Neglect

11165.2

As used in this article, "neglect" means the negligent treatment or the maltreatment of a child by a person responsible for the child's welfare under circumstances indicating harm or threatened harm to the child's health or welfare. The term includes both acts and omissions on the part of the responsible person.

(a) "Severe neglect" means the negligent failure of a person having the care or custody of a child to protect the child from severe malnutrition or medically diagnosed nonorganic failure to thrive. "Severe neglect" also means those situations of neglect where any person having the care or custody of a child willfully causes or permits the person or health of the child to be placed in a situation such that his or her person or health is endangered, as proscribed by Section 11165.3, including the intentional failure to provide adequate food, clothing, shelter, or medical care.

(b) "General neglect" means the negligent failure of a person having the care or custody of a child to provide adequate food, clothing, shelter, medical care, or supervision where no physical injury to the child has occurred. For the purposes of this chapter, a child receiving treatment by spiritual means as provided in Section 16509.1 of the Welfare and Institutions Code or not receiving specified medical treatment for religious reasons, shall not for that reason alone be considered a neglected child. An informed and appropriate medical decision made by parent or guardian after consultation with a physician or physicians who have examined the minor does not constitute neglect.

Police, judges, prosecutors, and CPS workers must have definitions with which to work. Researchers, likewise, must operationally define child maltreatment. Clearly, if we propose to write a book on child maltreatment, we must also attempt to define our subject matter.

Parent-Child Violence: Four Forms

It quickly becomes obvious that defining and assessing specific forms of child maltreatment constitute one of the most extensive and controversial areas of inquiry in the study of family violence (see Hamberger, 1994). Although specific definitions are discussed in more detail in subsequent chapters, the following paragraphs examine some of the general issues critical to the process of defining child maltreatment.

One reasonable starting point in defining child maltreatment is with the word *violence,* "an act carried out with the intention of, or an act perceived as having the intention of, physically hurting another person" (Steinmetz, 1987, p. 729). To further illuminate the matter, Gelles and Straus (1979) proposed that family violence can be conceptualized along two continuums, as depicted in Table 1.1. The *legitimate-illegitimate* continuum represents the degree to which social norms legitimize violence. Legitimate violence is an act that is culturally condoned (e.g., slapping the hand of a 3-year-old), whereas illegitimate violence is condemned (e.g., punching the face of a 3-year-old). The *instrumental-expressive* continuum represents the degree to which violence is used as a means to an end (instrumental), as opposed to an end in itself (expressive). Instrumental violence is an attempt to "induce another person to carry out or refrain from an act" (Gelles & Straus, 1979, p. 557). This could include spanking a child who has run out into the street, or slapping a wife who burns the dinner, as long as the aggressor's motivation is to curb the behavior. Expressive violence is essentially hitting someone out of anger and has no utilitarian value, except perhaps as a catharsis for the aggressor.

These four types of violence (legitimate-instrumental, illegitimate-instrumental, legitimate-expressive, and illegitimate-expressive) are reflected in the words of a young mother, who shares her views of discipline with family violence researcher Suzanne Steinmetz (1987):

> I've heard that you shouldn't spank when you're angry, but I can't agree with that because I think that's the time you should spank; before you have a chance to completely cool off, too. I think that the spanking helps the mother or dad as well as impresses the child that they did something wrong, and when they do something bad, they are going to be physically punished for it. You don't hit them with a stick or a belt, or a hairbrush, but a good back of the hand. . . . They remember it. (p. 729)

Think about what this mother is saying. She spanks her child, at least in part, because it is a catharsis—it helps her get the frustration out of her system (a presumably legitimate act, with an expressive motivation). She also spanks

TABLE 1.1 Four Types of Parent-Child Violence

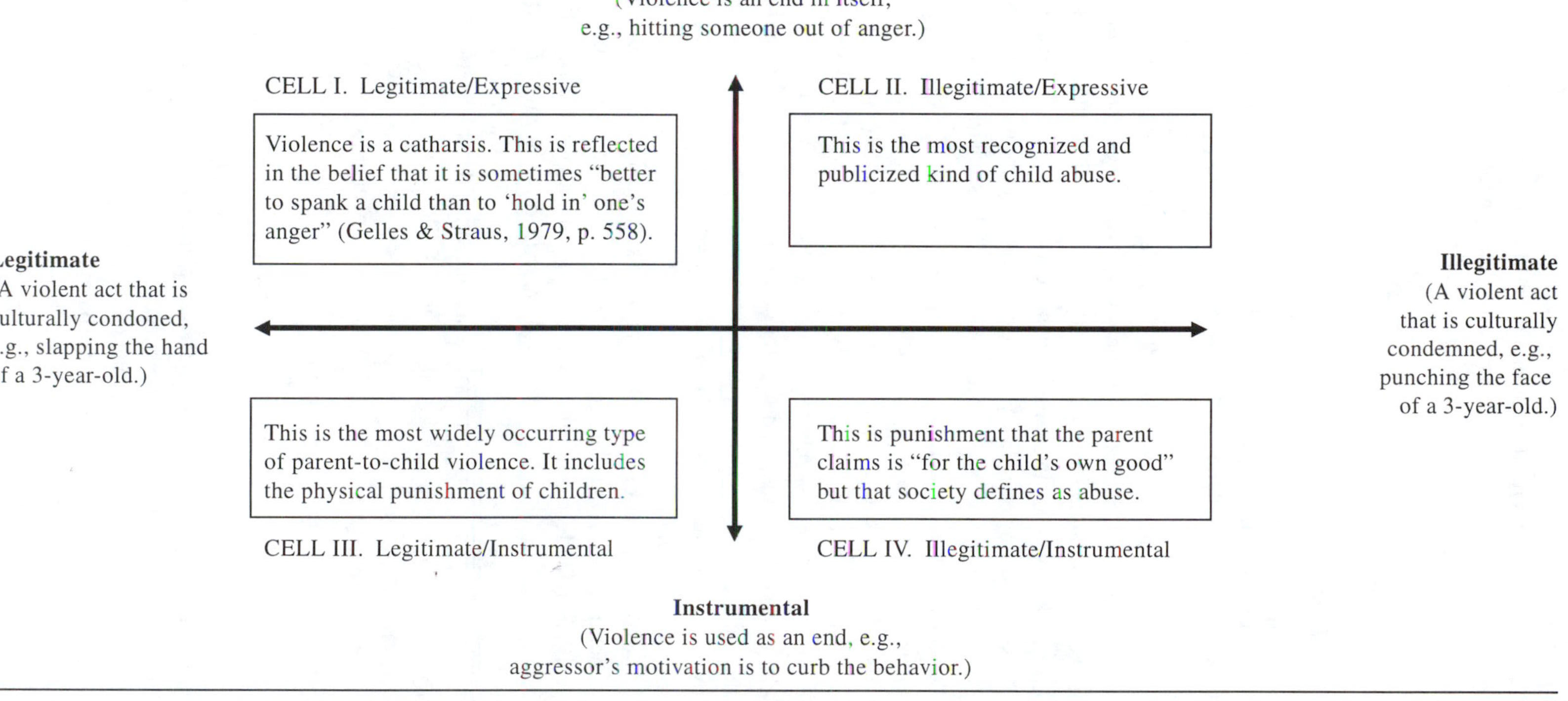

Expressive
(Violence is an end in itself,
e.g., hitting someone out of anger.)
CELL I. Legitimate/Expressive
Violence is a catharsis. This is reflected in the belief that it is sometimes "better to spank a child than to 'hold in' one's anger" (Gelles & Straus, 1979, p. 558).
CELL II. Illegitimate/Expressive
This is the most recognized and publicized kind of child abuse.
Legitimate
(A violent act that is culturally condoned, e.g., slapping the hand of a 3-year-old.)
Illegitimate
(A violent act that is culturally condemned, e.g., punching the face of a 3-year-old.)
This is the most widely occurring type of parent-to-child violence. It includes the physical punishment of children.
CELL III. Legitimate/Instrumental
This is punishment that the parent claims is "for the child's own good" but that society defines as abuse.
CELL IV. Illegitimate/Instrumental
Instrumental
(Violence is used as an end, e.g.,
aggressor's motivation is to curb the behavior.)

SOURCE: Adapted from "Determinants of Violence in the Family: Toward a Theoretical Integration," p. 558, by R. J. Gelles and M. A. Straus (1979), in *Contemporary Theories About the Family,* Vol. 1, edited by W. R. Burr, R. Hill, F. I. Nye, & I. L. Reiss, New York: Free Press. Reprinted and adapted with the permission of The Free Press, a division of Simon & Schuster, Inc. Copyright © 1979 by The Free Press.

because she wants to impress on the child that he has done something wrong (an instrumental motivation). This mother also indicates where she draws the line between legitimacy and illegitimacy, stating that some behaviors (spanking with a stick, belt, or hairbrush) are not acceptable (Steinmetz, 1987).

Legitimate Versus Illegitimate Acts

Remember that each of these four cells represents physical violence. Our interest, however, is in violence that crosses the legitimacy line—violence that society regards as abusive. Norms concerning legitimate versus illegitimate treatment of children do not exist "out there." They are socially constructed. Child maltreatment, therefore, is behavior that is successfully labeled *abusive* by claims-makers. Ultimately, societal norms concerning illegitimate violence are formalized in the form of laws, and every state has laws concerning child maltreatment. These laws, however, do vary from state to state, because different legislators have differing views of what constitutes abuse. The boxed insert "California Penal Code and Child Maltreatment" provides an example of how child maltreatment has been defined in California.

Table 1.1 is an attempt to illustrate definitional issues specific to physical child abuse, but one can certainly imagine similar tables for child sexual abuse, child neglect, and psychological maltreatment. The model is perhaps less applicable to sexual abuse and neglect because there is no expressive versus instrumental continuum. The fine line between legitimate and illegitimate acts, however, remains ambiguous. For example, when does a father's demonstration of affection become inappropriate?

Not all forms of child maltreatment are equally difficult to define legally. In general, child sexual abuse laws tend to focus on *perpetrator actions,* which results in far less ambiguity concerning the legitimate-illegitimate distinction than with other forms of child maltreatment. Notice that the California laws on sex abuse include considerable detail about a variety of specific illegal acts.

> When does a father's demonstration of affection become inappropriate?

The laws on physical abuse, neglect, and psychological abuse, on the other hand, tend to focus on *injury outcomes* and, as a result, are far less clearly defined. In many ways, the definitional issues surrounding child neglect and psychological maltreatment are the most ambiguous of all. As with physical violence, definitions focus on harm done to the child (i.e., injury outcomes), yet with neglect and psychological abuse, the harm is rarely externally visible. As a result, the distinction between the legitimate and illegitimate forms of verbal punishment, for example, is far from clear.

SUMMARY

The United States is the most violent industrialized country in the world (Siegel, 1995), and children are often victims of this violence. A remarkably high proportion of the maltreatment of children, furthermore, occurs within the family (Hotaling et al., 1990), with mounting evidence that family victimization is causally connected to street violence (OJJDP, 1995).

It is also important to understand the history of the child maltreatment problem. History illustrates how social conditions come to be defined as social problems, being filled with accounts of the physical and sexual mistreatment of children (e.g., deMause, 1974). Remarkably, however, the mistreatment of children did not begin to receive serious attention until the child-saving movement of the mid- to late 1800s (Pleck, 1987), and the research community essentially ignored child abuse until the 1960s (Kempe et al., 1962). Today, as a result of successful claims-making by many advocates and organizations, child maltreatment is generally recognized as a serious social problem.

Defining child maltreatment is inherently problematic because definitions are both subjective and constantly changing. Although words such as *abuse, maltreatment,* and *assault* are often used as if everyone agrees on their meaning, no such consensus exists. Despite disagreement, however, definitions are a crucial part of any research endeavor. Child protection, as well as social scientific progress, largely depends on shared definitional understandings.

GOALS OF THE BOOK

There are many reasons for writing a book such as this. Certainly, we intend to present and summarize available information on the topic of child maltreatment so that readers will gain substantive knowledge. Second, we wish to foster understanding of the magnitude of the problem and the devastation it causes (see Box 1.3, "Personalizing Child Maltreatment Research"). Along the way, we confront a number of controversial issues sparking debate among experts and numerous areas in which future research is crucial. We trust that by providing numerous sources of information, student researchers, academics, and advocates who have an interest in child maltreatment will thus have a better foundation for their work. Last, of course, we continue the process of outlining possible solutions. Just as we have felt compelled to write this book, we also anticipate generating the interest and concern of readers. We want the readers' exploration of the field to be stimulating and worthwhile.

BOX 1.3 Personalizing Child Maltreatment Research

Scientific study has a way of depersonalizing the tragedy of family violence. Indeed, when reading research, it is easy to distance oneself from the words on the page, to think of the victims and perpetrators as merely participants in a research study. It is important to remember, then, that behind every research finding are real people. In reading the following chapters, don't forget that child maltreatment affects real victims, real people.

Robert Sandifer was a real 11-year-old boy, nicknamed "Yummy" because of his love for cookies. Robert's story, which ended when he was shot in the head by his own gang, attracted national attention in the fall of 1994. Illinois children's services first came into contact with Robert when he was less than a year old. At age 3, he was removed from his home, with bruises (apparently from an electrical cord) and burns (from cigarettes) covering his body. From that point on, he lived with his grandmother in a home that sometimes contained as many as 19 children. What was the reason for his murder? Robert had killed a 14-year-old neighbor, and his gang, fearing he would become a liability, gunned him down (Braun & Pasternak, 1994).

Elisa Izquierdo was another real-life person. Her life and death, at age 6, also attracted national attention when her picture appeared on the cover of *Time* magazine (Van Biema, 1995). To all who knew her, Elisa was a bright, happy, beautiful girl with limitless potential. For most of her life, she had lived with her father, Gustavo, who loved and doted over his daughter. On weekend visits with her mother, Awilda Lopez, however, she was being abused. Elisa began to urinate and defecate uncontrollably, and she developed sores on her vagina. Gustavo petitioned the court to deny Awilda visitation rights, but before he could follow through on the petition, he died of cancer in 1994. Despite the evidence of abuse and the pleas from Gustavo's family, Awilda was granted permanent custody. Living with her mother, Elisa quickly deteriorated. School officials noticed she was often bruised and had trouble walking. Neighbors reported hearing her pleas: "Mommy, Mommy, please stop! No more! No more! I'm sorry!"

The Child Welfare Administration investigated but reported that everything looked fine. Elisa eventually stopped attending school altogether. On November 23, police were called to Elisa's home.

> When the police arrived, she [Awilda] confessed to killing Elisa by throwing her against a concrete wall. She confessed that she had made Elisa eat her own feces and that she had mopped the floor with her head. The police told reporters that there was no part of the six-year-old's body that was not cut or bruised. Thirty circular marks, that at first appeared to be cigarette burns, turned out to be impressions left by the stone in someone's ring. (Van Biema, 1995, p. 36)

These stories about Robert and Elisa are tragedies, so horrific that they made headlines in the national press. There are, of course, thousands upon thousands of other tragedies that never attract media attention. Consider Markus, a cute and precocious 7-year-old boy who went to live with his father and stepmother after his biological mother abandoned him at age 5. Markus's father asked that the boy be admitted to the inpatient psychiatric unit because he and his wife were unable to keep him from running away from their home in the middle of the night. Markus's father admitted that they had sometimes resorted to "shackling" Markus to his bed so he would not run away. His stepmother also revealed that she and her husband had never really wanted Markus to move into their home because they already had two of their own children. Young Markus, at age 7, had now been rejected by both his mother and father. Imagine being 7 years old and facing the realization that your mother and father neither love you nor want you. No wonder he wanted to run away (our case history)!

2

The Study of Child Maltreatment

Theoretical and Methodological Issues

CHAPTER OUTLINE

AN INTERVIEW WITH DAVID FINKELHOR

"If I had a large amount of money, I would do studies to extend the National Crime Victimization Survey to include children of all ages (that is, below age 12). This would help us get a better understanding of the full spectrum of child victimization even at very early ages."

David Finkelhor, a renowned family violence researcher with wide-ranging interests, is Professor of Sociology and Director of the Crimes Against Children Research Center at the University of New Hampshire. Here, he recently served as conference chair of the 6th International Family Research Conference. He has written extensively on topics such as sexual abuse of children and marital rape. Of the 11 books he has edited or written, the latest are *Nursery Crimes: Sexual Abuse in Daycare* (1989), coauthored with Linda Williams and Nanci Burns, and *Missing, Abducted, Runaway, and Thrownaway Children in America* (1990), coauthored with Gerald Hotaling and Andrea Sedlak. He also serves as an associate editor of three family violence journals. He is currently working on the Second National Study of Missing, Abducted, Runaway, and Throwaway children, under a contract with the U.S. Department of Justice. He received his B.A. in social relations, his Ed.M. in sociology (from Harvard), and his Ph.D. in sociology (from the University of New Hampshire).

Q: How did you become interested in child maltreatment?

A: It was a field in which I felt I could combine my scientific orientation with an opportunity to solve a pressing social problem. What has kept me involved is the continuing need for valid scientific information. I've studied a number of different, interrelated topics within the field partially out of my own curiosity. From the beginning, I've espoused the point of view that we should be interested in an integrated approach to these problems. In fact, I've tried to model this approach in my own research.

Q: What has shaped your approach to the field?

A: Practitioners have been very important for me in specifying issues that needed attention. Some heated public controversies, such as the debate over stranger abductions, have also been influential in making me think that someone ought to be looking at these ideas more objectively. Also, my disciplinary training as a sociologist has affected my work. I've been very impressed with the ability of contemporary survey research to talk to people candidly about sensitive subjects. There have been a number of breakthroughs in methodology, and I feel that these methods can be applied in the area of child maltreatment.

Q: What is your current research focus?

A: My current research interest is in child victimization, in general, and all the different ways that children get victimized inside and outside the family.

Q: What would you do if you had a large research grant?

A: If I had a large amount of money, I would do studies to extend the National Crime Victimization Survey to include children of all ages (that is, below age 12). This would help us get a better understanding of the full spectrum of child victimization even at very early ages.

Q: What other types of research or advocacy should be done?

A: I'd like to see a bit of redress in the balance between the interest in children as perpetrators of crime and the interest in children as victims of crime. We spend far more time discussing juvenile delinquency than we spend on discussing juvenile victimization, yet children and youth are more disproportionately victims than perpetrators.

Q: What can society do to diminish child maltreatment?

A: I recommend early intervention programs that support parents. One avenue of approach is to offer these programs within a comprehensive health care system.

Q: What is the biggest problem in trying to eliminate child maltreatment?

A: The greatest problem is at the sociological level. The American public is not able to "swear off" violence. We tolerate violence. We believe that it is an effective method for solving problems. Violence is a part of male identity. We tend to romanticize violence. We need to discourage the use of corporal punishment, eliminate exposure to violence in the media, and help teenagers learn nonviolent problem resolution skills.

Q: What should the government do to combat child maltreatment?

A: Government at all levels ought to fund more demonstration programs to stimulate innovative practices. I'd also like to see the government establish clearinghouses for dissemination of scholarly articles and a resource bank of statistics from survey data. I'd also like to see more money for the training of specialists.

Prior to the "discovery" of the battered child syndrome in the early 1960s (Kempe et al., 1962), there was essentially no research on child maltreatment. Even by the early 1970s, there was so little research on child maltreatment that it could, according to well-known researchers Richard Gelles and Murray Straus (1988), "be read in one sitting" (p. 11). In the last 20 years, interest in child maltreatment has grown with the field, expanding well beyond its initial academic borders of psychology and sociology to encompass a large number of academic and professional fields such as criminology, medicine, legal studies, social work, and law enforcement. In addition, advocates working with victims and perpetrators of child maltreatment have emerged as a forceful group of activists with a specific moral and political agenda. Perhaps no other social scientific field provides this diverse mix of advocates and "pure" researchers.

Each group brings its own perspective to bear on the problem, and the results are predictable. Experts schooled in different academic disciplines often employ different research methodologies, collect different types of data, and formulate different theoretical frameworks. In addition, various professionals, whether they be academicians, clinicians, or advocates, often approach the issue of child maltreatment from polarized perspectives, which results in diverse definitions, explanations, and solutions of the problem. As we stated in Chapter 1, disagreements about these issues are important because the group that is most persuasive in its arguments typically earns the right to define the problem, offer solutions, and secure funds to help alleviate the problem.

Further complicating matters is that child maltreatment is challenging to study and to explain. Theory is not well developed, and the research evidence is often inconclusive. Our task in this chapter is to examine the important theoretical and methodological issues in child maltreatment research. We begin with a summary of several theories, primarily from sociology and psychology, that help explain child maltreatment. Next, we consider the problems associated with measuring child maltreatment, and finally, we examine some methodological problems that continue to plague research in the field.

THEORIES OF CHILD MALTREATMENT

Macrotheory: Sociological Patterns

To many people, child maltreatment is incomprehensible. The idea that parents intentionally and knowingly inflict injury on their children is counterintuitive. A parent is supposed to protect and care for a child. Research suggests, nevertheless, that child maltreatment is far from uncommon. All families have tension, and *all* families sometimes resolve these tensions in inappropriate ways. Even the best parents may lose their tempers, for example, and squeeze an arm harder than they should, say something intentionally hurtful, or yell louder than they need to.

It is probably counterproductive, however, to label all inappropriate interactions between parents and children as child maltreatment because in doing so, the term becomes so broad that it loses its usefulness. It is important to know, nevertheless, that most parents sometimes behave in inappropriately aggressive ways. Given this empirical reality, it is fruitful to consider the many social and cultural conditions contributing to physically violent and verbally aggressive family interactions. As we will see, in many respects, aggression is a "normal" (i.e., common and culturally approved) part of family life. Why is this so?

Sociologists have identified a number of structural factors that make families prone to verbal and physical aggression. These broad macroexplanations of violence include cultural factors and structural characteristics of the family. In addition, several significant sociological theories of deviance also help explain child maltreatment.

Cultural Explanations

In many ways, violence is an accepted, encouraged, and even glorified form of cultural expression (Heath, Kruttschnitt, & Ward, 1986). One does not have to watch many movies, cartoons, or sporting events to see that physical violence, as a way of expressing one's emotions, is clearly acceptable. Some social scientists argue that there is *spillover effect,* in which the acceptance of violence in the culture contributes to criminal violence rates in society and at home (Straus, 1977; Tolan & Guerra, 1998). It certainly seems reasonable to argue that aggression and violence in the home mirror society's tolerance for aggression (Wyatt, 1994).

One obvious way that societal violence might influence the family is through the media (see also Chapter 7). The effects of media violence on both the behavior and victimization of children have been thoroughly researched during the past

20 years (see Comstock & Strasburger, 1990; Eron, Huesmann, Lefkowitz, & Walder, 1987; Felson, 1996), and much of this research points to media violence as contributing to aggression in children (Tolan & Guerra, 1998). Many researchers further argue that aggressive children are more likely to be violent toward peers and siblings and, presumably, more likely to grow up to be aggressive adults. Although the negative influence of the media is only one of the many factors contributing to societal violence, well-designed studies conclude that exposure to media violence contributes to aggression (Comstock & Strasburger, 1990).

> The negative influence of the media is one of many factors contributing to societal violence.

Family norms also condone a certain amount of family aggression. Parenting experts agree that children need discipline and that "good parents" are, at least in part, parents who are effective disciplinarians. Discipline, from a social scientific perspective, is the implementation of costs. The costs that parents impose on their children can vary from a spanking (i.e., a physical cost) to a time-out (i.e., a psychological cost). The costs can also range from those considered legitimate to those considered illegitimate. Most consider a slap on the hand or 2 minutes of time-out as legitimate forms of discipline for a 5-year-old. A slap across the face and 24 hours of time-out, however, are not usually considered legitimate forms of discipline.

A problem arises because legitimate punishments (a slap on the hand) and illegitimate punishments (a fist to the face) exist on the same continuum (i.e., violent behavior). It stands to reason that the more society encourages normative aggression and violence, the more likely that abusive aggression will also occur. This is one of the main reasons some child advocates argue for a strict no-spanking policy (e.g., Straus, 1994a). Although they acknowledge that most parents, in most situations, probably use corporal punishment in nonharmful ways, society's *condoning* and *encouragement* of spanking indirectly contribute to abuse. Many abusive parents report, for example, that they lost their temper while disciplining their child and did not "mean" to cause physical harm (Straus, 1994a).

Structural Characteristics of the Family

Many researchers have studied the structural factors that make families particularly prone to violence (Brinkerhoff & Lupri, 1988; Gelles & Straus, 1979). One factor is the *time risk* of spending considerable time with family members, which increases the opportunity for violence. Another factor is that family interactions are often tense and emotional, the intensity of which can make family relationships especially volatile. In addition, a power differential exists between family members. Children are subordinate to parents and, as a result, sometimes become targets of aggression. Children cannot, for example, fight back. Nor can they always choose with whom they will or will not interact. One way adults relieve conflict in interpersonal interactions is simply to dissolve the relationship. Parent-child relationships, however, are involuntary and difficult to dissolve. Most states are reluctant to break up families, and parents are often given every opportunity to change. The privacy of families also contributes to child maltreatment by making violence relatively easy to hide and by dictating a hands-off policy when it comes to family matters (Brinkerhoff & Lupri, 1988).

All these family structure factors combine to make child protection difficult. Imagine, for example, what you would do if you saw a mother violently slap the face of her 3-year-old child. Most observers would probably do nothing. After all, parental aggression is condoned in our culture, and corporal punishment is not only permissible but protected by law. In addition, family privacy norms provide parents with considerable autonomy in deciding how to discipline children.

Strain Theory

Strain theories maintain that deviance is common in societies that emphasize and promise financial success (e.g., the "American Dream") but do not provide equal access to legitimate opportunities for achieving that success (Merton, 1938). When their goals for financial gain are blocked, people in such societies experience strain and frustration, becoming more prone to deviant behavior.

Strain theories are supported by the recognition that rates of child maltreatment are higher in lower-income families, unemployed families, and families receiving Aid to Families With Dependent Children (AFDC; Limber & Nation, 1998). These patterns are consistent in both self-report studies and officially reported abuse, suggesting that the maltreatment-class connection is not simply a result of a tendency to define the acts of the less successful as abusive (Milner, 1998). The unequal distribution of opportunities, along with the inevitable stressors associated with poverty (e.g., financial worries, ill health, and crowded living conditions), produces high levels of frustration in lower-income families (Farrington, 1980; Straus, 1980). When this stress becomes overwhelming, aggression may be directed at innocent, yet convenient, victims (i.e., children and spouses). Largely as a result of historic patterns of strain and frustration, some criminologists argue that a culture of acceptance of violence has emerged in the lower socioeconomic groups. Proponents of this "subculture of violence" theory maintain that the lower-class violence is, to some extent, a cultural norm—a way of life (Wolfgang & Ferracuti, 1972).

Strain and frustration may also contribute to violence through what psychologists refer to as the frustration-aggression hypothesis (Dollard, Doob, Miller, & Sears, 1939). Suppose the person or situation associated with the frustration is not available as a target of someone's aroused aggression. The aggression might be displaced onto an innocent person, or scapegoat. When life is hard, you can't pay the bills, or you have just lost your job, who do you hit?

You can't hit "life" or the creditors, and if you hit your ex-boss, you could be thrown in jail. In this case, family members become convenient victims.

Social Bonding Theory: The Low Social Costs of Child Maltreatment

Most theories of deviance assume that social structural factors or psychological factors explain variation in the motivation to commit deviant acts. The question most theories attempt to answer is this: "Why do people involved in relationships, presumably based on love, physically assault each other?" (Williams & Hawkins, 1989, p. 595). Social bonding theory, however, asks a different question: Given the cultural and structural factors that encourage family violence, why aren't all families violent? That is, given that social bonding theory assumes that most people are sufficiently motivated to commit deviant acts (e.g., abuse their children), what social forces *prevent* certain people from committing those act?

According to Travis Hirschi (1969), people do *not* commit deviant acts when they have a *stake in conformity.* This stake is determined by the strength of the social bond. People who have strong bonds are constrained, and people with weakened bonds are free to commit deviant acts. Three components of the social bond are most relevant to child maltreatment discussions. *Commitment* refers to the degree to which the individual is invested in conventional activities and conventional success. People with a lot to lose (e.g., home, family, career, and standing in the community) have a tremendous stake in conformity and are less likely to abuse children. *Attachment* refers to the bonds people feel with significant others. Attachments create strong bonds to society because we do not want to disappoint people who are important to us. People with few significant attachments are more free to commit deviant acts. Finally, *belief* is the degree to which one feels the laws on child abuse are justified and "right." There are people, for example, who believe that children are their property and that society has no right to tell them what they can or cannot do to their child (Hechler, 1988). Obviously, this belief results in an increased probability of deviant behavior.

> Families who are involved in the community are less likely to be violent.

Much of the research on child maltreatment reveals empirical patterns consistent with social bonding theory. Young, single parents typically have less of a stake in conformity, along with higher rates of child maltreatment (Gelles, 1989). Persons who are poor are also less likely to have a stake in conformity, which might in part explain their higher rates of abuse. In particular, the poor have less to lose in career and material possessions and are, therefore, less likely to be invested in conventional activities (commitment bond). Socioeconomic status (SES) also contributes to child maltreatment through its impact on social integration (attachment bond). Social integration refers to the degree to which individuals are involved in church, community, and civic life or have successfully formed attachments within these communities. Because persons who are poor tend to be less integrated in church and community, they experience more social isolation. Research shows that abusive parents also experience high levels of isolation (Garbarino & Gilliam, 1980).

The key issue from a social bonding perspective, however, is social isolation, not poverty per se. The theory predicts that people who lack important attachments have less of a stake in conformity and are, therefore, more likely to be abusive. In neighborhoods where people know one another, where there is a sense of community pride, where people are involved in community organizations, and where people feel they can ask their neighbors for help, child maltreatment rates tend to be low, even if the neighborhood is poor (Emery & Laumann-Billings, 1998). The same pattern holds at the family level. Families with positive views of the community and who are active in the community are less likely to be violent (Garbarino & Kostelny, 1992).

Deterrence Theory: The Low Legal Costs of Child Maltreatment

Hirschi's social bonding theory focuses on the influence of *informal* social controls such as family, schools, churches, and work. Deterrence theory is also a control theory, but it focuses on the influence of *formal* social controls (i.e., the criminal justice system). Deterrence theory assumes that humans will rationally weigh the costs and benefits of a behavior (Gibbs, 1975). In this case, *costs* are defined as the perceived probability of getting caught (*certainty* of punishment) and the perceived seriousness of the punishment (*severity* of punishment). From the deterrence perspective, when there are few legal costs to antisocial behavior, the behavior is more common. Many scholars argue that the potential criminal cost of committing a violent act against a family member is too low, which partly explains the high rates of child maltreatment (Gelles & Straus, 1988).

Gelles and Straus (1988) illustrate the deterrence principle in their book *Intimate Violence.* They argue that one of the reasons family members hit other family members is "because they can." That is, there are insufficient controls or costs to keep them from hitting one another when they are inclined to do so. To illustrate, they tell the story of David, who is at the hospital with his son Peter. Peter had been playing with the family's new television set and had knocked it over. In anger, David "lost it" and hit Peter, who fell into the coffee table. Gelles and Straus maintain that the popular notion that parents just "lose control" is really more of a justification than an explanation. They remind us that people are far less likely to lose control when they cannot afford to do so, which raises the question of what exactly it means to lose control. What would happen, for example, if David and Peter were not related? What if David runs an automobile agency and 3-year-old Peter overturns the agency's television: "Does David slap, spank, or even beat the wayward 3-year-old? Absurd" (p. 21). If David does lose control and decides to beat Peter, he is likely to be in jail, in the hospital (if Peter's father is larger than David), or both.

From a deterrence perspective, parents abuse children when there are insufficient legal structures to keep them from losing control. Obvious extralegal controls (i.e., social costs) do come into play here (as social bonding theory reminds us), yet our primary intent is to focus on *legal* social controls. Although the legal cost of street violence is typically high, similar costs are "rarely paid by those violent in the home" (Gelles & Straus, 1988, p. 23). The title of the well-known book by Straus, Gelles, and Steinmetz (1980) reminds us that child maltreatment often takes place *Behind Closed Doors,* where physical separation from society and family privacy norms provide parents considerable autonomy. Thus, the cultural acceptance of parent-to-child violence helps blur the line between legitimate discipline and child maltreatment.

Let us remember that if one adult hits another adult, it is criminal assault. Children, however, are not afforded the same protection (Straus & Hamby, 1997). In rare cases in which an arrest of a parent is made and taken before the courts, judges are put in the no-win position of either ignoring the problem or breaking up the family, which is something they have been reluctant to do (Gelles, 1983). Taken together, these factors make the *perceived certainty* of getting caught and the *perceived severity* of punishment quite low.

Of course, the costs of child maltreatment have risen dramatically in recent years, and there is every reason to believe they will continue to rise. Mandatory reporting laws and the increasing awareness of the public mean that child maltreatment is more often recognized today than it has been at any other time in history. There is also increasing pressure to remove children from dangerous homes and to prosecute abusive parents (Besharov, 1996).

Microtheory: Psychological and Biological Predictors

Sociological theories may successfully explain why child maltreatment exists in a society, or why some segments of society experience more violence than others, but they fail to explain why individual family members are violent. Because sociological theories explain child maltreatment in primarily structural terms, they do not explain variation in individual motivation. Research consistently identifies poverty and social isolation, for example, as correlates of child maltreatment, and these correlates are consistent with sociological theories. The theories, however, predict only that rates of abuse are higher among the poor. Because most poor people are not abusive, and abusive people are not uniformly poor, sociological theories clearly do not explain everything (Emery & Laumann-Billings, 1998). Sociological theories do not tell us why some *individuals* are violent, whereas others are not. Explaining the behavior of individuals is more difficult than explaining structural patterns, and, as a result, the answers tend to be much more ambiguous. We cannot know all the reasons adults mistreat

> At best, we can identify certain risk factors that make maltreatment more understandable and somewhat predictable.

children, and, therefore, we cannot definitively predict who will be violent. At best, we can identify certain risk factors that make maltreatment more understandable and somewhat predictable.

Psychopathology

One common explanation of child maltreatment is psychopathology, which generally refers to mental disorder. Psychopathology theories propose that various forms of child maltreatment are committed by individuals who are seriously disturbed by some form of mental illness or personality disorder. An individual's psychopathology might distort his or her view of the world or serve as a disinhibitor to prohibited behavior. Some research has supported the psychopathology model of child maltreatment by demonstrating higher rates of various psychological disorders in offenders relative to comparison groups (e.g., Hunter, Childers, Gerald, & Esmaili, 1990). Most experts argue, however, that psychopathology is present in only a small percentage of the adults who physically or sexually abuse children (Groff & Hubble, 1984; Milner, 1998; Williams & Finkelhor, 1990).

Psychological and Behavioral Traits

Although only a minority of child maltreatment perpetrators display severe forms of psychopathology, many reports demonstrate that child maltreatment offenders display *elevated scores* on measures of cognitive distortions, depressive symptoms, stress, low self-esteem, and substance abuse or dependence compared with nonoffenders (e.g., Chan, 1994; Culp, Culp, Soulis, & Letts, 1989; Ethier, Lacharite, & Couture, 1995; Hayashino, Wurtele, & Klebe, 1995; Milner, Halsey, & Fultz, 1995). Other psychological and behavioral factors are specific to particular types of maltreatment. Parents who physically abuse their children, for example, display more anger control problems, hostility, and low frustration tolerance compared with nonabusive parents (e.g., Bauer & Twentyman, 1985; Milner et al., 1995). And child sexual abuse perpetrators display deviant patterns of sexual arousal compared with nonoffending men (e.g., Freund & Langevin, 1976). The mechanisms through which certain psychological and behavioral factors lead to child maltreatment vary, depending on the type of child maltreatment, and are not well understood (see Chapters 3 and 4 for discussions of these mechanisms).

Biological Factors

There are any number of ways that biological factors might be related to child maltreatment. For instance, perpetrators of physical child abuse show hyperresponsive physiological activity to both positive and negative child stimuli. Such unusual hyperresponsiveness might make child abusers more physiologically reactive in stressful situations with children and lead to abuse (Milner & Chilamkurti, 1991). Perpetrators of child sexual abuse demonstrate differences in hormonal levels relative to comparison groups (Langevin, 1993). Other correlates of child maltreatment are also presumably physiologically based, including low IQ, neuropsychological deficits, attention deficit disorder, physical disabilities, and physical health problems (Crittenden, 1992; Elliott, 1988; Milner, 1998). Although a greater number of studies are focusing on biological factors present in child maltreatment perpetrators, this area needs further study.

Parent-Child Interaction Theories

In attempting to discern the cause of child maltreatment, some researchers have focused on the reciprocal nature of the parent-child relationship, particularly in the context of physical child abuse and child neglect. Such theories propose that difficult child behaviors (e.g., continual whining and complaining) interact with behavioral problems and deficits of parents (e.g., anger control problems and poor parenting skills) and result in child maltreatment (DHHS, 1993; Milner, 1993; Whipple & Webster-Stratton, 1991).

There is also support for the presence of negative parent-child interactions in abused and neglected children. Abusive and neglecting families are characterized by disturbed patterns of infant attachments (Egeland, Sroufe, & Erickson, 1983; Kolko, 1992). Attachment is an enduring emotional bond that develops progressively during the first year of an infant's life while the infant is completely dependent on his or her caregiver for survival. This enduring bond serves an important function because through the caretaker-child relationship, the infant develops a sense of trust and security, a sense of self, and an ability to learn and explore (Ainsworth, 1973; Bowlby, 1980). Failure to form a secure attachment early in life may contribute to difficulties in adulthood such as the inability to develop close personal relationships (Ainsworth & Bowlby, 1991; Bowlby, 1980; Frankel & Bates, 1990). Research has consistently observed insecure patterns of attachment in physically abused, neglected, and psychologically maltreated children (Crittenden, 1992; Erickson & Egeland, 1987; Kolko, 1992). Insecure attachments are characterized by parental unresponsiveness to the physical and emotional needs of the child. Vulnerability in the parent-child relationship may lead to further difficult child behaviors and increased challenges for the parent as the child develops, resulting in a negative escalation of abusive parent-child interactions (see Cerezo, 1997; Crittenden, 1998).

Social Learning Theory

A widely accepted explanation of how socialization plays a role in child maltreatment rests on social learning theory. A process called *modeling,* in which a person learns social and cognitive behaviors by simply observing and imitating others, resides at the core of this theory (Bandura, 1971). When children are exposed to violence, either as direct victims of physical assault or as witnesses of violence, they are exposed to a set of norms and rationalizations that justify violence. Children learn that violence is an acceptable way, or perhaps even *the* acceptable way, of resolving family conflict and expressing emotions. In addition, learning in the observer is strengthened through observation of rewards and punishment dispensed to the model. As applied specifically to child maltreatment, observation of violence (e.g., father hits mother for "mouthing off") and reinforcement of violence within a social context (i.e., mother "shuts up") teach children exactly how to be abusive. In this case, violence is reinforced as a way of getting what one wants.

The popularity of social learning theory rests on several observations. First, violence tends to perpetuate itself from one generation to the next, "like father, like son," "like mother, like daughter" (Straus et al., 1980). Second, a wealth of laboratory experiments with humans (e.g., schoolchildren) lend strong validation to the claim that aggression can be learned through modeling (e.g., Bandura, Ross, & Ross, 1961). Finally, a large number of studies have successfully linked exposure to violence in one's childhood, either directly or through observation, to violence in adulthood (e.g., Cappell & Heiner, 1990; C. S. Widom, 1989; Williams & Finkelhor, 1990). Although the intergenerational pattern is far from perfect, research consistently demonstrates that abusive parents have been exposed to significantly more childhood violence than have nonabusive parents (Egeland, 1993).

Although intergenerational correlations are high, C. S. Widom (1989) points to many methodological problems with the research. First, there has been an overreliance on self-report and retrospective data. Retrospective reports are problematic because they rely on the memories and perceptions of violent adults concerning their childhood experiences. Second, there has been a general lack of comparison groups of nonviolent adults also asked to provide retrospective reports. Finally, in the popular eye, childhood maltreatment is perceived as *the* cause of adult perpetration, and this generalization is clearly far too simplistic. Childhood abuse is neither a necessary nor sufficient cause of adult violence. At best, the data suggest that children who were abused, or who witnessed abuse, are more *likely* to be abusive adults. They are not predetermined to be abusive. The majority of abused children do not grow up to be abusive adults (Kaufman & Zigler, 1987; C. S. Widom, 1989).

SECTION SUMMARY

Cultural explanations for child maltreatment focus on broad, cultural forces that may allow or promote negative parent-child interactions. In many ways, North American culture accepts and, in some sense, even mandates parental aggression and violence. Violence is so generally acceptable that low levels are considered normative. Parents, for example, regularly spank their children. The acceptance of this type of violence creates a climate in which abuse can occur as well as contributes to ambiguous boundaries between abusive and acceptable behavior.

Structural characteristics of the family may also contribute to child maltreatment. The continual interaction, intensity of emotions, and power imbalances inherent in most family living make children especially vulnerable targets. Furthermore, family privacy conceals violence from other members of society, thus making its occurrence more probable.

The *sociological theories* of deviance that seem most applicable to child maltreatment are *strain theory, social bonding theory,* and *deterrence theory.* Strain theory predicts that people who are frustrated by their inability to attain culturally defined goals of success (i.e., those who are poor and unemployed) are more likely to commit deviant acts. Social bonding theory suggests that people without much of a stake in conformity (e.g., attachments, conventional commitments, and beliefs) will face fewer social costs when they commit deviant acts. Finally, from a deterrence theory perspective, as long as the legal costs of child maltreatment are low (e.g., low perceived certainty and low perceived severity of punishment), child maltreatment rates will be high.

To consider why some individuals are violent whereas others are not, we examine various *psychological* and *biological* theories. One possible explanation is that people who mistreat children suffer from some sort of *psychopathology* or mental disorder, yet most experts argue that only a small percentage of child abusers suffer from a mental disorder. More relevant is a variety of *psychological and behavioral* factors, such as depression, stress, low self-esteem, and substance abuse, which are correlated with abuse perpetration. *Biological* factors, such as a physiological reaction to stress, might also play a role, as do parent-child interaction factors. The most important psychological theory is *social learning theory,* which predicts that children who are victims of assault or who witness assault learn that violence is an acceptable way of resolving family conflict and expressing emotions.

DETERMINING THE EXTENT OF CHILD MALTREATMENT

The study of child maltreatment, like the study of other deviant and criminal behavior, is plagued by inevitable estimation challenges. To illustrate the problems inherent in estimating crime, criminologists sometimes use the metaphor of a funnel. Figure 2.1 illustrates what this funnel might look like with respect to child maltreatment. At the top sits the actual amount of child maltreatment present within society (Level I). This number, which can become dramatically larger or smaller depending on how society defines maltreatment, is obviously unknown and unknowable. Level II includes all child maltreatment that comes to the attention of the various professionals who are mandated to report abuse (e.g., doctors, nurses, teachers, social workers, counselors, day care workers, and police) *plus* the child maltreatment that comes to the attention of authorities within CPS. In principle, because certain professionals are mandated to report abuse, all the abuse they encounter should appear in CPS data (Level III).

In actual practice, however, mandated professionals do not always report abuse. A therapist, for example, may become convinced that her client has been a victim of abuse but may not want to violate client-therapist trust. In addition, many mandated reporters have little faith in CPS, which makes them less motivated to report the abuse (Melton et al., 1995; Sedlak & Broadhurst, 1996). In crime research, the gap between crime that is reported and the amount of crime actually committed is referred to as the "dark figure," because researchers cannot know how large it is. Child maltreatment has its own dark figure, represented by the large and unknown number of actual cases (Level I) and the relatively smaller number of cases that are officially reported to CPS (Level III).

Level IV represents an even more narrow estimate of child maltreatment: the number of cases that are substantiated. A case of child maltreatment is substantiated when child protection agencies determine that a preponderance of evidence suggests that the abuse did in fact occur. Clearly, this is a less stringent criterion than that required in criminal courts, and, as a result, substantiation figures are a matter of some debate (Emery & Laumann-Billings, 1998). According to the National Committee to Prevent Child Abuse, only about one third of the cases reported to CPS were substantiated in 1995 (Wang & Daro, 1996). Just because a case is unsubstantiated, however, does not mean that abuse did not occur. Some unsubstantiated cases represent false allegations of abuse, whereas others remain unsubstantiated because of insufficient evidence where abuse may have actually occurred (see Chapter 4 for a discussion of false allegations of abuse).

Once a case is substantiated, the assumption is that the state will mandate services (e.g., counseling for the parents, foster care for the child, or permanent removal of the child). In reality, however, the state often does not intervene, so the funnel narrows even more at Level V. McCurdy and Daro (1993) argue that social services agencies are so overwhelmed that CPS intervenes in only 60% of substantiated cases. The remaining 40% of families are typically encouraged to get counseling on their own (Emery & Laumann-Billings, 1998).

Anywhere along this process, cases may also be turned over to the criminal justice system (Levels VI, VII, and VIII). Most child maltreatment cases, however, are not treated as criminal cases. Estimates are that less than 20% of substantiated cases involve formal court action (Emery & Laumann-Billings, 1998).

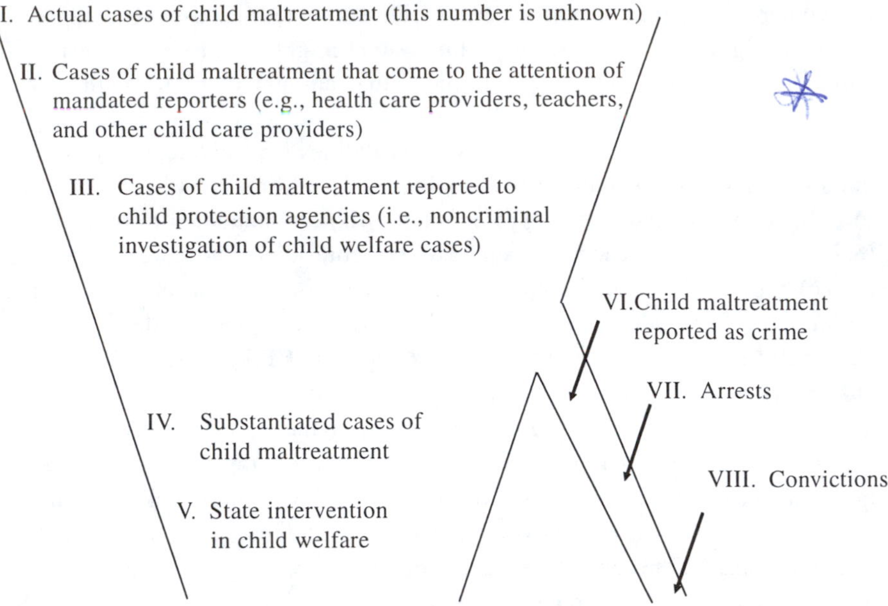

Figure 2.1. Problems in Estimating the Amount of Child Abuse: The Child Maltreatment Funnel

The funneling metaphor is helpful as we turn our attention to a discussion of the specific sources of data on child maltreatment. Each source examines a different level in the funnel. No data source is inherently superior to the others; rather, each has its own strengths and weaknesses. The primary distinction we make in this section is between *official statistics* and *self-report surveys.*

Official statistics come from the FBI, social service agencies, or professionals and represent the amount of child maltreatment that comes to the attention of those officially mandated to protect children. This includes maltreatment that is reported as a crime (Level VI), maltreatment that is reported to CPS (Level III), and maltreatment that is reported to any mandated professional (Level II; this includes CPS and other professionals such as health care workers, social workers, and teachers, who are mandated to report child maltreatment but may not do so). Self-report surveys are mail, phone, or face-to-face surveys of the general public concerning violence in the family. Self-reports are essentially *perpetration* or *victimization* surveys, in which researchers promise confidentiality and anonymity and hope that respondents will honestly answer questions about their own use of violence or victimization. Self-report surveys are the only way to estimate the dark figure of child maltreatment.

> Self-report surveys provide access to information about violence that is not included in official statistics.

Official Estimates

Official statistics reflect rates of reported intimate violence, for example, the number of cases reported to the police or to public social service agencies. There are essentially three types of official estimates: the National Incidence Study (NIS), child protective services (CPS) data, and the Uniform Crime Reports (UCR).

National Incidence Study

The NIS is the most inclusive of the three types of official data, being a congressionally mandated survey conducted by the National Center on Child Abuse and Neglect. There have been three NIS studies—in 1981, 1988, and 1996. NIS-3 (Sedlak & Broadhurst, 1996) was designed to meet the following four congressional mandates: (a) estimate the amount of neglect and abuse in the United States; (b) examine a number of demographic correlates of maltreatment; (c) estimate the number of substantiated cases that result in civil or criminal action; and (d) develop an understanding of how a case of maltreatment is detected, why it is or is not reported to CPS, and what actions are taken.

The NIS goes beyond the estimates provided by CPS. We know that many professionals who are mandated to report suspected cases of child maltreatment to CPS do not do so. Such professionals may have conflicting responsibilities, may not want to get involved with CPS, or may not trust the reporting system. The NIS is an attempt to estimate the amount of child maltreatment based on both CPS and non-CPS sources (Sedlak & Broadhurst, 1996).

The NIS-3 data come from 800 interviews of mandated reporters, including public school staff, day care centers, hospitals, police departments, voluntary service agencies, juvenile probation, and public health departments. Researchers then extrapolate from these random samples to create national estimates. Participants in the study were trained concerning definitions of abuse and neglect and asked to look for cases of maltreatment during the study. The important information from each case of suspected abuse was then turned over to NIS researchers, who used specific definitional standards to determine whether the case should be counted as child maltreatment.

The NIS is a widely respected data source for two reasons. First, NIS researchers employ uniform definitions of abuse and are, therefore, able to standardize the abuse label. The second advantage is that the NIS employs a relatively broad definition of abuse that includes a *harm standard* and an *endangerment standard.* The endangerment standard allows researchers to include children who have not been physically harmed but who have experienced maltreatment such that they are in danger of being harmed (Sedlak & Broadhurst, 1996). Table 2.1 displays the definitional standard used by the NIS-3.

(Text continued on p. 43)

TABLE 2.1 National Incidence Study: Definitions of Abuse

Physical Abuse: The category of physical abuse is unique in that it is not broken down into subtypes. Acts constituting physical abuse include hitting with a hand, stick, strap, or other object; punching; kicking; shaking; throwing; burning; stabbing; or choking a child.

In the NIS-3, children who were classified as physically abused included a 1-year-old who died of cerebral hemorrhage after being shaken by her father, a teen whose mother punched her and pulled out her hair, a child who sustained second- and third-degree "stocking" burns to the feet after being held in hot water, a preteen whose grandfather gave her a black eye, a teen who sustained bruises after being beaten with an extension cord, and a 3-year-old who had welts and bruises from being beaten with a belt by his father.

Sexual Abuse: Children who experienced any one of three specific forms of sexual abuse are counted in estimates of the overall incidence of sexual abuse. The three forms of sexual abuse reflect different types of acts:

Intrusion

Evidence[1] of oral, anal, or genital penile penetration or anal or genital digital or other penetration was required for this form of maltreatment.

Molestation with genital contact

This form of maltreatment involved acts in which some form of actual genital contact had occurred but where there was no specific indication of intrusion. When intrusion had been coded for a given child, molestation also was not coded, unless it reflected a distinctly different type of event in the child's experience (e.g., involved different perpetrators).

Other or unknown sexual abuse

This category was used for unspecified acts not known to have involved actual genital contact (e.g., fondling of breasts or buttocks and exposure) and for allegations concerning inadequate or inappropriate supervision of a child's voluntary sexual activities.

Emotional Abuse: The category of emotional abuse encompasses three distinct forms of maltreatment:

Close confinement (tying or binding and other forms)

Torturous restriction of movement, as by tying a child's arms or legs together or binding a child to a chair, bed, or other object, or confining a child to an enclosed area (such as a closet) as a means of punishment.[2]

Verbal or emotional assault

Habitual patterns of belittling, denigrating, scapegoating, or other nonphysical forms of overtly hostile or rejecting treatment, as well as threats of other forms of maltreatment (such as threats of beating, sexual assault, abandonment, etc.).[3]

Other or unknown abuse

Overtly punitive, exploitative, or abusive treatment other than those specified under other forms of abuse, or unspecified abusive treatment. This form includes attempted or potential physical or sexual assault;[4] deliberate withholding of food, shelter, sleep, or other necessities as a form of punishment; economic exploitation; and unspecified abusive actions.

Physical Neglect: There are seven specific varieties of physical neglect. Of these, the first two reflect inattention to remedial health care needs, the next three involve custody-related maltreatment, and the last two forms involve inadequate supervision and other types of physical neglect. The acts or omissions that are classified under each of these forms of maltreatment are

TABLE 2.1 Continued

Refusal of health care

Failure to provide or allow needed care in accord with recommendations of a competent health care professional for a physical injury, illness, medical condition, or impairment.[5]

Delay in health care

Failure to seek timely and appropriate medical care for a serious health problem that any reasonable layperson would have recognized as needing professional medical attention.[6]

Abandonment

Desertion of a child without arranging for reasonable care and supervision. This category included cases in which children were not claimed within 2 days and cases in which children were left by parents/substitutes who gave no (or false) information about their whereabouts.

Expulsion

Other blatant refusals of custody, such as permanent or indefinite expulsion of a child from the home without adequate arrangement for care by others or refusal to accept custody of a returned runaway.

Other custody issues

Custody-related forms of inattention to the child's needs other than those covered by abandonment or expulsion. For example, repeated shuttling of a child from one household to another, due to apparent unwillingness to maintain custody, or chronically and repeatedly leaving a child with others for days or weeks at a time.

Inadequate supervision

Child left unsupervised or inadequately supervised for extended periods or allowed to remain away from home overnight without the parent/substitute knowing (or attempting to determine) the child's whereabouts.[7]

Other physical neglect

Conspicuous inattention to avoidable hazards in the home; inadequate nutrition, clothing, or hygiene; and other forms of reckless disregard of the child's safety and welfare, such as driving with the child while intoxicated, leaving a young child unattended in a motor vehicle, and so forth.[8]

Educational Neglect: Educational neglect is broken down into three specific forms, as follows:

Permitted chronic truancy

Habitual truancy averaging at least 5 days a month was classifiable under this form of maltreatment if the parent/guardian had been informed of the problem and had not attempted to intervene.

Failure to enroll/other truancy

Failure to register or enroll a child of mandatory school age, causing the child to miss at least 1 month of school; or a pattern of keeping a school-age child home for nonlegitimate reasons (to work, to care for siblings, etc.) an average of at least 3 days a month.

Inattention to special education need

Refusal to allow or failure to obtain recommended remedial education services, or neglect in obtaining or following through with treatment for a child's diagnosed learning disorder or other special education need without reasonable cause.

Emotional Neglect: The category of emotional neglect includes seven specific forms of maltreatment:

TABLE 2.1 Continued

Inadequate nurturance/affection
Marked inattention to the child's needs for affection, emotional support, attention, or competence.[9]

Chronic/extreme spouse abuse
Chronic or extreme spouse abuse or other domestic violence in the child's presence.

Permitted drug/alcohol abuse
Encouragement or permitting of drug or alcohol use by the child; cases of the child's drug/alcohol use were included in this category if it appeared that the parent/guardian had been informed of the problem and had not attempted to intervene.[10]

Permitted other maladaptive behavior
Encouragement or permitting of other maladaptive behavior (e.g., severe assaultiveness and chronic delinquency) under circumstances where the parent/guardian had reason to be aware of the existence and seriousness of the problem but did not attempt to intervene.

Refusal of psychological care
Refusal to allow needed and available treatment for a child's emotional or behavioral impairment or problem in accord with competent professional recommendation.

Delay in psychological care
Failure to seek or provide needed treatment for a child's emotional or behavioral impairment or problem that any reasonable layperson would have recognized as needing professional psychological attention (e.g., severe depression or suicide attempt).

Other emotional neglect
Other inattention to the child's developmental/emotional needs not classifiable under any of the above forms of emotional neglect (markedly overprotective restrictions that foster immaturity or emotional overdependence, chronically applying expectations clearly inappropriate in relation to the child's age or level of development, etc.).

SOURCE: Reprinted from *Third National Incidence Study on Child Abuse and Neglect,* by A. J. Sedlak and D. D. Broadhurst, 1996, Washington, DC: U.S. Department of Health and Human Services.

NOTES:

1. Evidence means credible information (e.g., the perpetrator acknowledged his actions). As in the previous studies, the term does *not* have a technical meaning here, either legal or medical.
2. Does *not* include generally accepted practices such as use of safety harnesses on toddlers, swaddling of infants, or discipline involving "grounding" a child or restricting a child to his or her room.
3. This category was not used if verbally assaultive or abusive treatment occurred simultaneously with other abusive behavior (e.g., during a physical beating) unless adverse effects occurred that were separate and distinct from those in the other category.
4. Where actual physical contact did not occur (e.g., throwing something at the child).
5. This category does not apply to treatment needs concerning educational, emotional, or behavior problems, which were classified under educational neglect and/or emotional neglect, as described in subsequent sections.
6. Lack of preventive health care, such as failure to have the child immunized, is not included here. It is classified under "general neglect," defined in a later section.
7. This form of maltreatment also covers cases in which the child is temporarily locked out of the home.
8. This does *not* include situations that result from the parents' financial inability to provide (or obtain through AFDC) reasonably safe, hygienic living conditions.
9. Cases of nonorganic failure to thrive are classified under this form of maltreatment in addition to other instances of passive emotional rejection of a child or apparent lack of concern for a child's emotional well-being or development. Not included here were overt expressions of hostility and rejection, which are classified under verbal/emotional abuse.
10. Administering drugs to a child for nonmedical or nontherapeutic purposes (e.g., giving a child alcohol or marijuana) is classified here if the child was of school age (and hence likely to predispose the child behaviorally to self-administer the drugs) but is classified under "other or unknown abuse" for younger children.

Child Protective Services Data

CPS agencies are "noncriminal child welfare investigatory units" charged with the task of protecting children who are living in an unsafe environment (Finkelhor, 1994a, p. 35). CPS accumulates reports on the amount of child maltreatment and the outcomes of child maltreatment investigations.

There are two important CPS data sources. Although the two are similar, each is conducted by a different organization and is slightly different in research focus. The first contains extensive aggregate-level data reported by the states and compiled by the National Child Abuse and Neglect Data System (NCANDS). NCANDS was established following the 1974 Child Abuse Prevention and Treatment Act, which called for the creation of a national data collection system (DHHS, 1998). The NCANDS team produces an annual study, *Report From the States to the National Child Abuse and Neglect Data System,* now in its seventh edition (DHHS, 1998). The NCANDS survey focuses on the number of child abuse and neglect reports, the source of child abuse reports, investigation outcomes, types of maltreatment, description of the victims of maltreatment, and the relationship of perpetrators to victims.

The second data source comes from the National Committee to Prevent Child Abuse (NCPCA). The NCPCA produces its own annual report, referred to as *The Fifty State Survey* (Wang & Daro, 1998). This survey compiles data on the number of *reported* and *substantiated* victims of child maltreatment (e.g., physical abuse, neglect, sexual abuse, and emotional abuse), the number of confirmed child abuse fatalities, information on the reporting system used in each state, and the level of funding of CPS.

As a measure of prevalence, CPS data are probably less useful than NIS data. One problem, of course, is that CPS data are further down the funnel, which means they are further from the true prevalence of child maltreatment. The second problem is that definitions of abuse, investigative procedures, and data collection procedures are determined at the state level (DHHS, 1998). Because definitions of abuse are ambiguous, they will inevitably vary from agency to agency, which means that what is or is not counted as abuse will vary from agency to agency. In addition, CPS workers are invariably burdened with large caseloads, which makes thorough assessment all but impossible (Straus & Hamby, 1997).

Uniform Crime Reports

The UCR is the most commonly cited official data source on crime in the United States. It is an annual compilation by the FBI of all reported crimes as well as arrests made for those crimes. The UCR provides information on reported cases of criminal maltreatment (Level VI) and on arrests made in those cases (Level VII). Except for homicide, however, the UCR does not record the age of the victim, which means that for crimes such as sexual assault, it is difficult to distinguish adult assaults from child assaults (Finkelhor, 1994a). In addition, because only a small percentage of child maltreatment is reported, and an even smaller percentage is reported *as crime,* the UCR is of limited usefulness in child maltreatment studies.

Self-Report Surveys

There are two types of self-report surveys. Self-report *perpetration* surveys ask respondents about their own abusive and neglectful behavior. Self-report *victimization* surveys ask respondents about their experiences as victims of child maltreatment. Often, child maltreatment surveys contain elements of both, so in many respects there is less of a reason to distinguish between the two here. The Parent-Child Conflict Tactics Scale (CTSPC; Straus, Hamby, Finkelhor, Moore, & Runyan, 1998), for example, not only asks parents to report their own violent behavior but also elicits from them disclosure of sexual victimization that might have occurred to them in childhood. There are, however, slight differences in the potential methodological problems associated with victimization and perpetration surveys, and that is why we consider them separately here.

The obvious advantage of both types of self-report surveys is that they provide access to information about violence that is not reported to official agencies. These surveys are especially useful for information on normative violence (e.g., corporal punishment and sibling aggression). Problems (e.g., memory lapses and distortions) arise, however, because of the retrospective nature of the reports. This is especially true when adults are asked to recall childhood victimization. One of the debates about child sexual abuse, for example, is the controversy over adult accounts of childhood abuse. Although some point to the "recovered" memories of adults (e.g., Briere & Conte, 1993), others question the accuracy of these recovered memories and motivations of the therapists who have helped in their recovery (e.g., Ganaway, 1989; Loftus, 1993; see also Chapter 4).

Another problem with self-report data is that respondents might not be truthful. This is always a potential problem, but it is especially so in perpetration surveys in which respondents disclose their own abusive and neglectful behavior. Respondents may perceive their own violence as justified and therefore not reportable. They may also be psychologically motivated to underestimate their own level of violence or may minimize the severity of the violence (see Baumeister, Stillwell, & Wotman, 1990; Kruttschnitt & Dornfeld, 1992).

Conflict Tactics Scales (CTS)

The CTS (Straus, 1979) are the most widely used scales in self-reported family violence research, representing an impressive leap forward in the identification and quantification of specific, violent behaviors. The original CTS was designed to measure marital or dating violence, but it could be easily altered to measure child maltreatment by changing the reference from "your partner" to a specific child. In an attempt to alleviate additional problems with the CTS as a measure of child maltreatment, however, Straus and his colleagues (1998) created a modified version of the CTS: the Parent-Child Conflict Tactics Scale.

The questions in the CTSPC are more appropriate indicators of parent-child interactions. The CTSPC specifically measures the tactics or behaviors that parents might use when they are upset with a child. The survey begins with this statement:

> Children often do things that are wrong, disobey, or make their parents angry. We would like to know what you have done when your (SAY age of referent child) year-old child did something wrong or made you upset or angry. I am going to read a list of things you might have done in the past year, and I would like you to tell me whether you have: done it once in the past year, . . . (Straus et al., 1998, p. 267)

The interviewer then reads a list of 22 types of conflict resolution strategies parents might employ, including 4 *nonviolent* responses (e.g., "discussed the issue calmly"), 5 *psychological aggression* responses (e.g., "threatened to hit or throw something"), and 13 *physical aggression* responses (e.g., "threw something"; Straus & Hamby, 1997). Table 2.2 lists these 22 responses and divides them into the definitional categories.

The CTSPC also includes supplemental questions on *neglect, corporal punishment,* and *sexual abuse.* These items are listed in Table 2.3.

Straus and his colleagues acknowledge that measuring self-reported parental violence, psychological aggression, and neglect presents several problems. First, although the test-retest reliability is good, the internal consistency of the CTSPC is low, possibly because parents who engage in one form of maltreatment do not necessarily engage in others (Straus & Hamby, 1997). A bigger problem is that few parents want to portray themselves in a bad light, even in an anonymous survey. To minimize this social desirability problem, the survey attempts to create a "context of legitimization" by beginning with two socially acceptable discipline techniques. The rest of the items are listed randomly so that the researchers' perception of severity does not bias the respondent (Straus et al., 1998). Despite these precautions, parents no doubt often underreport their violence. Even with this assumed underreporting, however, prevalence studies based on the CTSPC suggest rates of maltreatment that are considerably higher than those reported by the NIS-3 (Straus et al., 1998).

National Crime Victimization Survey (NCVS)

The most commonly cited victim survey is the NCVS, a semiannual survey of 60,000 households conducted by the Bureau of the Census. We mention the NCVS only briefly here because although it is an important measure of criminal activity in the United States, children under the age of 12 are not interviewed. Thus it is only marginally useful in the study of child maltreatment. Despite this significant limitation, NCVS data are helpful in examining the victimization of older children.

TABLE 2.2 Parent-Child Conflict Tactics Scale (CTSPC)

Nonviolent Discipline
A. Explained why something was wrong
B. Put him/her in "time out" (or sent to his/her room)
Q. Took away privileges or grounded him/her
E. Gave him/her something else to do instead of what he/she was doing wrong

Psychological Aggression
N. Threatened to spank or hit him/her but did not actually do it
F. Shouted, yelled, or screamed at him/her
J. Swore or cursed at him/her
U. Called him/her dumb or lazy or some other name like that
L. Said you would send him/her away or kick him/her out of the house

Minor Physical Assault (Corporal Punishment)
H. Spanked him/her on the bottom with your bare hand
D. Hit him/her on the bottom with something like a belt, hairbrush, a stick or some other hard object
P. Slapped him/her on the hand, arm, or leg
R. Pinched him/her
C. Shook him/her (this is scored for Very Severe if the child is < 2 years)

Severe Assault (Physical Maltreatment)
V. Slapped him/her on the face or head or ears
O. Hit him/her on some other part of the body besides the bottom with something like a belt, hairbrush, a stick or some other hard object
T. Threw or knocked him/her down
G. Hit him/her with a fist or kicked him/her hard

Very Severe Assault (Severe Physical Maltreatment)
K. Beat him/her up, that is, you hit him/her over and over as hard as you could
I. Grabbed him/her around the neck and choked him/her
M. Burned or scalded him/her on purpose
S. Threatened him/her with a knife or gun

SOURCE: Reprinted from "Identification of Child Maltreatment With the Parent-Child Conflict Tactics Scales: Development and Psychometric Data for a National Sample of American Parents," p. 268, by M. A. Straus, S. L. Hamby, D. Finkelhor, D. W. Moore, & D. Runyan, 1998, *Child Abuse & Neglect, 22,* 249-270.

TABLE 2.3 CTSPC Supplemental Questions on Corporal Punishment, Neglect, and Sexual Abuse

Weekly Discipline (recommended when corporal punishment is a focus)

Sometimes it's hard to remember what happened over an entire year, so we'd like to ask a few of these questions again, just about the last week. For each of these questions, tell me how many times they happened *in the last week.*

WA. Put him/her in "time out" (or sent to his/her room)
WB. Shouted, yelled, or screamed at him/her
WC. Spanked him/her on the bottom with your bare hand
WD. Slapped him/her on the hand, arm, or leg

TABLE 2.3 Continued

Neglect

Sometimes things can get in the way of caring for your child the way you would like to, for example, money problems, personal problems, or having a lot to do. Please tell me how many times in the last year this has happened to you in trying to care for your child. Please tell me how many times you

NA. Had to leave your child home alone, even when you thought some adult should be with him/her
NB. Were so caught up with your own problems that you were not able to show or tell your child that you loved him/her
NC. Were not able to make sure your child got the food he/she needed
ND. Were not able to make sure your child got to a doctor or hospital when he/she needed it
NE. Were so drunk or high that you had a problem taking care of your child

Sexual Maltreatment

Now I would like to ask you something about your own experiences as a child that may be very sensitive. As you know, sometimes, in spite of efforts to protect them, children get sexually maltreated, molested, or touched in sexual ways that are wrong. To find out more about how often they occur, we would like to ask you about your own experiences when you were a child.

SA. Before the age of 18, were you personally ever touched in a sexual way by an adult or older child, when you did not want to be touched that way, or were you ever forced to touch an adult or older child in a sexual way—including anyone who was a member of your family, or anyone outside your family? *(If "Yes," ask:)* Did it happen more than once?
SB. Before the age of 18, were you ever forced to have sex by an adult or older child—including anyone who was a member of your family, or anyone outside your family? *(If "Yes," ask:)* Did it happen more than once?
SC. What about the experience of your own child. As far as you know, IN THE PAST YEAR, has your child been touched in a sexual way by an adult or older child when your child did not want to be touched that way, or has (he/she) been forced to touch an adult or an older child in a sexual way—including anyone who was a member of your family, or anyone outside your family? *(If "Yes," ask:)* Has it happened more than once? *(If "No," ask:)* Has it ever happened?
SD. In the last year, has your child been forced to have sex by an adult or an older child—including anyone who was a member of your family, or anyone outside your family? *(If "Yes," ask:)* Has it happened more than once? *(If "No," ask:)* Has it ever happened?

SOURCE: Reprinted from "Identification of Child Maltreatment With the Parent-Child Conflict Tactics Scales: Development and Psychometric Data for a National Sample of American Parents," pp. 269-270, by M. A. Straus, S. L. Hamby, D. Finkelhor, D. W. Moore, & D. Runyan, 1998, *Child Abuse & Neglect, 22,* 249-270.

SECTION SUMMARY

It is not easy to determine the prevalence of child maltreatment in society. The cultural acceptance of parent-to-child aggression and family privacy norms make child maltreatment easy to hide—and easy to ignore. There are various sources of data on child maltreatment, but none is perfect. In general, researchers rely on two types of child maltreatment data, *self-report surveys* and *official statistics.* Self-report surveys such as the *Parent-Child Conflict Tactics Scale* ask parents about their violent behaviors and their own sexual victimization. Despite significant limitations (e.g., faulty memory and dishonesty), surveys such as this are the only way to estimate the actual amount of child maltreatment in society. The *National Crime Victimization Survey* is only marginally useful because children under the age of 12 are not interviewed.

Official statistics estimate the amount of reported child maltreatment. Child maltreatment that is reported as crime is reflected in the *Uniform Crime Report,* the primary source of information on reported crime in the United States. Child maltreatment reported to protection agencies is reflected in *child protective services* data. CPS data are collected at the state level, but because states typically use different definitions of abuse, have different standards of substantiation, and have different financial commitments to child protection (which affect the number of staff available to investigate cases), these data tend to be inconsistent across states (Finkelhor, 1994a). The *National Incidence Studies* are an attempt to avoid some of the problems by interviewing child protection workers and others mandated to report child maltreatment. Each of these data sources has its strengths and weaknesses, and none is superior to any other.

METHODOLOGICAL ISSUES: CONDUCTING BETTER RESEARCH

Historically, little child maltreatment research has appeared in rigorously refereed journals in sociology, psychology, social work, and criminal justice. According to Rosenbaum (1988), several years ago editors of major social science journals were asked why they seemed unwilling to publish this research. They responded that they would like to publish about child maltreatment but that the research they had seen generally did not meet minimal standards of scientific rigor.

Researchers and advocates interested in child maltreatment, therefore, were faced with two alternatives: either improve the quality of the research or find alternative outlets. In many respects, the past 20 years have seen both alternatives occur. Today, numerous journals are devoted primarily to child maltreatment (e.g., *Child Abuse & Neglect, Journal of Family Violence, Child Abuse and Neglect: The International Perspective, Journal of Interpersonal Violence, The Future of Children, Journal of Child Sexual Abuse,* and *Child Maltreatment*). Some of these journals trace their roots back to the late 1970s (e.g., *Child Abuse & Neglect*), whereas others are only a few years old (e.g., *Child Maltreatment* and *Journal of Child Sexual Abuse*). With so many journals focusing on child maltreatment, there are many options for publication, which means that the research does not necessarily have to be of the highest quality to be published.

At the same time, however, the increasing interest in child maltreatment has fostered stronger emphasis on high-quality research. The federal government, for one, has become active in collecting and disseminating important data (e.g., the *National Incidence Study, Reports From the States to the National Child Abuse and Neglect Data System,* and the *Fifty State Survey*) and in funding high-quality research (e.g., the National Family Violence Survey and the National Family Violence Re-Survey were both federally funded). As a result, better research is produced today than at any other time in history.

Victims are vulnerable and difficult to study, and perpetrators are reluctant to be included in studies.

Overall, however, because of the overreliance on small, selective samples and the lack of comparison groups, many experts find the literature on family violence extensive but not definitive (Ohlin & Tonry, 1989). Part of the problem is the nature of the subject matter. Victims are vulnerable and difficult to study, and perpetrators are reluctant to be included in studies. Experimental designs are rarely feasible, and long-term longitudinal studies are difficult and costly (Rosenbaum, 1988). In the following section, we consider several specific problems that continue to plague child maltreatment research.

Definitional Ambiguity

Despite increased public and research attention, definitions of abuse have "proven to be frustratingly difficult to illuminate" (Emery, 1989, p. 321). The definitional criteria (i.e., severity or frequency of the act, consequences of the act, and intent of the perpetrator) deemed important vary from one audience to the next, as do distinctions between illegitimate and legitimate aggression. As a result, terms such as *abuse, maltreatment,* and *neglect* are merely labels used to describe an indeterminate range of negative behaviors. The behaviors that categorize abuse are often difficult to define objectively, and, as a result, certain acts are seen differently by different people.

Definitional ambiguity has played a key role in delaying the development of effective interventions and solutions.

Definitional ambiguity presents several other problems. Cross-cultural comparisons are challenging because of the variety of definitions. Even in North America, comparisons across various studies are not easy because researchers have operationalized variables so uniquely. Prevalence estimates of how much abuse exists in society are also affected by definitional variation. This lack of definitional consensus has significantly impeded understanding about the very meaning of child maltreatment. It has limited the interpretations of findings and restricted generalizations across studies as well. In the final analysis, definitional ambiguity has played a key role in delaying the development of effective interventions and solutions (Ohlin & Tonry, 1989).

As an example, think about how the word *abuse* is used in the popular and professional literature, as if everyone agrees on its meaning. Clearly, no such consensus exists. We hear it all the time: "New study finds that one out of four children is abused!" This statement is absolutely meaningless unless we know how *abuse* is operationally defined. It is certainly not surprising that the media sometimes oversimplify complicated issues; unfortunately, sometimes the professional community is guilty of the same thing. Perhaps the only solution is to remind all concerned of the continuing need to clearly articulate the operational definitions of abuse used in a given study.

Problems in Conducting Experimental Research

Most of the research in child maltreatment is retrospective and correlational. If a researcher wanted to study the effects of physical child abuse, for example, he or she might examine a sample of abused children for emotional, behavioral, or cognitive problems. These children might then be compared with a group of similar children matched for presumably relevant characteristics (e.g., age, gender, class, and race). In general, this is how research on the effects of abuse is conducted. Predictably, most of this research reveals that abused children have more cognitive problems (e.g., IQ, academic, memory, and verbal), behavior problems (e.g., aggression, drug use, and juvenile delinquency), and emotional problems (e.g., problems with peers, depression, and low self-worth) than do the comparisons (Azar, Ferraro, & Breton, 1998). In other words, abuse is correlated with a number of emotional and behavioral patterns. Yet two variables can be correlated without necessarily being causally related. Certainly, that child maltreatment victims are more likely than nonvictims to suffer from adult depression, for example, lends some support to the hypothesis that child abuse can cause depression. It is possible, however, that other factors that are also correlated with abuse (e.g., living in a chaotic family environment, living in poverty, and few social supports), rather than childhood abuse, might be more important causal determinants of emotional problems. Another possibility is that children with emotional problems are more likely to be abused. With retrospective correlational research, it is impossible to clearly identify causal relationships, and this means that conclusions are usually tentative.

Retrospective correlational research cannot clearly identify causal relationships.

Longitudinal Outcome Studies

Of course, researchers generally have little choice but to conduct correlational, rather than experimental, research. It is hardly feasible, for example, to take a sample of 200 children and randomly assign 100 into abusive families and 100 into nonabusive families. In some cases, however, methodologically sophisticated longitudinal studies might replace experimental designs. With longitudinal designs, the researcher can track the effects of child maltreatment through time. Unfortunately, these studies are expensive, participants are difficult to obtain, and attrition rates for participants are high. In addition, researchers are under pressure to produce immediate results (Azar, 1988). As a result, most research designs are cross-sectional, using retrospective, self-report survey data. Only a few researchers have successfully conducted longitudinal studies (e.g., Erickson, Egeland, & Pianta, 1989). It is also true that academic training for execution of large-scale longitudinal studies has been inadequate (Stouthamer-Loeber, van Kammen, & Loeber, 1992).

Only a few researchers have successfully conducted longitudinal studies.

Comparison Groups

Many studies have suffered from a failure to include satisfactory comparison groups of participants (see Rosenbaum, 1988). Comparison groups allow researchers to determine how perpetrators or abuse victims might be different from, or similar to, other people. When comparison groups have been used, moreover, they have often been insufficient (Wolfe & Mosk, 1983). The best way to evaluate the success of a sexual abuse treatment plan, for example, is to compare a randomly selected treatment group with a nontreatment control group (see Plotkin, Azar, Twentyman, & Perri, 1981). Researchers, however, seldom conduct research of this type.

When comparison group data cannot easily be obtained, researchers sometimes use normative data (i.e., published standards). As an illustration, researchers might initially obtain mothers' ratings of abused children on the Child Behavior Checklist (CBCL), a standardized checklist of a variety of behavior problems (Achenbach & Edelbrock, 1983). The investigators could then compare this sample of mothers' ratings with those obtained previously from a large sample of mothers from the general population (the normative sample) who had also rated their children using the CBCL.

The advantage to researchers in using the normative data from the CBCL is the ability to compare participants' scores without recruiting a comparison group of mothers who would be willing to rate their children. The disadvantage is that a researcher cannot generally control for confounding variables (e.g., prenatal drug exposure) with normative data. As a result, establishing cause-and-effect relationships is difficult. If the abused children in the above illustration, for instance, are rated as displaying more behavioral problems than children rated from the published norms, there is no way of determining what has caused this difference.

Problems With Samples

Researchers have used widely divergent samples, including random samples of the population, convenience samples of available parents, and clinical samples. Obviously, systematic differences among these samples are likely, and their noncomparability further hampers cross-comparison.

The representativeness of samples is also an important issue in social science research, with the area of child maltreatment no exception. When samples are representative, such as in the National Family Violence Surveys and the National Crime Victimization Surveys, they can be used to make inferences about the population. Nationally representative surveys thus provide the only types of data that allow an examination of patterns of child maltreatment in the United States as a whole.

Much of the child maltreatment research, however, is based on clinical samples rather than on representative samples. Clinical samples tend to be small, nonrepresentative, or convenience ("handy") samples that provide little information about the general patterns of behavior in a broader population. Data derived from clinical samples often lack generalizability even within small subgroups of the population. Despite serious limitations, studies based on clinical samples provide useful information about the dynamics and causes of abuse and often provide *preliminary* notions about prevention and treatment (Weis, 1989).

Some researchers have been inclined to misapply findings derived from one type of sample to another (Straus, 1993). Specifically, Straus (1991b) describes the problem as the *clinical fallacy* and the *representative sample fallacy.* The clinical fallacy refers to inappropriate generalization of clinical samples to the entire population. Generalizations may not hold because persons who seek or receive treatment are often not representative of the entire population. On the other hand, automatically assuming that large population samples are superior to smaller clinical samples (the representative sample fallacy) is unwarranted if the two groups are different. Clinicians, for example, often need information about specific groups of people, such as male sex offenders. In this case, clinicians would like to obtain a representative sample of male sex offenders, not just a representative sample of males.

SUMMARY

This chapter summarizes the theoretical and methodological issues that make child maltreatment one of the most difficult and problematic areas of social science research. The theory in child maltreatment is not well developed, and research discussions are typically reduced to structural and individual-level correlates of child maltreatment. Many sociological factors contribute to physically violent and verbally aggressive family interactions. The culture encourages and condones verbal and physical aggression by parents that, arguably, could indirectly contribute to maltreatment. Family structure factors also are thought to contribute to child maltreatment. Family members spend a great deal of time together, and interactions tend to be intense. The subordination and dependency of children make them vulnerable to abuse, and family privacy norms make child maltreatment easy to conceal.

Several sociological theories of deviance are relevant to child maltreatment discussions. Strain theories maintain that child maltreatment will be most common among people who are blocked in their attempts to achieve economic success. Strain theory is supported by evidence that suggests higher levels of maltreatment among those with lower incomes and the unemployed. Social bonding theory assumes that various social constraints—including intimate attachments to significant others, commitments to conventional activities and goals, and beliefs that violence is wrong—keep people from mistreating children. In the absence of these stakes in conformity, rates of abuse will be high. Deterrence theory predicts that as long as the legal risks of abuse are low (i.e., low perceived certainty and low perceived severity), abuse will be common.

Psychological and biological theories help identify risk factors that make child maltreatment somewhat predictable. One psychological explanation is that perpetrators possibly suffer from a mental disorder, but psychopathology seems to be present in only a small percentage of adults who physically or sexually abuse children. Perpetrators do often suffer from a variety of less severe psychological and behavioral problems, including stress, low self-esteem, substance abuse, hostility, and anger control problems. Many perpetrators are also physiologically reactive to high-stress situations, have a low IQ, suffer from attention problems, and have physical problems. The most important psychological theory is social learning theory, which suggests that children exposed to violence, either as direct victims or as witnesses of marital violence, are likely to see violence as an acceptable way of expressing frustration.

The many difficulties associated with determining the extent of child maltreatment are illustrated in Figure 2.1. The top of the funnel (Level I) is the actual amount of child maltreatment that exists in society. Although this figure is obviously unknown and unknowable, it can be estimated with self-report surveys such as the Parent-Child Conflict Tactics Scale. The CTSPC asks parents about a variety of conflict resolution tactics they might employ when upset with a child (e.g., nonviolent responses, psychological responses, and physical aggression responses). The CTSPC also includes supplemental questions on neglect, corporal punishment, and sexual abuse.

The most versatile and inclusive source of official statistics is the National Incidence Study, a congressionally mandated survey of child protection workers and other mandated professionals. This widely respected data source employs a standardized definition, plus a harm standard and an endangerment standard. CPS estimates are somewhat more limited because many mandated professionals choose not to report suspected cases of abuse. CPS data are also limited because they are collected at the state level, where definitions and investigative procedures are not standardized.

Despite the growing volume of published research, problems continue to plague the field. The most glaring of these may be definitional ambiguity. For example, the phrase "child abuse" is commonly used in popular and professional circles, but there is little agreement on exactly what it means. Without specific information on how abuse is operationalized, findings are difficult to compare across studies. Another problem is that most child maltreatment research is retrospective and correlational. This makes it all but impossible to establish cause-effect relationships. One possible solution is longitudinal research, but this is expensive and difficult to conduct. Many studies also lack appropriate comparison groups, making it difficult to know how perpetrators of abuse are different from, or similar to, other people. Finally, child maltreatment research suffers from an overreliance on clinical samples, which means the results cannot be generalized to the entire population.

3

Physical Child Abuse

CHAPTER OUTLINE

AN INTERVIEW WITH MURRAY STRAUS

"We have to change the culture of communities before parents will feel free to bring up children without violence."

Murray Straus, one of the world's preeminent family violence researchers, can be credited with organizing the field after the initial impetus provided by medical research on child abuse. He is Professor of Sociology and Codirector of the interdisciplinary Family Research Laboratory at the University of New Hampshire. He has authored or coauthored more than 200 articles and 15 books related to the family. An early and significant book, published in 1980 and coauthored with Richard Gelles and Suzanne Steinmetz, is *Behind Closed Doors: Violence in the American Family.* His latest book is *Beating the Devil Out of Them: Corporal Punishment in American Families* (1994). He has served as President of several professional organizations, such as the National Council on Family Relations, and has received one prestigious honor after another, including the 1992 Distinguished Contribution Award from the New Hampshire Psychological Association. He received both his B.A. in international relations and his Ph.D. in sociology (1956) from the University of Wisconsin.

Q: What sparked your interest in family violence?

A: It was the old scientific principle: If you come across something interesting, drop everything else and study it. In my case, it was the discovery in 1979 that one quarter of my students had been hit by their parents during their senior year in high school, and another quarter had been threatened with being hit. Somehow, it clicked with me that this kind of parental violence might be one of the roots of the violence that came to national attention during the Vietnam War era, a period of riots and assassinations, and the rising murder rate.

Q: Why did your work meet with such wide acceptance?

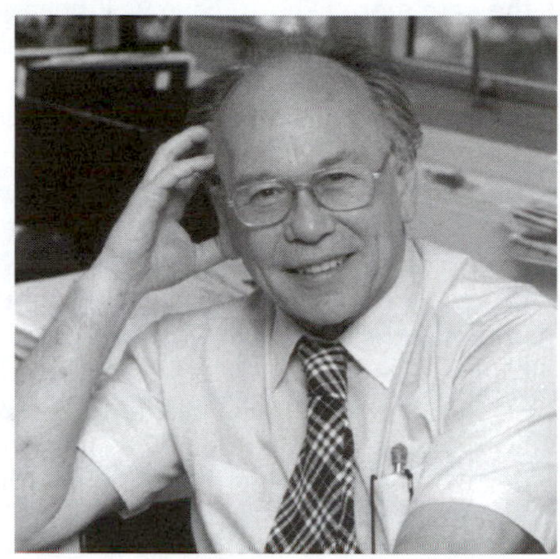

A: I think it was because my research on wife beating coincided with the establishment of battered women's shelters. They needed data on how pervasive the problem was, and our National Family Violence Surveys provided the statistics. A major accomplishment of the shelter movement was to create consciousness of and concern about wife beating.

Q: What has been your most influential article in the field?

A: The article on the Conflict Tactics Scales [CTS]. The CTS was a technological breakthrough. Up until then, psychologists and sociologists tended to think that they had to rely on official statistics or case studies to get data on family violence. The CTS showed that it was possible to get valid data from questionnaires in an ordinary clinical or research interview.

Q: What is your current research focus?

A: After more than 20 years of studying wife beating, I returned to just where I started in family violence 27 years ago—research on spanking and other legal forms of corporal punishment. I'm also developing new measures for use in family violence research. We have just finished a major revision of the CTS, and we are well along on developing another test. It is going to be called the Personal and Relationships Profile.

Q: What would you like to do if you had a large grant?

A: I would do a community experiment on corporal punishment. Corporal punishment will take a long time to end if we deal only with parents. Convincing them that they are more likely to have well-behaved children if they *never* spank tends to get undone when the inevitable misbehaviors occur and their friends and relatives say that what that child needs is a good spanking. We have to change the culture of communities before parents will feel free to bring up children without violence.

Q: What research would you like to see others undertake?

A: I think it is important to study violence *by women* against their partners. Almost everyone is afraid to deal with this issue despite data showing that women strike out physically against their partners as often as do men, and they also hit first just as often as men. My concern with the issue is partly because I think the evidence is clear that when women engage in what they call "harmless" violence, it is not. True, the man is rarely harmed, but it tremendously increases the risk that the woman will be.

Q: What social institutions must get involved to end family violence?

A: Unless churches get involved, things are going to progress much more slowly. When was the last time you heard a sermon saying that spanking is violence and we should stop bringing up our kids violently?

They cry in the dark so you can't see their tears.
They hide in the light so you can't see their fears.
Forgive and forget.
All the while, love and pain become one in [sic] the same
in the eyes of a wounded child.

Because hell, hell is for children.
And you know that their little lives can become such a mess.
Hell! Hell is for children.
And you shouldn't have to pay for your love with your bones and your flesh.

It's all so confusing this brutal abusing.
They blacken your eyes and then apologize.
Be Daddy's little girl and don't tell Mommy a thing.
Be a good little boy and you'll get a new toy.
Tell Grandma you fell off the swing.

Benatar, Geraldo, and Capps (1981)[1]

In 1980, Pat Benatar recorded the lyrics to the song titled *Hell Is for Children* to describe the world of an abused child. Until the 1960s, society was relatively unaware of the "hell" characteristic of abused children's lives. Child maltreatment was considered a mythical or rare phenomenon that occurred only in individuals' imaginations or at best in "sick" families from lower-social-class groups. Child maltreatment, however, is an ugly reality for millions of children each year and a problem the U.S. Advisory Board on Child Abuse and Neglect (1990) has described as a national emergency.

This chapter focuses on one form of child maltreatment: physical child abuse (PCA). In the first part of the chapter, we examine issues related to defining the physical abuse of children and determining the magnitude of the problem with official estimates and self-report surveys. Our attention then shifts to the typical characteristics of physically abused children and the adults who abuse them in terms of age, gender, and additional characteristics. We then evaluate the short-term as well as long-term consequences associated with PCA. The chapter concludes with a discussion of the major theories proposing causes of PCA and recommendations for addressing the problem.

SCOPE OF THE PROBLEM

What Is Physical Child Abuse?

One of the most significant issues in attempting to understand the problem of PCA is defining the term *physical child abuse.* Consider the following situations:

> Three-year-old Jimmy was playing with his puppy near a pond in his backyard. He tried to make his puppy drink from the pond by roughly holding his face to the water. Jimmy's father saw him forcing the puppy to drink and yelled at him to stop. After Jimmy did not respond, his father pulled Jimmy away from the dog and began holding his head under water to "teach him a lesson" about the appropriate way to treat his dog.

> Angela's baby, Maria, had colic from the day she was born. This meant that from 4:00 in the afternoon until 8:00 p.m., every day, Maria would cry inconsolably. No matter what Angela did, nothing would help Maria to stop crying. One evening, after Maria had been crying for 3 straight hours, Angela began shaking Maria from frustration. The shaking caused Maria to cry more loudly, which, in turn, caused Angela to shake the 5-month-old more vigorously. Angela shook Maria until she lost consciousness.

> Ryan and his brother Matthew were playing with their Power Rangers when they got into a disagreement. Both boys began hitting each other and calling one another names. Alice, the mother of the boys, came running into the room and pulled the boys apart. She then took each boy, pulled down his trousers, put him over her knee, and spanked him several times.

These vignettes portray a range of behaviors, some of which are clearly abusive, others that may or may not be considered abusive. Acts of violence by adults against children and adolescents range from mild slaps to extremely injurious attacks. Researchers and practitioners are also discovering that violence against children, in rare instances, can take significantly unusual forms (see Box 3.1, "Munchausen Syndrome by Proxy"). Prior to the 1960s, however, few, if any, of these situations would have been labeled abusive.

With the "discovery" of child abuse during the 1960s (Kempe et al., 1962), and the increased interest in child protection that followed, child abuse definitions changed rapidly. For the most part, the definitions that emerged during this time focused on acts of violence that caused some form of observable harm. Therefore, although recognition of PCA was increasing, the definition of physical

BOX 3.1 Munchausen Syndrome by Proxy

Increasing attention has focused on an unusual manifestation in adult perpetrators of PCA termed *Munchausen syndrome by proxy.* Munchausen syndrome, commonly referred to as factitious disorder, is a condition in which adults seek medical treatment for no apparent purpose other than to assume the role of a patient. The term *Munchausen syndrome by proxy* was first described by Meadow (1977) and is used to characterize adults who use a child as the vehicle for fabricated illness. The most recent version of the *Diagnostic and Statistical Manual of Mental Disorders* (American Psychiatric Association, 1994) defines the essential features of the condition as the "deliberate production or feigning of physical or psychological signs or symptoms *in another person* who is under the individual's care" motivated by "a psychological need to assume the sick role by proxy" (p. 725, emphasis added).

Typically, the children are "paraded before the medical profession with a fantastic range of illnesses" (D. A. Rosenberg, 1987, p. 548). Jones (1994) recently described the principal routes taken by caregivers to produce or feign illness, including the fabrication of symptoms by caregivers, alteration of laboratory specimens (e.g., urine or blood), and the direct production of physical symptoms or disease in the child. Caregivers have been known to contaminate children's urine specimens with their own blood and present the specimen to their doctor, claiming that the child had been urinating blood (D. A. Rosenberg, 1987). One mother repeatedly administered laxatives to her child, causing severe diarrhea, blood infection, and dehydration (Peters, 1989). In another case, a mother injected feces into her child's intravenous line to produce illness in the child (D. A. Rosenberg, 1987).

Until recently, virtually nothing was known about Munchausen syndrome by proxy outside of anecdotal case reports. As recognition of the condition has increased, several studies assessing the characteristics of adults with this syndrome and their child victims have appeared. The children are typically quite young, most in their preschool years (D. A. Rosenberg, 1987). The adult is most often the child's mother, and these women often have considerable experience or knowledge in health-related areas (Meadow, 1990). Recent evidence suggests that such individuals frequently suffer from additional disturbances such as Munchausen syndrome and personality disorders (Bools, Neale, & Meadow, 1994). The majority of conditions inflicted on these children involve the gastrointestinal, genitourinary, and central nervous systems (American Psychiatric Association, 1994). Some have suggested that another characteristic of these families is the unusual circumstances surrounding the deaths of siblings (e.g., multiple sibling deaths; Meadow, 1990).

The production or feigning of illness in dependent children is considered abusive, in large part, because of the serious physical consequences to children. The procedures used by caregivers to produce illness often cause physical discomfort or pain for the child. McClung, Murray, and Braden (1988), for example, described the intentional administration of ipecac to produce symptoms in children (e.g., recurrent and chronic vomiting and diarrhea). Such behavior on the part of caregivers sometimes results in the death of a child. In one review of Munchausen syndrome by proxy cases, the authors concluded that 9% of children died as a result of the procedures inflicted on them by their parents (D. A. Rosenberg, 1987). Children are often subjected to unnecessary and sometimes painful and potentially harmful medical procedures, such as surgery, X rays, and medications, as physicians unwittingly attempt to diagnose and treat the symptoms described by caregivers (Malatack, Wiener, Gartner, Zitelli, & Brunetti, 1985; Meadow, 1977). Such children are also at risk for short- and long-term physical illness and dysfunction (D. A. Rosenberg, 1987) as well as psychological problems (McGuire & Feldman, 1989).

abuse was still restrictive. As Gelles and Cornell (1990) point out, "If a father takes a gun and shoots at his child and misses, there is no physical injury. There is, of course, harm in a father's shooting and missing, but the act itself does not qualify as abuse" (p. 21).

In 1988, the National Center on Child Abuse and Neglect broadened the definition of abuse to include both a *harm standard* and an *endangerment standard* (DHHS, 1988, 1996). Using the harm standard, children are recognized as PCA victims if they have observable injuries lasting at least 48 hours. Children without observable injuries may also be recognized as abuse victims if they are deemed substantially *at risk* for injury or endangerment.

Despite more inclusive definitions, such as those used by the National Center on Child Abuse and Neglect, controversy continues to exist regarding the specific behaviors that should be labeled "violent" or "abusive." As we discussed in Chapter 1, most experts and researchers in the field define *violence* as an act carried out intentionally (or nonaccidentally) to cause physical pain or injury to another person (Gelles & Cornell, 1990). *Acts* of violence, however, can range from a slap on the hand to a cigarette burn on the face to an act so violent that the result is death. What range of behaviors should be included under the umbrella of PCA?

Physical Punishment and Child Rearing

In Chapter 1, we made a distinction between legitimate and illegitimate violence. At one extreme of the continuum are those practices considered to be "normal" violence, including commonplace physical acts such as slapping, pushing, or spanking. Many people consider such acts to be an acceptable part of punishment and child rearing. Indeed, survey data suggest that such behaviors are not labeled as abusive by most and are actually quite common. Surveys of parents, for example, show that 90% have used some form of physical punishment on their children (Straus, 1983; Wauchope & Straus, 1990). Similar studies of young adults show comparable rates, and 93% to 95% report experiencing some physical punishment as children or adolescents (Bryan & Freed, 1982; Graziano & Namaste, 1990). As Graziano and Namaste state,

> Slapping, spanking, paddling, and, generally, hitting children for purposes of discipline are accepted, pervasive, adult behaviors in U.S. families. In these instances, although anger, physical attack, and pain are involved between two people of vastly different size, weight, and strength, such behavior is commonly accepted as a proper exercise of adult authority over children. (pp. 459-460)

For many who study child maltreatment, the level of acceptance of this "normal" violence is appalling. Perhaps the most significant critic of the cultural acceptance of corporal punishment is Murray Straus, who is highlighted at the beginning of this chapter. In recent years, Straus (e.g., 1991c, 1994a) has attracted considerable attention for his research and views on spanking. Spanking is harmful, Straus argues, for two reasons. First, it legitimizes violence. When authority figures spank, they are, in essence, condoning the use of violence as a way to deal with frustration and to settle disputes. Second, the implicit message of acceptance contributes to violence in other aspects of society. To explain this extension of violence, Straus (1991c) employs a "cultural spillover theory," arguing that violence "in one sphere of life tends to engender violence in other spheres" (p. 137).

Spanking is positively correlated with other forms of family violence.

The research evidence tends to support this perspective that spanking is positively correlated with other forms of family violence, including sibling abuse and spouse assault. On the basis of the first Family Violence Survey, Straus (1991c) estimated that children who had been physically punished during the previous year were three times more likely to have assaulted a sibling during that year. Spanking is also correlated with crime outside the home, including self-reported delinquency, arrest, and homicide (Straus, 1991c). Straus's most recent research focuses on the relationship between spanking and antisocial behaviors such as cheating, telling lies, and disobedience in school. This research suggests that parents who use spanking to punish antisocial behavior are actually contributing to subsequent antisocial behavior in their children (Straus, Sugarman, & Giles-Sims, 1997). Especially problematic, according to Straus and Mouradian (in press), is impulsive corporal punishment, which is lashing out in anger without forethought or control.

As Straus (1994a) himself recognized, two variables can be correlated without necessarily being causally connected. Perhaps children with problem behaviors tend to be spanked and then go on to a life of crime. It is also possible that the main reason spanking and other forms of violence are correlated is because PCA and violence are correlated. Because children who are physically abused are presumably likely to be spanked, spanking might appear to be a causal contributor when it is not.

Despite the potential limitations of the research, many experts are convinced by the data that spanking is harmful, and many label spanking a form of child abuse. To a majority of Americans, however, it remains a common practice and is certainly not considered a behavior worthy of the abuse label in the minds of the general public. As will become clear in the next section, many states explicitly exclude corporal punishment from child abuse statutes (see Chapter 7 for a more detailed summary of the debate about corporal punishment).

Legal Perspectives

Legal definitions of PCA are different from conceptual definitions but come with their own set of difficulties. Daro (1988) has identified several problems involved in developing and operationalizing state statutes, including but not limited to the following: (a) defining abuse in as objective a manner as possible, (b) balancing children's rights with parental rights, and (c) applying the legal system to the solution of such a complex human problem.

Unfortunately, there is no uniform law that defines PCA for all jurisdictions within the United States. Instead, each of the 50 states, and the District of Columbia, has its own legal definition of PCA and corresponding reporting responsibilities. In general, all states acknowledge that PCA is physical injury caused by other than accidental means that results in a substantial risk of physical harm. Other key features of definitions vary according to the specificity of the acts included as physically abusive (Myers & Peters, 1987; Stein, 1993). Most emphasize the overt consequences of abuse such as bruises or broken bones (Wolfe, 1987). In addition, most states generally allow parents to use "reasonable" corporal punishment with children (Myers, 1992). The California state statute, as outlined by Westat in 1991, for example, indicates that PCA "does not include reasonable and age appropriate spanking to the buttocks where there is no evidence of serious physical injury" (cited in Myers, 1992, p. 141). (See Box 1.2 in Chapter 1, "California Penal Code and Child Maltreatment".)

How Common Is Physical Child Abuse?

Despite problems in defining PCA, researchers have made numerous efforts to determine the scope of the problem. Within the United States, researchers generally use one of two methods of estimation. In the first method, *official estimates* represent the number of cases of physical abuse *reported* to governmental social service agencies. In the second method, *self-report surveys* analyze the proportion of PCA in a population.

Official Estimates

The number of children who are officially reported to child protection agencies because of child abuse has increased each year. Recall from Chapter 2 that the three National Incidence Studies (NIS-1, NIS-2, and NIS-3), conducted by the National Center on Child Abuse and Neglect, are designed to measure the number of cases of PCA reported to investigatory agencies, schools, hospitals, and other social service agencies (see Table 2.1 in Chapter 2 for the definitions of PCA employed by NIS-3). The first of these surveys, published in 1981, estimated that there were 199,100 reported cases of PCA for a rate of 3.1 per 1,000 children (DHHS, 1981). In 1986, the second survey found that the figure had risen to approximately 311,500 children for a rate of 4.9 per 1,000 children (Sedlak, 1990). The third survey, published in 1996, found that the number of reported cases of PCA nearly had doubled since 1986 with 614,000 children reported for PCA in 1993 for a rate of 9.1 per 1,000 children (Sedlak & Broadhurst, 1996).

Other organizations have attempted to determine the scope of PCA through the aggregation of CPS reports across the 50 states and the District of Columbia. Since 1976, the American Association for Protecting Children (AAPC), a division of the American Humane Association, has conducted an annual National Study of Child Neglect and Abuse Reporting. This study, an annual survey of official reports of child maltreatment documented by CPS agencies, similarly estimated that between the years 1976 and 1987 there was a threefold increase in child maltreatment reporting overall (AAPC, 1989). In the majority of cases, caseworkers classified injuries as minor (e.g., minor cuts, bruises, and welts) rather than major (e.g., brain damage, bone fracture, internal injuries, poisonings, and burns and scalds; e.g., AAPC, 1988).

The most recent figures available, published by the National Committee to Prevent Child Abuse, estimated that CPS agencies received 3,195,000 reports of child maltreatment (including physical and sexual abuse, neglect, and psychological maltreatment) in 1997, which converts to a rate of 47 children of every 1,000 children in the United States (Wang & Daro, 1998). Almost 1 million of these cases (e.g., 830,700) were specific instances of PCA, which accounted for 26% of all child maltreatment reports. The National Committee to Prevent Child Abuse also estimated that in 1996, approximately 616 children died as a result of PCA, and another 510 children died as a result of physical neglect (Wang & Daro, 1998). Similar estimates have been obtained from the National Child Abuse and Neglect Data System (NCANDS) database (DHHS, 1998).

Self-Report Surveys

Estimates based on nationwide surveys of families across the United States provide another source of information on the rates of PCA. The self-report surveys discussed in this chapter are estimates from surveys of parents in the general population who report using some form of physical violence on their children. The most significant study of this type is the second National Family Violence Survey, conducted in 1985 (Gelles & Straus, 1987, 1988). In this telephone survey, which used the Conflict Tactics Scale (CTS) to measure abuse, parents reported on the conflict tactics techniques they used with their children in the past year. The techniques respondents could select ranged from mild forms of violence (e.g., slapped or spanked child) to severe forms of violence (e.g., beat up child, burned or scalded child, or used a knife or gun).

> Three fourths of parents admit at least one violent act during the rearing of their children.

Results indicated that as many as 75% of the reporting sample admitted at least one violent act in rearing their children. Approximately 2% of parents engaged in one act of abusive violence (a high probability of injuring the child) during the year prior to the survey. The most frequent type of violence in either case was slapping or spanking the child. Thirty-nine percent of respondents reported slapping or spanking their children more than two times in the past year.

A new version of the CTS, the Parent-Child Conflict Tactics Scale (CTSPC), was designed to improve on the limitations of the CTS (Straus et al., 1998). The original CTS was created to assess behavior between partners in adult relationships, rather than behavior between parents and children. The Parent-Child Conflict Tactics Scale improves and expands on the CTS by including revised psychological aggression and physical assault scales as well as new scales to measure nonviolent discipline, child neglect, and sexual abuse (see Chapter 2 for additional discussion of the CTSPC, and Table 2.2 for a list of PCA items).

The CTSPC was recently administered to a nationally representative sample of 1,000 parents who reported on the disciplinary methods they use with their children as part of a survey sponsored by the Gallup Organization. The CTSPC distinguishes between three levels of physical assault including *minor* assault (i.e., corporal punishment), *severe* assault (i.e., physical maltreatment), and *very severe* assault (i.e., severe physical maltreatment). Nearly two thirds of parents reported using at least one physical assault tactic during the previous year, and three fourths of parents reported using some method of physical assault during the rearing of their children. The items that accounted for most of the physical assaults by parents were those that were considered minor assaults such as spanking, slapping, and pinching (Straus et al., 1998). As Straus and colleagues point out, however, although the majority of physical assaults were in the minor assault category and included corporal punishment tactics, nearly *half of all parents* engaged in behaviors from the severe physical assault subscale at some point during their parenting. These included hitting the child with an object such as a stick or belt, slapping the child on the face, hitting the child with a fist, kicking the child, or throwing/knocking down the child. Each of the very severe physical assault tactics (e.g., "beating up" or burning the child or threatening the child with a knife or gun) was used by less than 1% of the sample.

Is the Rate of Physical Child Abuse Increasing?

Whether the rate of PCA is increasing is a difficult question to answer because there are several problems in estimating the frequency of PCA. Perhaps the most significant problem is the lack of definitional consensus. Because definitions of abuse change through time and across studies, estimates also vary. Depending on the *definition of abusive acts,* for example, the rate of abuse could range from nearly all children (i.e., those who are spanked) to very few children (e.g., those who are threatened with a gun). The rate of abuse also varies depending on the *definition of harm* that is used. Abuse estimates that include children who are at risk for harm are higher than estimates that include only those children with observable injury. With specific regard to official estimates, there is the obvious problem that PCA is a hidden crime and often goes unreported. There is also a problem in the way cases of abuse are counted. Some states, for instance, count individual children in estimating the amount of PCA. Others use the family as the unit of analysis, which underestimates abuse because more than one child may be maltreated per family. In addition, the retrospective nature of self-report studies and the possibility that parents may forget, or fail to admit, their abusive behavior limit their validity.

These methodological problems contribute to the difficulty in determining whether PCA is increasing, and they produce considerable debate among scholars (e.g., Besharov, 1990; Finkelhor, 1990). Is PCA increasing? The answer to the question seems to depend on whether one examines evidence from official or self-report studies. Official estimates indicate that rates of PCA are increasing dramatically. Between 1980 and 1993, the number of reported cases more than tripled (DHHS, 1981, 1988; Sedlak & Broadhurst, 1996). Gelles and Straus (1987) suggest that official rates of PCA have increased because the attention focused on the problem of child abuse has resulted in higher rates of reporting in recent years. Changes such as broader definitions of abuse, mandatory reporting laws, 24-hour hotlines, and state and national media campaigns have all contributed to increases in reported violence.

Although the increasing numbers of reports for PCA primarily reflect greater public awareness and concern, there has likely been some *actual increase* in PCA, particularly in recent years. The results of the most recent National Incidence Study, for example, indicate that although the number of less severe cases of child abuse remained stable between 1986 and 1993, the number of serious cases quadrupled (Sedlak & Broadhurst, 1996). These findings seem to suggest an increase in reporting due to more than enhanced awareness and concern; otherwise, the increase in reporting would be evident across all levels of abuse severity.

Although official statistics show an increase in the number of reports of PCA, particularly for serious cases, in recent years, the *rate* of increase has declined (Gelles & Cornell, 1990; Wang & Daro, 1997). In addition, statistics from self-report studies have not shown increases in parental reports of violence directed at children. Gelles and Straus (1987), for example, replicated their 1975 nationwide survey 10 years later and found that the estimated rate of violence toward children actually declined from 1975 to 1985. The most substantial decline was in the use of severe and very severe violence, which was 47% lower in 1985. Severe violence, defined as "kicking, biting, punching," "hitting or trying to hit with an object," "beating, threatening with a knife or a gun," or "using a knife or a gun over the past 12 months," declined from 1975 to 1985. It is unclear, however, to what degree *reporting* rates reflect *true* rates of PCA. Presumably, many parents who are abusive would not make this admission to researchers. Because child abuse arguably became more socially condemned between 1975 and 1985, one has to wonder if decreasing self-report rates of child abuse reflect increasing instances of dishonesty in reporting.

SECTION SUMMARY

Society has not always recognized physical violence directed at children as abusive. Despite delays in recognizing that abuse of children is wrong, today PCA is illegal in every state. Most state statutes and experts in the field recognize that PCA includes a range of acts carried out with the intention of harm that puts a child at considerable *risk for physical injury.* Disagreement continues to exist, however, in regard to behaviors that do not result in any physical signs of injury (e.g., spanking) or that lie in the borderland between "normal" corporal punishment and that which is excessive (e.g., resulting in broken bones). Effective *legal statutes* depend on objective definitions, balancing children's rights with parental rights, and enforcement of workable solutions for such a complex human problem.

Protective services receive hundreds of thousands of reports of PCA each year, and the number of reports has steadily increased during the past two decades. *Official estimates* as well as *self-report surveys* indicate that violence toward children in the home occurs frequently. As many as 75% of Americans report using at least one violent act toward their children at some point during child rearing. Debate about whether the rate of PCA is increasing has focused on official reporting statistics, which show a yearly increase in reports of PCA, compared with self-report survey data, which generally show stable, or declining, rates of PCA.

SEARCHING FOR PATTERNS: CHARACTERISTICS OF VICTIMS AND PERPETRATORS

Are girls or boys more likely to be the victims of PCA? Are children with particular behavioral characteristics or from specific ethnic backgrounds more vulnerable to physical abuse? What are the specific characteristics and traits of the adults who perpetrate violent acts against children? Agencies that receive official reports of abuse and survey data collected from representative samples of the population have provided much of the information on the sociodemographic characteristics of victims and perpetrators of PCA. Clinical as well as empirical studies have also provided information relevant to the psychological characteristics of PCA perpetrators. Although these sources of information are limited by the biases discussed in the previous section, they nonetheless provide some insight into the characteristics of child victims and adult perpetrators of PCA.

Characteristics of Victims of Physical Child Abuse

Age

Much evidence suggests that the risk of child maltreatment declines with age (DHHS, 1996, 1998). A similar pattern has also been noted specifically for cases of PCA. Statistics from the American Association for Protecting Children (1985), for example, indicate that for all types of officially reported physical abuse, the majority of child victims fall between the ages of 0 and 5 years (51%), followed by children aged 6 to 11 (26%), and then children aged 12 to 17 (23%). Although age differences in child maltreatment have become somewhat attenuated in recent years, nearly half of all physical abuse victims are aged 7 years or younger (DHHS, 1998; Sedlak & Broadhurst, 1996).

> Nearly half of all physical abuse victims are aged 7 years or younger.

Self-report surveys, on the other hand, suggest no decrease in PCA as children grow older (Straus et al., 1998; Wauchope & Straus, 1990). One explanation for this inconsistency could be that higher rates of PCA in official estimates reflect the greater risk of *injury* present among young children rather than greater risk of *assault* (Wauchope & Straus, 1990). Assaults that produce injury are certainly more likely to be reported to professionals.

Young children are not the only age group at risk for abuse. The most recent information from official estimates (DHHS, 1998), for example, indicates that approximately 32% of all PCA reports are for adolescents between 12 and 17 years. Gelles and Cornell (1990) suggest that the absence of attention toward adolescent victims, until recently, may result from societal perceptions that adolescents share some complicity in their abuse because of their size, strength, or difficult behaviors that may provoke the violence they receive. Consequently, such violent interactions may not be viewed as abusive but rather as legitimate methods of parental control. In addition, adolescents may appear to be less physically vulnerable or in danger of bodily harm (Powers & Eckenrode, 1988).

Gender

In regard to gender, research suggests that males are generally at a slightly greater risk for PCA than are females. Results from the second National Family Violence Survey found that for both minor and major forms of violence, males were at greater risk (Wolfner & Gelles, 1993). Official reports from 1996 data summarized by the National Center on Child Abuse and Neglect (DHHS, 1998) also indicate that males are more likely than females to be victims of PCA. Statistics from the AAPC (1988) indicate that for minor acts of physical abuse, males and females are equally at risk, but for major acts of physical abuse, boys are slightly more at risk than are females. Consistent with these data, findings from the NIS-3 indicated that boys were at somewhat greater risk for serious injuries compared with girls (Sedlak & Broadhurst, 1996).

Socioeconomic Status

Although maltreatment occurs in all socioeconomic groups, official reporting statistics have consistently shown that PCA occurs disproportionately more often among economically and socially disadvantaged families (DHHS, 1981, 1988; Sedlak, 1991; Sedlak & Broadhurst, 1996; Zuravin, 1989). Physically abused children were 12 times more likely to come from families with annual incomes less than $15,000 (Sedlak & Broadhurst, 1996). According to the most recent data from the AAPC (1988), 49% of all families reported for maltreatment were receiving public assistance in the form of AFDC such as food stamps or Medicaid. Low income also appears to be related to the severity of abuse, with serious or fatal injuries being more likely among families whose annual income is below the poverty level (e.g., Gil, 1970; Pelton, 1994; Wolfner & Gelles, 1993). This finding does not appear to be a consequence of bias in reporting, especially because it has emerged consistently across various databases during the past 20 years (Drake & Zuravin, 1998).

> Victims of physical child abuse are disproportionately represented among economically disadvantaged families.

Race

Studies evaluating the relationship between race and PCA are fraught with methodological difficulties (Asbury, 1993) and, as a result, should be interpreted cautiously. These methodological difficulties no doubt contribute to the equivocal findings in studies attempting to determine racial differences in rates of PCA. According to the most recent official reporting statistics from the National Committee to Prevent Child Abuse (Wang & Daro, 1998), 56.1% of PCA reports involved Caucasian children, 27.7% involved African American children, and 13.6% involved Hispanic children. Compared with 1996 census data (U.S. Bureau of the Census, 1997), these figures suggest that African and Hispanic Americans appear to be slightly overrepresented and Caucasians underrepresented in PCA reports. Results from the NIS, however, which are subject to fewer reporting biases, indicate an absence of race differences in rates of PCA (DHHS, 1981, 1988; Sedlak & Broadhurst, 1996).

Findings from national self-report studies of PCA are mixed. The first National Family Violence Survey found that rates of PCA for Caucasians and African Americans were consistent with their rates in the U.S. population at large

(Straus et al., 1980). Being of Native American or Asian heritage was a risk factor. In the second National Family Violence Survey, African American families were at greatest risk for PCA (Wolfner & Gelles, 1993).

Additional Risk Factors

Many researchers in the field of PCA have argued that special characteristics of children may put them at increased risk for abuse and neglect (e.g., Kirkham, Schinke, Schilling, Meltzer, & Norelius, 1986). Several studies, for example, suggest an association between PCA and birth complications such as low birth weight and premature birth (Brown, Cohen, Johnson, & Salzinger, 1988; Parke & Collmer, 1975). Studies have also implicated physical, mental, and developmental disabilities as risk factors for PCA (e.g., Ammerman, Van Hasselt, Hersen, McGonigle, & Lubetsky, 1989; Friedrich & Boriskin, 1976). In contrast, other research has failed to find prematurity and disabilities as risk factors for abuse (e.g., Benedict, White, Wulff, & Hall, 1990).

The National Center on Child Abuse and Neglect (DHHS, 1993) addressed the incidence of child abuse among children with disabilities (e.g., mental retardation, physical impairments such as deafness and blindness, and serious emotional disturbance) by collecting data from a nationally representative sample of 35 CPS agencies. Results indicated that the incidence of child maltreatment was almost twice as high (1.7 times higher) among children with disabilities compared with the incidence among children without disabilities. For children who were physically abused, the rate of disability was 2.1 times the rate for maltreated children without disabilities (vs. 1.8 for sexually abused and 1.6 for neglected children). The most common disabilities noted included emotional disturbance, learning disability, physical health problems, and speech or language delay or impairment.

A major difficulty in interpreting these data hinges on the specification of the sequence of these events. Were children disabled before the abuse, or is the disability the result of abuse? CPS caseworkers reported that for 47% of the maltreated children with disabilities, the disabilities directly led to or contributed to child maltreatment (DHHS, 1993). For 37% of children, abuse presumably caused the maltreatment-related injuries.

Characteristics of Perpetrators of Physical Child Abuse

Age

There is some evidence that younger parents are more likely to physically maltreat their children than are older parents (Brown et al., 1998; Connelly & Straus, 1992; Straus et al., 1998). Another finding is that abusive parents often begin their families at a younger age than do families in the general population, with many being in their teens at the birth of their first child (American Humane Association, 1984; DHHS, 1981).

Gender

Authorities receive slightly more PCA reports for females than for males (55% female, 45% male; DHHS, 1998). Some have suggested that the gender disparity found in official reporting statistics is because mothers spend more time with their children (Gelles & Cornell, 1990). The gender distribution of PCA perpetrators may depend, however, on the specific relationship between perpetrator and child. Children who had been physically abused by birth parents, for example, were more likely to be abused by mothers (60%) than by fathers (48%), but the reverse was true when the perpetrator was a nonbiological parent or parent substitute (90% male and 19% female; Sedlak & Broadhurst, 1996). Self-report studies have also found that gender results vary depending on other factors. In the second National Survey on Family Violence, for example, female caretakers reported a higher rate of minor violence compared with male caretakers, but gender differences for severe violence were nonexistent (Wolfner & Gelles, 1993).

Relationship to the Victim

Official statistics indicate that the child's birth parents are the perpetrators of physical abuse in the majority of reported cases (72%; Sedlak & Broadhurst, 1996). Cases involving strangers or outsiders involve only a small minority of child maltreatment cases (10%; DHHS, 1998). Official statistics are difficult to interpret, however, because many states, by definition, include reports only for perpetrators who are in a caretaking role.

Speculation about whether single parents and stepparents are at particular risk of abusing their children has prompted several investigations. Official report data and survey data show that single parents are overrepresented among abusers (Brown et al., 1998; Gelles, 1989; Sedlak & Broadhurst, 1996). In the NIS-3, children living in single-parent families had a 63% greater risk of PCA than children living in two-parent families (Sedlak & Broadhurst, 1996). Gelles (1989), however, has argued that the greater risk among single parents is not a function of raising children alone but rather a function of the high rate of poverty and high stress levels in such families. Societal stereotypes also suggest that stepparents are more likely to abuse their nonbiological children. The fairy tale about Cinderella is a prime example of the evils of stepparenting. Both self-report surveys and official estimates, however, do not indicate that stepparents are more likely to physically abuse children than are biological parents (Gelles & Harrop, 1989; Sedlak & Broadhurst, 1996).

Psychological Characteristics

Many studies have evaluated the psychological characteristics of adults who physically abuse children (for reviews, see Milner, 1998; Milner & Dopke, 1997). Early studies of perpetrators identified several characteristics of abusive adults such as emotional and behavioral difficulties, interpersonal problems, low levels of intelligence, and a lack of child development knowledge (e.g., Hunter, Kilstrom, Kraybill, & Loda, 1978; Smith, Hanson, & Noble, 1974; Steele & Pollock, 1968). These early studies were primarily descriptive in nature, based on the observations of clinicians. As a result, such studies provided little information about whether these characteristics were unique to physically abusive parents. Later studies were more scientifically sound and included control groups of nonabusive parents as well as standardized measurement instruments. Although the use of more sophisticated methodology cannot definitively establish whether parental characteristics *cause* a parent to physically abuse a child, such information can be helpful in guiding treatment efforts. Table 3.1 lists the most common characteristics of physically abusing adults described by researchers.

Studies comparing nonabusive parents with physically abusive parents have confirmed several characteristics typical of abusive parents that were noted in earlier clinical studies, such as anger control problems, hostility, low frustration tolerance, depression, low self-esteem, substance abuse or dependence, deficits in empathy, and rigidity (e.g., Christensen et al., 1994; Dore, Doris, & Wright, 1995; Kelleher, Chaffin, Hollenberg, & Fischer, 1994; Lahey, Conger, Atkeson, & Treiber, 1984; Milner et al., 1995). Many studies have also found that physical abusers report more anxiety, life stress, and personal distress (e.g., Chan, 1994; Lahey et al., 1984; Whipple & Webster-Stratton, 1991). These negative emotional states may increase the risk of PCA by interfering with the way parents perceive events, by decreasing parenting abilities, or by lowering parents' tolerance for specific child behaviors (Hillson & Kupier, 1994; Lahey et al., 1984; Milner, 1998).

Physically abusive adults are also more likely than nonabusive individuals to exhibit family and interpersonal difficulties such as isolation from family and friends, spousal conflict, and negative family interactions. With regard to family interactions, abusive and high-risk individuals report more verbal and physical conflict among family members, spousal disagreement, and deficits in family cohesion and expressiveness (e.g., Justice & Calvert, 1990; Mollerstrom, Patchner, & Milner, 1992). In addition, abusive parents engage in fewer positive interactions with their children such as playing together, providing positive responses to the child, and demonstrating affection (e.g., Bousha & Twentyman, 1984; Lahey et al., 1984). Abusive parents also report more conflict in their families of origin (e.g., their own child abuse) compared with nonabusive parents (Cappell & Heiner, 1990). Studies also indicate that perpetrators of PCA report more interpersonal problems outside the family such as social isolation and loneliness (Chan, 1994; Kelleher et al., 1994; Starr, 1982; Trickett, Aber, Carlson, & Cicchetti, 1991).

TABLE 3.1 Characteristics of Adults Who Physically Abuse Children

Emotional and behavioral difficulties
Self-expressed anger
Depression
Low frustration tolerance
Low self-esteem
Rigidity
Anger control problems
Deficits in empathy
Anxiety
Perceived life stress and personal distress
Substance abuse/dependence
Family and interpersonal difficulties
Spousal conflict
History of abuse in childhood
Deficits in positive interactions with child and other family members
Isolated from friends and the community
Parenting difficulties
Unrealistic expectations of children
Disregard for child's needs/abilities
Deficits in child management skills
Viewing parenting role as stressful
Negative bias/perceptions regarding child
Poor problem-solving ability with regard to child rearing
Intrusive/inconsistent parenting
Less communication, interaction, stimulation
Biological factors
Reports of physical health problems
Physiological overreactivity
Neuropsychological deficits

SOURCE: Information for this table was obtained from the following references, which are representative but not exhaustive: Azar, Barnes, & Twentyman (1988); Bousha & Twentyman (1984); Cappell & Heiner (1990); Chan (1994); Christensen et al. (1994); Dore, Doris, & Wright (1995); Justice & Calvert (1990); Kelleher et al. (1994); Milner, Halsey, & Fultz (1995); Tuteur, Ewigman, Peterson, & Hosokawa (1995); Whipple & Webster-Stratton (1991); Wolfe (1991).

Studies comparing abusive and nonabusive parents have evaluated other psychological variables such as the context of the abusive family and characteristics of parenting. Compared with nonabusive adults, abusive individuals have unrealistic expectations and negative perceptions regarding their children (Azar, Barnes, & Twentyman, 1988; Bauer & Twentyman, 1985; Larrance & Twentyman, 1983; Milner & Robertson, 1990). Such parents often regard their child as bad, slow, or difficult to discipline and view the child's behavior as if it were intended to annoy them. A parent may expect a child to be toilet trained at an unreasonably early age, for instance, and then interpret the child's continual lack of training as deliberate misbehavior.

Abusive parents tend to view the parenting role as stressful and dissatisfying, and they exhibit numerous deficits in child management skills (Mash, Johnston, & Kovitz, 1983; Trickett et al., 1991; Trickett & Kuczynski, 1986). Physically abusive parent-child interactions, for example, involve a lower rate of interaction; a higher rate of directive, critical, and controlling behavior; and a higher frequency of verbal and physical aggression (Bousha & Twentyman, 1984; Mash et al., 1983; Whipple & Webster-Stratton, 1991). Tuteur, Ewigman, Peterson, and Hosokawa (1995) observed mother-child dyads for 10 minutes in a private room of a public health clinic equipped with toys, a table, and paper and crayons. Mothers sat at the table with their child, who was allowed to use the paper and crayons but was not permitted to play with the toys. Tuteur and his colleagues found that abusive mothers, when compared with nonabusive mothers, used more negative and rigid control (e.g., chased child under the table) rather than positive (e.g., comfortably directed child), and requests were either neutral (e.g., Keep going) or negative (e.g., Draw a circle right now) rather than positive (e.g., Can you please draw a circle for Mommy?).

Biological Factors

Several researchers have suggested that biological factors may distinguish physically abusive parents from nonabusive parents. Some theorists, for example, have proposed that physically abusive parents possess a physiological trait that predisposes them to a hyperreactive response to stimuli (Bauer & Twentyman, 1985; Knutson, 1978). This theory suggests that parents who possess this trait have a heightened physiological reaction when confronted with a stressful situation, such as a crying child. Research studies examining physiological reactivity in perpetrators of PCA are abundant and consistently demonstrate that perpetrators of PCA are hyperresponsive to child-related stimuli (e.g., Disbrow, Doerr, & Caulfield, 1977; Frodi & Lamb, 1980; Milner & Chilamkurti, 1991). Frodi and Lamb, for example, presented physically abusive mothers and a control group of nonabusive mothers with three videotapes: (a) a crying infant, (b) a quiet but alert infant, and (c) a smiling infant. Comparisons between the two groups revealed that although both groups responded to the crying infant with increased heart rate, blood pressure, and skin conductance, the abusive mothers displayed greater increases in heart rate. In addition, only the abusive mothers showed increased physiological reactivity in response to the smiling infant, suggesting that abusive parents view their children as aversive regardless of the child's emotional state.

These findings have been duplicated in studies comparing nonabusive but high-risk participants with low-risk participants and in studies using stressful non-child-related stimuli (e.g., Casanova, Domanic, McCanne, & Milner, 1992; Crowe & Zeskind, 1992). Although it appears that abusive parents exhibit a general physiological overreactivity, it is unclear exactly how this pattern contributes to parents' physical maltreatment of their children. It may be that heightened physiological reactivity influences the way a parent cognitively processes or perceives a child's behavior or the way a parent subsequently reacts to a child (Milner, 1993). It is also difficult to determine whether this physiological pattern is a genetic trait that predisposes parents toward abusive behavior or whether the physiological pattern developed as a *result* of continuing negative parent-child interactions.

In evaluating additional biological risk factors, several studies demonstrate that adults who abuse children report more health problems and physical disabilities than nonabusing adults (e.g., Conger, Burgess, & Barrett, 1979; Lahey et al., 1984). Research is also appearing that describes neuropsychological factors that are characteristic of physically abusive parents. Nayak and Milner (1996), for example, found that mothers at high risk for PCA performed worse on measures of problem-solving and conceptual ability as well as measures of cognitive flexibility compared with mothers defined as at low risk for abuse (cited in Milner, 1998). The variables of physical health and neurological functioning need further evaluation before the precise nature of the link between biological risk factors and PCA can be determined.

SECTION SUMMARY

Sociodemographic characteristics of children who are victims of PCA do not suggest that any particular subpopulation of children is the sole target of violence. Girls as well as boys are reportedly maltreated, and all age groups are represented in the literature. A diversity of ethnic backgrounds also characterizes the victims of PCA. There is evidence, however, that some characteristics place certain individuals at more risk than others. Young children, for example, between 0 and 7 years of age are at particularly high risk for PCA. Victims of physical abuse are also disproportionately represented among economically disadvantaged groups. Children with special needs such as those with physical or mental disabilities also appear to be at higher risk for abuse. With regard to race, most studies show that African American and Hispanic children are more frequently reported for PCA, although a cautious interpretation of such data is warranted.

A relatively large volume of literature addresses the *characteristics of perpetrators* of PCA. Although no single profile of PCA perpetrators exists, research supports several attributes that represent elevated risk for PCA. High rates of abuse are associated with individuals who begin their families at a young age. In the overwhelming majority of reported cases, perpetrators are the parents of the victim. Single parenthood is also associated with abuse; the contribution of stepparenting as a risk factor is less clear. Data regarding perpetrator gender are mixed, although it is clear that PCA is committed by males as well as by females. Studies evaluating psychological characteristics and biological factors associated with perpetrators have found numerous factors that differentiate abusive parents from nonabusive parents, such as depression, anger control problems, parenting difficulties, family difficulties, and physiological overreactivity. Although many characteristics of perpetrators have been identified, it is important to note that not every individual possessing such risk factors is abusive.

TABLE 3.2 Effects Associated With Physical Child Abuse for Children, Adolescents, and Adults

Children

Medical complications: bruises; head, chest, and abdominal injuries; burns; fractures

Cognitive difficulties: decreased intellectual and cognitive functioning; deficits in verbal faculty, memory, problem solving, perceptual-motor skills, and verbal abilities; decreased reading and math skills; poor school achievement; increase in special education services

Behavioral problems: aggression, fighting, noncompliance, defiance, property offenses, arrests

Socioemotional deficits: delayed play skills, infant attachment problems, poor social interaction skills, deficits in social competence with peers, avoidance of adults, difficulty making friends, deficits in prosocial behaviors, hopelessness, depression, low self-esteem

Adolescents

Antisocial behavior: violent interpersonal behavior, delinquency, violent offenses, substance abuse

Other: attentional problems, depressed school performance, increased daily stress, low self-esteem, homosexuality

Adults

Criminal/violent behavior: arrests for delinquency, adult criminal behavior, poor self-concept, violent criminal behavior, marital violence (for adult males), received and inflicted dating violence, physical abuse of own children

Substance abuse: abuse of alcohol and other substances

Socioemotional problems: self-destructive behavior, suicidal ideation and behavior, anxiety, hostility, dissociation, depression, unusual thoughts, interpersonal difficulties

SOURCE: Information for this table was obtained from the following references, which are representative but not exhaustive: Ammerman (1991); Chu & Dill (1990); Cicchetti & Barnett (1991); Eckenrode, Laird, & Doris (1993); Fantuzzo (1990); Gold (1993); Kaufman & Cicchetti (1989); Kolko (1992); Lopez & Heffer (1998); Malinosky-Rummell & Hansen (1993); Marshall & Rose (1990); Myers (1992); Smith (1994); K. S. Widom (1989); Williamson, Borduin, & Howe (1991); Wodarski, Kurtz, Gaudin, & Howing (1990).

CONSEQUENCES ASSOCIATED WITH PHYSICAL CHILD ABUSE

Children who experience physical maltreatment are more likely to be physically, behaviorally, and/or emotionally impaired, compared with their nonabused counterparts (for reviews, see Ammerman, 1991; Cicchetti & Toth, 1995; Fantuzzo, 1990; Kolko, 1992). In some cases, the negative consequences associated with abuse continue to affect the individual well into adulthood (for reviews, see Gold, 1993; Malinosky-Rummell & Hansen, 1993). Table 3.2 displays the most frequently reported problems associated with PCA for children as well as for adolescents and adults.

Effects Associated With the Abuse of Children

Research examining the effects associated with PCA of children has, until relatively recently, been limited to physical harm. The more subtle, yet significant, social and psychological effects were ignored in evaluations that focused only on visible signs of trauma such as physical injuries. More recent research indicates that PCA is also associated with detrimental effects on the child's emotional, social, and intellectual functioning.

It is important that we interpret this research on the consequences associated with PCA with considerable caution. The issue of effects is complicated, and, as a result, the consequences of abuse are not well understood. Most of the research we will discuss in this section is correlational, which means that one cannot necessarily assume that PCA is the cause of the various problems observed in PCA victims. Physical abuse, for example, often occurs in association with other problems within the family or in the environment such as marital violence, alcohol or drug use by family members, parental depression, psychological maltreatment, and low SES. It is therefore difficult to conclude with any certainty that the psychological problems associated with PCA result solely, or even primarily, from the violent interactions between parent and child. Certainly, it would not surprise us to find that an abused child who regularly witnesses violence between his or her drunk parents, who is abused by an older sibling, and who is poor, is having problems in school. We would be surprised if such a child were *not* having difficulty. Determining which of the individual environmental factors, or combination of factors, is responsible for the child's school problems is a difficult task.

Medical Problems

The medical consequences of PCA are numerous and can range from minor physical injuries (e.g., bruising) to serious physical disfigurements and disabilities. In extreme cases, abuse can result in the death of a child (see Box 3.2, "Killing Our Children"). Bruises are one of the most common types of physical injuries associated with PCA. Although nonabused children also incur bruises, physically abused children have bruises in uncommon sites (e.g., buttocks, back, abdomen, and thighs; Schmitt, 1987). Other markings can result from grabbing; squeezing; or using belts, switches, or cords. A series of unusual injuries is often an indication of nonaccidental injury or PCA (Myers, 1992).

One of the most dangerous and life-threatening types of injury is head injury, the most common cause of death in abused children (e.g., Smith, 1994). Various actions can result in head injury, including a blow to the head by an object, punching the head with a fist, or throwing a child against a hard surface. Another dangerous form of abuse that can result in head injury is grasping the child and vigorously shaking the child back and forth. This type of injury, known as *shaken baby syndrome* or *shaken impact syndrome,* can result in the child's brain moving

BOX 3.2 Killing Our Children

On October 25, 1994, Susan Smith loaded her two small boys into the back seat of her Mazda. As Susan drove along county roads in South Carolina, Michael, age 3 years, and his brother, Alexander, age 14 months, fell asleep. Susan Smith pulled the car up to a boat ramp by a lake and got out of the car. The mother of the two children then watched as the car rolled into the lake, floated for a few minutes, and then sank beneath the surface with the boys still strapped into their car seats (Adler, Carroll, Smith, & Rogers, 1994). Susan Smith murdered her two children and shocked the nation, reminding us once again that parents are indeed capable of killing their own children.

Roughly 1,185 children were killed as a result of child abuse or neglect in 1996 (Wang & Daro, 1998). The rates of fatalities reported to CPS, furthermore, have steadily increased during the past several years. Between 1985 and 1994, the rate of child deaths increased by 48% (Wiese & Daro, 1995). These statistics in and of themselves are cause for concern and become even more alarming in light of the belief that such figures represent underestimates of actual fatality rates. These numbers do not reflect, for example, child deaths due to maltreatment reported to other authorities such as law enforcement agencies, hospitals, or coroners (Wells, 1994b). Also excluded are cases that are improperly classified as accidental deaths or as sudden infant death syndrome rather than as maltreatment (See boxed insert in Chapter 1: "Infanticide or Sudden Infant Death Syndrome?"; Ewigman et al., 1993). In one study, McClain, Sacks, Froehlke, and Ewigman (1993) concluded that the overwhelming majority (85%) of deaths due to parental maltreatment are misclassified in this way.

Characteristics of child maltreatment deaths have been evaluated, and some consistencies have emerged. According to data derived from reporting agencies, approximately half of child fatalities result from physical abuse (Wang & Daro, 1998). These deaths might result from cumulative beatings or single violent episodes. The other half of victims die as a result of neglect when parents fail to provide for a child's basic needs (e.g., medical care or adequate supervision) or as a result of multiple forms of maltreatment (Wang & Daro, 1998). The leading cause of death among physically abused children is death associated with some type of injury to the head (Smith, 1994). The large majority (78%) of these children are under the age of 5 years, with more than one third of these children under the age of 1 year at the time of their death (Wang & Daro, 1998).

Children's deaths at the hands of their parents or other caregivers seem to represent the ultimate failure of CPS. Although Susan Smith was not previously identified by CPS, many cases of fatal child maltreatment did have prior or current contact with such agencies. Approximately 30% to 50% of children killed by parents or caretakers are killed after they have been identified by child welfare agencies and have been involved in interventions and were either left in their homes or returned home after a short-term removal (Besharov, 1991; Wang & Daro, 1996, 1998). Just because a child dies in a community, however, is not evidence of a faulty CPS system. As Carroll and Haase (1987) note, "Even in the best of social service departments and with the best of services, children, most tragically, will die. In this field of protective services, human judgments are being made; and being human, mistakes are inevitable" (p. 138). Carroll and Haase believe that the important determination in such cases is whether the child's death or injury resulted from a lack of response by CPS or as a result of an incorrect human judgment.

What can be done to help prevent child maltreatment fatalities? One response to the problem of child maltreatment fatalities that is receiving increasing support is the concept of child death review teams. Child death review teams are typically composed of a board of community professionals representing multiple agencies (Durfee, 1994). Child death review teams are forming across the United States, Canada, and other countries. Although the functions of such teams vary, most review child death cases to identify the prevalence of deaths from abuse and neglect and to improve the policies and procedures of CPS to prevent future abuse (Cavaliere, 1995; Thigpen & Bonner, 1994). Other prevention efforts have focused on the investigation of risk factors associated with child maltreatment fatalities. One study compared maltreatment fatality cases with nonfatal maltreatment cases and found several factors to be associated with fatality, such as paternal drug use, absence of a maternal grandmother in the home, ethnicity, young age of the child, presence in the home of a father or father substitute, a sibling with medical problems, and prior removal of the child from the home (Fontana & Alfaro, 1987). A recent review concluded that a child's young age was the best predictor of severe and fatal physical abuse (Hegar, Zuravin, & Orme, 1994).

Finally, Daro and Alexander (1994) have called for a broad public health approach to preventing childhood maltreatment deaths. They recommend efforts directed at federal, state, and local levels such as expanding available funding for programs and research, reforming judicial and child welfare policy, increasing professional and community education, and providing community-based support for at-risk families. Many believe that a comprehensive approach will be necessary to realize an actual reduction in child maltreatment fatalities. As Attorney General Janet Reno (1994) recently stated, "The problem of child maltreatment-related deaths is not a simple one, and the solutions require the coordinated efforts of many agencies and professionals as well as the commitment of the entire community" (p. 1).

---

within the skull, causing blood vessels to stretch and tear (Bruce & Zimmerman, 1989). The end result can be severe injury, coma, or death. Commonly, parents who bring their children into emergency rooms with nonaccidental head injury report that the child's injury was caused by a fall from an item of furniture (crib, couch, bed, etc.). Research evaluating injury from accidental falls, however, disputes such parental claims because accidental events typically result in minor injuries such as bruises or cuts or no injury at all (Lyons & Oates, 1993).

Other common injuries include chest and abdominal injuries, burns, and fractures (Myers, 1992; Schmitt, 1987). Abdominal injuries can be caused by hitting children with objects, grabbing children tightly, or punching or kicking children in the chest or abdominal areas, resulting in organ ruptures or compressions. Burns, which are often inflicted as punishment, can include immersion in scalding water or contact burns with objects such as irons, cigarettes, stove burners, or heaters. Finally, fractures of bones in various areas of the body often result from PCA. Fractures can be caused by any of a number of actions, including punching, kicking, twisting, shaking, and squeezing.

Cognitive Problems

Studies have documented that physically abused children exhibit lower intellectual and cognitive functioning relative to a comparison group of children on general intellectual measures as well as specific measures of verbal facility, memory, verbal language, communication abilities, problem solving, and perceptual motor skills (e.g., Fantuzzo, 1990; Friedrich, Enbender, & Luecke, 1983; Haskett, 1990; Hoffman-Plotkin & Twentyman, 1984). Academic performance is another area of substantiated difficulty in physically abused children. Compared with nonabused children, physically abused children display poor school achievement and adjustment, receive more special education services, score lower on reading and math tests, exhibit more learning disabilities, and are more likely to repeat a grade (de Paul & Arruabarrena, 1995; Eckenrode, Laird, & Doris, 1993; Salzinger, Kaplan, Pelcovitz, Samit, & Krieger, 1984). Many of these differences in cognitive ability remain, even after the effects of socioeconomic disadvantage are controlled (Kurtz, Gaudin, Wodarski, & Howing, 1993; Wodarski, Kurtz, Gaudin, & Howing, 1990).

Behavioral Problems

Physical aggression and antisocial behavior are among the most common correlates of PCA (Wolfe, 1987). In most studies, abused children show more aggression, even after the poverty, family instability, and wife battering that often accompany abuse are statistically controlled (e.g., Fantuzzo, 1990). In other words, abuse seems to have an effect on behavior independent of the potential contribution of other factors. This negative behavioral pattern has appeared across a wide variety of settings, such as summer camp (Kaufman & Cicchetti, 1989) and preschool and day care programs (Alessandri, 1991), using a variety of data collection procedures (i.e., adult ratings: Hoffman-Plotkin & Twentyman, 1984; observations: Bousha & Twentyman, 1984). Other behavioral difficulties include drinking and drug use, noncompliance, defiance, fighting in and out of the home, property offenses, and arrests (e.g., Hotaling et al., 1990).

> Physical aggression and antisocial behavior are among the most common correlates of physical child abuse.

Socioemotional Difficulties

Some researchers argue that victims of PCA suffer from problems related to attachment to caregivers and social interactions (Cicchetti & Barnett, 1991; Conaway & Hansen, 1989; Youngblade & Belsky, 1990). The quality of the parent-child bond, for example, consistently reflects insecure attachments (e.g., increased avoidance of and resistance to the parent) in infants exposed to PCA (Cicchetti, Toth, & Bush, 1988; Kolko, 1992).

These early patterns of parent-child interaction may also lay the foundation for subsequent difficulties in social interactions for older children (Kolko, 1992).

Physically abused children exhibit poor social interactions with peers as well as adults (e.g., Fantuzzo, 1990; Kinard, 1982; Salzinger, Feldman, Hammer, & Rosario, 1993). Difficulties include trouble making friends, deficits in prosocial behavior (e.g., smiling) with peers, and delays in interactive play skills (Alessandri, 1991; Howes & Eldredge, 1985; Prino & Peyrot, 1994).

Studies have also demonstrated a higher incidence of emotional difficulties in physically abused children relative to comparison children. School-age children, for example, have been found to display lower levels of self-esteem (Allen & Tarnowski, 1989; Kaufman & Cicchetti, 1989). Finally, evidence suggests that victims of PCA exhibit feelings of hopelessness, depression, and low self-worth (Allen & Tarnowski, 1989; Fantuzzo, 1990).

Effects Associated With the Abuse of Adolescents

Although the consequences associated with PCA for young children have received extensive interest in the empirical literature, much less attention has focused on the physical, social, and psychological effects of PCA on adolescents. Some cases of PCA begin in adolescence, whereas others begin in childhood, contributing to the difficulty in understanding the effect of PCA on adolescents. Nonetheless, some have argued that the effects of PCA may be expressed somewhat differently in adolescents (e.g., Williamson, Borduin, & Howe, 1991).

The few reports that have examined the consequences of maltreatment in adolescents suggest that deviant or problematic behavior is often found among adolescents who were abused in childhood. Such individuals often display antisocial as well as violent interpersonal behavior such as dating violence (Dodge, Bates, & Pettit, 1990; Reuterman & Burcky, 1989) and aggression toward parents and siblings (Kratcoski, 1984). Abused children also have higher rates of delinquency compared with general population as well as poverty samples (e.g., Alfaro, 1981; Kratcoski, 1984; Zingraff, Leiter, Myers, & Johnsen, 1993). One study found higher rates of homosexuality in individuals who experienced physical abuse during adolescence compared with nonabused adolescents (Harry, 1989). Consequences associated with PCA for adolescents also include externalizing behavior problems, attention problems, poor self-esteem, substance abuse, depressed school performance, and more daily stress (Cavaiola & Schiff, 1988; Truscott, 1992; Williamson et al., 1991; Wodarski et al., 1990).

Possible Long-Term Effects

Understanding the effects associated with the abuse of children is important because such problems may lead to long-term difficulties. It is evident that many of the psychological and social difficulties that emerge in childhood are also evident in adults who have a history of PCA (Malinosky-Rummell & Hansen, 1993). It is further believed that many of the social and behavioral impairments that begin in childhood and persist in adulthood may contribute to the intergenerational transmission of abuse (Wolfe, 1987). Unfortunately, only a few studies have empirically examined the long-term sequelae associated with PCA.

Criminal and Violent Behavior

One of the most frequently discussed long-term consequences of PCA is criminal behavior. K. S. Widom (1989) compared a sample of validated cases of child abuse and neglect (identified 20 years earlier by social service agencies) with a sample of matched controls. She evaluated juvenile court and probation department records to establish occurrences of delinquency, criminal behavior, and violent criminal behavior. Although the study did not distinguish between various forms of maltreatment, results indicated that the abused-neglected group had a higher likelihood of arrests for delinquency, adult criminality, and violent criminal behavior than did the control group. The majority of individuals with a history of PCA did not have any offenses or violations, however, reminding us that the link between abuse and criminality is far from perfect.

Childhood abuse is neither a necessary nor sufficient cause of adult perpetration.

Other research suggests that adults with a childhood history of physical abuse are more likely to both receive and inflict dating violence (Marshall & Rose, 1990; Riggs, O'Leary, & Breslin, 1990). In addition, male adults who were physically abused as children are more likely to physically abuse their marital partners (Rosenbaum & O'Leary, 1981). Researchers have also found that adults who were victims of physical abuse as children are more likely to be perpetrators of PCA as adults. The percentage of adults abused as children who later go on to abuse others, however, is not 100% (Kaufman & Zigler, 1987; C. S. Widom, 1989). Once again, it is important to remember that childhood abuse is neither a necessary nor sufficient cause of adult perpetration.

Substance Abuse

The rate of substance abuse in adults with a history of physical abuse has also attracted scientific attention. Examination of substance abuse, however, has focused on alcohol abuse in men, which limits its generalizability. In a recent review of the literature linking substance abuse with a history of PCA, Malinosky-Rummell and Hansen (1993) reached the following conclusions: (a) Adults who abuse substances report a higher incidence of childhood physical abuse compared with the general population; (b) physically abused male alcoholics, relative to nonabused alcoholics, report more problematic drinking and social and medical difficulties; and (c) physically abused inpatients tend to experience more alcoholism and substance abuse compared with nonabused inpatients.

Socioemotional Difficulties

Less information is available on the long-term socioemotional consequences of physical maltreatment compared with other forms of abuse (e.g., sexual). Nonetheless, some recent research suggests a relationship between PCA and psychological adjustment in adults. Evidence to date indicates that adults with a history of PCA exhibit more significant emotional problems (e.g., higher incidence of self-destructive behavior, suicidal thoughts and behavior, anxiety, hostility, and depression) compared with nonabused controls (Bryer, Nelson, Miller, & Krol, 1987; Chu & Dill, 1990; Downs & Miller, 1998; Kroll, Stock, & James, 1985; Wind & Silvern, 1994; Yesavage & Widrow, 1985). Reports also confirm that a history of PCA is associated with greater dissociation, suicidal ideation, poor self-concept, and negative feelings about interpersonal interactions (e.g., Briere & Runtz, 1988; Downs & Miller, 1998; Lopez & Heffer, 1998; Wind & Silvern, 1994).

Mediators of Abuse Effects

To add to the uncertainty in understanding the effects of PCA, it is also true that the experience of PCA does not affect each victim in a consistent or predictable way (Cicchetti & Rizley, 1981). For some, the effect of PCA may be pervasive and long-standing, whereas for others the experience may not be invariably negative or disruptive. The small sample of severely abused children initially described in 1967 by Elmer and reevaluated in 1992, for example, evidenced scores within the normal range on measures of mood, self-esteem, and aggression (Martin & Elmer, 1992). What factors might contribute to the variability in the effects that are associated with PCA?

One mediating factor is the severity and duration of the abuse. The assumption is that more severe and/or chronic maltreatment will lead to more severe outcomes. Although empirical data are sparse, some evidence supports this contention (e.g., Erickson et al., 1989; Kinard, 1982; Wind & Silvern, 1992). In addition, some researchers have suggested that the greater the number of subtypes of maltreatment (e.g., physical abuse, sexual abuse, and neglect), the more negative the outcome will be for the child as well as the adult with a history of PCA (Kurtz, Gaudin, Howing, & Wodarski, 1993; Wind & Silvern, 1992).

Other research suggests that the negative effects of abuse are greatest for children in families in which there are high levels of stress and parental psychopathology (e.g., schizophrenia) or depression (Kurtz, Gaudin, Howing, et al., 1993; Walker, Downey, & Bergman, 1989). Reports are also beginning to appear that demonstrate the influence of sociocultural and family variables (e.g., SES and the quality of the parent-child interaction) on negative outcome (Herrenkohl, Herrenkohl, Rupert, Egolf, & Lutz, 1995). Finally, recent studies have implicated the protective influence of certain factors such as high intellectual functioning (Herrenkohl, Herrenkohl, Egolf, & Wu, 1991) and the presence of a supportive parent figure (Herrenkohl et al., 1995).

SECTION SUMMARY

The problems associated with PCA are multiple and far-reaching and include negative physical and psychological effects for child and adolescent victims as well as adults who report a childhood history of PCA. Possible negative *effects for children* include medical (e.g., head injury), cognitive (e.g., school problems), behavioral (e.g., aggression), and socioemotional (e.g., poor social skills) problems. Although less is known about the negative consequences associated with the abuse of adolescents, available research indicates that the possible *effects for adolescents* range from antisocial and violent behavior to poor self-esteem and substance abuse. Many of the same social and behavioral impairments found in childhood are also possible *effects for adults,* including criminal and violent behavior, substance abuse, and socioemotional difficulties. The experience of PCA, however, does not affect each individual in a consistent or predictable way. Specific characteristics of victims' families or their abuse experiences can serve to *mediate the effects* of abuse. Victims whose families are characterized by high stress and whose abuse experiences are more severe tend to exhibit greater levels of psychological distress. On the other hand, victims who benefit from high levels of intelligence and a supportive parent figure appear to be protected in some way and demonstrate fewer psychological symptoms.

EXPLAINING PHYSICAL CHILD ABUSE

Unfortunately, it is impossible at this time to specify the exact circumstances that lead to PCA. Several factors have contributed to the difficulty in explaining and predicting physical abuse. First, PCA is a complex set of interacting behaviors and factors. Second, methodological problems have plagued the research in this area. Because most studies are retrospective, information could be biased by the memory or perceptions of individuals. In addition, sample sizes are often small and nonrandom, calling into question the validity and generalizability of findings. The definition of what constitutes abuse has also varied across studies, contributing to difficulties in interpreting results. Little is known about cause-effect relationships because experimental designs, which could help establish cause-effect relationships, are rarely feasible. Researchers obviously cannot randomly assign some children to abusive parents and others to nonabusive parents. Finally, it is clear that the populations of abusers and victims are diverse in psychological, social, and demographic characteristics, limiting any widespread application of the causes of abuse that could account for all, or even most, cases of PCA.

TABLE 3.3 Risk Factors Associated With Physical Child Abuse

- *Factors associated with individual pathology*
  - Perpetrator characteristics
    - Self-expressed anger and anger control problems
    - Depression
    - Low frustration tolerance
    - Low self-esteem
    - Rigidity
    - Deficits in empathy
    - Substance abuse/dependence
    - Physical health problems
    - Physiological reactivity
- *Factors associated with parent-child relationship*
  - Characteristics of the child
    - Difficult child behaviors
    - Young age
    - Physical and mental disabilities
  - Characteristics of the adult
    - Deficits in parenting skills
    - Unrealistic expectations of children
    - Viewing the parenting role as stressful
    - Negative bias/perceptions regarding child
- *Factors associated with family environment*
  - Characteristics of the family
    - Current abusive family practices (e.g., spouse abuse)
    - Intergenerational abusive family practices (e.g., child abuse)
    - Marital discord
    - Few positive family interactions
- *Factors associated with situational and societal conditions*
  - Situational
    - Low socioeconomic status
    - Single-parent household
    - Public assistance
    - Blue-collar employment
    - Unemployment or part-time work
    - Situational stress (e.g., large family size)
    - Social isolation
  - Societal
    - Cultural approval of violence in society, generally
    - Cultural approval of corporal punishment
    - Power differentials in society and the family

Despite such qualifications, several models have attempted to explain the causes of PCA. Since the early 1960s, views on the primary causes of child abuse have expanded to move beyond disturbed adults or children to include the more pervasive influences of parent-child relationships, the family environment, socioeconomic disadvantage, and cultural sanctioning of violence and corporal punishment. These models have been incorporated into multidimensional, interactional models that emphasize the interplay among these various factors (e.g., Belsky, 1993; Wolfe, 1991). Table 3.3 displays the multiple risk factors implicated in the empirical literature as playing a role in the physical abuse of children.

The Individual Pathology Model

As we discussed previously, many trace the discovery of child abuse to the 1962 publication of the "Battered Child Syndrome." Kempe and his colleagues (e.g., 1962) argued that child abusers were "psychopathic" and in need of psychiatric treatment. They also suggested that PCA was a rare social problem, which facilitated the assumption that perpetrators were disturbed individuals who must be "crazy" or "sick." As PCA has been defined more broadly to include a greater number of adults as perpetrators, however, it has been more difficult to see "child abusers" as people who suffer from a mental illness, personality disorder, alcohol or drug abuse, or any other individual defect. Although research has identified a subgroup of severely disturbed individuals who abuse children (Berger, 1985; Walker et al., 1988), only a small proportion of abusive parents (less than 10%) meet criteria for severe psychiatric disorders (Kempe & Helfer, 1972; Straus, 1980). As noted previously, however, perpetrators of PCA often do exhibit specific nonpsychiatric psychological, behavioral, and biological characteristics that distinguish them from nonabusive parents, such as anger control problems, depression, parenting difficulties, physiological hyperreactivity, and substance abuse.

> Physically abusive parents are more likely to have anger control problems and physiological overreactivity.

The Role of Child Behavior Problems

Other theorists have focused on child behavior as a contributing factor to PCA. As we noted previously, certain characteristics of the child place him or her at risk for abuse. Difficult behaviors, young age, and physical and mental disabilities are all child characteristics associated with abuse. It is sometimes difficult, however, to determine which of these traits are the result, rather than a precipitant, of abuse. A child's mental disability, for example, could have existed at birth or could have resulted from abuse (e.g., severe blows to the head). Regardless of the cause of a child's behavior, PCA is associated with child care that is more demanding and difficult. It should be noted, however, that legal statutes governing adult behavior do not grant adults the right to inflict physical injury on children *regardless* of the child's behavior. When an adult does inflict injury, he or she is legally responsible for his or her behavior. Children cannot be held responsible for their own victimization. In addition, there is considerable evidence that child characteristics alone do not adequately explain the occurrence of child maltreatment (Erickson & Egeland, 1996).

> Children cannot be held responsible for their own victimization.

Parent-Child Interaction

Parent-child interaction theories suggest that difficult child behaviors interact with specific parental behaviors to result in physical abuse (Cerezo, 1997; Crittenden, 1998). It is the behavior of both the parent and the child, rather than either of them alone, that promotes violence. Studies have repeatedly demonstrated, for example, that punitive parenting is associated with negative child behavior and outcomes (e.g., Denham, Renwick, & Holt, 1991; Dowdney & Pickles, 1991). Likewise, deviant child behaviors have contributed to parental abuse (Biringen & Robinson, 1991; Herrenkohl, Herrenkohl, & Egolf, 1983; Youngblade & Belsky, 1990). Such findings raise what is known as the directionality question: Who affects whom? Clearly, parenting practices have direct effects on children. A child's behavior, however, also contributes to a parent's response to that child (Bell & Chapman, 1986).

Some experts have suggested that the difficulties in parent-child relations develop during the abused child's infancy, when early attachments between parent and child are formed (Erickson & Egeland, 1996; Malinosky-Rummell & Hansen, 1993). A child may be born with a challenging characteristic such as a difficult temperament or a physical disability. Such difficulties may create an excessive challenge for a parent and interfere with the development of a secure attachment between the parent and child. This vulnerability may, in turn, lead to further difficult child behaviors and increased challenges for the parent. Such a pattern could escalate and result in physical abuse when challenges exceed a parent's tolerance or capability threshold. Several studies have found that maltreating parents more frequently have insecure attachments to their infants compared with nonmaltreating parents (e.g., Crittenden, Partridge, & Claussen, 1991; Egeland & Sroufe, 1981). In addition, several studies support a theory of negative escalation in abusive parent-child dyads (for reviews, see Cerezo, 1997; Crittenden, 1998).

Social Learning Theory

Many retrospective studies have demonstrated that a significant percentage of adults who abuse children were abused themselves as children (e.g., Cappell & Heiner, 1990; Gelles, 1973; Hunter et al., 1978). These adults presumably learned, through experiences with their own parents, that violence is an acceptable method of child rearing. In addition, adults with a history of PCA missed the opportunity to learn more appropriate and nurturing methods of adult-child interaction.

> A significant percentage of adults who abuse children were abused themselves as children.

Some prospective research supports the notion that parenting styles are passed from one generation to the next. Crittenden (1984) found that children as young as 2 years of age interacted with their sibling infants in a manner similar to that of their mothers, who demonstrated a range of parenting styles including abusive, neglecting, inept, and sensitive patterns of interaction. Others have found a relationship between the parental practices of grandparents and an adult's subsequent use of harsh parenting practices (Simons, Whitbeck, Conger, & Chyi-In, 1991).

Evidence also suggests that even children who do not experience abuse directly learn violent interpersonal interaction styles. Through witnessing the negative interactions between the significant adults in their lives, children learn maladaptive or violent methods of expressing anger, reacting to stress, or coping with conflict (Jaffe, Wolfe, & Wilson, 1990; Kalmuss, 1984; see Chapter 6 for a discussion of children who observe marital violence). Studies consistently demonstrate that adults who abuse children are more likely to come from homes characterized by considerable marital discord and violence (Gelles, 1980; Hotaling & Sugarman, 1986; Kalmuss, 1984).

As we discussed at great length in Chapter 2, however, the cycle of violence is not a universal law, and most abused children do not become abusive adults. Kaufman and Zigler (1987) reviewed the empirical literature on this question and concluded that the rate of intergenerational transmission is approximately 30%. This means that 70% of those who were abused as children do not go on to become abusive adults. Because not all children who experience PCA become physically abusive adults, there must be factors that mediate these intergenerational patterns. Egeland, Jacobvitz, and Sroufe (1988), for example, found that those mothers who were physically abused but did not abuse their own children were significantly more likely to have received emotional support from a nonabusive adult during childhood, participated in therapy during some period in their lives, and been involved in a nonabusive, stable, and emotionally supportive and satisfying relationship with a mate. Nonabusive mothers with a history of PCA are also reportedly less anxious, dependent, immature, and depressed and are more flexible in how they view their children (e.g., Caliso & Milner, 1994; Egeland et al., 1988). Hunter and Kilstrom (1979) found that parents who did not repeat child maltreatment were more likely to report childhood social support, such as a positive relationship with one parent.

Situational and Social Conditions

During the 1970s, interest in the context of abusive behavior led to research examining situational, social, and cultural factors that might foster abuse. Sociological models of abuse were developed that focused on factors such as economic conditions, societal and cultural values, and social systems (e.g., Gelles & Straus, 1988; Gil, 1970).

Gil (1970) was one of the first to point out the high proportion of abused children coming from poor and socially disadvantaged families. Recent research supports these earlier findings by indicating that PCA is more common among low-income families and families supported by public assistance (AAPC, 1988;

DHHS, 1996; Sedlak, 1991). Children whose fathers are unemployed or work part-time are also more at risk for abuse compared with children of fathers with full-time employment (AAPC, 1988; McCurdy & Daro, 1994b; Wolfner & Gelles, 1993). A study by Mills in 1982 compared the changes in county unemployment rates during 1981 with the annual child abuse and neglect official report figures during that same year (cited in Pelton, 1994). Of the 51 counties in the study that showed increased unemployment rates, approximately 69% had increases in child abuse and neglect reporting compared with 19% of the 21 counties with unemployment rate decreases. Blue-collar workers are more likely to engage in physical punishment and abuse than white-collar workers (Straus et al., 1980; Wolfner & Gelles, 1993).

Social isolation, including a lack of extended family or peer support network, has also been a social factor associated with abuse (Gil, 1970). Research suggests that abusive parents have relatively fewer contacts with peer networks, as well as with immediate family and other relatives (Disbrow et al., 1977; Whipple & Webster-Stratton, 1991; Zuravin & Grief, 1989). One possible illustration of social isolation is the finding that abusive parents are less likely to have a phone in the household (Dubowitz, Hampton, Bithoney, & Newberger, 1987).

Using official reporting statistics, Zuravin (1989) measured social isolation by evaluating community variables associated with maltreating families. Results indicated a significant relationship between physically abusive families and communities with high proportions of single-family dwellings and vacant housing. According to Garbarino and Crouter (1978), these variables serve as physical impediments to social networks by isolating families from one another and decreasing the number of social supports available. Other researchers have found that maltreating families engage in few social or recreational activities and do not use available community resources (e.g., Corse, Schmid, & Trickett, 1990; Smith, 1975).

Situational variables, particularly as they affect the level of stress within a family, have been associated with PCA. Stressful situations such as a new baby, illness, death of a family member, poor housing conditions, and larger than average family size are also risk factors in maltreatment (Gil, 1970; Johnson & Morse, 1968; Straus et al., 1980). Wolfner and Gelles (1993) found that households with two to four children at home were at increased risk for both minor and abusive violence. Other situational variables associated with PCA include high levels of stress from work-related problems and pressures, marital discord, conflicts over school performance, illness, and a crying or fussy child (Barton & Baglio, 1993; Gelles, 1973).

Cultural Approval of Physical Child Abuse

Specific cultural factors have been suggested as playing a role in conditions leading to PCA. The general pervasiveness of violence in America, as discussed previously, is a good example of an aspect of American culture that might create a context that fosters the physical abuse of children. The general acceptance of corporal punishment as a method of discipline is another aspect of American culture conducive to violence in general and to PCA more specifically. Because corporal punishment puts the child at risk for physical injury, it is at least indirectly connected to child abuse (Straus, 1994a, 1994b).

Unequal power differentials in the structure of society, particularly the family, might also contribute to PCA (Gelles & Cornell, 1990). Children are abused, in part, because they are unable to defend themselves against stronger and more powerful adults (e.g., financially, emotionally, and physically). Some evidence consistent with this idea is found in official estimates of physical abuse that suggest that the rates of PCA decrease with child age, as the child becomes older and stronger and more capable of self-defense (Gelles & Hargreaves, 1981).

SECTION SUMMARY

Views on the primary causes of PCA have included a *variety of models,* such as those that focus on the *psychiatric disturbance* of abusers (e.g., mental illness, personality disorder, and substance abuse) and those that suggest that the problem is rooted in dysfunctional *parent-child interactions* (i.e., increased risk of abuse because of parental frustration, stress, and impatience). Evidence suggests children *learn to model violent behavior* by merely witnessing negative interactions, perpetuating a cycle of violence. Nevertheless, qualifications regarding the reliability of information about the causes of PCA (e.g., methodological problems, sample sizes, definitions of abuse, ethical issues, and heterogeneous groups) have affected research in the field.

A significant shift in the conceptualization of the causes of PCA occurred with the birth of *sociological models* that focused on the situational and social context of abuse. These models emphasized the possible implications of socioeconomic disadvantage (e.g., low income), social isolation (e.g., less peer support), situational stressors (e.g., illness or poor housing), and cultural approval of violence (e.g., acceptance of corporal punishment) in contributing to PCA. At the present, PCA is conceptualized as a complex problem resulting from *multiple interacting factors* from many domains including the adult perpetrator, parent-child interactions, family environment, and situational and social conditions.

RESPONDING TO PHYSICAL CHILD ABUSE

Solutions to the PCA problem vary, depending on the etiological framework one adopts. Psychological treatment interventions focusing on the individual child or adult are proposed by those who explain PCA in individualistic terms. Those who explain PCA from an interactional or transactional perspective focus on disturbed marital relationships or the parent-child interaction. Others who explain PCA in structural or ecological terms have emphasized community interventions or the alleviation of social problems connected with PCA (e.g., poverty and social isolation). Regardless of the long-term solutions offered, the initial response must begin with protecting the children who are victims of PCA.

Protecting the Child

Federal and state laws provide for the protection of children who are at risk for child abuse or neglect. In most states, such responsibility falls on the local department of social services. In different states, this department may be called the department of public welfare, the department of human resources, or the department of human services (Carroll & Haase, 1987). Regardless of the label, the department of social services has a division responsible for the protection of children, usually referred to as child protective services. Protection may be implemented on either a voluntary or involuntary basis and may result in a child's remaining at home or being placed in some type of out-of-home care.

Child Protective Services

The role of CPS is to protect children via four services: investigation of reports of maltreatment, provision of treatment services, coordination of services with other agencies in the community, and implementation of preventive services (Carroll & Haase, 1987; Wells, 1994a). Ideally, the goal of CPS for all cases is to prevent child abuse and neglect in the child's own home through various crisis intervention and treatment services. These services may include crisis nursery or respite care, community-based family resource centers, counseling for children and parents, parenting education, lay therapy, home visitor services, and self-help or volunteer programs such as Big Brothers/Big Sisters, Parents Anonymous, and Parents United (Daro, 1988; Wells, 1994a).

In recent years, CPS agencies across the country have come under fire because of concern about the seeming inability of the system to provide adequate protection for those children reported for maltreatment (see boxed insert: "Killing Our Children"). This criticism reflects a growing number of problems faced by protective services agencies: the consistent increase in child abuse reports and resulting increases in workloads, low budgets, and a high turnover rate of well-trained social workers who are leaving the field (Carroll & Haase, 1987; McCurdy & Daro, 1994a). The recommended maximum workload for acceptable treatment services, for example, is 17 families per caseworker (Smolowe, 1995). Reports of current caseloads are often between 30 and 50 families per caseworker (Gelles & Cornell, 1990). Under these conditions, it is not difficult to understand why approximately one third of the state administrators contacted by the Child

Welfare League of America (1986) do not routinely investigate reports within the 24 to 48 hours mandated by child welfare legislation. In addition, the NIS-3 findings indicated that CPS investigated only approximately one fourth of children reported under the most stringent definitions of maltreatment (Sedlak & Broadhurst, 1996).

> Historically, CPS agencies have focused on reporting and investigation, rather than prevention and treatment.

Melton and Barry (1994) have argued that another reason the system fails is because it responds to allegations, not needs. Historically, CPS has narrowly focused on reporting and investigation to the exclusion of efforts directed at prevention and treatment. At the present time, approximately 30% to 40% of the families in which maltreatment has been substantiated do not receive any "service" other than investigation (McCurdy & Daro, 1994a; Wang & Daro, 1998).

In reaction to the problems with the system and its response to abused and neglected children, the U.S. Advisory Board on Child Abuse and Neglect formulated a new national strategy for the protection of children in 1993. Melton and Barry (1994) summarized this strategy, which includes the following elements:

1. Strengthening neighborhoods as environments for children and families
2. Refocusing the delivery of human services so that efforts are focused on services to prevent child maltreatment rather than almost exclusively on services provided after abuse has occurred
3. Reorienting the role of government in child protection so that incentives are offered for prevention and treatment rather than investigation
4. Targeting societal values that may contribute to child maltreatment such as cultural acceptance of violence and exploitation of children
5. Increasing the knowledge base about child maltreatment through federal research programs

Out-of-Home Care

Out-of-home care includes foster care placements, court placements to relatives, residential treatment centers, and institutions. In 1985, an estimated 276,000 children were living in out-of-home care settings, primarily as a result of child abuse, physical neglect, parental incompetency, or abandonment (Sudia, 1986). By the early 1990s, the number had escalated to more than 400,000, with approximately 75% of these children placed in foster care (George, Wulczyn, & Fanshel, 1994; Morganthau et al., 1994). The Adoption and Foster Care Analysis and Reporting System estimated that in 1996, more than 500,000 children were living in foster care (Children's Bureau, 1997). The rise in the number of children placed in out-of-home settings has led to considerable debate in recent years about placement decisions (see Box 3.3, "Out-of-Home Placement Dilemmas").

BOX 3.3 Out-of-Home Placement Dilemmas

The U.S. Advisory Board on Child Abuse and Neglect (1993) recently concluded that "the system the nation has devised to respond to child abuse and neglect is *failing*" (p. 2). One component of that system receiving increasingly more and more criticism is out-of-home placement. One problem is that decreasing numbers of families are participating as foster parents, which limits the number of placements available for children (Morganthau et al., 1994). Other concerns focus on the potentially negative psychological effects that might result from out-of-home placement such as emotional and behavioral problems. Critics also argue that the system is harmful for children because it puts them at increased risk for abuse in out-of-home settings.

Concerns voiced about out-of-home placement create a dilemma about what to do with children without homes—those who are abused, neglected, or unwanted. Reform of this system has been the topic of debate in Washington (Morganthau et al., 1994). Former House Speaker Newt Gingrich has recommended bringing back orphanages as one solution (Fornek & O'Donnell, 1994). Public perceptions of orphanages are generally negative and conjure up images of lonely and emotionally starved children. Orphanages have been likened to prisons, useful for warehousing large numbers of children unable, for whatever reason, to live at home (Blankenhorn, 1994). In addition to distasteful images, the notion of resurrecting the orphanage has also raised concern about the resulting effect on the physical, social, and emotional well-being of children living in such arrangements. Gates (1994), for example, reviewed the history of the orphanage, describing the overcrowded conditions, poor nutrition, and unreasonable labor characteristic of orphanages of the 1800s. The orphanages of today, however, are group homes or residential treatment centers that include smaller living quarters with higher staff-child ratios.

What, then, is the best alternative for maltreated children? In arriving at the best alternative, the costs and benefits of leaving the child in the home versus foster care versus residential living must be evaluated. An analysis of the financial costs of each alternative indicates that the least expensive alternative is to keep the child in the home, followed by placing the child in foster care. The maximum monthly federal program payments to parents range from $253 in Alaska to $192 in Vermont (Green, 1994, cited in Morganthau et al., 1994). These figures translate into approximately $6 to $8 a day per child. Foster care placement ranges from $12 to $16 a day per child (Spencer & Knudsen, 1992). The most expensive alternative is institutional care. Boys Town, a residential group home, spends approximately $111 to $133 a day per child (Morganthau et al., 1994).

Financial expenses are not the only consideration. What about the other potential costs associated with various alternatives, such as the potential for negative socioemotional consequences and the risk for further maltreatment? Some experts have argued that the social and emotional damage created by out-of-home placement may outweigh the potential harm a child faces by remaining in the home (Besharov, 1990). Others believe that the doctrine of family reunification should be abandoned for programs that focus on child protection and intervention aimed at the child's needs (Gelles, 1993b).

The research evidence evaluating these issues, unfortunately, is inconclusive. With regard to the potential psychological damage resulting from out-of-home placement, some studies have found better outcomes for children in foster care (Hensey, Williams, & Rosenbloom, 1983), whereas others have found better outcomes for children who remain at home (Lynch & Roberts, 1982). In a recent study, Kurtz, Gaudin, Howing, and Wodarski (1993) found no effect on child outcome for length of time spent in foster care, but they did find that greater numbers of foster care placements were associated with more negative child outcomes.

Research evaluating the risk for further maltreatment associated with in-home and out-of-home placement is also inconclusive. Cohn and Daro (1987) found that 30% to 47% of parents continued to abuse their children while receiving treatment services. Abuse, however, also occurs in out-of-home placements (Rosenthal, Motz, Edmonson, & Groze, 1991; Spencer & Knudsen, 1992). Some reports suggest that such abuse is uncommon, constituting less than 1% of confirmed abuse cases (McCurdy & Daro, 1994b), whereas other research suggests that abuse in out-of-home settings is more common than in-home abuse (Rabb & Rindfleisch, 1985). Spencer and Knudsen (1992) compared relative risk for maltreatment among a variety of out-of-home facilities and found that children in day care and school facilities were less likely to be maltreated than those in foster homes, residential homes, and state institutions and hospitals.

The best placement alternative for any given child will likely depend on the particular circumstances of that individual. Placement decisions must involve a flexible and comprehensive approach that respects the potential contributions of many types of interventions. In some instances, keeping the child in the home while the family receives intensive intervention has proven cost-effective (Daro, 1988; Walton, Fraser, Lewis, & Pecora, 1993). On the other hand, there is no question that out-of-home care will be necessary for some children. Ultimately, the solution to the placement dilemma will involve many challenges:

> Increased risk to children and families occurs when either protection or preservation is emphasized to the exclusion of the other. If prevention of placement or reunification is framed as the primary "success," we introduce an incentive which may endanger children. Conversely, an emphasis on protection, without providing parents in-home services at the level they need, may harm children. (Lloyd & Sallee, 1994, p. 3)

Although state laws permit placement in out-of-home care to protect children, all states have programs to prevent the dissolution of the family when desirable and possible (Stein, 1993). The recently enacted federal law titled the Adoption and Safe Families Act of 1997 reaffirms the principle of family reunification but also holds paramount the concern for children's safety (see Chapter 7 for a comprehensive discussion of this new law). Children may be placed in out-of-home care when danger to the child is imminent or when prevention attempts are unlikely to be effective. In addition, the new law defines specific situations in which states *are not* required to make "reasonable efforts" to return children to their families (e.g., when the parent has committed murder, manslaughter, or felony assault of the child or another child of the parent). Furthermore, the law affirms that children should not grow up in temporary living situations by establishing requirements for early permanency planning (e.g., timely adoption and a time frame for initiating termination of parental rights).

Psychological Treatment

The psychopathology-based view of PCA led to treatment efforts directed primarily at individual parents. Such methods have been criticized for being too narrow in scope, ignoring the other serious contributors to and consequences of PCA (Graziano & Mills, 1992). Current approaches are broader and include not only adult interventions but also child-focused and family interventions (Kolko, 1998; Oates & Bross, 1995; Wolfe & Wekerle, 1993).

Adult Interventions

Since the 1970s, adult interventions have increasingly used cognitive-behavioral approaches, including some form of skills training that focuses on anger-, child-, or stress-management skills (for reviews, see Azar, 1997; Schellenbach, 1998). The most frequently used behavioral approach is to train parents in nonviolent child management skills. Such training involves educating parents about the effects of reinforcement and punishment on behavior and the importance of consistency in discipline. Parents also learn how to appropriately deliver both reinforcement and punishment for child behaviors. Programs achieve these goals by providing written information, appropriate parenting models through demonstration (video or live), and problem-solving approaches for increasing child compliance. Parent programs also attempt to guide parental behavior by providing opportunities for role play to practice skills and feedback about performance (e.g., MacMillan, Olson, & Hansen, 1991).

Anger control techniques attempt to reduce negative emotional responses and thoughts and enhance coping ability (e.g., Acton & During, 1992). These programs achieve these goals by assisting parents in identifying events that increase negative emotions and helping parents replace anger-producing thoughts with more appropriate ones. Anger control programs also attempt to teach self-control skills in an effort to reduce uncontrolled expressions of anger. Stress management techniques typically involve education and training of parents with regard to relaxation techniques, ways to reduce psychological stress, and methods for coping with stressful interactions with their child (e.g., Egan, 1983).

Empirical studies evaluating the effectiveness of interventions for adults who abuse children indicate that parent-focused approaches consistently demonstrate improvements in parenting skills such as positive interactions with their children; effective control of unwanted behavior; and decreases in negative, coercive, or physically punitive management techniques (Azar & Siegel, 1990; Graziano & Mills, 1992; Wolfe & Wekerle, 1993). These techniques are also effective in enhancing anger control and stress management approaches by increasing coping and problem-solving skills (Acton & During, 1992). Parent-focused programs also exhibit some collateral effects by decreasing aggressive or negative behavior in the children of abusive parents and by increasing social skills and networks (Oates & Bross, 1995; Wolfe & Wekerle, 1993). Some evaluation studies have indicated that changes in parent behavior are maintained through time, although more researchers need to incorporate follow-up measures in their research designs (Schellenbach, 1998).

Child Interventions

In extreme cases, physically abused children may be exhibiting such severe psychological and behavioral difficulties that hospitalization is required. Most child interventions, however, involve therapeutic day treatment programs, individual therapy, and play sessions. Therapeutic day treatment programs typically provide group activities, opportunities for peer interactions, and learning experiences to address developmental delays (Culp, Little, Letts, & Lawrence, 1991; Parish, Myers, Brandner, & Templin, 1985). Individual therapy often incorporates relaxation skills, problem-solving strategies, anger management techniques, and efforts to improve self-esteem (Walker et al., 1988). Play sessions include opportunities for play interaction between abused children and adults and/or peers (e.g., Davis & Fantuzzo, 1989).

Available studies evaluating the effectiveness of child-focused treatment interventions indicate that these programs are successful in decreasing aggressive and coercive behaviors and in improving social behavior, cognitive development, and self-esteem in abused children relative to controls (Fantuzzo et al., 1996; Oates & Bross, 1995; Wolfe & Wekerle, 1993). Unfortunately, most of the studies evaluating treatment interventions directed at the child victim of PCA focus on preschool or young children to the exclusion of school-age and adolescent victims and do not make distinctions between various forms of maltreatment. In addition, few studies provide extended follow-up assessments to determine whether these benefits are maintained through time.

Family Interventions

Limited information is available regarding interventions that target the family such as marital or family therapy approaches. One exception is the study conducted by Brunk, Henggeler, and Whelan (1987), which compared 33 maltreating families randomly assigned to either parent training or family therapy. Results indicated that both treatments were associated with decreases in psychological complaints, perceived stress, and overall severity of identified problems. A more recent study conducted by Kolko (1996b) included physically abused children and their parents, who were randomly assigned to either family therapy or separate individual cognitive-behavioral treatments for the child and parent. These two groups were compared with families who received routine community services. The results of this study suggested that both family therapy and cognitive-behavioral treatment were superior to routine community services in reducing child-to-parent violence, child behavior problems, and parental distress. Family therapy was also shown to be effective in reducing levels of parental anger and physical discipline or force, although not as effectively as cognitive-behavioral treatment (Kolko, 1996a).

Intensive family preservation programs are another family-oriented approach offering some promise for physically abusive families. Such home visitation programs involve professionals or community volunteers who provide a variety of intervention approaches during regular visits to abusive parents. Intensive family preservation programs were developed in an effort to prevent out-of-home placement of abused and neglected children by providing short-term, intensive therapeutic and supportive interventions. Most such programs focus on training parents in child development and parenting skills, as well as in stress reduction techniques and anger management (Wasik & Roberts, 1994). Several evaluations of intensive family preservation programs demonstrate their success in preventing out-of-home placement of children (e.g., Bath & Haapala, 1993; Schwartz, AuClaire, & Harris, 1991). Home visitation programs are also recommended for the prevention of PCA (U.S. Advisory Board on Child Abuse and Neglect, 1993) and are discussed further in Chapter 7.

Community Interventions

Several community interventions commonly serve as adjuncts to some of the other intervention methods reported in this section. The idea behind community interventions is to directly address the multiple factors believed to contribute to PCA such as social isolation, financial stress, and excessive child care demands.

Social Networks

Because many abusive parents are socially isolated, researchers have suggested providing them assistance in developing a social network (Gaudin, Wodarski, Arkinson, & Avery, 1990; Walker et al., 1988). These networks include personal friends as well as community contacts. Community contacts vary depending on a particular family's needs but might include crisis hotlines, support groups (e.g., Parents Anonymous), or educational classes (e.g., Wolfe, Edwards, Manion, & Koverola, 1988). Home visitation programs offer another avenue of support to abusive parents. Home visits not only provide parents with knowledge about child development and management but also serve as a source of social support for parents (see Amundson, 1989; Roberts, Wasik, Casto, & Ramey, 1991).

Economic Assistance

Abusive families often need assistance to establish basic necessities such as food and shelter. Unfortunately, programs aimed at macrolevel concerns, such as poverty, are almost nonexistent (Hay & Jones, 1994). Local service organizations, the family's caseworker, or the Salvation Army might be able to provide such assistance. Professionals might also make job and educational referrals, although additional support may be necessary to combat the economic difficulties faced by these families (Hay & Jones, 1994). Parents may also need assistance completing government forms to obtain state funds for food stamps, child support, and Temporary Assistance for Needy Families (TANF, which has replaced AFDC).

Child Care Programs

Because abusive parents often find the parenting role challenging and have fewer child care options, child care programs can provide relief for overly burdened parents who need a break (Hay & Jones, 1994). Therapeutic child day care centers provide an environment similar to traditional day care programs but additionally provide services to target developmental delays and behavioral disorders associated with child maltreatment. Children can also be enrolled in preschool programs or Head Start centers, or families can take advantage of respite care services (e.g., home aides). Research has shown that such programs are successful in enhancing abused children's functioning (Daro & McCurdy, 1994).

Multiservice Approaches

Multiservice interventions recognize the complex and interactive nature of PCA by targeting multiple systems and integrating complementary services. Most multiservice interventions have an ecological emphasis and include interventions aimed at the child, parent, family, and social environment that focus on the use of diverse community services and interventions. Such approaches attempt to alter social factors that increase stress and affect a family's ability to function effectively (e.g., Lutzker & Rice, 1987). Project 12-Ways is a noteworthy example of such an approach and includes a variety of services for families such as parent-child training, stress reduction, marital counseling, employment assistance, and money management (Lutzker, 1990b; Lutzker, Frame, & Rice, 1982). Although improvements have been documented in some parent behaviors, and reabuse rates are lower in families participating in the program compared with controls, initial evaluations have found that improvements are not maintained through time (Lutzker, 1990b; Nelson, 1994).

SUMMARY

The physical abuse of children is a complex problem that is not well understood despite nearly four decades of research efforts. The complexity of PCA is evident in attempts at defining what specific circumstances constitute abuse. Although most experts recognize that PCA includes a range of behaviors that cause observable harm to children, the boundary between PCA and "normal" parenting practices, or behaviors that do not result in observable harm, is less clear. Despite definitional ambiguities, it is clear that thousands of children are subjected to the harm associated with PCA each year. The majority of Americans report using at least one violent act toward their children at some point during child rearing.

Research examining the characteristics of the victims and perpetrators of PCA demonstrates the heterogeneity of victim and offender populations. Child victims, as well as adults who perpetrate PCA, represent all gender, age, race, and socioeconomic groups. A number of risk factors, however, have been consistently associated with PCA. Victims are often young children between 0 and 7 years of age. Children with special needs such as those with physical or mental disabilities also appear to be at higher risk for abuse. Perpetrators of PCA are disproportionately represented among economically disadvantaged groups, and their environments include additional stressors such as having children at a young age and single parenthood. Adults who inflict violence against children also display other psychological characteristics including depression, anger control problems, parenting difficulties, family difficulties, and physiological overreactivity.

PCA has been associated with a number of negative effects including negative physical and psychological effects for child and adolescent victims as well as for adults who report a childhood history of PCA. Such negative consequences affect a variety of areas of functioning including the physical, emotional, cognitive, behavioral, and social domains. The experience of PCA, however, does not affect each individual in a consistent or predictable way. Specific factors can mediate the effects of PCA, either increasing or decreasing its detrimental effects. Factors associated with an increased effect of PCA include the severity of abuse, the duration, and the number of forms of abuse experienced.

The causes of PCA are not well understood, although a number of models have been proposed in an attempt to understand the violence that occurs between adults and children. Early theories focused on psychiatric disturbances in abusers, whereas later theories have implicated dysfunctional parent-child interactions. A significant shift in the conceptualization of PCA occurred with the birth of sociological models, which emphasized the situational and social factors associated with abuse, including the role of socioeconomic disadvantage, social isolation, situational stressors, and cultural approval of violence.

Early solutions to the PCA problem focused on the abusing parent to the exclusion of other potentially helpful interventions. More recently, CPS agencies, under the administration of both federal and state systems, have provided assistance (e.g., child care, community centers, counseling and education, and visitor and self-help programs) for children who are at risk for child abuse or neglect. Because of the complexity of PCA, any single intervention or treatment is unlikely to be successful, particularly with high-risk families. Psychological approaches for children and their families target parenting skills; anger control and stress management; social and developmental skills; and child-centered, marital, and family interactions. Some families may need additional treatment interventions that focus on psychiatric disorders, substance abuse problems, or in-home services (e.g., crisis intervention and assertiveness training). Furthermore, community interventions have expanded to address situational and social factors that might contribute to PCA, namely, social isolation and economic stressors. In such cases, home visits, hotlines, support groups, local service organizations, family caseworkers, and government programs such as TANF or distribution of food stamps are called on for support. Although evaluation studies suggest that these interventions appear promising, additional research is needed to enhance efforts directed at solving the PCA problem.

NOTE

1. From "Hell Is for Children" [Record], by P. Benatar, N. Geraldo, and R. Capps, 1981. Rare Blue Music, Inc./Neil Geraldo (ASCAP), Red Admiral Music Inc./Big Tooth Music Co. (BMI), Rare Blue Music Inc./Muscletone Music (ASCAP). (1980). Used with permission.

4

Child Sexual Abuse

CHAPTER OUTLINE

AN INTERVIEW WITH LUCY BERLINER

"I think that what is needed to solve the problem of child maltreatment, in addition to particular policies, are better ways of going about achieving policy goals. We are too quick to see passing a law, getting the government to give more money, or imposing a particular model as the solutions to child maltreatment."

Lucy Berliner is a certified social worker and Clinical Associate Professor at the University of Washington Graduate School of Social Work and Department of Psychiatry and Behavioral Sciences and Research Director at the Harborview Center for Sexual Assault and Traumatic Stress in Seattle, Washington. She has published extensively on topics associated with child sexual abuse victimization and perpetration and is actively engaged in administering clinical interventions to sexual assault victims and their families, conducting research on various aspects of sexual victimization of children, and promoting public policy on behalf of sexual assault victims. She serves as an associate editor of two interpersonal violence journals and also serves on the board of a number of child maltreatment organizations such as the *National Center for Missing and Exploited Children*. She received her B.A. in Spanish from Earlham College in Indiana and her M.S.W. from the University of Washington.

Q: What sparked your interest in the area of child maltreatment?

A: As a graduate student intern in the early 1970s, by sheer serendipity, I ended up working graveyard shifts in the emergency department of Harborview Medical Center, Seattle's regional trauma center. I also worked days in the hospital's newly established program for sexual assault victims. The program was funded to provide crisis support to rape victims to increase the women's cooperation with the criminal justice system. These experiences provided me with up-front, personal exposure to the impact of interpersonal violence and ignited an enduring interest in developing effective clinical and social policy responses to such violence. Although children were not my initial focus, it soon became apparent that children constitute a substantial percentage of victims. I have always been concerned with child maltreatment within the larger context of interpersonal violence.

Q: What would you describe as your most influential contribution to the field of child maltreatment?

A: I think my strength, and unique contribution, is my ability to integrate clinical experience, research findings, and social policy considerations to create better ways of helping child victims and their families recover from abuse experiences and obtain justice. My ideas almost always come directly from personal experiences with victims, encounters with other professionals involved within the field, or my work in the community focused on improving system responses or legislation. As a result, my ideas are grounded in real life and usually have credibility, even with those who may have a different point of view. In addition, I think I have been a good model for the importance of learning from other disciplines, seeing the other side of arguments, acknowledging when mistakes have been made, and being open to new ways of approaching issues.

Q: What should be done to help solve the problem of child maltreatment?

A: Professionals need to come up with better methods to obtain the common citizen's support for efforts to prevent and respond to child maltreatment. To make this happen, professionals need to be more effective in addressing the contrast between how the public feels about child abuse in the abstract versus the personal reactions to child maltreatment when it occurs in one's own family or immediate community. One mistake professionals can make, for example, is to be righteous and assume that others are not as concerned about child maltreatment as themselves. Although legislatures and citizens may not always accept or support policy recommendations, it is not necessarily because they do not care about maltreated children. Everyone realizes that abuse happens and that it is bad, yet it is clear we have not hit on the best way to get broad community support for solutions. Finding ways to get on "the same page" with regular citizens would help professionals' efforts to prevent and respond to child maltreatment.

Q: What type of policy recommendations are most needed in the field of child maltreatment?

A: I think that what is needed to solve the problem of child maltreatment, in addition to particular policies, are better ways of going about achieving policy goals. We are too quick to see passing a law, getting the government to give more money, or imposing a particular model as the solutions to child maltreatment. I prefer to see more support for system and service solutions that are effective at the local level. More attention should be focused on identifying the important principles of these successful efforts, and such programs should then be exported to other communities. I would also like to see greater reliance on professional societies and other organizations in setting standards for competent practice for those who work with abuse victims and their families.

INTRODUCTION

CASE HISTORY: SASHIM'S SECRET

Sashim was 6 years old and an only child when her parents divorced. Her father had been physically violent with both Sashim and her mother, and all subsequent ties with him were eliminated after the divorce. The next 3 years were difficult for Sashim because she rarely saw her mother, who worked two jobs in an attempt to make ends meet. When Sashim was 9 years old, her mother met a man named Bhagwan, a 39-year-old construction foreman. Shortly after Sashim's mother met him, Bhagwan moved in with the family and took a serious interest in Sashim. He took her to movies, bought her new clothes, and listened to the difficulties she was having at school. He seemed to provide her with the parental attention that she had missed for so many years.

After several months, Bhagwan's behavior toward Sashim began to change. He became much more physical with her, putting his arm around her when they were at the movies, stroking her hair, and kissing her on the lips when he said good night. He began to come into her bedroom or the bathroom without knocking (e.g., when she was changing or bathing). Bhagwan then began "checking on her" in the middle of the night. During his visits, he would stroke and caress her body. In the beginning, he touched only her nonprivate areas (e.g., shoulders, arms, and legs), but after several visits, he began to touch her breasts and genitals. Eventually, he began to kiss her sexually during his touching, all the while telling her how much he loved her and enjoyed being her father. He warned her that she should not tell anyone about their time together because others would not understand their "special" relationship.

One night, Bhagwan attempted to have sexual intercourse with Sashim, and she refused. A few days later, one of Sashim's favorite teachers asked if something was bothering her. Sashim began crying and told her teacher everything that had happened. Sashim's teacher reassured her that she believed her and would help her. Sashim's teacher called child protective services and reported her conversation with Sashim. Two social workers came to school and listened to Sashim as she told her story. Bhagwan was arrested. Sashim's mother was incredulous and could not believe that Bhagwan could do such a thing or that such a thing could occur without her knowing about it. She refused to believe Sashim, calling her a liar and a "home-wrecker." As a result, Sashim was placed in a foster home. Shortly thereafter, Sashim was diagnosed with leukemia and was told that she had only 6 months to live. Her only request was that she be able to die at "home" with her foster parents, to whom she had become quite attached. The hospital required that Sashim have parental consent before they could grant her request. Her biological mother still had legal custody of Sashim, however, and refused to grant the request unless Sashim agreed to recant her story about Bhagwan. (first author's case history)

As this case history demonstrates, child sexual abuse (CSA) is a multifaceted problem that is extraordinarily complex in its characteristics, dynamics, causes, and consequences. This chapter examines the major issues that contribute to such complexity. The chapter opens by addressing issues related to defining the scope of CSA, including definitions and rates of the problem. Attention then focuses on the typical characteristics of CSA victims as well as perpetrators regarding age, gender, the relationship between perpetrator and victim, and additional factors. Next, a discussion follows of the dynamics of CSA and the consequences of this form of maltreatment for the victim. Finally, the chapter concludes with an analysis of potential causes of CSA and responses to the problem. Although the discussion focuses on CSA in the broader context of family violence, attention will not be limited to intrafamilial (i.e., incestuous) sexual abuse because a substantial proportion of sexual abuse is extrafamilial.

SCOPE OF THE PROBLEM

What Is Child Sexual Abuse?

As discussed previously, one of the greatest barriers to understanding different forms of child maltreatment is the difficulty inherent in defining the problem. The issue is no less problematic with CSA. Which of the following case examples, for instance, deserve the label *CSA*?

Jamie, a 15-year-old adolescent, frequently baby-sat his neighbor, 4-year-old Naomi. Each time Jamie baby-sat Naomi, he had her stroke his exposed penis while they watched her favorite video.

Manuel and Maria frequently walked around nude at home in front of their 5-year-old son, Ernesto.

Matt, a 10-year-old boy, was repeatedly forced to have anal intercourse with his uncle when Matt was between the ages of 5 and 9 years. After his abuse stopped, Matt frequently sneaked into his 6-year-old sister's room and had anal intercourse with her.

Sally was a 16-year-old, self-proclaimed "nymphomaniac." Sally had numerous boyfriends from school with whom she had physical relationships (e.g., kissing, fondling, and sexual intercourse). One evening while Sally was home alone with her 45-year-old stepfather, he asked her if she would like to "mess around." Sally willingly agreed to have sexual intercourse with him.

Dexter, a 30-year-old man, invited 7-year-old Jimmy to his house frequently for an after-school snack. After their snacks, Dexter had Jimmy undress and assume various sexual poses while he made videotapes, which he distributed for profit.

The interactions described in each of these vignettes raise several important questions about defining CSA. First, what behaviors are defined as *sexual*? Second, under what circumstances do sexual interactions become *abusive*?

Cultural Context

In Chapter 1, a review of the discovery of CSA indicated that sexual interactions between children and adults have occurred throughout history, beginning in ancient times. Only recently has CSA been recognized as a social problem. It is thus apparent that any definition of CSA is dependent on the historical period in question, the cultural context of the behavior, and the values and orientations of specific social groups (Wurtele & Miller-Perrin, 1992). To define CSA today, it is essential to know something about what types of behavior are generally regarded as acceptable in American families. Is it abusive for Manuel and Maria to walk around nude in front of their 5-year-old son? What if their son were 13 years of age? How much variation in nudity, touching various body parts, or kissing on the lips is socially acceptable?

Unfortunately, researchers have conducted few studies on normal patterns of touching and physical contact. One exception is the research of Rosenfeld and colleagues, which examined typical family patterns of bathing and touching (Rosenfeld, Bailey, Siegel, & Bailey, 1986; Rosenfeld, Siegel, & Bailey, 1987). Survey responses of 576 parents revealed that parents rarely bathed with their children at any age, particularly with the opposite sex (e.g., mothers with sons), after the children were 3 to 4 years of age. The touching of mothers and fathers (e.g., genitals or breasts) by children was relatively common among preschoolers, but declined as the children became older. More recent research confirms these findings and indicates that some types of sexual behavior are common in non-abused children (e.g., children touching their own sex parts), whereas more explicit sexual behaviors (e.g., inserting objects into the anus or vagina and oral-genital contact) are extremely rare (Friedrich, Grambsch, Broughton, Kuiper, & Beilke, 1991). Additional research is necessary to determine the frequency of other family behaviors such as sleeping patterns, nudity, privacy, and other types of touching (e.g., kissing and hugging) as well as cultural differences in such behaviors.

Conceptual Issues

The National Center on Child Abuse and Neglect (1978) defined child sexual abuse as

> contacts or interactions between a child and an adult when the child is being used for the sexual stimulation of the perpetrator or another person. Sexual abuse may also be committed by a person under the age of 18 when that person is either significantly older than the victim or when the perpetrator is in a position of power or control over another child. (p. 2)

This definition is consistent with most legal and research definitions of CSA and incorporates four key components that are generally regarded today as essential in defining CSA. First, definitions of CSA are typically broad enough to include not only cases of intrafamilial abuse (i.e., incest) but also cases of extrafamilial abuse. Second, definitions of CSA often include sexual experiences with a child involving both physical contact and noncontact activities. CSA, for example, may include physical contact such as fondling or intercourse as described in the vignette interactions involving Jamie, Matt, and Sally. Sexual abuse can also include noncontact forms as illustrated in the last scenario depicting Dexter making a pornographic video of Jimmy.

Controversy continues to exist, however, regarding the specific behaviors deemed abusive, regardless of whether those behaviors are classified as contact or noncontact experiences. Parental nudity is clearly a noncontact behavior, but is it an abusive behavior? One way to distinguish between abusive and nonabusive behaviors is to evaluate the intent of the perpetrator. Many definitions of CSA, for example, define abuse as sexual activities that are intended for sexual stimulation, thus excluding normal family or caregiving interactions (e.g., nudity, bathing, and displays of affection). In practice, however, determining whether a behavioral intention is sexual or nonsexual can be difficult. How can one determine whether a grandfather's kiss to his granddaughter is innocent affection or sexual contact meant for his sexual gratification? Furthermore, some experts argue that caregiving behaviors can go beyond normal experiences and become abusive, such as when children are repeatedly exposed to genital examinations or cleanings (Berson & Herman-Giddens, 1994).

A third important component of CSA definitions emphasizes the exploitation of adult authority and power to achieve the adult's sexual ends. Implicit in this definition is the assumption that children are incapable of providing informed consent to sexual interactions with adults for two reasons. First, because of their developmental status, children cannot give informed consent because they are not capable of fully understanding what they are consenting to and what the consequences of their consent might be. Second, children's ability to provide informed consent is limited because they might not be in a position to decline involvement because of the adult's authority status. The incident between Sally and her stepfather is abusive because despite Sally's sexual experience and "consent" in this situation, she is not mature enough to understand the ramifications of having sexual intercourse with her stepfather. As Haugaard and Reppucci (1988) point out, "The total legal and moral responsibility for any sexual behavior between an adult and a child is the adult's; it is the responsibility of the adult not to respond to the child" (p. 193).

Children are incapable of providing informed consent to sexual interactions with adults.

A final component of CSA definitions addresses the age or maturational advantage of the perpetrator over the child. Although many definitions limit abuse to situations involving an age discrepancy of 5 years or more between perpetrator and victim (e.g., Conte, 1993), others include children and adolescents as potential perpetrators if a situation involves the exploitation of a child by virtue of the perpetrator's size, age, sex, or status. Broader definitions of CSA include circumstances such as those described in the second scenario between 10-year-old Matt and his 6-year-old sister. An increasing number of reports involving both adolescent offenders and children victimizing children younger than themselves are beginning to appear (e.g., Abel & Rouleau, 1990; Gomes-Schwartz, Horowitz, & Cardarelli, 1990; Johnson, 1989).

Estimates of Child Sexual Abuse

Despite problems in defining CSA, researchers have made numerous efforts to determine the scope of the problem. In the United States, researchers generally use one of two methods of estimation: official estimates based on reported cases and self-report surveys of adults who report having experienced sexual victimization during childhood.

Official Estimates

One source of information about official estimates of CSA comes from annual surveys conducted to assess the number of official reports of CSA documented by CPS in the United States (AAPC, 1988; DHHS, 1998; Wang & Daro, 1998). Data from 1986 indicated that approximately 50,714 children were *reported* to CPS for child sexual abuse (AAPC, 1988). This figure increased to 223,650 children in 1997 (Wang & Daro, 1998).

As discussed in Chapter 2, official estimates such as those provided by the DHHS are difficult to interpret because most child maltreatment never comes to the attention of CPS. Victims and families often do not report abuse, and many professionals who are mandated to report abuse often fail to do so (e.g., Kalichman, Craig, & Follingstad, 1989; Russell, 1983). Estimates are that mandated professionals (e.g., psychologists, social workers, and physicians) fail to report approximately half of the maltreatment cases they identify (Sedlak, 1990).

The National Incidence Studies attempt to avoid some of the problems associated with underreporting by including reports to CPS as well as cases of abuse encountered by community professionals (see Table 2.1 in Chapter 2 for the definitions of sexual abuse employed by the NIS-3). Three National Incidence Studies (NIS-1, NIS-2, NIS-3) have estimated the frequency of CSA in the United States (DHHS, 1981, 1988; Sedlak, 1990; Sedlak & Broadhurst, 1996). NIS-1 estimated that 42,900 children under the age of 18 were sexually abused in 1980 (a rate of 0.7 per 1,000 children). NIS-2 estimated that 133,600 children were sexually abused in 1986 (a rate of 2.1 per 1,000 children). NIS-3 estimated that 300,200 children were sexually abused in 1993 (a rate of 4.5 per 1,000 children).

Data from both CPS reports and the NIS suggest an increase in reporting rates for child sexual abuse. An increase in *reporting rates,* however, is not necessarily equivalent to an increase in the *actual rate* of child sexual abuse (a discussion of this issue follows). Many factors can contribute to fluctuating reporting rates, which makes the interpretation of official statistics difficult. The definition of CSA that is employed is one factor that influences reporting rates. In the second NIS (DHHS, 1988), for example, rates were higher when teenagers, in addition to adults, were considered perpetrators of abuse. Official statistics also often include duplicate reports or reports made only to CPS, contributing to the difficulty in interpreting findings.

Self-Report Surveys

Self-report victimization surveys examine the proportion of a population that acknowledges having experienced sexual abuse during childhood. Self-report surveys include samples of college students, clinical or special groups (e.g., psychiatric inpatients and runaway youths), and community members (e.g., Finkelhor, 1979; Finkelhor, Hotaling, Lewis, & Smith, 1990; Powers, Eckenrode, & Jaklitsch, 1990). Compared with official statistics, self-report surveys probably do a better job of estimating the true rate of victimization. Self-report surveys of sexual abuse, however, also underestimate actual rates because some men and women who were victimized as children may not remember their experiences or may be reluctant to report them as adults (see Williams, 1994).

The sensitive nature of the topic, problems with recall, and definitional problems make sexual abuse difficult to estimate from data generated via victim surveys. Furthermore, many of the studies that have been conducted rely on clinical samples that cannot be generalized to the public. Because of these problems, estimates vary dramatically. A review of college student and community studies, for example, indicated that the prevalence of sexual abuse ranged from 7% to 62% for females and from 3% to 16% for males (Wurtele & Miller-Perrin, 1992).

Self-report surveys of sexual abuse may also underestimate actual rates of victimization.

Self-report estimates were recently obtained from a national random sample of 1,000 adults who participated in a telephone survey sponsored by the Gallup Organization (Finkelhor, Moore, Hamby, & Straus, 1997). Adults were asked two questions about their own childhood experiences of sexual abuse (see items SA and SB in Table 2.3 of Chapter 2). Results indicated that overall, 23% of respondents reported being "touched in a sexual way" or "forced to have sex" before the age of 18 by a family or nonfamily member. The results regarding gender ratio for this survey indicated that women were nearly three times as likely as men to self-report child sexual abuse. These results are similar to the most representative and methodologically sound self-report surveys in the literature, which indicate that at least 20% of women and between 5% and 10% of men in North America have experienced some form of sexual abuse as children (Finkelhor, 1994a).

Is Sexual Abuse Increasing?

Official estimates indicate that reports of CSA have increased dramatically since 1980. Does this increase in official reports indicate a true rise in the rate of CSA? It is certainly possible that sexual abuse could be increasing because of changes taking place within the family such as divorce, both parents working outside the home, and the greater presence of stepfathers and baby-sitters. It is also possible that what has increased is public awareness about sexual abuse resulting in a greater number of reports of abuse. Others argue that official reports are inflated as a result of false allegations and social hysteria (Rabinowitz, 1990). There has been considerable controversy among researchers and in the media surrounding the issue of fabricated reports of CSA, although the research evidence suggests that false allegations by children are rare (e.g., Jones & McGraw, 1987; Romer, 1990; see Box 4.1, "Do Children Fabricate Reports of Child Sexual Abuse?").

It seems most likely that the actual occurrence of CSA is not increasing but rather that CSA is reported more often as a result of legislative changes and

(text continued on p. 113)

BOX 4.1 Do Children Fabricate Reports of Child Sexual Abuse?

> Each year, there are persons who go to jail and lose their life savings, their homes, their reputations, and their jobs because social workers, psychologists, prosecutors, jurors, and judges believe what young children tell them about being sexually molested. Hundreds of thousands of individuals each year are accused falsely of child abuse. (Emans, 1988, p. 1000)

The origin of the statement that "hundreds of thousands of individuals each year are accused falsely" is typically attributed to Douglas Besharov, the first director of the National Center on Child Abuse and Neglect and keynote speaker at the first Victim of Child Abuse Laws conference (Hechler, 1988). Besharov attributes the large number of false allegations to massive publicity surrounding child abuse accompanied by a dramatic increase in reporting (Besharov, 1985). Is there an epidemic of false allegations? Do parents and other individuals who interact with children need to be concerned that they may be accused of CSA?

After watching the television news or reading the newspaper, it might be easy to conclude that the answer to both questions is a resounding yes. A number of well-publicized cases have contributed to the perception among many that there is an epidemic of false allegations. Celebrities Woody Allen and Michael Jackson, for example, have recently argued that they were falsely accused of CSA. Another case that has received a great deal of attention involved Dale Akiki, a mentally and physically disabled child care worker in San Diego. Akiki was acquitted of sexually abusing, torturing, and kidnapping nine preschool-age children. In their report, the grand jury rebuked therapists, parents, and prosecutors for being "overzealous" and using improper investigation procedures. The grand jury concluded that "lawyers should try cases, not causes" (Mydans, 1994, p. A7).

A few years earlier, one of the longest and most costly criminal trials in U.S. history, the McMartin Preschool case, similarly ended without convictions. In the 1983 McMartin case, Ray Buckey; his mother, Peggy McMartin Buckey; and five other child care workers were accused of sexually abusing some 360 children over several years (Victor, 1993). As in the Akiki case, the defendants were said to be "devil worshipers" and were accused of many bizarre and unspeakable acts. The district attorney's office, citing the "leading questions" of many of the social workers who counseled the children, eventually dropped the charges on everyone except Ray and Peggy Buckey. In January 1990, the Buckeys were acquitted on 52 of the 65 counts against them. Later that year, the prosecution dropped the remaining charges against Ray Buckey.

Highly publicized cases such as these might lead one to conclude that *most* accusations of CSA made by children are fabricated. Research, however, suggests otherwise. One line of research has examined whether children have the general capacity to lie. Current research suggests that children under age 7 are unlikely to be successful at telling a lie (Morency & Krauss, 1982). Other experts have examined the capacity of children to lie about CSA specifically and have concluded that nonsexually abused prepubescent children simply do not have the sexual knowledge or vocabulary to describe many of the explicit sexual acts experienced during abuse. Other research has evaluated whether children have the capacity to form and recall detailed memories of events. Current research and theory regarding memory in children indicate that children's memory ability depends on their language skills and ability to order and interpret events, skills that are particularly difficult for young children (Hewitt, 1998; Perry, 1992). In some situations, however, younger children can provide more accurate recall than adults (e.g., for a particularly salient event; Lindberg, 1991). In addition, children as young as 2 or 3 years of age can reconstruct events with 75% accuracy when they mentally re-create a scene to be remembered (reported in Perry, 1992).

Critics suggest that children are not *intentionally fabricating* stories or memories but that false reports result from parents and professionals who create such memories in children. Studies have examined the suggestibility of children by exposing them to some event and questioning the child about it. Most studies find that young children, especially preschoolers, are more suggestible than older children and adults (Ceci & Bruck, 1993). By age 10 to 11 years, however, children are no more suggestible than adults (Saywitz & Snyder, 1993).

The memory of young children, as a result, can be contaminated by misleading information. Loftus and Ketcham (1991) described research whereby preschool and kindergarten children were shown 1-minute films and subsequently interviewed. Children were asked suggestive questions such as "Did you see a boat?" and "Didn't you see a bear?" and responded affirmatively that they had seen these objects in the film. Because there was no boat or bear in the films, the researchers concluded that they were able to alter the children's responses or possibly create a memory simply by asking a suggestive question. Others have criticized the connection between this research and false allegations of sexual abuse, arguing that the circumstances in such experimental situations are different from an actual event of sexual abuse.

Investigators have also evaluated interview techniques relevant to sexual abuse investigations and found that in general, the techniques are not unduly suggestive. The majority of children do not disclose sensitive material in response to open-ended questions about a medical exam (Saywitz, Goodman, Nicholas, & Moan, 1991). Studies evaluating the use of anatomically correct dolls indicate that they are unlikely to elicit erroneous information (Everson & Boat, 1990). Other research has shown that the use of reinforcement during an interview does not affect accuracy of recall negatively (Goodman, Bottoms, Schwartz-Kenney, & Rudy, 1991). Evaluating an interview technique for research purposes, however, may not reflect the way in which some interviews are conducted in the "real world." Asking a child the same question repeatedly could make the child feel pressure to respond affirmatively (e.g., "Did he touch any of your private parts?"). Making reference to the responses of other children potentially involved in sexual exploitation might also unduly influence a child's response and result in a false allegation (e.g., "José said that Jimmy touched his penis. Did anything like that happen to you?").

The most direct research evidence associated with false allegations comes from studies that have examined samples of cases reported to child protection agencies or other professionals. Most studies of official estimates of CSA indicate that approximately 40% to 50% of CSA cases are unsubstantiated (Wang & Daro, 1998; Wiese & Daro, 1995). Confusion continues to exist, however, regarding what constitutes an unsubstantiated case. Some have equated "unsubstantiated" with false allegations. This definition is misleading because there are several reasons why a case may be labeled unsubstantiated. Unsubstantiated cases include both reports that are fabricated (false) and reports involving insufficient evidence. Unsubstantiated cases theoretically include true reports with insufficient evidence as well as false allegations of abuse.

Estimates of false allegations of abuse range from 3% to 8% of sexual abuse reports (Everson & Boat, 1989; Jones & McGraw, 1987). For example, Jones and McGraw reviewed 576 reports of alleged sexual abuse made to the Denver Department of Social Services in 1983. Of those 576 reports, 53% were confirmed as substantiated reports of abuse. Seventeen percent were unsubstantiated but categorized as representing a legitimate suspicion by the reporter. Another 24% were categorized as having insufficient information to make a determination about the abuse. The remaining 6% of reports were categorized as false allegations. Of the false allegations, 26 were reports from adults, and 8 were made by children or adolescents (5 of these 8 reports were made by disturbed adolescents who had been sexually victimized by an adult in the past). Of the adult cases, the large majority were allegations that arose in the context of custody or visitation disputes, although other studies have indicated that the overwhelming majority of custody disputes do not involve sexual abuse allegations (Faller, 1993). The most recent official estimates available suggest that in those states that identify malicious reports, approximately 1% of unsubstantiated reports constitute intentionally false reports (DHHS, 1998).

There are several reasons to be cautious about results from such studies because rates of false allegations vary, depending on the type of population sampled (Everson & Boat, 1989). In addition, whether a report is considered true or false depends on the criteria used, which can vary from the consensus of clinicians to the disposition of CPS to a judge's opinion. Such judgments are fallible, and as a result, the "true" rate of false allegations could be either somewhat higher or lower. Despite these methodological limitations, the rate of false allegations across studies is consistently low, representing a minority of reports. Even the smallest percentage of false positives, however, warrants continued research focusing on the methods of validating sexual abuse such as increasing the accuracy of validation attempts, improving interview techniques, and enhancing training for evaluators. By preventing false allegations, we not only avoid harming those falsely accused but also refocus attention on identified victims of abuse.

---

increases in public and professional awareness. A study conducted by Feldman and colleagues (1991) examined self-report estimates by comparing English-language studies from the 1970s and 1980s with those of the 1940s. When the variations in methodology across studies were controlled (e.g., definitions of abuse and upper age limits used for victims), results indicated that prevalence figures in 1940 were not significantly different from prevalence estimates of the 1970s and 1980s (e.g., 12% vs. 10% to 12%, respectively, of females younger than 14 years of age). Another study surveyed various age cohorts regarding childhood experiences of CSA and found that the 18- to 19-year-olds recalled proportionately less sexual abuse than the 20- to 27-year-olds, suggesting that in recent years there has been a significant decline in CSA (Bagley, 1990). These data are consistent with information from official reports of CSA that show declines in the proportion of reported cases involving child sexual abuse beginning in the early 1990s (DHHS, 1998; Wang & Daro, 1998).

> It seems likely that child sexual abuse is reported more often because of legislative changes and increased awareness.

Sexual Abuse in Other Cultures

The view that CSA is a social problem of significant magnitude has largely been an American phenomenon. Until recently, CSA has received a great deal more attention in the United States than in other countries, particularly relative to other forms of maltreatment. Studies from other countries that address the problem of CSA internationally, however, are beginning to appear (e.g., Ho & Kwok, 1991; Krugman, Mata, & Krugman, 1992; Sariola & Uutela, 1994). Finkelhor (1994b) summarized the international rate of CSA in a review of 21 nonclinical population studies primarily from English-speaking and northern European countries but also included studies from Costa Rica, the Dominican Republic, Spain, and Greece. Finkelhor's analysis revealed international rates of CSA comparable with North American studies including Canada and the United States.

SECTION SUMMARY

Sexual interactions between children and adults have existed throughout history. Society has not recognized these types of interactions as abusive and harmful, however, until relatively recently. Although any definition of CSA is time and culture bound, today's definition focuses on the *types of behaviors* and the *intent* involved, as well as the *age and/or power discrepancy* between offender and victim. Legally, it is assumed that children are incapable of or limited in providing *informed consent* to sexual interactions with adults. CSA includes both contact (e.g., fondling and intercourse) and noncontact (e.g., taping a pornographic video) experiences; events that occur within and outside the family; and behaviors that involve the exploitation of authority, status, and physical size to achieve the perpetrator's sexual interests.

Although the true number of children victimized by CSA is unknown, it is apparent that sexual victimization in childhood is a common experience. Indeed, there is good reason to speculate that official and self-report estimates *underestimate* the extent of the problem. The actual rate of child sexual abuse remains elusive because of the reluctance of victims and families, as well as professionals, to report abuse. The *variability* of both official and self-report estimates is due to a number of factors including the *type of population sampled* and the *definition of abuse* that is employed. Research during the past several years has documented significant increases in reporting rates; nevertheless, it is likely that increasing rates, both in the United States and elsewhere, are the result of social factors rather than of an increase in the actual incidence of abuse.

SEARCHING FOR PATTERNS: CHARACTERISTICS OF VICTIMS AND PERPETRATORS

Characteristics of Victims of Child Sexual Abuse

Research evaluating demographic characteristics associated with CSA addresses several questions about the victims and perpetrators of this form of abuse. Studies focus on the age and gender of the adults and children involved in abuse, the relationship between perpetrator and victim, and specific risk factors associated with CSA.

Age

Definitional restrictions limit the upper age range typically to 16 to 18 years, but at the lower age range, children as young as 3½ months have been reported for CSA (Ellerstein & Canavan, 1980). Cases on the extreme ends of this continuum are less common, and most clinical studies and official estimates indicate the mean age of children reporting abuse as 9 to 11 years (e.g., AAPC, 1988; Gomes-Schwartz et al., 1990). Retrospective studies of adults support the findings that middle childhood (approximately 7 to 12 years of age) is the most vulnerable period for CSA (Finkelhor, 1993; Finkelhor et al., 1990). It is probable, however, that abuse of young children goes undetected because young children are less likely, or able, than older children to report abuse (Hewitt, 1998), and adults in self-report surveys may not remember abuse that occurred early in childhood (Williams, 1994). Indeed, the most recent official reporting statistics indicate that the rates of sexual abuse show little variability across ages for children 3 years or older (DHHS, 1998; Sedlak & Broadhurst, 1996).

Gender

Official estimates and self-report surveys indicate that the majority of CSA victims are female (DHHS, 1996, 1998; Finkelhor, 1993; Finkelhor et al., 1990). Girls were three times more often sexually abused than boys, according to results of the NIS-3 (Sedlak & Broadhurst, 1996). Many experts believe that this gender discrepancy reflects, in part, that males are simply less likely to report abuse. Some self-report surveys of adult males, for example, indicate that male victims are less likely to disclose abuse (e.g., Finkelhor, 1981). Several societal norms may contribute to the underreporting of males, including (a) the expectation for boys to be dominant and self-reliant, (b) the notion that early sexual experi-

> A higher proportion of male children are sexually abused than previously thought.

ences are a normal part of boys' lives, (c) fears of being considered homosexual because most boys who are abused are abused by men, and (d) pressure on males not to express helplessness or vulnerability (Nasjleti, 1980; Rew & Esparza, 1990). New evidence suggests that a higher proportion of males are being abused than previously thought. The rates of abuse for males appearing in self-report surveys of adults, for example, are higher than rates obtained from official reporting statistics (Larson, Terman, Gomby, Quinn, & Behrman, 1994).

Additional Risk Factors

In an effort to identify and describe other risk factors associated with CSA, several researchers have compared victims and nonvictims on additional characteristics (e.g., Finkelhor, 1984; Finkelhor et al., 1990; Gruber & Jones, 1983). A number of family and social characteristics, such as the presence of a stepfather or living without one's natural parents for extended periods, have been associated with an increased risk for CSA (Brown et al., 1998; Finkelhor, 1984; Finkelhor et al., 1990; Paveza, 1988). Other risk factors include having a mother who was employed outside the home or who was disabled or ill; living with parents whose relationship was conflicted; living with parents having alcohol, drug abuse, or emotional problems; having few close friends; and having a poor relationship with one or both parents (Brown et al., 1998; Finkelhor, 1984; Gruber & Jones, 1983). There is also some evidence that children who have a cognitive vulnerability are at increased risk for CSA. The incidence of CSA among children with a disability, for example, is 1.75 times the rate for children with no disability (National Center on Child Abuse and Neglect, 1993). Other variables presumably linked to CSA (e.g., social isolation, ethnicity, and socioeconomic status) have been evaluated but have produced mixed results (e.g., see Bagley, 1991; Doll, Joy, & Bartholow, 1992; Finkelhor, 1984; Finkelhor et al., 1990; Laumann, Gagnon, Michael, & Michaels, 1994; Sedlak & Broadhurst, 1996; Wyatt, 1985).

Characteristics of Perpetrators of Child Sexual Abuse

When contemplating an image of a CSA perpetrator, many people picture a stranger or "dirty old man." Research examining the demographic characteristics of CSA perpetrators suggests that these stereotypes are rarely accurate.

Age

Research shows that offenders vary widely in age, although the AAPC (1988) reported 32 years as the mean age of reported perpetrators. Growing research evidence, however, suggests that juvenile perpetrators may be underestimated among reported cases and constitute a significant segment of the CSA offender population (Barbaree, Marshall, & Hudson, 1993; Ryan & Lane, 1991). Finkelhor (1979), for example, estimated from self-report surveys that one third of all offenders are under age 18. Clinical data from victims also suggest that a substantial proportion of their offenders are adolescents (Gomes-Schwartz et al., 1990). Other studies of perpetrator samples suggest that most sexual offenders *develop* deviant sexual interests prior to age 18 (e.g., Abel & Rouleau, 1990). Furthermore, increasingly large numbers of adolescents are being referred for treatment for sexual offenses against children (Ryan & Lane, 1991). For the most part, the characteristics of the juvenile offender are similar to the adult offender. The juvenile offender, for example, is primarily male and represented by all ethnic, racial, and socioeconomic groups (Margolin & Craft, 1990; Ryan & Lane, 1991).

Gender

Most perpetrators are male. Most studies indicate, for example, that among reported perpetrators, three quarters or more are male (DHHS, 1996, 1998; Finkelhor, 1984; Russell, 1983). In addition, there is evidence that a significant minority of the general male population has committed a sexual offense against a child. In their nationwide random sample survey, Finkelhor and Lewis (1988) found that between 4% and 17% of the male population acknowledged having molested a child. Similarly, Briere and Runtz (1989) found that 21% of male undergraduate students reported having experienced sexual attraction to children, and 7% indicated some likelihood of having sex with a child if they could avoid detection and punishment.

> Most perpetrators are male, but female perpetration may be more common than surveys suggest.

Female perpetration may be more common than surveys suggest. Lack of recognition of females as potential offenders may occur because of culturally prescribed definitions of child sexual abuse that do not include women (see Box 4.2, "The LeTourneau Case: Is It Love or Abuse?"). Females may go unnoticed, for example, because inappropriate sexual contact may occur in the context of culturally approved routine child care and may simply be labeled as "inappropriate affection" (Lawson, 1993; Saradjian, 1996; Schetky & Green, 1988).

Studies are beginning to evaluate various characteristics of the female perpetrator of CSA, and preliminary results suggest that female offenders can be described by any of a number of typologies (see Elliott, 1993; Mathews, Matthews, & Speltz, 1989; Mitchell & Morse, 1998; Saradjian, 1996). Most female perpetrators are either accomplices to male perpetrators, lonely and isolated single parents, adolescent baby-sitters, or women who develop romantic

(text continued on p. 120)

BOX 4.2 The LeTourneau Case: Is It Love or Abuse?

When a 36-year-old teacher at Shoreline Elementary school confessed to having sex with an ex-student in the summer of 1997, the community of Burien, Washington, was understandably shocked. The teacher was married and had four children, was well liked in the community, and was considered one of the better teachers in the school. The sexual affair had been "consensual," but the child, who had just turned 13 when the affair started, was hardly in a position to offer consent. In the state of Washington, sex with a minor aged 12 to 16 is "rape of a child," a serious felony with a maximum penalty of 89 months (Cloud, 1998). Because both the teacher and student acknowledged the affair, there was no doubt about the guilt of the teacher.

Although the sexual abuse of students is not widely studied, and is certainly not the most common form of sexual abuse, it is probably more common than many people might realize. In one of the few studies on the topic, Shakeshaft and Cohan (1995) report that more than 50% of the superintendents in the state of New York indicated that they have had to deal with sexual abuse between school personnel and students. In Washington State, the superintendent of public instruction receives between 75 and 100 accusations of teacher sexual misconduct annually (Montgomery, 1996). Indeed, cases such as the one in Burien, although unusual, are not unheard of. Only 1 year earlier in the neighboring community of Kirkland, junior high teacher Mark Billie was convicted of raping a 15-year-old student (Bartley, 1998).

The Burien case, however, has received far more attention than other similar cases of sexual abuse in the schools. It was told and retold in all the nation's major newspapers and magazines and was the subject of countless news magazine television shows. From the *Globe* to the *Washington Post* and from *20/20* to *Dateline,* the Burien case was big news. Why the interest? Because the rapist was a woman.

Mary LeTourneau first met Jimmy[1] when he was a student in her second-grade class at Shoreline Elementary School. Four years later, Jimmy was in her class again, this time as a sixth grader. During his sixth-grade year, Jimmy and LeTourneau became quite close. When Jimmy had problems at home or at school, he could always talk with LeTourneau. She was his mentor and confidant. Their relationship had become so close that when Jimmy's mother had to work late, he would sometimes spend the night at LeTourneau's home. During the time she had known Jimmy, LeTourneau may have been in need of a confidant herself. She and her husband, Steve, for example, had been forced to file for bankruptcy and were having marital problems. On top of that, her father had grown ill with cancer (Cloud, 1998).

During the latter part of Jimmy's sixth-grade year, their relationship began to change. He began to write love letters to LeTourneau and apparently asked her to have sex. At first she refused. Then, in the aftermath of a particularly heated fight with her husband, Steve, she and Jimmy had sex for the first time (Cloud, 1998). The relationship lasted for 8 months and was discovered only after LeTourneau told her husband she was pregnant. Knowing he was not the father, Steve LeTourneau confronted Jimmy, who confessed to the affair and to being the father. The police arrested Mary LeTourneau in February of 1997.

LeTourneau plead guilty to second-degree child rape and was sentenced to 7½ years in prison. Judge Linda Lau, however, was reluctant to put her in prison for so long. LeTourneau's defense lawyer had argued that she suffered from bipolar disorder, otherwise known as manic depression, and that she was more in need of treatment than punishment. LeTourneau had no criminal record, and she seemed unlikely to reoffend. Not even the boy's mother was pushing for prison time. Standing before Judge Lau, LeTourneau begged for mercy: "I did something that I had no right to do morally or legally," she said. "It was wrong, and I am sorry. I give you my word that it will not happen again" (quoted in Fitten, 1997, p. 3). The judge ultimately showed leniency, suspending all but 6 months of the sentence. There were, however, two conditions: LeTourneau would have to undergo treatment in the Special Sex Offender Sentencing Alternative, and she could have no contact with Jimmy (Santana, 1998).

Despite her confessions before the judge, LeTourneau apparently saw herself more as a victim than a criminal. She resented the label "child rapist," as well as the court-mandated counseling she received in the sex offender treatment program. She had fallen in love with a 13-year-old, and he had fallen in love with her. What was so wrong with that (Cloud, 1998)? Only 4 weeks after her release, police found LeTourneau and Jimmy together in her car. LeTourneau had violated the condition of her release. Judge Lau immediately reimposed the 7½-year prison sentence, saying, "These violations are extraordinarily egregious and profoundly disturbing. This case is not about a flawed system. It is about an opportunity that you foolishly squandered" (Santana, 1998, p. 5). Finally, in March of 1998, just when the case seemed as if it could not get any more bizarre, LeTourneau's attorney announced that Mary was 6 weeks pregnant (Santana, 1998).

At first glance, the story of Mary LeTourneau and Jimmy may seem like a strange case to include in a book on child maltreatment. After all, this case does not represent a typical example of child sexual abuse. The LeTourneau case is atypical because it involves a male victim and female perpetrator, demographic characteristics especially uncommon with reported cases of sexual abuse (DHHS, 1996). Many professionals in the field, however, argue that female perpetration of CSA is underrecognized (e.g., Saradjian, 1996).

One reason that female perpetration may go unrecognized is society's reluctance to define sexual interactions between women and children as abuse. The LeTourneau case provides a good illustration of the process by which societies come to define some interactions between adults and children as abusive. From the beginning, societal reactions as to whether the LeTourneau case was *really* sexual *abuse* were mixed. Media accounts emphasized that Jimmy pursued LeTourneau, that he was especially mature, and that he knew exactly what he was doing. Likewise, some speculated that she was not a sex offender. She was a vulnerable woman in a shaky marriage who happened to fall in love. Although societal reaction to the case suggests a reluctance to define the interaction between Jimmy and LeTourneau as abusive, many child advocates who observed the case were not nearly so reluctant. Regardless of whether she was pretty or was psychologically disturbed, and regardless of whether he was precocious, this was child abuse:

> Lots of 13-year-old kids are physically mature, very intelligent. But this business of a 35-year-old woman making a love commitment with a 13-year-old boy is hard to fathom. What 13-year-old has the capacity for that kind of love. . . . I have no sympathy for her. When we hear it here—the proclamation of love—it is a rationalization. Did she care about his welfare, about what could happen to him by becoming a father at 13? I don't see where she's acted in (the boy's) best interest. That's not love—that's a big emotional party. (Florence Wolfe, codirector of Seattle-based Northwest Treatment Associates, as quoted in Fitten, 1997, pp. 2-3)

That the vast majority of reported sexual abuse perpetrators are male may have significantly contributed to the reluctance to recognize the LeTourneau case as abuse. It is men, for example, who are supposedly physiologically programmed to seek as many partners as possible (McDermott, 1997). On the surface, it seems nearly impossible for a woman to be sexually attracted to a 13-year-old boy. This may have been the thought of police who initially found the couple together in June of

1996, some 8 months before LeTourneau's eventual arrest. The police found LeTourneau and Jimmy late at night lying together underneath a blanket in the back of LeTourneau's parked van. After talking with LeTourneau, and Jimmy's mother, they became convinced by LeTourneau's claims that nothing had happened, and the police decided to let her go. Had a 35-year-old *male* teacher been lying in the back of a parked van with a 13-year-old *female* student, the reaction by the police would likely have been different.

Note

1. Jimmy is not the boy's real name, although his identity was eventually revealed by the *Globe* and later in several other news magazines.

---

relationships with adolescent boys (Elliott, 1993; Finkelhor, Williams, & Burns, 1988; Margolin & Craft, 1990; Saradjian, 1996). There is some evidence that female offenders are more likely to be caretakers (vs. strangers) and to abuse younger-aged children compared with male offenders, although the severity of abuse does not appear to differ for male versus female perpetrators (Rudin, Zalewski, & Bodmer-Turner, 1995). Studies attempting to examine causal factors associated with female perpetration have uncovered common characteristics including a troubled childhood (e.g., sexual victimization), specific personality traits (e.g., need for nurturance and control), mental illness, drug addiction, and disturbed sexual and social relationships (see Saradjian, 1996, for a review). Caution in interpreting the results of studies investigating female perpetrators of CSA is necessary, however, because most research is based on case studies. Additional research using appropriate comparison groups and adequate samples is needed before firm conclusions can be drawn.

Relationship to the Victim

The most comprehensive information regarding the victim-perpetrator relationship in sexually abusive encounters comes from large-scale community surveys of women reporting childhood histories of abuse (e.g., Finkelhor et al., 1990; Russell, 1983). In Russell's survey, 11% of victimizations involved experiences with fathers or stepfathers; 45% involved acquaintances, friends, or family friends; 20% involved other relatives; and 11% involved strangers. In the first national survey of adults reporting histories of CSA (Finkelhor et al., 1990), percentages for victim-perpetrator relationships for both female and male victims, respectively, were as follows: strangers (21%, 40%), friend or acquaintance (41%, 44%), and family member (29%, 11%). In this sample, males were more likely to have been abused by a stranger, whereas females were more likely to have been abused by a family member. These data suggest that the perpetrator is a person familiar to the child in the majority of cases.

SECTION SUMMARY

Research suggests that it is unwise to stereotype the demographic characteristics of CSA perpetrators. One of the most consistent findings from research evaluating risk factors associated with CSA, however, is *gender differences*. Females are more likely to be victims of CSA, and males are more likely to be perpetrators of CSA. On the other hand, new research suggests that the female perpetrator, and the male victim in particular, may represent a significant proportion of these populations that goes undetected by researchers, practitioners, and reporting agencies. CSA perpetrators vary by age, but they consistently develop a trusting relationship with their victims and commonly include acquaintances or friends, fathers or other parental figures, and other family members. *Child and family variables* that increase the risk of CSA include such factors as a victim's age (i.e., 7 to 12 years old), family composition (e.g., presence of a stepfather), maternal availability, and family conflict (e.g., parents with emotional or drug-related problems).

A review of these findings shows that the populations of victims and offenders are *heterogeneous,* suggesting that sexual abuse occurs in virtually all demographic, social, and family circumstances. Furthermore, the majority of research has focused on female victims and male perpetrators, and, as a result, most research findings do not pertain to male victims or female perpetrators. As a final caveat, it is important to acknowledge the difficulty in determining whether these variables are actual risk factors for abuse, consequences of abuse, or correlates of abuse history.

DYNAMICS OF CHILD SEXUAL ABUSE AND CONSEQUENCES ASSOCIATED WITH VICTIMIZATION

Dynamics of Child Sexual Abuse

To develop a comprehensive understanding of CSA, it is also necessary to examine the characteristics of the victimization experience itself. Much of what is known about the victimization experience comes from cases reported to protective services or studies of CSA victims and perpetrators.

Type of Sexual Activity

Both adults and children have provided descriptions of the types of sexual behavior they encountered in abusive situations. Although the range of sexual activities theoretically extends from exhibitionism to intercourse, the questions posed by researchers have influenced the variability in the types of activities actually reported. In addition, the procedures employed (e.g., face-to-face vs. anonymous interviews or surveys) and the type of sample studied (e.g., community samples of adults or children reported for abuse, clinical populations, and college students) can affect the proportion of victims reporting various types of abuse.

Russell (1983) distinguished between three types of sexual activity: *very serious* abuse (e.g., completed or attempted vaginal, oral, or anal intercourse; cunnilingus; and analingus); *serious* abuse (e.g., completed and attempted genital fondling, simulated intercourse, and digital penetration); and *least serious* abuse (e.g., completed and attempted acts of sexual touching of buttocks, thighs, legs or other body parts, clothed breasts, or genitals; or kissing). Of the sample of 930 women, 38% reported a childhood experience involving one of these forms of sexual abuse. Of these women reporting a childhood experience of abuse, 38% experienced very serious abuse, 34% serious abuse, and 28% less serious abuse. In another study of 156 sexually abused children, Gomes-Schwartz et al. (1990) assessed specific sexual behaviors and found that 28% experienced either vaginal or anal intercourse; 38% experienced oral-genital contact or object penetration; 23% experienced fondling or mutual stimulation; and 6% experienced some form of attempted sexual contact (e.g., the offender requesting that the child touch his genitals), touching, or voyeurism.

Initiation of the Abuse

Preliminary reports from men incarcerated for CSA or participating in treatment programs for CSA offenders have provided some information about the techniques perpetrators use to identify and recruit child victims (e.g., Budin & Johnson, 1989; Conte, Wolf, & Smith, 1989; Elliott, Browne, & Kilcoyne, 1995). Perpetrators do not molest every child to whom they have access but instead generally select children who are vulnerable in some way. Vulnerable children include those who are passive, quiet, trusting, young, unhappy in appearance, needy, or living in a divorced home.

Once the perpetrator has identified the child, he or she may desensitize the child to sexual activity through a grooming process that involves a progression from nonsexual to sexual touch in the context of a gradually developing relationship. The typical scenario begins with seemingly accidental or affectionate touches and then proceeds to sexual touches. Offenders tend to misrepresent moral standards or misuse their authority or adult sophistication to seduce children (e.g., "It's OK, you're my daughter"). In addition, perpetrators report employing a range of coercive tactics to initiate the relationship, such as separating children from other protective adults, conditioning children through reward (e.g., money, toys, candy, and clothes) and punishment (e.g., threatening to hit the child or to hurt loved ones), forcing children to observe violence against their mothers, or using physical force or threatening gestures.

To avoid overreliance on data derived solely from acknowledged perpetrators, researchers have also asked victims directly about their abuse experiences. Berliner and Conte (1990), for example, interviewed child victims (10 to 18 years of age) about the process of their own sexual victimization. The children's accounts closely resembled those provided by the perpetrators. The children reported that their perpetrators initiated sexual activity by gradually shifting from normal affectionate contact or physical activities (e.g., bathing, hugging, massaging, wrestling, and tickling) to more sexual behaviors (e.g., genital touching). The children also reported that their perpetrators made statements attempting to justify the sexual contact. The most common themes of such statements were to suggest that the behavior was not really sexual or to acknowledge that the behavior was sexual but that it was acceptable (e.g., "I'm just going to look, I won't touch"; "I'm teaching you about sex").

Maintenance of the Abuse

Studies evaluating victim and perpetrator perspectives on the process of abuse also shed light on strategies used to maintain children in sexual activities for prolonged periods. Central to maintaining sexual activities with children is the ability to convince the child that the activities should be kept secret so that other adults cannot intervene to terminate the abuse. Studies of child victims as well as adults victimized as children indicate that the majority of victims do not disclose their abuse immediately, and a significant number do not disclose for years (Elliott & Briere, 1994; Gomes-Schwartz et al., 1990; Timnick, 1985).

Perpetrators report a range of coercive activities used to maintain the abusive relationship including bribes, threats, and physical aggression. The child may maintain silence about the abuse, for example, because the offender has offered the child attention, money, or purchases of special toys in exchange for his or her silence (e.g., Elliott et al., 1995). To maintain a child's silence, perpetrators often use threats such as harming or killing the child, a significant other, or a pet; sending the victim to a frightening place; or showing pictures of the child involved in sexual acts to the parents. Finally, overt acts of aggression, such as physically overpowering the child, are often used to reinforce secrecy (Budin & Johnson, 1989; Conte et al., 1989; Lang & Frenzel, 1988). Until recently, sexual offenses against children were largely characterized as nonviolent, with most experts estimating that physical violence accompanies approximately 20% of incidents (e.g., Timnick, 1985). Newer studies, however, suggest that offenders are more frequently aggressive and often use physical threats (Becker, 1994; Briere & Elliott, 1994; Stermac, Hall, & Henskens, 1989).

Effects Associated With Child Sexual Abuse

Since the initial recognition of CSA, authorities have debated the effects of adult-child sexual interactions in the context of a secret relationship. Some have suggested that children who are sexually exploited by adults do not suffer mental harm—either while children or later as adults (e.g., Yorukoglu & Kemph, 1966). The majority of research evidence, however, suggests that a variety of negative psychological, behavioral, and interpersonal problems are more prevalent among CSA victims compared with individuals without such a history (see reviews by Beitchman, Zucker, Hood, daCosta, & Akman, 1991; Beitchman et al., 1992; Berliner & Elliott, 1996; Kendall-Tackett, Williams, & Finkelhor, 1993; Neumann, Houskamp, Pollock, & Briere, 1996; Trickett & Putnam, 1998). The consequences associated with CSA can be classified as either initial effects (occurring within 2 years following the abuse) or long-term effects (consequences beyond 2 years subsequent to the abuse).

Initial Effects

For initial effects, investigators have identified a wide range of emotional, cognitive, physical, and behavioral problems. The specific manifestations of symptomatology appear to depend on the developmental level of the victim (Beitchman et al., 1991; Hewitt, 1998; Kendall-Tackett et al., 1993; Wurtele & Miller-Perrin, 1992). Table 4.1 displays the most common symptoms associated with CSA for preschool, school-age, and adolescent children.

TABLE 4.1 Possible Short-Term Effects Associated With Sexual Abuse in Preschool, School-Age, and Adolescent Children

Behavioral	*Emotional*	*Cognitive*	*Physical*
Preschool			
Regression/immaturity	Anxiety*	Learning difficulties	Bruises
Social withdrawal	Clinging		Genital bleeding
Sexualized behavior*	Nightmares*		Genital pain
Sexual preoccupation*	Fears		Genital itching
Precocious sexual knowledge	Depression		Genital odors
Seductive behavior*	Guilt		Problems walking
Excessive masturbation*	Hostility/anger		Problems sitting
Sex play with others*	Tantrums		Sleeping disturbance
Sexual language*	Aggression		Eating disturbance
Genital exposure*			Enuresis
Sexual victimization of others*			Encopresis
Family/peer conflicts			Stomachache
Difficulty separating			Headache
Hyperactivity			

TABLE 4.1 Continued

Behavioral	*Emotional*	*Cognitive*	*Physical*
School age			
Regression/immaturity*	Anxiety	Learning difficulties*	Stomachache
Social withdrawal	Phobias	Poor concentration	Headache
Sexualized behavior	Nightmares*	Poor attention	Genital pain
Sexual preoccupation	Fears*	Declining grades	Genital itching
Precocious sexual knowledge	Obsessions	Negative perceptions	Genital odors
Seductive behavior	Tics	Dissociation	Problems walking
Excessive masturbation	Hostility/anger		Problems sitting
Sex play with others	Aggression*		Sleep disturbance
Sexual language	Family/peer conflicts		Eating disturbance
Genital exposure	Depression		Enuresis
Sexual victimization of others	Guilt		Encopresis
Delinquency	Suicidal		
Stealing	Low self-esteem		
Poor peer relations			
Hyperactivity*			
Adolescent			
Social withdrawal*	Anxiety	Learning difficulties	Stomachache
Self-injurious behavior*	Phobias	Poor concentration	Headache
Sexualized behavior	Nightmares	Poor attention	Genital pain
Sexual preoccupation	Obsessions	Declining grades	Genital itching
Precocious sexual knowledge	Hostility/anger		Genital odors
Seductive behavior	Depression*		Problems walking
Promiscuity	Guilt		Problems sitting
Prostitution	Suicidal*		Pregnancy
Sexual language	Low self-esteem		Eating disturbance*
Sexual victimization of others			Possible immune system dysfunction
Delinquency*			Dysregulated cortisol
			Increased catecholamine level
Running away*			Sleep disturbance*
Early marriage			
Substance abuse*			
Truancy			
Dropping out of school			
Stealing			
Poor peer relations			

SOURCE: Information for this table was obtained from the following references, which are representative but not exhaustive: Beitchman, Zucker, Hood, daCosta, & Akman (1991); Boney-McCoy & Finkelhor (1995); DeBellis, Burke, Trickett, & Putnam (1996); DeBellis, Chrousos, et al. (1994); DeBellis, Lefter, Trickett, & Putnam (1994); Dubowitz, Black, Harrington, & Verschoore (1993); Everson, Hunter, Runyon, & Edelson (1990); Friedrich, Grambsch, & Damon (1992); Friedrich, Urquiza, & Beilke (1986); Gil & Johnson (1993); Gomes-Schwartz et al. (1990); Lanktree, Briere, & Zaidi (1991); Mannarino, Cohen, Smith, & Moore-Motily (1991); Mannarino, Cohen, & Berman (1994); Mennen & Meadow (1994); Putnam, Helmers, & Trickett (1993); Trickett, McBride-Chang, & Putnam (1994); Wells, McCann, Adams, Voris, & Ensign (1995); Wozencraft, Wagner, & Pellegrin (1991).
* Indicates most common symptoms for age group.

In a review of 45 of the most recent empirical studies on initial effects, Kendall-Tackett et al. (1993) concluded that one of the two most common symptoms identified in sexually abused children is sexualized behavior (e.g., overt sexual acting out toward adults or other children, compulsive masturbation, excessive sexual curiosity, sexual promiscuity, and precocious sexual play and knowledge). Sexualized behavior is also believed to be the behavioral symptom that is most predictive of the occurrence of sexual abuse (Friedrich, 1993). The other most frequent problem is posttraumatic stress disorder (PTSD) symptomatology, which includes difficulties such as nightmares, fears, feelings of isolation and an inability to enjoy usual activities, somatic complaints, symptoms of autonomic arousal (e.g., easily startled), and guilt feelings.

> The most common symptoms of CSA are sexualized behavior and posttraumatic stress disorder symptoms.

In addition to the myriad symptoms documented in sexual abuse victims, CSA has been associated with a wide range of psychopathology. Of the victimized children studied by Gomes-Schwartz et al. (1990), 17% of the preschool group (4 to 6 years of age), 40% of the school-age group (7 to 13 years of age), and 8% of adolescent victims (14 to 18 years of age) evidenced clinically significant pathology, indicating severe behavioral and emotional difficulties. Using a checklist of parent-reported behaviors to assess the effects of sexual abuse on 93 prepubertal children, Dubowitz, Black, Harrington, and Verschoore (1993) found that 36% had significantly elevated scores on the Internalizing Scale (e.g., depression and withdrawn behavior), and 38% had elevated scores on the Externalizing Scale (e.g., acting-out behaviors). Similar levels of dysfunction would be expected in only 10% of the general population of children.

Overall, evidence to date strongly suggests that CSA results in disturbing psychological sequelae in a significant portion of child victims. In their review, Browne and Finkelhor (1986) concluded that from 20% to 40% of abused children seen by clinicians manifest pathological disturbance. Most of the types of symptoms demonstrated in victims of CSA, however, are no different from the difficulties seen in clinical samples of children and adolescents more generally. In degree of symptomatology, sexually abused children generally exhibit significantly more psychological symptoms than nonabused children, but fewer symptoms than clinical children. The only exceptions to this pattern are the findings indicating that sexually abused children exhibit more sexualized behavior and PTSD symptomatology than both nonabused and clinical groups of children (Beitchman et al., 1991; Kendall-Tackett et al., 1993).

Long-Term Effects

The psychological consequences of childhood sexual victimization can extend into adulthood and affect victims throughout a lifetime. A history of CSA has been associated with a variety of symptoms, such as emotional reactions including depression and anxiety (e.g., Chu & Dill, 1990; Elliott & Briere, 1992; Peters

& Range, 1995; Swett, Surrey, & Cohen, 1990). According to Browne and Finkelhor (1986), depression is the most common symptom reported by adults sexually abused as children. Additional effects include problems with interpersonal relationships, PTSD symptomatology (i.e., reexperiencing traumatic events through intrusive thoughts, flashbacks, or nightmares), sexual adjustment, and behavioral dysfunction (i.e., substance abuse, eating disorders, and self-mutilation; e.g., Bagley, Wood, & Young, 1994; Boyd, Guthrie, Pohl, Whitmarsh, & Henderson, 1994; Briere & Conte, 1993; Elliott, 1994; Springs & Friedrich, 1992). Table 4.2 summarizes the long-term symptoms found in adult victims of CSA.

Although investigators of the long-term effects of CSA have generally obtained data from clinical populations, they have also conducted studies using nonclinical populations, such as college students (e.g., Briere & Runtz, 1990; Fromuth, 1986) and randomly selected subsamples of adults abused as children (e.g., Burnam et al., 1988; Saunders, Villeponteaux, Lipovsky, & Kilpatrick, 1992; Siegel, Sorenson, Golding, Burnam, & Stein, 1987) and detected significant negative effects. In their review, Browne and Finkelhor (1986) concluded that approximately 20% of adults who were sexually abused as children evidence serious psychopathology as adults.

Explaining the Variability in Effects

Perusal of these research findings suggests that no single symptom or pattern of symptoms is present in all victims of CSA. Many CSA victims exhibit no symptoms at all, at least in the short term. In their review of CSA effects, Kendall-Tackett et al. (1993) concluded that approximately 20% to 50% of children are asymptomatic at initial assessment, and only 10% to 25% become symptomatically worse during the 2 years following victimization. Why is it that some victims are severely affected, others are moderately affected, and still others are left relatively unscathed? Furthermore, why do some victims manifest anxiety in response to their abuse and others show physical symptoms or depression?

One problem in answering these questions is that methodological weaknesses have plagued the research in this area (see Briere, 1992b). The definition of sexual abuse, for example, varies across studies. In addition, several studies have failed to include comparison groups, whereas others have employed subjective, unstandardized interviews and assessment devices. The samples used in research on the effects of CSA are also problematic. College student samples, for example, tend to be biased regarding intelligence, social class, and motivational aspects. Clinical samples of CSA victims are also biased because they include only CSA cases referred for treatment services and, therefore, may not be generalizable to all cases of CSA (e.g., such samples may not include less symptomatic children or undisclosed victims). Finally, studying the psychological effects of adolescents or adults abused as children does not allow the establishment of a definitive causal relationship between symptoms and a history of CSA. In the absence of longitudinal studies that begin before abuse occurs, it

TABLE 4.2 Possible Long-Term Effects Associated With Child Sexual Abuse

Type of Effect	*Specific Problem*	*Specific Symptoms*
Emotional	Depression	Depressed affect
		Suicidality
		Low self-esteem
		Guilt
		Poor self-image
		Self-blame
	Anxiety	Anxiety attacks
		Fears
		Phobias
		Somatic symptoms
		Migraine
		Stomach problems
		Aches and pains
		Skin disorders
Interpersonal		Difficulty trusting others
		Poor social adjustment
		Social isolation
		Feelings of isolation, alienation, insecurity
		Difficulty forming/maintaining relationships
		Parenting difficulties
		Sexual revictimization
		Physical victimization
Posttraumatic stress disorder (PTSD) symptomatology	Reexperiencing	Intrusive thoughts
		Flashbacks
		Nightmares
	Numbing/avoidance	Dissociation
		Amnesia for abuse events
		Disengagement ("spacing out")
		Emotional numbing
		Out-of-body experiences
	Associated symptoms	Poor concentration
Sexual adjustment		Anorgasmia
		Arousal/desire dysfunction
		Sexual phobia/aversion
		Sexual anxiety
		Sexual guilt
		Promiscuity
		Prostitution
		Dissatisfaction in sexual relationships
Behavior dysfunction	Eating disorders	Bingeing
		Purging
		Overeating
	Substance abuse	Alcoholism
		Illicit drugs
	Self-mutilation	Cutting body parts
		Carving body areas
		Hitting head or body with or against objects

SOURCE: Information for this table was obtained from the following references, which are representative but not exhaustive: Briere (1992a); Brier & Conte (1993); Briere & Runtz (1987, 1990); Burkett (1991); Chu & Dill (1990); Cole, Woolger, Power, & Smith (1992); Elliott (1994); Elliott & Briere (1992); Morrison (1989); Neumann, Houskamp, Pollock, & Briere (1996); Springs & Friedrich (1992); Steiger & Zanko (1990); Swett, Surrey, & Cohen (1990); Urquiza & Goodlin-Jones (1994); Widom (1995).

is difficult to determine whether the observed characteristics result from early sexual abuse or some other variable such as family dysfunction. Although studies conducted within the past 10 years are achieving greater empirical precision by using larger numbers of participants, multiple measures, comparison groups, and longitudinal designs (e.g., Briere & Runtz, 1987; Erickson et al., 1989; Gomes-Schwartz et al., 1990), more research is needed to clarify the specific effects of CSA for a given individual victim.

Researchers attempting to understand the effects associated with childhood sexual victimization have explored the association between characteristics of the sexually abusive situation or its aftermath and differential psychological effects. Are the psychological effects of CSA, for example, more severe when a child is abused by a father figure versus an uncle? Are the effects more severe when the child's disclosure is met with disbelief? Researchers have evaluated the relationship between CSA effects and a number of factors, including the circumstances of the abuse, postabuse characteristics, and victim perceptions of the abuse. Table 4.3 lists the variables that have been examined and their influence on the effects of CSA.

Several aspects of the abuse situation are associated with increased symptomatology in both child victims and adult survivors. Perhaps the most consistent finding is that threats, force, and violence by the perpetrator are linked with increased negative outcome (Beitchman et al., 1992; Browne & Finkelhor, 1986; Gomes-Schwartz et al., 1990). Studies have also demonstrated that the least serious forms of sexual contact (e.g., unwanted kissing or touching of clothed body parts) are associated with less trauma compared with more serious forms of genital contact (e.g., vaginal or anal intercourse; Bagley & Ramsay, 1986; Elwell & Ephross, 1987; Mennen & Meadow, 1995). Most studies indicate that abuse perpetrated by fathers, father figures, or individuals having an intense emotional relationship with the victim is associated with more severe consequences (Beitchman et al., 1991; Beitchman et al., 1992; Briere & Elliott, 1994; Feinauer, 1989). In addition, when victims are exposed to multiple forms of child maltreatment (e.g., sexual and physical abuse), they exhibit increased symptomatology (e.g., Egeland & Sroufe, 1981; Ney, Fung, & Wickett, 1994).

Specific postabuse events (i.e., how family and institutions respond) have also shown a relationship to the effects of CSA. It is well established that responses toward the victim by parents, relatives, teachers, and other adults have a significant effect on the trauma and recovery associated with CSA. Studies have consistently found that negative responses tend to aggravate the trauma experienced by children (e.g., Gomes-Schwartz et al., 1990; Runyan, Hunter, & Everson, 1992). In contrast, the availability of social supports following the disclosure of abuse, such as maternal support or a supportive relationship with an adult, appears to mitigate negative effects and plays a protective role (e.g., Conte & Schuerman, 1987; Gomes-Schwartz et al., 1990). The unavailability of social supports has also been associated with increased psychological problems in adults (Herman, 1992; Springs & Friedrich, 1992).

New areas of research are examining other potential mediators of abuse such as the victim's subjective perceptions of the event (e.g., Hazzard, 1993; Miller-Perrin, 1998; Williams, 1993). For example, Williams found in her sample of 531

TABLE 4.3 Potential Mediators of the Effects of Child Sexual Abuse

Potential Mediators	*Influence on Child Sexual Abuse Effects*
Abuse characteristics	
Duration and frequency	Results are mixed for research evaluating child victims; increased duration is associated with more negative effect for adults abused as children.
Type of sexual activity	More severe forms of sexual activity (e.g., penetration) are associated with more negative effect.
Age at onset	Results are mixed.
Child/perpetrator relationship	More negative effect is associated with fathers, father figures, or intense emotional relationships.
Number of perpetrators	Results are mixed for research evaluating child victims; a greater number of perpetrators is associated with more negative effect for adults abused as children.
Victim gender	Results are mixed, with some findings showing similarities between genders and some suggesting more externalizing symptoms for males and internalizing symptoms for females.
Force or physical injury	Presence of force or physical injury is associated with greater negative effect.
Multiple forms of abuse	Different combinations of child maltreatment are associated with more negative effect.
Postabuse characteristics	
Response toward the victim	Negative reactions are associated with greater negative effect.
Court involvement	Results are mixed.
Out-of-home placement	Results are mixed.
Available social support	Increased social support is associated with less severe effect.
Perceptions of abuse	
Perceived severity	Increased perceived severity of abuse is associated with greater negative effect.

SOURCE: Information for this table was obtained from the following references, which are representative but not exhaustive: Bagley & Ramsay (1986); Beitchman et al. (1991); Beitchman et al. (1992); Browne & Finkelhor (1986); Conte & Schuerman (1987); Feinauer (1989); Gomes-Schwartz et al. (1990); Kendall-Tackett et al. (1993); Mennen & Meadow (1995); Williams (1993); Young, Bergandi, & Titus (1994).

adult victims that victims' perceived severity of the abuse was the major determinant of subsequent adjustment or maladjustment. In children, greater distress was found in those who blamed themselves for their abuse and in those who viewed their abusive experiences as threatening (Johnson & Kenkel, 1991; Morrow, 1991). Future research should examine additional potential mediators, particularly those that might decrease the negative effects of CSA.

SECTION SUMMARY

Greater numbers of empirical studies evaluating the dynamics of CSA victimization are beginning to appear that describe the *types of sexual activity* involved, the methods used to initiate the abuse, and how the abuse is maintained. Specific sexual activities (e.g., categorized as *least serious* to *very serious*) range from exhibitionism to various forms of penetration. Perpetrators appear to *target children who are vulnerable* in some way and *initiate the abuse* by desensitizing children to increasingly more sexual types of contact. To both initiate and *maintain the abuse,* perpetrators may use coercive tactics such as verbal threats or overt aggression.

Numerous empirical studies have documented the myriad psychological consequences associated with childhood sexual victimization. Difficulties of an emotional, physical, cognitive, and behavioral nature can result in the *short term* (e.g., sexualized behavior and anxiety) as well as the *long term* (e.g., troubled interpersonal relationship and PTSD symptomatology). There is a wide range of psychopathology (e.g., acting out, depression, and withdrawn behavior) among victims, with some exhibiting few problems and others experiencing significant psychopathology. This heterogeneity in symptomatology of CSA victims and degree of psychopathology plus methodological weaknesses in the field (e.g., lack of standard definitions, comparison groups, adequate samples, and longitudinal studies) have led researchers to *equivocal findings.* Nevertheless, it appears that the factors most likely to increase trauma include increased duration and multiple forms of abuse, the presence of force and/or violence during the abuse, abuse by someone who is a father figure or emotionally close to the victim, abuse that involves more invasive forms of sexual activity, and negative reactions by significant others once the abuse has been revealed. Recent research has also examined *potential mediators* of abuse such as the victim's subjective perceptions of the events and the availability of social support following disclosure.

EXPLAINING CHILD SEXUAL ABUSE

The victims and perpetrators of CSA are characterized by a great deal of diversity, and the dynamics and consequences of abuse show similar variability. Such heterogeneity contributes to the difficulty in answering one of the central questions in understanding CSA: Why do some individuals sexually abuse children? Another factor contributing to the difficulty in answering this question is the paucity of quality research on the topic (Crittenden, 1996). Despite these limita-

TABLE 4.4 Risk Factors Associated With Child Sexual Abuse

System Level	*Risk Factor*
Child	Female gender Prepubescent age Few close friends Passive Quiet Trusting Unhappy appearance Depressed affect Needy
Perpetrator	Male gender Childhood history of sexual and physical victimization Antisocial disregard for concerns of others Poor impulse control Passive Sensitive about performance with women Deficient heterosexual skills Feelings of dependency, inadequacy, vulnerability, loneliness Sexually attracted to children Use of alcohol/drugs Use of cognitive distortions to justify behavior Fantasizing about sexual activity with children
Family	Spouse abuse Divorced home Unhappy family life Poor relationship with parents Parents in conflict Living in a family with a stepfather or without natural father Mother employed outside home Mother has not completed high school Mother disabled or ill History of sexual abuse in mother
Sociocultural	Sanctioning sexual relations between adults and children Neglecting children's sexual development Male-dominated household Oversexualization of normal emotional needs Socializing men to be attracted to younger, smaller, more vulnerable sexual partners Blocking the development of empathy in males Socializing stoicism in males Objectifying sexual partners Child pornography

tions, experts have developed theoretical formulations that focus on different individuals or systems that are involved in CSA, including the victim, the perpetrator, an abusive family, and society. Table 4.4 displays the risk factors associated with each of these systems.

Focus on the Victim

Early explanations for the occurrence of CSA focused on the role of the victim and his or her culpability in encouraging or "allowing" the sexual abuse to occur. Researchers described victims as seductively encouraging the perpetrator or as enjoying the abuse (see Faller, 1988a, for a discussion of this issue). Little evidence, however, exists to support these positions. Admittedly, many CSA victims exhibit sexualized behavior, but most experts believe that such behavior is the result, rather than the cause, of abuse. In addition, the idea that children encourage or "want" the abuse experience is contradicted by research evidence suggesting that only a minority of victims report that their abuse had pleasurable or positive characteristics (e.g., victims reporting that they felt loved during the abuse; Faller, 1988a). Whether the victim in CSA can be viewed as culpable also depends on how the definition of sexual abuse is conceptualized. As previously discussed, current perspectives of CSA preclude victim culpability because children are viewed as developmentally incapable of allowing or permitting the abuse to occur.

> Young, female children who have many unmet needs appear to be particularly susceptible to potential molesters.

Culpability is distinct from vulnerability, however, and it is possible to argue that certain attributes of children might make them special targets for molesters. Young, female children who have few close friends or who have many unmet needs appear to be particularly susceptible to the attention and affection of a potential molester. At particular risk are children described as passive, quiet, trusting, young, unhappy or depressed, and needy. CSA victims also appear to have strong needs for attention, affection, and approval (Berliner & Conte, 1990; Erickson et al., 1989; Finkelhor et al., 1990).

Focus on the Offender

Theorists also implicate the perpetrator in their efforts to determine the roots of CSA. The majority of research attempting to discern why particular individuals sexually abuse children has included only males and, as a result, cannot be generalized to female perpetrators. Researchers attempting to delineate traits of perpetrators initially relied on the psychiatric model, assuming that the causes of abuse stem from the individual psychopathology of male abusers. Later attempts additionally focused on deviant patterns of sexual arousal and childhood history.

Offender Pathology

Early theories viewed abusers as psychotic, brain-damaged, senile, or mentally retarded individuals who could not control their own behavior (Weinberg, 1955).

Subsequent research, however, suggests that severe psychiatric, intellectual, and neurological problems characterize only a small minority of offenders (National Center for Prosecution of Child Abuse, 1993; Williams & Finkelhor, 1990).

A variety of less severe forms of psychopathology do typify sexual abusers, including antisocial tendencies such as disregard for the interests and concerns of others and lack of impulse control (Bresee, Stearns, Bess, & Packer, 1986; Groth, Hobson, & Gary, 1982; Yanagida & Ching, 1993). Such findings suggest that offenders have a willingness to exploit others and to violate social norms (Williams & Finkelhor, 1990). Other studies describe molesters as passive; having feelings of vulnerability, inadequacy, and loneliness; being overly sensitive about their sexual performance with women; and exhibiting deficits in heterosocial skills (Hayashino et al., 1995; Katz, 1990; Milner & Robertson, 1990; Seidman, Marshall, Hudson, & Robertson, 1994). Presumably, these problems may lead offenders to turn to children to have their social and relationship needs met while avoiding the demands of adult relationships.

Deviant Sexual Arousal

Other theories propose that perpetrators seek out sexual encounters with children primarily because they are sexually attracted to children (Abel, Becker, & Cunningham-Rathner, 1984; Marshall, Barbaree, & Butt, 1988). The origins of such deviant sexual arousal, however, are undetermined. Some researchers have suggested that deviant sexual arousal is the result of biological factors such as abnormal levels of male hormones called *androgens* (Bradford, 1990). Learning theorists, on the other hand, have proposed that deviant sexual arousal develops when it is reinforced through fantasies of sexual activity with children and masturbating to those fantasies (Laws & Marshall, 1990; Marshall & Eccles, 1993). Although some support exists for each of these theories, other studies have yielded inconsistent results (e.g., Bradford, 1990; Hunter, Goodwin, & Becker, 1994; Langevin, Lang, & Curnoe, 1998; Salter, 1988).

Regardless of the cause of deviant sexual arousal, the procedure most often used to determine whether CSA perpetrators have an unusual sexual arousal to children is penile plethysmography. This procedure involves the placement of a gauge around the base of the penis, in the privacy of a lab or clinic. The participant then views slides or videotapes of different types of sexual partners (e.g., same-age, opposite-sex partners, young male children, and adolescent females) or listens to audiotaped descriptions of different types of sexual encounters (e.g., consenting nonviolent sex with a same-age opposite-sex partner and nonconsenting violent sex with a male child). The penile gauge is sensitive to small increases in the circumference of the penis, and the percentage of arousal is recorded by the plethysmograph.

Investigators have compared the sexual responses of child molesters, incest offenders, and nonoffending men with mixed results. Freund and his colleagues (e.g., Freund & Langevin, 1976) conducted some of the first studies and found that molesters were significantly more aroused by slides of both female and male children interacting with adults than were nonoffending males. Subsequent studies examining sexual arousal in specific categories of perpetrators have yielded conflicting results. Quinsey, Chaplin, and Carrigan (1979) found that incestuous fathers exhibited more appropriate adult sexual arousal than nonincestuous child molesters. In contrast, Marshall, Barbaree, and Christophe (1986) found that although incest offenders paralleled normals by showing low arousal to children, they showed no dramatic arousal increase to adult females. Indeed, the incest offenders exhibited less arousal to adult females than did the control group. The nonincestuous offenders, on the other hand, showed considerable arousal to children up to age 9, minimal arousal for 11- to 13-year-olds, and increased arousal again to adult females. Taken together, these findings suggest that compared with control group males, some subgroups of CSA perpetrators, primarily extrafamilial child molesters, exhibit deviant sexual arousal toward children. The pattern of sexual arousal exhibited by incestuous offenders is less clear.

Complicating the role of deviant sexual arousal in CSA even further is evidence that nonoffenders also exhibit some level of sexual arousal toward children. Freund, McKnight, Langevin, and Cibiri (1972) found that nonoffending adult males had higher arousal to pictures of nude pubescent and younger girls than to landscapes or pictures of nude boys. Because not all individuals who are sexually aroused by children act on their feelings, researchers have hypothesized that other factors, usually referred to as *disinhibitors,* must be operating.

One possible disinhibitor is alcohol, which may affect the perpetrator's ability to maintain self-control over sexual impulses toward children (Abel et al., 1984; Finkelhor, 1984). Other possible disinhibitors are cognitive distortions. From this viewpoint, perpetrators rationalize and defend their behavior through distorted ideas or thoughts. "Having sex with children," for example, "is a good way to teach them about sex," or "Children need to be liberated from the sexually repressive bonds of society" (Abel et al., 1984; Abel et al., 1989; Segal & Stermac, 1990). Research evidence is accumulating that supports the presence of cognitive distortions in CSA perpetrators (Hayashino et al., 1995; Segal & Stermac, 1990).

In evaluating research on deviant sexual arousal, it is important to view such studies within the confines of their conceptual and methodological limitations. Many studies, for example, have mixed the types of perpetrators within groups (e.g., natural fathers, stepfathers, and adoptive fathers into a single incest sample; Marshall et al., 1986). Other limitations include the use of small and unrepresentative samples. The penile plethysmography procedure itself has also been questioned because of false positives and false negatives and the ability of some molesters to inhibit sexual arousal in the lab (Conte, 1993). In examining the role of deviant sexual arousal, alcohol and drug use, and cognitive distortions, it is important to note that these factors may not play a role in all cases of CSA. It is also unclear to what degree such variables cause, rather than result from, the abuse.

Childhood History of Victimization

Many researchers have suggested that childhood sexual victimization contributes to adult perpetration. The sexual abuse may have been directly experienced by the perpetrator in the past or may have occurred to another family member while the perpetrator observed or was aware. Overholser and Beck (1989) noted that 58% of their sample of child molesters reported being molested as children, compared with 25% of the rapist group and only 5% of matched controls. The relationship between perpetration and a history of previous sexual victimization holds for adolescent sexual offenders as well (Becker, Kaplan, Cunningham-Rathner, & Kovoussi, 1986; Johnson, 1989; Katz, 1990). Several studies have also demonstrated frequent reports of sexual abuse against some other family member in the offender's family of origin, and others have noted a relationship between sexual perpetration of children and high rates of physical abuse in the backgrounds of offenders (Williams & Finkelhor, 1990).

Why would a history of victimization lead to perpetrating sexual offenses? One possible explanation is that individuals abuse children in an effort to resolve, assimilate, or master the anxiety resulting from their own abuse (Groth, 1979; Hartman & Burgess, 1988). As we noted previously in this chapter, victims of CSA often engage in inappropriate sexual behaviors with others (see Table 4.1). Another interpretation refers to the lack of a nurturing parental relationship, betrayal as a child, and the subordination of one's own needs to those of an abuser, factors that preclude the development of empathy or sensitivity toward others (Ginsburg, Wright, Harrell, & Hill, 1989). Still others have suggested that repeatedly having one's needs subordinated and having one's body invaded or manipulated may result in feelings of powerlessness and a later need to exploit others to regain personal power and control (Wurtele & Miller-Perrin, 1992). A final possibility is that by experiencing victimization, the offender learns through modeling that children can be used for sexual gratification (Laws & Marshall, 1990).

Research on the intergenerational transmission of sexual abuse has been questioned on methodological grounds, such as overreliance on retrospective designs, self-report data, and correlational studies. Lack of appropriate comparison groups and the possibility that perpetrators report histories of abuse as rationalizations for their behaviors are also factors that contribute to difficulty in interpreting findings. It is likely that although some association exists, most children who are sexually abused do not grow up to abuse other children, and some individuals without a history of abuse become CSA perpetrators.

Focus on the Family

Family dysfunction models view CSA as a symptom of a dysfunctional family system. These theories hold that the family in general, or one of its members (e.g., typically the perpetrator or a nonoffending adult), contributes to an environment that permits and possibly encourages the sexual victimization of children.

A number of family theories focus on how a mother's behavior may contribute in some way to her child's victimization. Early theories held mothers responsible for the abuse by blaming them for poor marital relationships or infrequent marital sex. In this view, infrequent marital sex increased a husband's sexual frustration, thus "driving" him to seek satisfaction elsewhere in the family (e.g., Justice & Justice, 1979). Other theories viewed mothers as culpable for the abuse because of their inability to protect the victim from the offender. As noted previously, maternal employment outside the home and maternal disability or illness are risk factors for CSA. Such theories, however, have often relied on clinical impressions or retrospective data or have not been supported by research. In addition, many of the so-called contributing characteristics ascribed to mothers could be the result of living with a perpetrator.

Contemporary explanations view the mother's role in the context of contributing to a child's vulnerability, rather than of being responsible for the abuse. Research suggests that mothers may actually be co-victims, rather than co-conspirators. Mothers from incestuous families are often physically and emotionally abused by the perpetrator themselves and also frequently have a childhood history of CSA (e.g., Faller, 1989; Gomes-Schwartz et al., 1990; Truesdell, McNeil, & Deschner, 1986). According to this view, mothers may contribute to their children's vulnerability by withdrawing from their children or being unavailable to them (either emotionally or physically) because they lacked an adequate representation of a secure mother-child relationship themselves (Friedrich, 1990). Faller (1988a, 1989) also suggested that these women may gravitate toward men who are similar to their own abusers or who will not make sexual demands on them because they are sexually attracted to children.

Other family systems theorists have focused on general characteristics of the family as a unit rather than on individual members and have identified significant levels of dysfunction in families of CSA victims, although the nature of the dysfunction is unclear because of conflicting research findings (Crittenden, 1996). Considerable research indicates that abusive families exhibit conflicted relationships including marital conflict in the home, poor relationships between children and parents, divorce in the home, and spouse abuse (e.g., Lang, Flor-Henry, & Frenzel, 1990; Paveza, 1988; Sirles & Franke, 1989). Other research has confirmed that CSA families are frequently disorganized, lacking cohesion and involvement between members, deficient in community involvement, and generally more dysfunctional (e.g., Elliott, 1994; Jackson, Calhoun, Amick, Maddever, & Habif, 1990; Madonna, Van Scoyk, & Jones, 1991; Ray, Jackson, & Townsley, 1991). The most common difficulties in CSA families are problems with communication, lack of emotional closeness, and inflexibility (Dadds, Smith, Weber, & Robinson, 1991).

Experts have proposed several explanations for how poor family relations might be related to CSA. To reduce the tension that exists within the marital relationship, for example, a father might distance himself from his wife by turning his sexual and emotional attention to his daughter. This distancing stabilizes the marital conflict and reduces the likelihood of a breakup. Gruber and Jones (1983) attempted to explain the role of marital conflict in extrafamilial abuse by suggesting that victims living in an unstable home may seek some sense of emotional stability through relationships outside the home, such as with a potential offender. Others have suggested that families that lack cohesion, concern between members, and organization may fail to supervise children adequately, thus exposing them to more opportunities for sexual abuse (Ray et al., 1991; Sgroi, 1982).

Focus on Society and Culture

Social and cultural factors include the broad context of society and community forces that play an etiological role in CSA. Current theories target social attitudes and child pornography. Sociocultural theories remain largely speculative, awaiting confirmation from empirical investigation.

Social Attitudes

One theory views CSA as a problem stemming from the inequality between men and women that has been perpetuated throughout history by the patriarchal social system (e.g., Birns & Meyer, 1993). Rush (1980) extends the boundaries of inequality to include children by pointing out that traditionally, both women and children have shared the same minority status, and, as a result, both have been subject to sexual abuse by men. Some limited support for the feminist theory of CSA comes from a study conducted by Alexander and Lupfer (1987). These researchers found that female university students with a history of incest rated their family structure as having greater power differences in male-female relationships than did female university students with a history of extrafamilial sexual abuse or those with no history of abuse.

Child Pornography

Other sociocultural theories of CSA implicate media portrayals of children as a factor in CSA (e.g., Rush, 1980; Wurtele & Miller-Perrin, 1992). Child pornography is one type of media that may stimulate sexual interest in children and ranges from photographs to films or videotapes to magazines and books that depict children in sexually explicit acts (see Chapter 6 for a discussion of child pornography as a form of child maltreatment). Research evaluating the relationship between child pornography and CSA is mixed, with some studies failing to support the hypothesized relationship and others finding that child molesters do use pornography (see review by Murrin & Laws, 1990).

SECTION SUMMARY

Despite the work of numerous researchers in the field of CSA, it is still unclear what causes an individual to sexually abuse a child. Some theories *focus on the child* and characteristics that may make a child more vulnerable (e.g., being passive, quiet, trusting, young, unhappy, and needy). Other theories *focus on the perpetrator* and describe him or her as having psychological dysfunction, deviant sexual arousal patterns, or a childhood history of victimization (e.g., physical, emotional, or social) that leads to adult perpetration. Numerous *family characteristics* are also associated with CSA, including family conflict (from poor relationships to divorce), dysfunction (e.g., use of violence, alcohol, and withdrawal behaviors), and families with a mother who has a history of childhood sexual abuse. Recent theories further suggest that mothers may be co-victims as well. Other theories propose that sociocultural forces such as *social attitudes* (e.g., inequality between men and women) and *child pornography* (that stimulates sexual interest in children) are responsible for CSA. No one theory by itself or in combination with other theories can effectively explain CSA.

RESPONDING TO CHILD SEXUAL ABUSE

Throughout the chapter, descriptions about what is known about CSA have been provided in an attempt to explore the relevant issues more thoroughly. A comprehensive understanding of any problem is a necessary first step in attempting to intervene in that problem. Once authorities receive a report of CSA, several systems become involved in the responses and interventions directed at the problem, including the mental health and criminal justice systems.

Treatment Interventions

One of the earliest responses to the CSA problem was to provide therapeutic services to victims and offenders, as well as to their families. Several programs originated in the early 1970s, although they were restricted in number and focus. More recently, there has been a renewed interest in the treatment of sexual abuse victims as well as perpetrators that better reflects an understanding of the complexity of the CSA problem.

Basic Issues in Treatment

Whether treatment centers on the child victim, the adult survivor, or the perpetrator of abuse, there are several basic treatment issues. First, victims and perpetrators of CSA are diverse in their preabuse history, the nature of the abuse experience, and available social supports and coping resources. As a result, any treatment program needs to be tailored to meet the particular needs of each individual (Chaffin, 1994; Courtois & Watts, 1982). There is no canned treatment program that will be effective for all victims, all perpetrators, or all families.

Second, therapists and others working in the field of CSA need to be aware of issues associated with countertransference (their own personal reactions) toward victims, perpetrators, and their families. Individuals working with a child's perpetrator, for example, may have feelings of anger or hatred toward him or her that make it difficult to respond in a therapeutic manner. Or as Haugaard and Reppucci (1988) put it, "The image of a 5-year-old girl performing fellatio on her father in submission to his parental authority does not engender compassion" (p. 191). Clinicians may also feel uncomfortable when working with child victims who sometimes behave sexually toward their therapists. In addition, studies have revealed that a significant number of professionals who work with victims have a history of child abuse themselves (Feldman-Summers & Pope, 1994; Nuttall & Jackson, 1994). These experiences might affect practitioners' views of CSA and its victims, contributing to distorted perceptions of patients and also possibly to therapy-induced memories (Beutler, Williams, & Zetzer, 1994). (For further discussion, see Box 4.3, "The Repressed Memory Controversy.")

Therapy for Child Victims and Adult Survivors

A number of professionals, including master's-level therapists, clinical social workers, psychologists, and psychiatrists, conduct therapy for child victims and adult survivors of CSA. Treatment can take a variety of forms, such as individual counseling, family treatment, group therapy, and marital counseling, and often includes various combinations (e.g., individual counseling and group therapy).

Despite the diversity of treatment modalities, several goals of therapy are common to most approaches. One goal of therapy is to alleviate any significant symptoms presented by the individual child or adult (Courtois & Watts, 1982; Lipovsky & Elliott, 1993; Osmond, Durham, Leggett, & Keating, 1998; Rust & Troupe, 1991). The variability of responses to CSA dictates the development of specialized treatment strategies to meet each individual's needs. A child victim might present with self-injurious behavior, for example, and might benefit from a behavior modification program tailored specifically to help alleviate such behaviors. An adult might present with a specific sexual dysfunction that might respond to a modified sex therapy technique.

Other symptoms of abuse are so common that therapists should expect to address them in the majority of child victims and adult survivors. The guilt,

BOX 4.3 The Repressed Memory Controversy

1989: The California Courts of Appeal extended the statute of limitations under the doctrine of "delayed discovery," allowing individuals claiming, as adults, a history of CSA during childhood to sue their parents. Individuals must be able to demonstrate that memories of the event were repressed (by providing certification from a licensed mental health professional).

1990: Nineteen-year-old Holly Ramona accused her father, Gary Ramona, of repeatedly raping her between the ages of 5 and 8. Holly's memories of the abuse surfaced while she was a college student receiving therapy for depression and bulimia. During several months of therapy, Holly experienced flashback memories of her father sexually molesting her. Just before accusing her father, Holly received the hypnotic drug sodium Amytal and recounted multiple episodes of abuse by her father. After the allegations surfaced, Gary Ramona lost his $400,000-a-year job, his daughters refused to interact with him, and his wife divorced him.

1992: The False Memory Syndrome Foundation was established to provide information and support to more than 2,300 families. The group contends that there is a "rash" of individuals who have been falsely accused of sexual abuse.

1994: The Napa Valley Superior Court jury ruled that Holly Ramona's memories were "probably false" and that although her therapists had not implanted the memories, they had negligently reinforced them (Butler, 1994). Gary Ramona was awarded $500,000 of the $8 million he sought in damages.

This chronology of events illustrates some of the dilemmas associated with the repressed memory debate. Are Holly and others like her victims of CSA? Or are the accused adults the victims of false memories? There is little consensus regarding these questions among legal, medical, and mental health professionals. In one camp are experts who believe that repressed memories are common and result from either repression of negative feelings associated with the abuse or amnesia associated with dissociative defenses (i.e., multiple personality disorder) of a traumatic event (Briere & Conte, 1993). In the other camp are the critics of repressed memories who claim that such memories may be due to fantasy, illusion, subsequent contextual cues, or the result of implantation by a therapist or other perceived authority figure (Ganaway, 1989; Loftus, 1993).

In support of the argument that repressed memories exist, Herman and Schatzow (1987) found that 64% of female incest survivor patients did not have full recall of their sexual abuse and reported some degree of amnesia. One fourth of these women reported severe memory deficits or complete amnesia for the event. Approximately 75% of the women obtained evidence to corroborate their abuse reports such as confirmation from other family members, discovering that a sibling had also been abused, or a confession by the perpetrator. A more recent study conducted by Briere and Conte (1993) showed a substantial rate of repressed memories in a clinical sample of sexual abuse victims (59%). Such studies, however, are limited because of the retrospective and self-report nature of the data and because the individuals were in therapy. An additional study followed a community sample of 100 documented sexual abuse cases whose victims were between the ages of 10 months and 12 years. When these CSA victims were questioned, as adults, about their childhood histories 17 years later, 38% did not recall the previously substantiated incident (Williams, 1994).

Critics of repressed memories, on the other hand, emphasize the limitations of such studies: specifically, the problem that participants in clinical samples are attempting to remember "a memory for forgetting a memory" (Loftus, 1993, p. 522). Other potential sources of repressed memories have been suggested. For example, some claim that popular writings exaggerate sexual abuse as "nearly universal" (Bower, 1993b) and contain unvalidated claims such as "If you are unable to remember any specific instances but still have a feeling that something abusive happened to you, it probably did" (Bass & Davis, 1988, p. 21). Proponents of false memories claim that such statements are dangerous given the malleability of memory. Research has shown that memory is subject to distortion from stress, incentives to keep secrets, and suggestion (Loftus, 1993; Perry, 1992).

Others contend that popular writings encourage emotional confrontations with alleged perpetrators (Loftus, 1993) and in general are written as part of a "sexual abuse industry" to create victims (Travis, 1993). Since 1989, 19 states have passed legislation allowing people to sue for recovery of damages for injury suffered as a result of CSA remembered for the first time during adulthood, and an estimated 300 lawsuits involving formerly repressed memories had been filed as of September 1993 (Bower, 1993a). Some have suggested that the motivation behind these lawsuits is fame and fortune (Davis, 1991; Lachnit, 1991), rather than justice.

The final argument offered by critics of repressed memories is the notion that therapists may "implant" memories through either overt or covert suggestions. Therapists may inadvertently communicate to their clients their own beliefs that repressed memories are common, and clients might subsequently assume that it is likely to have happened to them (Loftus, 1993). Others have suggested that therapists may overtly implant a memory of CSA by diagnosing abuse after too brief an evaluation, the use of leading questions, or the use of questionable assessment or therapeutic techniques such as hypnosis and sodium Amytal (Butler, 1994; Loftus, 1993).

Unfortunately, the debate about whether memories of CSA are repressed or false remains unresolved, and it is unlikely that the question will receive a clear answer in the near future. To date, there is no definitive way of knowing whether a given memory is true or false. Both sides do agree, however, in the importance of improving methods to assess and treat victims of CSA and of continuing to seek empirical knowledge to uncover the realities regarding repressed memories. An American Psychological Association task force was recently appointed to examine what is known about repressed memories and included a panel of both skeptics and believers. A preliminary report from the group indicated that they had reached a consensus regarding the extremes of the debate:

> Both ends of the continuum on people's memories of abuse are possible. . . . It is possible that under some cue conditions, early memories may be retrievable. At the other extreme, it is possible under some conditions for memories to be implanted or embedded. (DeAngelis, 1993, p. 44)

---

shame, and stigmatization experienced by the victim, for example, need to be addressed by helping the victim change his or her perception about being "different" as well as somehow to blame for the abuse. Here, therapists often undertake some form of cognitive restructuring to appropriately relocate the responsibility of the abuse to the offender (Cahill, Llewelyn, & Pearson, 1991; Jehu, Klassen, & Gazan, 1986; Osmond et al., 1998). Many experts believe that group therapy is a particularly effective modality in which to counter self-denigrating beliefs and to confront issues of secrecy and stigmatization because participants are able to discuss their experiences with peers who have also been abused (Berman, 1990; Cahill et al., 1991; Celano, 1990; Corder, Haizlip, & DeBoer, 1990).

Anxiety and fear are also common symptoms, and one task of therapy is to give victims the opportunity to diffuse these feelings by talking about their abuse experience in the safety of a supportive therapeutic relationship (Berliner, 1991; Courtois & Watts, 1982). Adults are often able to process the abusive experience simply by discussing it with their therapists. For children, however, other avenues may be necessary, such as reenacting the abuse through play. For both the adult survivor and child victim, it is necessary to teach strategies for managing the fear and anxiety that may accompany the processing of the abuse, such as relaxation training, problem-solving skills, the use of positive coping statements, and the use of imagery (Berliner, 1991; Meichenbaum, 1977).

Another goal of therapy is to teach the client to express anger in appropriate ways (Blake-White & Kline, 1985; Jones, 1986). To combat depression and low self-esteem, many experts use cognitive and interpersonal exercises and role plays and emphasize the victim's survival skills and personal strengths (e.g., Corder et al., 1990; Courtois & Watts, 1982). In addition, providing the victim with sex education and self-protection skills may lead to a sense of empowerment and may prevent any further victimization (Berliner, 1991; Damon, Todd, & MacFarlane, 1987).

To date, relatively little is known about the success of victim-oriented interventions for CSA because of the dearth of systematic evaluations (for reviews, see Becker et al., 1995; Berliner & Elliott, 1996; Finkelhor & Berliner, 1995). Most reports of therapy outcome consist of descriptive data and nonstandardized approaches that show only modestly positive or nonsignificant results (Beutler et al., 1994; Kolko, 1987). Although the amount of research examining treatment efficacy is limited, available studies suggest the efficacy of both individual and group treatments for child and adult victims of CSA (Becker et al., 1995; Finkelhor & Berliner, 1995). Some studies have found positive self-reported behavioral change, whereas others have demonstrated improvement in social, emotional, and behavioral functioning on standardized measures (e.g., Cohen & Mannarino, 1993; Friedrich, Luecke, Beilke, & Place, 1992; Roth & Newman, 1991; Rust & Troupe, 1991). Researchers have also begun to evaluate variables that enhance or inhibit treatment efficacy and have found that therapist and victim gender, current social supports, educational level, and the victim's relationship to his or her perpetrator affect treatment outcome (Alexander, Neimeyer, & Follette, 1991; Follette, Alexander, & Follette, 1991; Fowler & Wagner, 1993; Friedrich, Berliner, Urquiza, & Beilke, 1988; Friedrich, Luecke, et al., 1992).

Treatment Interventions for Offenders

The primary treatment goal in working with CSA offenders is to reduce the likelihood of recidivism or repeated offenses. Studying treatment outcome and measuring recidivism are difficult tasks. It is often difficult, for example, for a researcher to determine whether convicted offenders commit a subsequent offense unless long-term follow-ups to monitor reoffenses are extended indefinitely. In one study, 27% of offenders did not reoffend for at least 4 or more years after release (Romero & Williams, 1995). Numerous methodological problems also characterize the research examining treatment outcome with CSA offenders, including nonrandom assignment to treatment conditions, biased samples, and attrition among treatment participants (see Becker, 1994; Marshall & Pithers, 1994). Despite these difficulties, one review of the treatment literature concluded that recent advances in treatment approaches "provide definite grounds for optimism about the responsiveness of some segments of the offender population to existing treatment modalities" (Becker, 1994, p. 188). A variety of treatment approaches exist for CSA offenders, including physiological approaches, traditional and family systems therapies, and cognitive-behavioral techniques (e.g., Becker, 1994; Marshall, Jones, Ward, Johnston, & Barbaree, 1991).

Physiological Approaches

Physiological approaches include castration (surgical removal of the testicles), brain surgery, and drug therapy (e.g., Bradford, 1990; Heim & Hursch, 1979; Marshall et al., 1991). Most physiological treatments are based on the notion that there is some sort of biological mechanism affecting the offender's sex drive and causing the abusive behavior. Early approaches focused on castration and removal of certain brain areas (e.g., hypothalamus) in an attempt to control sexual behavior. Although some outcome studies show a reduction in sex offenses, the presence of methodological problems, ethical concerns, and negative side effects cast doubt on the usefulness of these techniques (Heim & Hursch, 1979; Marshall et al., 1991).

Newer approaches focus on the use of drugs to treat child molesters in an attempt to reduce sexual-offending behavior (Marshall et al., 1991). This type of treatment, sometimes referred to as *chemical castration,* has largely employed drugs called *antiandrogens,* agents that reduce sexual drive. Outcome studies have revealed contradictory results (e.g., Berlin & Meinecke, 1981; Kiersch, 1990; Lugavere, 1996; Wincze, Bansal, & Malamud, 1986). In a review of the literature, Marshall et al. (1991) concluded that drug therapy may be beneficial for some offenders but should be used conservatively in conjunction with other treatments or as a temporary method until psychological treatments can begin.

Traditional and Family Systems Approaches

Insight-oriented therapies, another approach designed to treat CSA offenders, primarily involve individual counseling for the offender. The general purpose of these therapies is to assist the perpetrator in understanding the role sexual abuse plays in his or her life. Outcome studies evaluating various insight-oriented approaches have been mixed (Prendergast, 1979; Sturgeon & Taylor, 1980), probably because of methodological differences across studies. According to a recent survey of sex offender treatment programs, individual counseling techniques are used in only approximately 2% of treatment programs (Knopp, Freeman-Longo, & Stevenson, 1992).

Other treatment programs for offenders emphasize family systems approaches. Giarretto (1982) pioneered the Child Sexual Abuse Treatment Program, a comprehensive program that uses a sequence of therapies for incest families including individual counseling for the child victim, mother, and perpetrator; mother-daughter counseling; marital counseling; perpetrator-victim counseling; group counseling; and family counseling. Hewitt (1998) also described a family approach that includes a series of meetings with individuals within the family (e.g., nonoffending parent, the child victim, and the alleged abuser) and between family members (e.g., nonoffending parent and child victim; alleged abuser and child victim) in an effort to reunify families in which sexual abuse has occurred. Typical themes addressed in family-oriented therapies include parents' failure to protect the victim from abuse, feelings of guilt and depression resulting from the abuse, the inappropriateness of secrecy, the victim's anger toward parents, the perpetrator's responsibility for the abuse, appropriate forms of touch, confusion about blurred role boundaries, poor communication patterns, and the effect the abuse has had on the child (Giarretto, 1982; Hewitt, 1998; Osmond et al., 1998; Sgroi, 1982; Wolfe, Wolfe, & Best, 1988). Family therapy may also address the needs of family members indirectly affected by the abuse, such as those of the nonoffending parent and siblings, as well as disruptions caused by the disclosure of abuse, such as incarceration, financial hardship, and parental separation (Wolfe et al., 1988). Whenever victims and abusers are seen together in therapy, however, special attention should be paid to protecting the victim from intimidation. Although the research evaluating the outcome of the family therapy approach is scant and does not include long-term follow-up, available reports do demonstrate the effectiveness of the approach (Giarretto, 1982).

Cognitive-Behavioral Techniques

Cognitive-behavioral approaches represent an additional method of treatment and are the most widely available and actively researched forms of therapy for CSA offenders (for a review, see Marshall et al., 1991). Behavioral interventions primarily emphasize deviant sexual arousal patterns of CSA perpetrators and attempt to alter them. Most behavioral approaches have used some form of aversive therapy. Abel, Becker, and Skinner (1986) report on a process called masturbatory satiation. In this technique, the perpetrator is instructed to reach orgasm through masturbation as quickly as possible using *appropriate* sexual fantasies (e.g., sexual encounters between two mutually consenting adults). Once he has ejaculated, the offender is to switch his fantasies to images involving children and continue to masturbate until the total masturbation time is 1 hour. This technique supposedly reinforces the appropriate fantasies through the pleasurable feelings of orgasm and diminishes the fantasies involving children because they are associated with nonpleasurable masturbation that occurs after ejaculation. Cognitive therapies, by contrast, are designed to teach offenders how to recognize and change their inaccurate beliefs (e.g., that the perpetrator is simply "teaching" the victim about sex; Abel et al., 1986).

Many treatment programs combine both cognitive and behavioral techniques with other components (e.g., improving social and life skills) to create a multidimensional approach (e.g., Marshall & Barbaree, 1988). Some experts advocate that treatment, consistent with a multidimensional approach, should focus on additional nonsexual difficulties, such as antisocial behavior and a history of sexual victimization (e.g., Chaffin, 1994; Scavo, 1989). One final treatment component that is gaining increasing support is relapse prevention. Programs that include a relapse prevention component include assisting perpetrators in identifying patterns in their behavior that are precursors to abuse and providing long-term, community-based supervision (Marques, Nelson, West, & Day, 1994; Miner, Marques, Day, & Nelson, 1990; Pithers & Kafka, 1990). In a recent review of the treatment literature, Marshall and Pithers (1994) endorsed multidimensional treatment programs by stating that "implementation of a single therapeutic intervention, even by the most highly skilled practitioners, cannot be considered sufficient treatment for most sex offenders" (p. 25).

Most experts agree that the therapeutic value of cognitive-behavioral approaches has been clearly demonstrated (Marshall et al., 1991; Marshall & Pithers, 1994). Others have argued that such a conclusion is premature given the methodological limitations of studies (Quinsey, Harris, Rice, & Lalumiere, 1993). One criticism of outcome studies is that although some treatment approaches have been shown to alter arousal patterns to pictures and/or stories of children, such changes do not necessarily apply to actual children. Other methodological limitations include limited follow-up information, overreliance on self-report data, and lack of appropriate comparison groups. In his recent review of the treatment outcome literature, Chaffin (1994) concluded,

> Despite previous skepticism regarding the efficacy of offender treatment, there are good data to support its effectiveness with the kinds of patients often seen in outpatient settings. This suggests that practitioners can justify favorable prognoses for less severe patients. The data are less optimistic regarding the outlook for severe populations. (p. 233)

The Criminal Justice System

The criminal justice system primarily centers on the punishment of perpetrators of CSA. Researchers and practitioners, however, have also focused on the effect of the criminal justice system on the victim and methods to assist the child victim or witness.

Perpetrators

The criminal justice response toward the perpetrator who is accused or convicted of CSA can take many forms, including prison sentences, plea bargaining, diversion programs, and probation. Although there are no national statistics on the number of CSA prosecutions or the number of perpetrators who receive diversion programs or probation, research on selected jurisdictions provides some information about the criminal justice system response to CSA.

Criminal prosecutions for CSA offenders are not always initiated. In 1987, Chapman and Smith found that approximately 42% of sexual abuse allegations substantiated by CPS or reported to the police were forwarded for prosecution (cited in Finkelhor, 1994a). Many factors influence whether prosecution is initiated (e.g., Tjaden & Thoennes, 1992). Cases involving victims younger than age 7 are less likely to be prosecuted, for example, whereas cases of abuse that are severe, involve force, and include perpetrators with a prior criminal record are more likely to be prosecuted (e.g., Myers, 1994; Tjaden & Thoennes, 1992).

As is true of other crimes, plea bargaining is common in cases of CSA. Approximately two thirds of cases result in the perpetrator pleading guilty in exchange for reduced charges (e.g., Tjaden & Thoennes, 1992). Diversion or probation programs are often used, which include agreements between prosecutors and defendants whereby the defendant participates in some form of counseling or treatment with the understanding that charges will be dismissed if the defendant complies (Myers, 1993). In Smith, Hillenbrand, and Govestsky's study (1990), 80% of convicted child molesters were sentenced to probation, which usually included court-mandated treatment as a condition for probation.

Some have suggested that a failure to prosecute and jail CSA offenders reflects a lack of social recognition and commitment to the problem (Wurtele & Miller-Perrin, 1992). There are many reasons, however, why CSA cases are not prosecuted. In 1987, the U.S. Supreme Court stated that "child abuse is one of the most difficult crimes to detect and prosecute because there often are no witnesses except the victim" (quoted in Myers, 1993, p. 573). In addition, physical evidence in cases of CSA is rarely available (Bays & Chadwick, 1993). The child's testimony is often the only evidence in the case, and the public, prosecutors, and judges are often concerned about the credibility of the child witness (Finkelhor, 1994a; Myers, 1993, 1994).

Despite the difficulty in prosecuting cases of CSA, there is some evidence that child abuse is treated much like other crimes within the criminal justice system. The percentage of CSA cases that proceed to trial, for example, is approximately 10%, which is similar to criminal cases in general (Goodman et al., 1992; Tjaden & Thoennes, 1992). A strong criminal justice system response is also evidenced by the fact that the majority of CSA prosecutions that go to trial result in convictions (Gray, 1993). Research has also demonstrated that the percentage of child maltreatment cases for which criminal prosecutions are initiated is higher for CSA cases than for other types of maltreatment (e.g., Tjaden & Thoennes, 1992).

The criminal justice system has also responded to CSA offenders in other ways. In 1993, President Bill Clinton signed the National Child Protection Act, requiring states to report information on child abuse arrests and convictions to the national criminal history record system of the Federal Bureau of Investigation. Three years later, President Clinton signed a federal version of "Megan's Law," a law requiring states to create a system of sexual offender community notification (see boxed insert: "Megan's Law" in Chapter 7). In addition, some states require that registered sex offenders submit specimens of body fluids that can be genetically compared with specimens taken from victims (Myers, 1994).

There is considerable debate regarding the punitive role of the criminal justice system in responding to CSA. Some argue that prevention and therapy, rather than litigation and sentencing, are ultimately important in responding to the problem (U.S. Advisory Board on Child Abuse and Neglect, 1993). Advocating prosecution of offenders, however, is not necessarily inconsistent with prevention and treatment efforts and has the added value of validating the victim's innocence and society's view that CSA is unacceptable (Myers, 1994; Peters, Dinsmore, & Toth, 1989; Wurtele & Miller-Perrin, 1992). Unfortunately, systematic research studies examining the effects of various criminal justice system responses (e.g., incarceration vs. plea bargaining vs. mandated treatment) on rates of recidivism are rare.

Child Victims

Another concern associated with the criminal justice system has centered on how to protect child victims from the stress associated with case investigation and court proceedings. Several experts have suggested that stress results from activities that the child must endure, such as multiple interviews and face-to-face confrontations with the perpetrator (Goodman et al., 1992; Montoya, 1993). Imagine the fear of a 4-year-old, for example, who must sit on the witness stand, in a strange courtroom in front of strangers, and describe an event as potentially upsetting as sexual abuse. Or imagine the 7-year-old child who is expected to testify against the perpetrator who happens to be the child's parent. In addition, child witnesses must often endure cross-examination from the defense that is usually directed at destroying the child's credibility. Most adults might find such an experience distressing.

In addition to increasing the discomfort of the victim, stress associated with the criminal justice system response is also believed to increase a child's distractibility, reduce his or her motivation, and possibly interfere with memory recall (Saywitz & Snyder, 1993). In a study of child witnesses of CSA, Saywitz and Nathanson (1993) found that a courtroom environment impaired memory performance and was associated with increased child reports of stress. Legal professionals and mental health experts have suggested a number of approaches designed to minimize the stress and discomfort experienced by CSA victims.

One positive development has been the practice of minimizing both the number of interviews and the number of interviewers that a child experiences. One method that accomplishes this task is the use of videotaped investigative interviews with children (see Montoya, 1993). This practice is effective because the numerous professionals involved can view the tape rather than subject the child victim to multiple interviews by different professionals. The use of multidisciplinary teams may also be helpful in reducing the number of interviews that a child is subjected to, thus reducing additional stress to the child victim (Pence & Wilson, 1994). Multidisciplinary teams consist of various professionals involved in the investigation and adjudication of CSA cases, including law enforcement officials, health professionals, and CPS workers, who work together to pool and coordinate resources. Children are typically interviewed by only one highly trained professional while other members of the team observe from behind a one-way mirror. Most states have laws authorizing or mandating the use of such teams.

The practice of courtroom accommodations for child witnesses is another positive development designed to reduce criminal justice system-related stress. Some courts have allowed the child witness to testify outside the direct presence of the offender by permitting videotapes at trial in lieu of the child's testimony (Montoya, 1993; Perry & McAuliff, 1993). The Sixth Amendment of the Constitution, however, protects the defendant's right to confront his or her accuser—in this case, the child witness. As a result, most states do not categorically allow the admissibility of videotaped testimony (Pence & Wilson, 1994). As an alternative, the use of closed-circuit television has been used in North America and other countries, allowing children to testify in the judge's chambers via a monitor (Bottoms & Goodman, 1996; Myers, 1992).

Another positive development is the use of preparation and support for victims of CSA as they experience criminal justice proceedings. Many practices, for example, can be implemented to help make the courtroom a less frightening place for children, such as familiarizing the child ahead of time with the courtroom (e.g., through tours of the courtroom or court schools), closing the courtroom to the public and press, and allowing a trusted adult to remain in the courtroom while the child testifies (Myers, 1994; Regehr, 1990; Saywitz & Snyder, 1993). Accumulating evidence suggests that such approaches are helpful in improving the completeness of children's reports, their ability to answer questions, and the consistency of their responses (Goodman et al., 1992; Saywitz & Snyder, 1993).

SUMMARY

No one knows the specific number of children who are victimized by child sexual abuse each year. The confusion in determining accurate rates of CSA is largely due to the difficulty inherent in defining and studying such a complex social problem. Although no precise estimates are available, it is clear that large numbers of children are sexually exploited by adults. Conservative estimates derived from the most methodologically sound studies suggest that 20% of women and between 5% and 10% of men experience some form of CSA during childhood.

Research examining the characteristics of CSA demonstrates the heterogeneity of victim and offender populations. Victims can be male or female, range in age from infancy to 18, and come from a variety of racial and socioeconomic backgrounds. Perpetrators are also heterogeneous and represent all possible demographic and psychological profiles. A number of risk factors, however, have been consistently associated with CSA. Victims are often female, have few close friends, and live in families characterized by poor family relations and the absence or unavailability of natural parents. Perpetrators of CSA are most often male and someone who is familiar to the child, such as a relative or an acquaintance.

The dynamics that characterize CSA situations are consistently described by both perpetrators and victims. Perpetrators usually target children who are vulnerable or needy in some way, such as those who are unhappy or come from a divorced home. Perpetrators typically involve the child in a grooming process that involves desensitizing the child to sexual abuse by gradually progressing from nonsexual to sexual touch. Perpetrators also use a variety of coercive tactics to initiate and maintain the abuse, such as threats, bribes, and physical force.

The psychological sequelae for victims associated with CSA are variable and consist of short-term as well as long-term effects. Difficulties associated with CSA include a variety of symptoms that affect emotional well-being (e.g., depression), interpersonal functioning (e.g., social withdrawal), behavior (e.g., substance abuse), sexual functioning (e.g., sexualized behavior), physical health (e.g., headaches), and cognitive functioning (e.g., poor concentration). Variability in outcome for victims is associated with a number of factors including the severity of the sexual behavior, the degree of physical force used by the perpetrator, the response the victim received following disclosure, and the identity of the perpetrator.

The heterogeneity of victim and perpetrator populations has contributed to the difficulty in establishing a single explanation for why sexual abuse occurs. One perpetrator may abuse a certain type of child for one reason, and another may abuse a different type of child for a different reason. Etiological theories have focused on different individuals and systems involved in CSA. Some theories have centered on the role of the victim or the mother, whereas the majority emphasize some form of offender dysfunction associated with personality, deviant sexual arousal, or childhood history. Some family theories have also proposed a set of specific characteristics of the family system (e.g., parental conflict and family disorganization) that might contribute to CSA. Finally, several theories have implicated sociocultural factors (e.g., social attitudes toward children and child pornography) that might play a contributory role.

In recognition of the significance of the CSA problem, a number of professionals have been involved in the response toward victims and perpetrators. Criminal justice system responses directed at the problem of CSA sometimes include punitive responses for the perpetrators of CSA as well as interventions designed to alleviate the stress associated with victim involvement in the investigatory and legal processes. Researchers and practitioners have also developed an array of treatment interventions in an effort to address the multiple causes and far-reaching consequences of CSA. Regardless of the type of approach that is used, the therapeutic goals for child victims and adult survivors generally include addressing significant symptomatology as well as common emotions associated with abuse such as guilt, shame, anger, depression, and anxiety. Group therapy has also been recommended as a beneficial intervention for victims to reduce self-denigrating beliefs, secrecy, and stigmatization. Treatment programs for offenders include a variety of approaches but most typically incorporate cognitive and behavioral components to reduce deviant sexual arousal and cognitive distortions associated with abuse. These approaches demonstrate some promise, although further studies are needed to address the limitations of extant research methodologies and potential alternative treatments (e.g., improving social and life skills) to accompany therapeutic interventions.

5

Child Neglect and Psychological Maltreatment

CHAPTER OUTLINE

AN INTERVIEW WITH PATRICIA CRITTENDEN

"Unfortunately, because we think of children as victims, parents are consequently labeled as perpetrators. As a result, we become tempted to punish such 'perpetrators' and thus reduce our ability to help either the parents or their children."

Patricia Crittenden is a prolific scholar who has published several books and more than 50 journal articles and book chapters concerning issues related to child maltreatment. In 1994, she received the Gimbel Award for her scholarship in family and child violence. She has a multidisciplinary background, earning an M.Ed. in special education and an M.A. in developmental psychology, both at the University of Virginia. She received her Ph.D. in family and developmental psychology from the University of Virginia in 1983 and held a postdoctoral fellowship at the University of New Hampshire in the Family Research Laboratory. She has been involved in a variety of professional activities including college and graduate-level instruction, social work case management, infant intervention, parent education, psychotherapy, administration of the Miami Child Protection Team, and instruction of normal and special education high school, elementary, and preschool students. Her present work involves theory development, clinical research and case consultation, graduate and postgraduate teaching, and development of clinical assessments for disorders of attachment.

Q: What sparked your interest in the area of child maltreatment?

A: Like many turns in my career, my interest in maltreatment was unintended but fortuitous. In the 1960s, I began working with low-income, disadvantaged children. As I worked my way down in age toward a greater focus on prevention, I began to work with infants at risk for developmental delay. As it turned out, most of the referrals were of maltreated infants and their mothers. Hence, I needed to learn about child abuse and neglect.

Q: What would you describe as your most influential contribution to the field of child maltreatment?

A: I wish I could say that I changed people's views of maltreating adults to a nonblaming, compassionate attitude toward these individuals who are distressed themselves and who have been victimized far longer than their children. I think the United States, however, is still predominantly concerned with who did what to whom and whether it was right or wrong. So, at one level, I think I have fallen short in my intended goal of helping others to understand developmental processes in a nonjudgmental and compassionate way. Possibly, however, I have assisted others to see patterns in children's behavior that were not formerly apparent. That is, I hope I have assisted professionals in seeing the strategic and self-protective organization that underlies some disturbed behavior, as well as the pain that underlies some apparently "resilient" behavior.

Q: What should communities do to assist child victims of maltreatment?

A: I think our society has become too focused on children as "victims" of child maltreatment. Conceptualizing oneself as a victim is not good for one's mental health and does not do justice to the active coping strategies used by children who have been endangered. We need to (a) look at what maltreated children do to cope with their situations, (b) create nonthreatening environments for maltreated children, and (c) teach maltreated children to recognize the difference between the two (thus, enabling them to develop strategies for safety). Further, any real help for the great majority of maltreated children must include assistance to their parents. Unfortunately, because we think of children as victims, parents are consequently labeled as perpetrators. As a result, we become tempted to punish such "perpetrators" and thus reduce our ability to help either the parents or their children. If we eliminate the notion of victims, we can view all people as individuals having to cope with a range of dangers. This perspective would promote supporting endangered parents and children so that they might live in safer environments and learn to use strategies suitable for safety. Put another way, I think we need a strengths approach to troubled families.

Q: What should be done to diminish child maltreatment?

A: I would focus on prevention by making environments safe at the cultural/community level, by supporting couples to make family life safe, and by teaching parents and children strategies for reducing danger. Although I resist single-issue approaches, this demands both severe reduction of firearms in homes and also wide use of birth control. The teaching of strategies for safe interpersonal behavior should begin in kindergarten and continue to graduation as a basic part of the curriculum on family life (in the positive sense, not as techniques for identifying, reporting, and protecting oneself from abuse). Universal screening of mother-infant dyads at 6 weeks, 15 to 18 months, and 30 months could help focus group and individual prevention efforts. In all cases, I would respect parents enough to understand their goals and to assist them to find more effective means of meeting them. Concurrently, I would cease to respond punitively toward parents who harm their children and would reduce greatly the use of foster care while increasing equally the availability of family-centered intervention. If forced to choose between prevention and extensive treatment, I would choose prevention. No other choice has the possibility of reducing the problem of child maltreatment in the future.

INTRODUCTION

Case History: Will and Mark: "Where Are the Parents?"

Will and Mark arrived at the psychiatric unit of the county hospital after being apprehended by the police the night before. Their clothes were covered with dirt, and the odor emanating from their bodies indicated that they had not bathed in quite some time. Both were thin and immediately asked the nursing staff for some food. An interview revealed that they were brothers and part of a family of seven, although many other "friends of the family" often stayed in their house. Neither parent worked, and Will and Mark stated that they often had the responsibility to bring home money for their parents. Their father had taught them how to beg for money on various street corners around the city.

After the interview, the events of the previous evening were clear. Mark and Will had been out "killing time" by wandering around the neighborhood. They had decided to "get some fresh air" when their father began swearing at them, as he frequently did, for failing to have his dinner ready on time. After roaming the city for hours, Mark and Will spotted a pickup truck and took it for a ride. After a short drive, they stopped at a local furniture store, broke in, and began to vandalize the merchandise by ripping the furniture with Will's knife. A woman from the community spotted the intruders and called the police. She told the police that two young boys, probably somewhere between 7 and 9 years of age, had broken into a local business. (first author's case history)

The events depicted in this vignette clearly reflect parenting practices that are less than ideal. Such behaviors, however, would not be characterized as physically or sexually abusive as previously defined. The interactions described in this vignette may not be labeled *abusive* at all but do illustrate two additional proposed forms of child maltreatment: *child neglect* and *psychological maltreatment.* This chapter addresses these two forms of child maltreatment, although much less is known about them. Child neglect has been referred to as the "most forgotten" form of maltreatment (Daro, 1988). Wolock and Horowitz (1984) coined the phrase "the neglect of neglect" to describe the disinterest in the topic by professionals as well as society. Likewise, psychological maltreatment was not recognized as a distinct form of child maltreatment until recently.

Why has most research focused on physical and sexual child abuse (PCA and CSA) with less emphasis on child neglect and psychological maltreatment? The most obvious answer is that physical abuse and, to a lesser degree, sexual abuse result in immediate and observable harm. Child neglect and psychological maltreatment are much more elusive in their negative consequences. In cases of child neglect or psychological maltreatment, for example, a single act is unlikely to result in significant and immediate harm. The cumulative effects of these forms of abuse, however, are insidious and are often associated with negative consequences that are just as serious, if not more so (Crittenden, 1992; Ney et al., 1994).

> Where should the line be drawn between parental error and negligence or psychological maltreatment?

Child neglect and psychological maltreatment are also evasive in terms of definitional issues. Although defining PCA and CSA involves some ambiguities, particularly at the less extreme ends of the continuum, understanding what constitutes child neglect and psychological maltreatment poses even greater problems. Where should the line be drawn between less than adequate parenting or parental error and negligence or psychological maltreatment? Many of the specific behaviors used to define child neglect or psychological maltreatment are less "deviant," that is, they are committed by many parents at one time or another. Ignoring or criticizing a child, for example, and being unsupportive are behaviors that most parents engage in during the normal course of parenting. As a result, it is necessary to consider under what circumstances these behaviors might constitute child neglect or psychological maltreatment.

Related to definitional ambiguities is the problem of overlap between child neglect and psychological maltreatment with other forms of child abuse. Child neglect and psychological maltreatment rarely occur in isolation as "pure" forms of maltreatment but rather often coexist with one another, as well as with other forms of child abuse (e.g., Claussen & Crittenden, 1991; Ney et al., 1994). Coexistence with other forms of maltreatment is particularly characteristic of psychological maltreatment, which in the broadest sense (e.g., parental actions that damage a child's self-worth and esteem) occurs as a component of all forms of maltreatment (e.g., Hart & Brassard, 1991).

The complex nature of child neglect and psychological maltreatment has contributed to a serious lack of information about the characteristics, consequences, and causes of these forms of child maltreatment. The realization that child neglect and psychological maltreatment may be the most pervasive and damaging forms of child maltreatment, however, has spurred research interests in these topics. In the first part of the chapter, we address what is currently known about child neglect; in the latter half of the chapter, we focus on psychological maltreatment. Much of the literature for both forms of maltreatment aims at clarifying definitional issues, and each section reflects this emphasis accordingly. Because research evaluating these forms of abuse is in its infancy, we address the causes, solutions, and interventions for each form of maltreatment simultaneously.

CHILD NEGLECT

As is true of all forms of child maltreatment, child neglect is not new. Not until the early 20th century, however, was the neglect of children's basic needs acknowledged or defined as a social problem (Wolock & Horowitz, 1984). In more recent times, widespread recognition of this form of child maltreatment, and subsequent empirical attention directed at it, has taken a back seat to physical and sexual forms of child abuse (Berliner, 1994; Dubowitz, 1994; Wolock & Horowitz, 1984). Historically, professionals have viewed child neglect as a less significant appendage of the more tangible forms of maltreatment, as a stepchild of PCA.

There may be several reasons for inattention to child neglect:

1. Some erroneously believe that neglect does not result in serious consequences.
2. Many may feel that it is inappropriate to judge parents involved in poverty-related neglect.
3. Many may be reluctant to become involved in child neglect because the problem seems insurmountable.
4. Some may find other forms of maltreatment more compelling.
5. Ambiguity and vagueness regarding what constitutes neglect cause confusion.
6. Child neglect provokes negative feelings. (Dubowitz, 1994)

The realization that child neglect is the most frequently reported form of child maltreatment (DHHS, 1996, 1998; Wang & Daro, 1998), however, has increased clinical and research efforts directed at the problem.

Scope of the Problem

In response to increased interest in child neglect, professionals have focused on defining the parameters of child neglect and determining the magnitude of the problem. As is true of other forms of child maltreatment, reaching a consensus regarding conceptual and operational definitions and determining the rates of the problem are two of the greatest challenges to the field.

What Is Child Neglect?

- Eight-year-old Mark is left to care for his 3-year-old sister, Maria.
- Margaret fails to provide medication for her 10-year-old, who has a seizure disorder.
- Jonathon refuses to allow his 16-year-old son into their house and tells him not to return.
- Tyrone and Rachel live with their three children in a home that is thick with dirt and dust, smells of urine, and has a refrigerator filled with rotting food.
- Alicia leaves her 10-month-old unattended in a bathtub full of water.

> Reaching a consensus regarding definitions of child neglect is one of the greatest challenges.

These scenarios portray a range of behaviors that are sometimes labeled as child neglect. The way child neglect is defined is critical because such definitions influence the way that the problem is conceptualized for purposes of conducting research, reporting neglect, understanding the causes of neglect, and formulating interventions as well as prevention strategies for the problem.

Current Definitions. Most experts generally agree that child neglect refers to deficits in the provision of a child's basic needs (e.g., Dubowitz, Black, Starr, & Zuravin, 1993; Munkel, 1994). Gaudin (1993) defined child neglect as follows: "Child neglect is the term used most often to encompass parents' or caretakers' failure to provide basic physical health care, supervision, nutrition, personal hygiene, emotional nurturing, education, or safe housing" (p. 67). This definition emphasizes parental blame, parental responsibility, or both, in child neglect. Such a narrow focus on the role of the caretaker in child neglect is inadequate because it might limit understanding of the problem. In the second scenario above, for example, Margaret may not provide her 10-year-old with medication for her seizure disorder not to intentionally harm her child but because she cannot afford the cost of the medication. By focusing exclusively on the failures of the parent, professionals might confine intervention strategies to improving parental behaviors, thereby excluding some other important contributors to neglect, such as poverty.

In response to this criticism, other researchers have called for a more comprehensive definition of child neglect that incorporates a variety of factors that might lead to neglect (e.g., Dubowitz, Black, Starr, et al., 1993; Helfer, 1990; Paget, Philp, & Abramczyk, 1993). The definition of child neglect used in the second and third National Incidence Studies (DHHS, 1988; Sedlak & Broadhurst, 1996), for instance, included various forms of physical neglect such as refusal of health care; abandonment; inadequate supervision; and inadequate nutrition, clothing, and hygiene (see Table 2.1 in Chapter 2 for the definitions of child neglect employed in NIS-3). In addition, this definition distinguished between parental failure to provide when options are available and failure to provide when options are not available. Certain situations were excluded whereby parents or caretakers were involved in acts of omission because of financial limitations (e.g., an inability to afford health care). The penal codes of several states include definitions of neglect that exclude neglect due to limited financial resources. Such definitions call attention to additional social factors potentially involved in neglectful behaviors, which encourages awareness about the complexity of child neglect. Understanding the multidimensional nature of child neglect may, in turn, help professionals be more effective in directing research and intervention efforts.

Variability exists regarding exactly what constitutes a child's basic needs. Are the parents of Mark and Maria, described in the first scenario, negligent because they leave 8-year-old Mark to care for his 3-year-old sister, Maria? Obviously, it depends on the specific circumstances. What if Mark were responsible for Maria's care for 5 minutes while she played on the floor? For 5 minutes while she played in the bathtub? For one evening between 9 p.m. and 1 a.m.? For every evening between 9 p.m. and 1 a.m.? What if Mark were responsible for Maria's care while their parents took a 2-week vacation? A given behavior can be interpreted as neglectful or not depending on several factors, including the consequences to the child, the duration and frequency of neglect, and the cultural context in which the behavior occurs.

Severity of Consequences. Many experts have argued that the severity of the consequences of the neglect is an important but overlooked variable in defining child neglect (Crouch & Milner, 1993; Erickson & Egeland, 1996). The severity of child neglect can be conceptualized along a continuum ranging from optimal care to that which is grossly inadequate. Severity is typically assessed according to the magnitude of outcomes to children or the degree of demonstrable harm (DHHS, 1981; Dubowitz, Black, Starr, et al., 1993). A case in which a child dies from bleach poisoning, for example, might rank as more severe than a case in which a child receives a minor burn from an iron, although the same parental behavior contributed to both injuries (i.e., lack of supervision).

One problem with the criterion of demonstrable harm is that some negative outcomes of child neglect are difficult to measure (e.g., emotional consequences), and at times there may be no immediate harm. The three children of Tyrone and Rachel, described in the fourth scenario, may suffer no demonstrable harm as a result of living in unsanitary conditions for a month. Although there may be no immediate negative effects, however, the parents' behavior could still be considered neglect. Zuravin (1988a) found that only 25% of neglected children reported to a protective services agency suffered immediate, physical harm. In recognition of this dilemma, the DHHS (1988) broadened its definition of child neglect in the NIS-2 to include a category titled *endangered.* This new category allowed for reporting children who demonstrated no actual harm (i.e., present evidence of injury) but for whom it was reasonable to suspect potential harm (i.e., future risk of injury). The laws in most states include risk of harm or endangerment in their definitions of neglect (Myers & Peters, 1987).

One difficulty in considering potential harm, as articulated by Dubowitz, Black, Starr, et al. (1993), is predicting the likelihood that harm will actually occur and whether that potential harm is significant. An illustration is the potential for harm present each time a person gets into a car, crosses a street, or consumes food with a high cholesterol content. In each case, there is uncertainty about whether actual harm will result and whether such harm will be significant. Professionals are faced with a continuum of behaviors that require human judgment in making child neglect determinations, resulting in a definitional process that may be even more subjective than other forms of child maltreatment discussed in this book. We agree with Dubowitz and colleagues that potential harm that is probable and severe in its consequences should be considered in definitions of neglect. Leaving a 10-month-old unattended in a bathtub full of water as Alicia did in the last scenario, for example, could likely result in severe injury or even death if the infant is left for a significant amount of time.

Frequency and Duration. The frequency and duration of neglecting behavior are also important definitional considerations (Claussen & Crittenden, 1991; Dubowitz, Black, Starr, et al., 1993; Zuravin & Taylor, 1987). Single incidents of neglectful behavior or occasional lapses in adequate care usually qualify as a normal characteristic of parenting or as parental error, rather than as an indication of serious child neglect. If a child occasionally misses a bath or skips a meal, few identify such a child as neglected. In contrast, a pattern of frequent and repeated deficits in child care (e.g., few baths and numerous skipped meals) is more likely to be considered neglectful (Daro, 1988; Dubowitz, Black, Starr, et al., 1993).

The frequency, severity, and duration of neglecting behavior are important definitional considerations.

Furthermore, some have argued that frequency and chronicity should be evaluated in the context of the severity of harm involved in a particular act (DHHS, 1988; Dubowitz, Black, Starr, et al., 1993; Zuravin, 1991). Some isolated incidents or brief omissions in care can result in serious consequences, for example, when a caretaker leaves a young child or infant alone near a swimming pool, or when a parent fails to use a seat belt or car seat for a young child who dies in a car accident. Serious omissions of this nature have led some to argue that "an omission in care that harms or endangers a child constitutes neglect, whether it occurs once or a hundred times" (Dubowitz, Black, Starr, et al., 1993, p. 18). In the third scenario whereby Jonathon throws his 16-year-old son out of their home and tells him not to return, the behavior occurs only once, but that single behavior could prove to be quite dangerous and harmful.

> Cultural and community values largely determine the adequacy or inadequacy of child care.

Distinctions based on frequency and chronicity are helpful not only in defining child neglect but in understanding characteristics and causes of child neglect. Research conducted by Nelson, Saunders, and Landsman (1990), for example, found differences between chronic and nonchronic neglectful families. Chronically neglectful families were characterized by multiple problems and deficits including lack of knowledge, skills, and tangible resources. Nonchronically neglectful or "new neglect" families had experienced recent significant crises (e.g., parental divorce or illness) that appeared to presently overwhelm normally sufficient coping abilities. Nelson et al. concluded that the characteristics of nonchronically neglectful families suggested short-term crisis, stress-management, and support group interventions, whereas characteristics of chronically neglectful families suggested the need for multiple treatment interventions for a long duration.

Cultural Issues. The point at which child care moves from the adequate to the inadequate is largely determined by cultural and community values. The acceptable age, for example, for a minor to be responsible for preparing his or her own meals might be different for various cultural groups and for various claims-making groups within any culture. Some groups might condemn the notion of a 12-year-old taking on this responsibility, whereas other groups might approve of it. Ultimately, societal reactions distinguish adequate from inadequate care.

Research examining North American communities indicates that cultural views of what constitutes household cleanliness, appropriate medical and dental care, and adequate supervision vary little across sociodemographic variables. Polansky and colleagues (Polansky, Ammons, & Weathersby, 1983; Polansky, Chalmers, & Williams, 1987; Polansky & Williams, 1978) have evaluated nonmaltreating mothers with various sociodemographic backgrounds using the Childhood Level of Living scale. This scale is designed to assess the importance of basic standards of child care, including cognitive, emotional, and physical care. Results have consistently indicated that there is strong agreement about the basic elements of child care, with similar standards of care found for rural, urban, working-class, and middle-class individuals.

Forms of Neglect. Additional efforts aimed at defining the precise nature of child neglect have led researchers to propose numerous typologies clarifying the various situations that constitute child neglect. Most authors agree that child neglect exists in many forms, such as physical neglect, educational neglect, developmental neglect, and emotional neglect (e.g., Hegar & Yungman, 1989; Sedlak & Broadhurst, 1996; Wolock & Horowitz, 1984). Some experts in the field have proposed an additional category termed *prenatal neglect* that occurs even before a child is born (see Box 5.1, "Neglecting the Unborn Child").

Despite general agreement regarding these broad categories of neglect, disagreement exists regarding the precise behaviors or subtypes included under physical, educational, developmental, and emotional neglect. The strongest consensus exists for *physical neglect,* generally defined as a deficit in basic necessities such as food, clothing, and shelter. The NIS-2 and NIS-3 broadened the concept of physical neglect to include refusal or delay in seeking health care, desertion or abandonment of a child, refusing custody (e.g., throwing a child out of the house or not allowing a runaway to return home), and inadequate supervision (DHHS, 1988; Sedlak & Broadhurst, 1996). In the NIS-3, an example of physical neglect included a 2-year-old who was found naked and alone wandering in a street late at night (Sedlak & Broadhurst, 1996). *Educational* or *developmental neglect* generally refers to deprivation of experiences necessary for growth and development, such as intellectual and educational opportunities. An example of educational neglect is a child who is chronically truant or not enrolled in school (Sedlak & Broadhurst, 1996).

The greatest disagreement exists in determining situations consistent with *emotional neglect.* Although most experts agree on broad conceptual parameters of emotional neglect that include failure to provide support, security, and encouragement, they disagree on the specific operationalization of such behaviors. Current attempts to delineate the behaviors that constitute emotional neglect include situations that others have traditionally viewed as physical, educational, or developmental. Emotional neglect has been defined in the NIS-3, for example, to include delay or refusal of psychological care, which others have classified as developmental neglect (e.g., Hegar & Yungman, 1989; Sedlak & Broadhurst, 1996). There is also considerable overlap between definitions of emotional neglect and psychological maltreatment. Some experts, for example, have included a parent's failure to express affection and caring for a child as psychological maltreatment, whereas others define inadequate nurturance and affection as emotional neglect (Hart, Brassard, & Karlson, 1996; Sedlak & Broadhurst, 1996).

Despite the disagreement and overlap in organizational frameworks, several subtypes of neglect are repeatedly reported in the literature. These are summarized in Table 5.1. At least 11 subtypes of child neglect have been consistently described: (a) health care neglect, (b) personal hygiene neglect, (c) nutritional neglect, (d) neglect of household safety, (e) neglect of household sanitation, (f) inadequate shelter, (g) abandonment, (h) supervisory neglect, (i) educational neglect, (j) emotional neglect, and (k) fostering delinquency.

(text continued on p. 166)

BOX 5.1 Neglecting the Unborn Child

Prenatal neglect generally includes actions that occur during the prenatal period that can potentially harm the unborn child. Most conceptualizations of prenatal neglect focus on women who abuse illicit drugs and alcohol during pregnancy, exposing infants to their harmful effects in utero. National estimates of the number of drug-exposed infants vary widely because no state requires the uniform testing of infants for drug exposure. In its annual national survey, the National Committee to Prevent Child Abuse found that 6,922 infants were reported for drug exposure in 1993 (McCurdy & Daro, 1994b). The figure increased to 7,469 drug-exposed infants in 1994 (Wiese & Daro, 1995). It is estimated that approximately 11% of all women have used illegal drugs while pregnant (Jones, 1992).

Most of the concern about prenatal drug exposure has been generated as a result of the increasing numbers of studies demonstrating a relationship between prenatal drug exposure and negative developmental outcomes for the fetus (see reviews by Chiriboga, 1993; Zuckerman & Bresnahan, 1991). Fetal alcohol syndrome, for example, is a well-recognized consequence of alcohol abuse during pregnancy. Babies born to mothers consuming large quantities of alcohol during pregnancy suffer from numerous difficulties, including growth deficiency, anomalies of brain structure and function, and abnormalities of the head and face (Sokol & Clarren, 1989). Research has also linked prenatal use of illicit drugs such as heroin, cocaine, and marijuana to fetal harm, including growth retardation, microcephaly, and increased rates of organ anomalies (e.g., Bays, 1990; Hadeed & Siegel, 1989).

In light of these research findings, many advocate for mandatory drug testing of newborns and criminal liability for substance-abusing pregnant women (e.g., Garrity-Rokous, 1994). Many methodological constraints to such research, however, limit the establishment of definitive cause-effect relationships between prenatal drug exposure and negative developmental outcome. Maternal drug use, for example, often occurs in association with poor maternal nutrition, and, as a result, it is difficult to determine which variable is responsible for negative developmental outcome (Chiriboga, 1993). The results of such studies are also difficult to interpret when the influence of the parenting environment subsequent to birth is not considered, a factor demonstrated to influence the developmental outcome of drug-exposed infants (Black, Schuler, & Nair, 1993). A child may be exposed to cigarette smoke in utero, for example, as well as in the environment after birth when the mother continues to smoke.

Despite these limitations, legal responses to the problem of prenatal neglect are appearing. Many states have mandated that professionals report drug-exposed infants or substance-abusing pregnant women to CPS. As of 1994, 27 states required the reporting of drug-exposed babies, an increase from 19 states in 1993 (Daro & McCurdy, 1994; Wiese & Daro, 1995). Although some states explicitly include infants born with a positive drug toxicology as abused or neglected children, most do not (National Clearinghouse on Child Abuse and Neglect Information, 1992). In addition, successful criminal prosecutions under child abuse and neglect statutes are rare (Garrity-Rokous, 1994; Sovinski, 1997). Civil proceedings, however, which result in removal of the child from the home rather than prison sentences, are a more likely outcome for substance-abusing pregnant women. Several recent cases have supported court intervention to protect drug-exposed newborns on the basis that such circumstances were probative of child neglect (Myers, 1992). Prosecutors have also sometimes used related state statutes (e.g., involuntary manslaughter and prohibitions against delivering drugs to minors) to charge women who abuse substances during pregnancy, although this approach has been generally unsuccessful in obtaining criminal convictions (Garrity-Rokous, 1994; Sovinski, 1997).

One reason for the lack of uniformity in response to prenatal neglect may involve the disagreement surrounding the relative significance of the rights of the unborn child versus the rights of the pregnant woman (Fleisher, 1987; Garrity-Rokous, 1994). Another source of confusion is the ambiguity of state statutes, which often leave considerable room for variability in interpreting what circumstances can be legally sanctioned. In addition, punitive responses toward substance-abusing pregnant women have been questioned on practical, constitutional, therapeutic, and empirical grounds (e.g., Garrity-Rokous, 1994; Sovinski, 1997). Although the problem of prenatal neglect continues to be the focus of much theoretical discussion and empirical research, solutions will likely remain elusive for some time.

TABLE 5.1 Subtypes of Child Neglect

Type	*Description*	*Examples*
Health care neglect	Refusal to, or delay in, providing physical or mental health care	Failing to obtain a child's immunizations Prescriptions not filled and provider's instructions not followed Dental needs left untreated Prescribed psychological help not obtained
Personal hygiene neglect	Standards of personal care and cleanliness are not met	Infrequent bathing Poor dental hygiene Clothing inadequate for weather conditions or size Sleeping arrangements that prohibit a child from obtaining adequate sleep
Nutritional neglect	Failure to provide a diet of quality nutritional balance	Insufficient calories Meals do not represent the basic food groups Food is stale or spoiled
Neglect of household safety	Safety hazards in or around the house	Structural hazards within the home, such as broken stairs or railings, broken windows, holes in floors or ceilings Fire hazards, such as frayed wiring, the presence of combustible materials, objects too close to heat sources posing a burn threat Chemicals or drugs accessible to children
Neglect of household sanitation	Standards of housekeeping care and cleanliness are not met	Excess accumulation of garbage and trash in home Vermin and insects are uncontrolled Surfaces are covered with dirt and filth Bedding is unclean

TABLE 5.1 Continued

Type	*Description*	*Examples*
Inadequate shelter	A physical shelter and/or stable "home" is not provided or is inadequate	Refusing custody responsibilities of one's child Not allowing a runaway to return home Inability to provide a stable and permanent home (i.e., homelessness) Overcrowded living conditions (e.g., 25 people living in a four-bedroom home) "Throwing" an adolescent out of the home
Abandonment	Physical desertion of one's child, including potentially fatal or nonfatal abandonment	Placing children in dumpsters, parks, and so on Abandoning children while in the care of others (e.g., baby-sitters, hospitals, relatives)
Supervisory neglect	Deficits in parental supervision that can lead to injury	Children are left in the home alone for prolonged periods Children are allowed to roam the streets at night
Educational neglect	Parents do not provide necessary care and supervision to promote education	Children of mandatory age are not enrolled in school Frequent and chronic truancy are permitted Inattention to special education needs
Emotional neglect	Child's need for emotional support, security, and encouragement are not provided	Caretaker is unavailable emotionally Caretaker is indifferent or rejects child
Fostering delinquency	Encouraging the development of illegal behaviors	Rewarding children for stealing

SOURCE: Information for this table was obtained from the following references, which are representative but not exhaustive: Hegar & Yungman (1989); Munkel (1994); Sedlak & Broadhurst (1996); Wolock & Horowitz (1984); Zuravin (1991).

Estimates of Child Neglect

During the past 15 years, child neglect has emerged as the most frequently reported and substantiated form of child maltreatment (Wang & Daro, 1998). Estimates of child neglect come primarily from official reports made to professionals and CPS agencies. Recent research has also appeared that employs a parent self-report technique to determine estimates of neglecting behavior.

Official Estimates. The AAPC (1988) reported that child neglect cases (i.e., deprivation of necessities) accounted for approximately 55% of all child maltreatment cases reported to CPS in 1986. Data from the National Center on Child Abuse and Neglect indicated that child neglect cases, including medical as well as other forms of neglect, accounted for 52% of reported cases (DHHS, 1998). Data from the National Committee to Prevent Child Abuse, consisting of the most recent statistics available, revealed that child neglect accounted for approximately 52% of reported cases (Wang & Daro, 1998).

The number of children reported for neglect has increased in recent years (DHHS, 1996; Wang & Daro, 1998). The National Incidence Studies (NIS-1, NIS-2, and NIS-3) have attempted to evaluate the incidence of child neglect and are illustrative of the increases in child neglect reports, as shown in Table 5.2. These figures also demonstrate the problems inherent in estimating child neglect. The increase in child neglect from NIS-1 to NIS-2 reflects, in part, the broadening of the definition of child neglect in the NIS-2 to include children at risk for harm in addition to those actually harmed. Definitional variability, however, cannot account for the increases between NIS-2 and NIS-3 because both studies used identical definitions of child neglect. Increases in the number of children reported for child neglect between 1986 and 1993 likely reflect an increased capability on the part of community professionals to recognize neglect, but they may also reflect a *real* increase in child neglect during this period (Sedlak & Broadhurst, 1996).

Self-Report Surveys. Estimates of child neglect have been obtained from a self-report study that employed a nationally representative sample of parents using the Parent-Child Conflict Tactics Scales (Straus et al., 1998). Neglect was defined by several questions that focused on lack of parental supervision, nutritional neglect, alcohol abuse, medical neglect, and emotional neglect (see Table 2.3 of Chapter 2 for items employed to measure child neglect). Survey results indicated that 27% of parents reported engaging in some form of child neglect at least once during the past year. The most common form of child neglect in this study was leaving a child alone even when the parent thought an adult should be present. Eleven percent of parents also reported that they were unable to ensure that their child obtained the food he or she needed, whereas approximately 2% of parents reported an inability to adequately care for their child because of problem drinking.

Searching for Patterns: Characteristics of Victims

Agencies that receive official reports of neglect provide information on the sociodemographic characteristics of victims such as age, gender, race, and SES. These official estimates, despite their limitations, provide most of the available information on the characteristics of neglected children.

TABLE 5.2 Number of Children Reported for Physical and Educational Neglect in the National Incidence Studies

	Physical Neglect		*Educational Neglect*	
	Number of Children	*Rate per 1,000 Children*	*Number of Children*	*Rate per 1,000 Children*
NIS-1	103,600	1.6	174,000	2.7
NIS-2	507,700	8.1	284,800	4.5
NIS-3	1,335,100	19.9	397,300	5.9

SOURCE: DHHS (1981, 1988); Sedlak (1990); Sedlak & Broadhurst (1996).

Age

The average age of neglected children is 6 years (AAPC, 1988). Several sources of estimates for child neglect indicate that the risk for child neglect generally declines with age (e.g., DHHS, 1998; Sedlak & Broadhurst, 1996). Recent data from the National Center on Child Abuse and Neglect indicate that 51% of reported child neglect victims are under 5 years of age and that 34% of those reports are for children under 1 year of age (DHHS, 1994). Serious injuries and fatalities from neglect are also more common for younger children (Wang & Daro, 1998). This general pattern, however, varies for different subtypes of neglect. In the NIS-3 (Sedlak & Broadhurst, 1996), older children were more likely to be victims of emotional neglect.

Gender

In regard to gender, few differences have been associated with rates of child neglect (Claussen & Crittenden, 1991; DHHS, 1988, 1994). The National Center on Child Abuse and Neglect (DHHS, 1998) found, for example, that 51% of reported cases were males and 49% were females. Research findings vary with regard to gender, however, when findings associated with subtypes of neglect are examined. The NIS-3, for example, found that boys were more likely to be emotionally neglected than girls (Sedlak & Broadhurst, 1996).

Race

Studies attempting to determine racial differences in rates of child neglect are fraught with methodological difficulties and, as a result, should be interpreted cautiously (Asbury, 1993). According to the most recent official reporting statistics from the AAPC (1988), 63% of child neglect reports involved Caucasian children, 20% involved African American children, and 12% involved Hispanic children. Comparison of these data with census data indicates that the risk of neglect appears to be higher for African American and Hispanic children. Indeed, 44% of all medical neglect reports involved African American children (DHHS, 1998). The significance of this pattern, however, is unclear because race is also associated with SES.

Socioeconomic Status and Family Structure

Although child neglect occurs at all levels of society, rates of neglect are higher in families characterized by very low income, unemployment, and dependence on social assistance (AAPC, 1988; Brown et al., 1998; DHHS, 1996). SES is a stronger predictor of child neglect than of physical abuse (Crittenden, 1988; Zuravin, 1986, 1989). The median income of neglectful families is significantly lower than the national average (American Humane Association, 1984). Income level has also been associated with severity of neglect, with higher-income families generally associated with less severe forms of neglect (see Claussen & Crittenden, 1991).

Family size and structure are also associated with neglect. Children of single parents are at greater risk for all types of neglect compared with children living with both parents (Brown et al., 1998; Sedlak & Broadhurst, 1996). In addition, at-risk percentages are considerably higher for neglected children compared with both sexually and emotionally abused children (Sedlak & Broadhurst, 1996). Child neglect is also related to the number of dependent children living in the family. In NIS-3, children in the largest families (four or more children) were two to three times more likely to be neglected (Sedlak & Broadhurst, 1996). Poverty, family size, and being a single parent are all interrelated and significantly increase a child's risk for neglect (Brown et al., 1998).

Consequences Associated With Child Neglect

Although there has been considerable research evaluating the negative consequences associated with other forms of child maltreatment, relatively little research is available that examines the unique effects of child neglect on children's functioning. This state of affairs is somewhat of a paradox, given the suggestion that the effect of child neglect can be both significant and long-lasting and may be associated with more serious harm than physical or sexual abuse (e.g., Crittenden, 1992; Erickson & Egeland, 1996; Ney et al., 1994).

In addition to the paucity of research on the effects of child neglect, what studies are available are marred by methodological problems (Crouch & Milner, 1993; Erickson & Egeland, 1996). Some of the same difficulties that characterize studies of other child maltreatment groups also plague studies of victims of child neglect. Limited sample sizes, the use of unstandardized measures, definitional variability, and the lack of comparison groups are limitations of research on the effects associated with child neglect. An additional problem is that samples are heterogeneous, consisting of victims not only of child neglect but also of other forms of abuse (e.g., Vondra, Barnett, & Cicchetti, 1990).

The limited number and quality of research investigations examining the effects associated with child neglect make the interpretation of findings difficult. Many samples include children who are victims of physical child abuse *and* child neglect, making it difficult, if not impossible, to sort out the effects of one form of child maltreatment from the other. An increasing number of sound investigations that focus specifically on child neglect victims, however, are beginning to appear (see Crouch & Milner, 1993, for a review). Collectively, these studies have consistently uncovered several problems associated with child neglect including social difficulties, intellectual deficits, emotional and behavioral problems, and physical consequences. Refer to Table 5.3 for a summary of possible negative effects associated with child neglect.

Social Difficulties

One of the most often cited problems associated with neglect is difficulty in social skills and adjustment. As evidence of social difficulties, a number of studies have revealed a relationship between neglect and disturbed patterns of infant-caretaker attachment (e.g., Bousha & Twentyman, 1984; Crittenden, 1992; Egeland & Sroufe, 1981). Egeland and colleagues (Egeland & Sroufe, 1981; Egeland et al., 1983; Erickson & Egeland, 1996) are conducting the Minnesota Mother-Child Project, a longitudinal study in which 267 women (and their children) are periodically assessed beginning in the last trimester of pregnancy and continuing through elementary school. Four maltreatment groups were identified including physical abuse, verbal abuse, emotional neglect (psychological unavailability), and neglect, as well as a control group of nonmaltreated children. The children and their mothers participated in a series of situations to assess the developmental consequences of maltreatment. Evaluation during the first 2 years of life focused on the quality of attachment between the mother and child. Investigators observed the mother-infant pairs during several interactions including feeding and play situations, a stressful situation in which a stranger was introduced into the environment, and a problem-solving task. Results indicated that a significantly higher proportion of neglected children were anxiously attached (e.g., overly dependent, clingy, and prone to crying) at both 12 and 18 months than children in the control group. In addition, the social difficulties these children experienced continued throughout elementary school (Erickson & Egeland, 1996).

Other indications of disturbed parent-child interactions have appeared, demonstrating the deficits in communication, increased aggression, and poor involvement characteristic of the interactions between neglecting mothers and their children (Bousha & Twentyman, 1984; Christopoulos, Bonvillian, & Crittenden, 1988; Crittenden, 1992). Additional research has also revealed other areas of social maladjustment in victims of child neglect such as socially withdrawn behavior and decreased prosocial behavior (Crittenden, 1992; Hoffman-Plotkin & Twentyman, 1984; Prino & Peyrot, 1994).

TABLE 5.3 Possible Negative Effects Associated With Child Neglect

Social difficulties
- Disturbed parent-child attachment
- Disturbed parent-child interactions
  - Child is passive, shows deficits in prosocial behaviors and communication, and displays physical aggression
  - Parent exhibits less sensitivity, appears more withdrawn and uninvolved, uses less general speech and phrases of acceptance, uses more direct imperatives, has or displays low rates of social interaction and verbal instruction
- Disturbed peer interactions such as deficits in prosocial behavior, social withdrawal, and isolation

Intellectual deficits
- Receptive and expressive language deficits
- Academic problems
- Intellectual delays
- Lower levels of overall intelligence
- Less creative and flexible in problem solving
- Deficits in language comprehension and verbal abilities

Emotional and behavioral problems
- Apathy and withdrawal
- Low self-esteem
- Ineffective coping
- Physical and verbal aggression
- General behavior problems
- Negative affect (e.g., anger, frustration)
- Conduct disorder
- Psychiatric symptoms

Physical consequences
- Death
- Failure to thrive

SOURCE: Information for this table was obtained from the following references, which are representative but not exhaustive: Bousha & Twentyman (1984); Christopoulos, Bonvillian, & Crittenden (1988); Crittenden (1992); de Paul & Arruabarrena (1995); Egeland & Sroufe (1981); Egeland, Sroufe, & Erickson (1983); Erickson & Egeland (1996); Prino & Peyrot (1994); Williamson, Borduin, & Howe (1991); Wodarski, Kurtz, Gaudin, & Howing (1990).

Intellectual Deficits

An additional area of functioning affected by neglect is intellectual ability. A large group of studies comparing neglected children and adolescents to matched comparison groups have indicated that neglect victims show deficits in language abilities, academic skills, intelligence, and problem-solving skills (e.g., Egeland et al., 1983; Hoffman-Plotkin & Twentyman, 1984; Wodarski et al., 1990). Wodarski and colleagues, for example, evaluated 139 school-age and adolescent physically abused, neglected, and nonmaltreated children and found that both neglected and abused children evidenced significantly poorer overall school performance and math skills. The neglected children, but not the abused children, also obtained lower language and reading skills scores than the group of nonmaltreated children. These intellectual deficits continued even after the researchers controlled the influence of socioeconomic disadvantage.

Emotional and Behavioral Problems

Emotional and behavioral difficulties are an additional area of maladjustment frequently found in neglect victims. Studies have demonstrated that neglectful mothers rate their children as having more behavior problems in general compared with nonmaltreating mothers (Erickson & Egeland, 1996; Rohrbeck & Twentyman, 1986; Williamson et al., 1991). Researchers have also documented differences in specific behavioral and emotional problems in neglected preschool and school-age children compared with controls (e.g., Bousha & Twentyman, 1984; de Paul & Arruabarrena, 1995; Williamson et al., 1991). In summarizing the findings of their longitudinal research on physically and emotionally abused and neglected children, Egeland et al. (1983) made the following conclusion about the neglect group: "This is an unhappy group of children, presenting the least positive and the most negative affect of all groups . . . and in general did not have the skills necessary to cope with various situations" (p. 469).

> The most serious physical consequence of child neglect is death.

In contrast, other researchers have failed to find differences in adjustment between neglected and nonmaltreated children when evaluating behavioral and emotional difficulties (e.g., Rohrbeck & Twentyman, 1986; Wodarski et al., 1990). These conflicting findings demonstrate the difficult and complex nature of studying effects associated with child neglect. One reason for the conflicting findings could be due to sampling variability. Studies that do not find differences in adjustment between neglected and nonmaltreated children could be composed of less severely neglected children than studies that find such differences. Studies that do find differences in adjustment between neglected and nonmaltreated children, on the other hand, may also be biased. Differences found between groups could be because neglected children are from low socioeconomic groups, which experience more environmental stress. The behavioral differences could be due to SES, rather than neglect per se. Wodarski and colleagues (1990), for example, found no differences between neglected and nonmaltreated children on measures of overall behavioral functioning as well as specific behaviors (e.g., self-concept, aggression, self-help skills, and delinquency) after controlling for SES.

Physical Consequences

A final consequence associated with child neglect includes physical effects. The most serious physical consequence of child neglect, of course, is death. In 1996, an estimated 1,185 children died from child abuse and neglect. Of these, approximately 43% died from child neglect (Wang & Daro, 1998). An additional physical consequence often associated with neglect is failure to thrive (FTT), a syndrome characterized by marked retardation or cessation of growth during the first 3 years of life (Kempe, Cutler, & Dean, 1980). Because FTT also includes nonphysical components, its designation as a consequence of physical neglect versus psychological maltreatment is controversial (see Box 5.2, "Failure to Thrive").

BOX 5.2 Failure to Thrive

One of the most extreme consequences of child maltreatment is a clinical disorder known as *failure to thrive* (FTT). The term was initially coined to describe infants and young children hospitalized or living in institutions in the early 1900s. Such children were described as exhibiting marked deficits in growth as well as abnormal behaviors such as withdrawal, apathy, excessive sleep, unhappy facial expressions, and self-stimulatory behaviors including body rocking or head banging (e.g., Bakwin, 1949; Kempe & Goldbloom, 1987; Spitz, 1945). Some cases of FTT are organic in nature, resulting from diseases such as kidney or heart disease. More controversial are FTT cases believed to be nonorganic in nature, resulting from "psychosocial diseases" such as physical neglect and psychological maltreatment.

Although most experts agree that nonorganic FTT results from psychosocial difficulties that reduce caloric intake, the nature of the psychosocial difficulties has been the subject of considerable debate. Some focus on the physical aspects of the syndrome, such as the lack of nutrients, and therefore view FTT as primarily a medical condition resulting from physical child neglect (e.g., inadequate food and nutrition). The physical aspects of FTT have been operationalized as height and weight gain below the third percentile on standardized growth charts of expected development (e.g., Lacey & Parkin, 1974). FTT has traditionally been viewed as a physical or medical condition because the physical problems associated with the syndrome (e.g., malnutrition) often bring the child to the attention of medical professionals.

Others, however, focus on the psychological aspects of FTT, such as isolation and the lack of stimulation in the child's environment, and therefore view FTT as primarily a psychological condition resulting from psychological neglect. The psychological aspects of FTT have been operationalized in the *Diagnostic and Statistical Manual of Mental Disorders* (*DSM-IV;* American Psychiatric Association, 1994), which uses the term *reactive attachment disorder of infancy or early childhood* to describe the behavioral consequences associated with FTT. Reactive attachment disorder is defined as follows:

> The essential feature of Reactive Attachment Disorder is markedly disturbed and developmentally inappropriate social relatedness in most contexts that begins before the age of 5 and is associated with grossly pathological care. The child shows a pattern of excessively inhibited, hypervigilant, or ambivalent responses (e.g., frozen watchfulness, resistance to comfort, or a mixture of approach and avoidance). (p. 116)

Numerous studies have demonstrated a relationship between nonorganic FTT and maternal deprivation or disturbed mother-infant interactions. Studies evaluating differences between nonorganic FTT infants and normally developing infants have found that the interactions between FTT children and their mothers are characterized by deficits in attachment, sensitivity toward the child, and degree of comfort between mother and child (Ayoub & Milner, 1985; Haynes, Cutler, Gray, O'Keefe, & Kempe, 1983; Hegar & Yungman, 1989). Drotar, Eckerle, Satola, Pallotta, and Wyatt (1990) also found that mothers of nonorganic FTT infants demonstrated less adaptive social interactional behavior, less positive affect, and more arbitrary terminations of feedings. Kempe and Goldbloom (1987) have described additional characteristics of FTT parent-child dyads. In feeding situations, for example, mothers may ignore the child's hunger and instead initiate play. In addition, mothers may misinterpret the child's refusal of food as defiance rather than as a sign of satiation. During play situations, mothers may be socially withdrawn (e.g., failing to look at or smile at the child) or refuse to interact with the child (e.g., placing the child in his or her crib).

Theoretical and research advances in the field have broadened conceptual understanding of nonorganic FTT. Kempe and Goldbloom (1987) have argued that the term *nonorganic FTT* should be dropped and replaced with *malnutrition due to neglect* to direct professionals to "more precise descriptions of deficits in nutrition and growth, weight and height levels, and the individual developmental and behavioral characteristics of a given child" (p. 312). Others have likewise argued the importance of a diversity of interacting factors in nonorganic FTT, including environmental variables related to feeding and nurturance in addition to organic factors (Ayoub & Milner, 1985; Hathaway, 1989; Lachenmeyer & Davidovicz, 1987). Although most studies investigating FTT have focused on mothers as parents, research suggests that fathers also play a significant role and that parental deprivation characterizes the family dynamics of nonorganic FTT (Gagan, Cupoli, & Watkins, 1984). A broader conceptual perspective should focus treatment efforts not only on enhancing a child's nutritional status and improving the parent-child relationship but on additional environmental variables as well.

SECTION SUMMARY

Although child neglect is not a new form of child maltreatment, traditionally it has not received as much attention, socially or empirically, as sexual and physical child abuse. Reasons for this disinterest might be because *neglect issues "seem less deviant"* than PCA or CSA and because of *reluctance by professionals to judge or blame* parents (especially in cases of poverty). Difficulties in *defining and identifying child neglect* have also contributed to the lack of attention toward this form of child maltreatment.

Current research efforts concentrate on defining the problem, both conceptually and operationally. Most experts agree that conceptually, child neglect refers to deficits in the provision of a child's *basic needs* (e.g., health care, nutrition, and supervision). Many experts have formulated a number of typologies of neglect in an effort to operationalize precisely what is meant by basic needs. Current typologies include physical, educational, developmental, and emotional neglect. Researchers have also emphasized the need to incorporate several characteristics of neglect into current definitions, such as the severity, frequency and duration, and community and cultural (e.g., socioeconomic) aspects of the neglecting situation. Despite considerable efforts, little consensus exists regarding the best definition for child neglect.

The true incidence of child neglect is unknown because of the many *inherent methodological problems* in trying to study rates of child maltreatment (e.g., reporting biases, definitional variability, and failure to differentiate among subtypes of neglect). Despite these difficulties, it is clear that hundreds of thousands of children are reported for child neglect each year—so many children that child neglect is the most frequently reported form of child maltreatment, accounting for 52% to 55% of reported maltreatment cases.

Official estimates of child neglect, despite their limitations, provide most of the available information on the subject. Research has demonstrated that the majority of children reported for neglect are under the age of 5 and that the risk for child neglect and the severity of neglect generally decrease with age. The importance of gender differences is not supported by the research, nor is there a clear pattern of the role of racial differences because of the existence of confounding factors such as SES and methodological difficulties. The strongest predictor of child neglect is *economic disadvantage,* because low-income children, children of unemployed parents, and children residing in a single-female-headed household are at greatest risk.

Relative to other forms of maltreatment, less research has examined the unique effects of child neglect on children's functioning, although an increasing number of methodologically sound investigations are appearing. Available research to date suggests that child neglect is associated with a variety of problems including *social difficulties* (e.g., disturbed parent-child interactions and socially withdrawn behavior), *intellectual deficits* (e.g., in language abilities, problem-solving skills, and academic skills), *behavioral and emotional problems* (e.g., low self-esteem and aggression), and *physical dysfunction* (e.g., failure to thrive). Specifically, studies have shown that very young children are adversely affected by maltreating mothers who are physically abusive, hostile or verbally abusive, or psychologically unavailable. Future studies should attend to additional variables potentially associated with child neglect outcome, such as the victim's age and gender, the severity of neglect, and various subtypes of neglect (Crouch & Milner, 1993). Research is also needed to evaluate the potential long-term effects of child neglect.

PSYCHOLOGICAL MALTREATMENT

- A mother locks her 3-year-old son in a dark attic as a method of punishment.
- A parent makes the following statement: "Amy, you are the most stupid, lazy kid on earth. I can't believe you're my child. They must have switched babies on me at the hospital."

- A father threatens his son by telling him that he will kill his new puppy if he misbehaves.
- A parent refuses to look at or touch his or her child.

Most individuals have witnessed interactions between a parent and a child that seem inappropriate. The children depicted in the scenarios above may not be physically or sexually abused. They may not be neglected. Despite the lack of overt physical aggression, sexual behavior, or physical signs of maltreatment, however, most people probably view this behavior as wrong or, at the least, less than optimal. Examples such as these have led researchers into a discussion of an additional form of child maltreatment: *psychological maltreatment.*

> Professionals have tended to marginalize psychological maltreatment.

Several authors are now suggesting that psychological maltreatment may be the most destructive and pervasive form of maltreatment (Brassard, Germain, & Hart, 1987; Garbarino, Guttman, & Seely, 1986). Imagine the potential consequences to children who grow up hearing that they are worthless or stupid or ugly. Or consider the potential damage to a child who is rejected by parents who refuse to demonstrate love through physical affection. In what has become known as the Thomas theorem, famed social psychologist W. I. Thomas once concluded, *Situations defined as real are real in their consequences* (Thomas & Thomas, 1928). In other words, if a child regularly hears that he is worthless, stupid, unlovable, or ugly, he will come to believe it. After all, sociologists and psychologists have discovered that individuals perceive themselves as others see them. Perhaps even more tragic, the child may begin to *act* as though she is worthless, stupid, unlovable, or ugly.

Historically, professionals have tended to marginalize psychological maltreatment in much the same way as they have marginalized neglect. Professionals have viewed psychological maltreatment as a side effect of other forms of abuse and neglect, rather than as a unique form of child maltreatment. Some reasons why psychological maltreatment may often be overlooked were recently articulated by O'Hagan (1993), who stated that psychological maltreatment is "slow and protracted, will create no stir, pose no threat of scandal nor media scrutiny, and has little political significance for the managers of child care bureaucracies" (p. 15).

Community surveys, however, indicate that the public is concerned about this type of maltreatment. The National Center for Prosecution of Child Abuse, for example, conducted a nationally representative public opinion poll between 1987 and 1992 and found that approximately 75% of adults who were surveyed during this 6-year period viewed "repeated yelling and swearing" at children as harmful to their well-being (Daro & Gelles, 1992). Within the past decade, psychological maltreatment has been increasingly recognized as worthy of scientific study as a form of child maltreatment existing as a discrete form (see Hart & Brassard, 1993; Loring, 1994; Wiehe, 1990).

Scope of the Problem

What Is Psychological Maltreatment?

Psychological maltreatment may be the most ambiguous form of child abuse (Daro, 1988). We speculate that nearly all parents, at some level, psychologically mistreat their children at some time by saying or doing hurtful things they later regret. Such mistakes are a characteristic of most intimate relationships. Few assert, however, that most children are "victims" of psychological maltreatment. How, then, does one determine when psychological maltreatment has occurred? Which verbal interactions are abusive, which behaviors are psychologically neglecting, and which interactions are a necessary part of parenting?

Conceptual Issues. Professionals have proposed many conceptual definitions for psychological maltreatment to guide research, clinical practice, and social policy. One generic definition offered by Hart et al. (1996) states that psychological maltreatment is a "repeated pattern of behavior that conveys to children that they are worthless, unloved, unwanted, only of value in meeting another's needs, or seriously threatened with physical or psychological violence" (p. 73). Much disagreement exists, however, about how to operationally define psychological maltreatment. This inconsistency stems, in part, from the variety of purposes for using definitions of psychological maltreatment (e.g., to make legal decisions, for conducting interventions with victims, and to determine incidence figures). As a result, there is much debate and confusion in the literature regarding what exactly constitutes psychological maltreatment.

> Psychological maltreatment may be the most difficult form of child maltreatment to define.

Some researchers offer broad definitions and argue that psychological maltreatment is pervasive. Some have suggested that psychological maltreatment is embedded in all major forms of child abuse and neglect (Garbarino et al., 1986; Hart et al., 1996; Hart, Germain, & Brassard, 1987). Others have suggested even broader definitions to include ecological factors such as racism, sexism, and war zone environments (Hart et al., 1987; Jones & Jones, 1987). Such broad definitions are clearly problematic because in the worst case, everyone is a victim of psychological maltreatment, and, at best, such definitions fail to distinguish psychological maltreatment as a unique form of child maltreatment. Other authors define psychological maltreatment more narrowly, focusing on specific abusive behaviors on the part of adults (e.g., repeatedly swearing at a child), which naturally leads to the identification of less abuse in society (e.g., American Humane Association, 1981). Several experts have recommended that the term *psychological maltreatment* be reserved for only the most extreme and severe parental behaviors that result in psychological damage to the child (Hart et al., 1996).

At the core of conceptual problems in defining psychological maltreatment is a lack of clarity in what is meant by the term *psychological.* There has been a great deal of confusion in the literature regarding whether this word refers to behavior on the part of perpetrators or to the consequences that result for the child victim. McGee and Wolfe (1991) proposed a matrix to explain the multiple conceptual perspectives emphasized by experts about psychological maltreatment. Table 5.4 displays a modified version of the matrix, which shows various combinations and possibilities, depending on the type of parent behavior and the consequences to the child.

In this matrix, parent behaviors can be physical or nonphysical and can result in either physical or nonphysical (e.g., psychological) consequences to the child. When parent behaviors are physical and result in physical consequences (e.g., touching a child with a cigarette that results in a burn), such a scenario illustrates a commonly accepted conceptualization of physical child abuse (McGee & Wolfe, 1991). According to McGee and Wolfe, researchers have defined psychological maltreatment using the remaining combinations of parenting behaviors and psychological outcomes. When a parent engages in physical behavior (e.g., touching a child with a cigarette) that results in physical as well as nonphysical outcomes (e.g., anxiety and fear), some have included this situation as psychological maltreatment (e.g., Garbarino et al., 1986). On the basis of this model, additional physical behaviors carried out by parents such as sexual abuse or physical neglect that results in negative psychological outcomes would also be considered psychological maltreatment.

In contrast, some parental behaviors can be nonphysical in nature and result in either physical or nonphysical harm to the child. Insensitive parenting (e.g., not responding to a child's needs for nurturance and attention), for example, has been linked to both physical (e.g., malnutrition; Lacey & Parkin, 1974) and nonphysical (e.g., cognitive development; Egeland et al., 1983) outcomes. The combination of nonphysical parental behavior (e.g., swearing at a child) and nonphysical outcomes (e.g., decreased self-esteem) reflects the conceptualization of psychological maltreatment as a distinct or "pure" form of child maltreatment (Garbarino et al., 1986; McGee & Wolfe, 1991).

McGee and Wolfe (1991) argue that psychological maltreatment should be defined primarily on the basis of specific parental behaviors, rather than on the effects these behaviors may produce. Others have supported this approach but emphasize the need to consider secondarily the effect of maltreatment (Hart & Brassard, 1991). It might be difficult to define psychological maltreatment, for example, in the absence of its effects on the child victim given that parental behaviors lie on a continuum. Although not all parental behaviors consisting of criticism are abusive, some may be. One way to distinguish between abusive and nonabusive behaviors might be to consider the behavior's negative effect on development. Effects on child functioning, however, need to be determined by research, as do additional variables such as the specific characteristics of neglecting behaviors (e.g., frequency, intensity, and duration; Hart & Brassard, 1991; McGee & Wolfe, 1991).

TABLE 5.4 Conceptual Perspectives on Psychological Maltreatment

	Parent Behaviors	
Consequences to the Child	*Physical*	*Nonphysical*
Physical	Physical abuse	Psychological maltreatment
Nonphysical	Psychological maltreatment	Psychological maltreatment

SOURCE: Modified from "Psychological Maltreatment: Toward an Operational Definition," p. 5, by R. A. McGee and D. A. Wolfe, 1991, *Development and Psychopathology, 3,* 3-18.

Subtypes of Psychological Maltreatment. In an effort to define specific parental behaviors more precisely, several authors have developed organizational frameworks that identify various subtypes of psychological maltreatment (e.g., Baily & Baily, 1986; Garbarino et al., 1986; Hart & Brassard, 1991; O'Hagan, 1995). Table 5.5 summarizes the various subtypes of psychological maltreatment reported in the literature. Eight forms of psychological maltreatment have been consistently identified: (a) rejecting, (b) degrading (i.e., verbal abuse), (c) terrorizing, (d) isolating, (e) missocializing (i.e., corrupting), (f) exploiting, (g) denying emotional responsiveness (i.e., ignoring), and (h) close confinement.

An example of an organizational framework is the typological system provided in the NIS-3 (Sedlak & Broadhurst, 1996), which distinguished between forms of psychological maltreatment (see Table 2.1 of Chapter 2 for the definitions of psychological maltreatment employed in NIS-3). Psychological abuse (referred to as emotional abuse in the study) included a variety of behaviors such as close confinement and verbal or emotional assault, as well as miscellaneous behaviors. Close confinement referred to torturous restriction of movement such as tying a child's limbs together or tying a child to an object, such as furniture. Verbal or emotional assault included such behaviors as belittling, denigrating, threatening harm, and other forms of hostile or rejecting treatment. Other miscellaneous behaviors included extreme forms of punishment (e.g., withholding food or sleep) and economic exploitation (e.g., prostitution). Psychological neglect in NIS-3 (referred to as emotional neglect) included a variety of behaviors ranging from inadequate nurturance and affection to permitted drug or alcohol abuse. In addition, psychological neglect was also defined as witnessing extreme or chronic domestic violence, permitting maladaptive behavior (e.g., chronic delinquency), and refusal or delay in obtaining needed psychological treatment.

The typologies in Table 5.5 illustrate the subjective nature of definitions of psychological maltreatment. Definitions and typological systems represent a compilation of the various behaviors and circumstances that have been identified by researchers in the field. As such, these conceptualizations reflect the values of those who created them, with various advocates and researchers determining the types of parent-child interactions that "should be" considered inappropriate. For example, "refusing to help a child" may be abusive in the eyes of a particular

TABLE 5.5 Subtypes of Psychological Maltreatment

Type	*Description*	*Example*
Rejecting	Verbal or symbolic acts that express feelings of rejection toward the child	Singling out a specific child for criticism and/or punishment Refusing to help a child Routinely rejecting a child's ideas
Degrading (i.e., verbal abuse)	Actions that deprecate a child	Insulting a child (calling a child names) Publicly humiliating a child Constantly criticizing a child Continually yelling or swearing at a child
Terrorizing	Actions or threats that cause extreme fear and/or anxiety in a child	Threatening to harm a child Threatening to harm a loved one Witnessing spouse abuse Setting unrealistic expectations with threat of loss/harm Punishing a child by playing on normal childhood fears Threatening suicide or to leave child
Isolating	Preventing the child from engaging in normal social activities	Locking a child in a closet or room Refusing interactions with individuals outside family Refusing interactions with other relatives
Missocializing (i.e., corrupting)	Modeling, permitting, or encouraging antisocial behavior	Encouraging delinquent behavior Encouraging alcohol or substance abuse Indoctrinating racist values

researcher but may be seen as important in helping a child gain independence from a parent's perspective.

McGee and Wolfe (1991) recently outlined several other criticisms of current typological systems. Psychological maltreatment subtypes, they argue, are not inclusive of all potentially psychologically abusive and neglectful behavior. Inconsistent parenting practices, for example, have not been included in typologies of psychological maltreatment despite their detrimental effects on a child's development. Another problem with classification systems is that the subtypes are not mutually exclusive: One behavior can be considered under more than one subtype. Insulting a child by shouting "You're nothing but a fat, lazy pig!", for example, could be considered not only as an act of degrading but also as an act of rejecting. A final criticism levied against typological systems is that these subtypes are sometimes defined by their outcomes. *Corrupting,* for example, is defined as stimulating the child to engage in destructive and antisocial behavior.

Research is beginning to address some of the problems associated with typological systems. Hart and Brassard (1991) have described five subtypes of

TABLE 5.5 Continued

Type	*Description*	*Example*
Exploiting	Using a child for the needs, advantages, or profits of the caretaker	Treating a child as a surrogate parent Using a child for child pornography or prostitution Using a child to live the parent's unfulfilled dreams
Denying emotional responsiveness (i.e., ignoring)	Acts of omission whereby caretaker does not provide necessary stimulation and responsiveness	Caretaker is detached and uninvolved with child Caretaker interacts with child only if absolutely necessary Failing to express affection, caring, and love toward child Does not look at child or call by name
Close confinement	Restricting a child's movement by binding limbs	Tying a child's arms and legs together Tying a child to a chair, bed, or other object
Other	Types of emotional maltreatment not specified under other categories	Withholding food, shelter, sleep, or other necessities as a form of punishment Chronically applying developmentally inappropriate expectations (sometimes referred to as overpressuring)

SOURCE: Information for this table was obtained from the following references, which are representative but not exhaustive: Baily & Baily (1986); Department of Health and Human Services (1988); Garbarino, Guttman, & Seely (1986); Hart & Brassard (1991); Hart, Germain, & Brassard (1987).

psychological maltreatment that have been empirically validated: spurning (verbal statements of rejection and hostile degradation), terrorizing, isolating, exploiting or corrupting, and denying emotional responsiveness. Other research has demonstrated empirical distinctions between broader subtypes of maltreatment (e.g., psychological abuse vs. psychological neglect; Brassard, Hart, & Hardy, 1993; Crittenden, 1990). In addition, some research has failed to confirm specific subtypes as distinct categories of psychological maltreatment. Hart and Brassard (1991), for example, reported that rejection is a component of both spurning and denying emotional responsiveness, rather than a unique form of psychological maltreatment.

Legal Issues. State reporting statutes do not always specifically cover psychological maltreatment, although most state statutes include some reference to the concept (see Chapter 1 boxed insert: "California Penal Code and Child Maltreatment"). The 1974 Child Abuse Prevention and Treatment Act refers to psychological maltreatment as "mental injury" and delegates the responsibility of more specific definitions to each individual state.

Most state definitions emphasize harm to the child rather than focusing on parental actions. Pennsylvania, for example, provides a specific and narrow definition for its category of "serious mental injury": "a psychological condition . . . caused by acts of omission . . . which render the child chronically sick and severely anxious, agitated, depressed, socially withdrawn, psychotic, or in fear that his/her life is threatened" (quoted in Garbarino et al., 1986). The state of Oregon added mental injury, more broadly defined, to its child abuse reporting law in 1985. This law states that any mental injury to a child shall include only observable and substantial impairment of the child's mental or psychological ability to function caused by cruelty to the child, with due regard to the culture of the child (ORS 418.740).

These legal statutes further illustrate the problems associated with defining psychological maltreatment, because the law generally requires that a given act result in identifiable harm. "It will not suffice for a reporter to imagine a child might possibly be injured later by a particular course of parental behavior" (State of Oregon Children's Services Division, 1991, p. 4). The effects of psychological maltreatment, however, may only rarely be identifiable, or they may be identifiable only after years of maltreatment.

Estimates of Psychological Maltreatment

Given the definitional complexities described above, it should be clear that the actual rate of psychological maltreatment is unknown. Despite definitional problems, several studies have attempted to investigate the scope of the problem.

Official Estimates. National reporting statistics have consistently demonstrated that psychological maltreatment is the least common form of reported and substantiated maltreatment. Estimates vary, however, and are influenced by definitional and methodological variability across studies. The AAPC (1988) found that psychological maltreatment (defined as *emotional maltreatment*) accounted for approximately 8% of all official reports of child maltreatment in 1986. Data from the National Center on Child Abuse and Neglect indicated that psychological maltreatment accounted for 6% of reported child maltreatment cases (DHHS, 1998). The most recent statistics available indicate that 4% of reported cases consist of psychological maltreatment as the primary (distinct from physical abuse, child neglect, etc.) form of abuse (Wang & Daro, 1998).

The National Incidence Studies (DHHS, 1981, 1988; Sedlak & Broadhurst, 1996) have obtained the highest rates for psychological maltreatment. In the NIS-2, the 391,100 reported cases of psychological maltreatment (including psychological abuse and emotional neglect) accounted for 28% of all cases of child maltreatment (Sedlak, 1990). NIS data indicate that between 1980 and 1986, the rate of psychological abuse increased by 43%, and the rate of emotional neglect more than doubled. Results of NIS-3 indicated that the rate of both psychological abuse and emotional neglect nearly tripled between 1986 and 1993

(Sedlak & Broadhurst, 1996). As is true for child neglect reports, rates of psychological maltreatment are higher when definitions are broadened to include potential harm.

As with other forms of child maltreatment, many professionals believe that psychological maltreatment is underreported. Although psychological maltreatment is the least common form of child maltreatment reported to protective service agencies, it is the most commonly reported form of child maltreatment among families involved in therapeutic treatment programs for child abuse and neglect (Daro, 1988). One reason that psychological maltreatment may be underreported is because its effects are rarely visible or immediate. In addition, psychological maltreatment has only recently been recognized as a reportable form of child maltreatment. As a result, many individuals in a position to report it may fail to do so because they do not define questionable parental behaviors as psychological maltreatment. Another reason to suspect underreporting is because psychological maltreatment often co-occurs with other forms of abuse (Claussen & Crittenden, 1991). That psychological maltreatment is the least reported may reflect nothing more than that it is not usually the most visible form of abuse experienced by a particular child.

Self-Report Surveys. Daro and Gelles (1992) reported on the parenting practices of a nationally representative sample of 1,250 parents surveyed each year between 1988 and 1992. Although rates fluctuated during the 6 years of data collection, 45% of parents reported insulting or swearing at their children in 1992.

Analysis of data from the second National Family Violence Survey provides additional information on self-report estimates of psychological maltreatment (Vissing, Straus, Gelles, & Harrop, 1991). Psychological maltreatment included both verbal (e.g., insulting or swearing) and nonverbal (e.g., sulking or refusing to talk) forms of interaction with a child. Results indicated that approximately 63% of parents reported using one of these forms of interaction with their children at least once during the past year. Vissing et al. also attempted to determine the frequency of these types of interactions and found that the average number of instances was 12.6 per year, with approximately 21% reporting more than 20 instances.

Parent self-reports of psychological maltreatment were even higher in a nationally representative sample of parents using the Parent-Child Conflict Tactics Scales (CTSPC; Straus et al., 1998). Straus and colleagues found that approximately 86% of parents reported using some form of psychological aggression (e.g., yelling, screaming or shouting, using threats, and swearing) at least once during the past year (see Table 2.1 of Chapter 2 for the list of psychological aggression items). Among parents who reported engaging in such behavior, parents reported using this behavior an average of 22 times during the preceding 12 months. The most common forms of psychological aggression used by parents in this study included shouting, yelling, or screaming at the child. In addition, psychological aggression was almost as common in their sample of parents as nonviolent means of discipline such as distraction or time-outs.

Searching for Patterns: Characteristics of Victims

Most of the available information about sociodemographic characteristics of psychological maltreatment victims comes from official reports made to CPS agencies. Because only a small percentage of psychological maltreatment cases are reported, however, knowledge about sociodemographic characteristics of psychological maltreatment victims is tentative at best.

Age and Gender

Findings from the NIS-2, with its broad definition of psychological maltreatment, found no association between psychological maltreatment and age (DHHS, 1988). The most recent data from the National Center on Child Abuse and Neglect, however, indicated that reports of psychological maltreatment increased with child age (DHHS, 1998). Official estimates also indicate gender differences associated with rates of psychological maltreatment with girls (53%) slightly more at risk than boys (47%) (DHHS, 1998).

Other Risk Factors

Researchers have also demonstrated a link between psychological maltreatment and other risk factors, such as the child's race or ethnicity and his or her family's income (AAPC, 1988; Jones & McCurdy, 1992). Victims of child maltreatment are more likely to be Caucasian relative to other forms of abuse. Caucasians account for 77% of psychological maltreatment cases and 67% of other forms of abuse (AAPC, 1988). Both the NIS-2 and NIS-3 also found an association between economic factors and psychological maltreatment. In both studies, lower-income families (i.e., yearly income less than $15,000) were significantly more likely to be characterized by psychological maltreatment (defined as *emotional abuse*) than higher-income families (Sedlak & Broadhurst, 1996).

Consequences Associated With Psychological Maltreatment

Both researchers and clinical practitioners have speculated about the potential short- and long-term consequences of psychological maltreatment, such as antisocial behaviors, depression, withdrawal, and low self-esteem (e.g., Gross & Keller, 1992). Descriptive clinical and case study research appears to confirm many of these difficulties, although methodologically sound research in this area is lacking (Cabrino, 1978; Kavanagh, 1982).

Many of the same methodological problems encountered in studying the effects of other forms of child maltreatment (e.g., lack of standardized definitions) also plague the research investigating the negative effects of psychological

TABLE 5.6 Possible Negative Effects Associated With Psychological Maltreatment

Interpersonal maladjustment
Insecure attachment to caregiver
Low social competence and adjustment
Few friends
Difficulties with peers
Intellectual deficits
Academic problems
Lower educational achievement
Deficits in cognitive ability
Deficits in problem solving
Lack of creativity
Affective-behavioral problems
Aggression
Disruptive classroom behavior
Self-abusive behavior
Anxiety
Shame and guilt
Hostility and anger
Pessimism and negativity
Dependent on adults for help, support, and nurturance

SOURCE: Information for this table was obtained from the following references, which are representative but not exhaustive: Brassard, Hart, & Hardy (1991); Claussen & Crittenden (1991); Crittenden & Ainsworth (1989); Egeland (1991); Erickson & Egeland (1987); Erickson, Egeland, & Pianta (1989); Hoglund & Nicholas (1995); Kent & Waller (1998); Vissing, Straus, Gelles, & Harrop (1991).

maltreatment. The use of samples of individuals experiencing multiple forms of abuse has also contributed to confusion in interpreting results. Despite these problems, some progress has been made in assessing the negative initial and long-term effects associated with psychological maltreatment.

Initial Effects

The short-term effects associated with psychological maltreatment receiving consistent empirical support are listed in Table 5.6. They include interpersonal maladjustment, intellectual deficits, and affective-behavioral problems.

In the interpersonal realm, researchers have documented maladjustment in psychologically maltreated children in the areas of attachment, social adjustment, and peer relationships. Psychologically maltreated children, for example, are significantly more likely than their nonmaltreated peers to be insecurely attached to a parent (e.g., Crittenden & Ainsworth, 1989; Egeland, 1991). Several investigators have also found that psychologically maltreated children exhibit lower levels of social competence and adjustment (e.g., have trouble making friends) relative to their nonmaltreated counterparts (e.g., Brassard, Hart, & Hardy, 1991; Claussen & Crittenden, 1991; Vissing et al., 1991).

Intellectual deficits also distinguish psychologically maltreated children from controls (e.g., Erickson & Egeland, 1987; Erickson, Egeland, & Pianta, 1989; Hart & Brassard, 1989). In a longitudinal study of educational achievement, researchers found lower achievement in psychologically maltreated children compared with matched controls (Erickson & Egeland, 1987). Other studies have uncovered academic problems and deficits in cognitive ability and problem solving (e.g., Erickson & Egeland, 1987; Erickson et al., 1989).

A final effect of psychological maltreatment includes a variety of affective and behavioral problems. Several studies have substantiated that psychologically maltreated children exhibit significantly more general behavior problems relative to control children (e.g., Hart & Brassard, 1989; Hickox & Furnell, 1989; Vissing et al., 1991). Psychologically maltreated children also demonstrate more specific problems such as aggression, delinquency, disruptive classroom behavior, self-abusive behavior, hostility and anger, and anxiety when compared with control children (e.g., Erickson & Egeland, 1987; Vissing et al., 1991).

Long-Term Effects

A limited number of studies have evaluated the potential long-term effects of psychological maltreatment. The available information indicates that adults who report a childhood history of psychological maltreatment exhibit psychological difficulties. Gross and Keller (1992) evaluated 260 university students identified as physically abused, psychologically abused, both physically and psychologically abused, or nonabused. On standardized instruments, psychologically abused respondents had lower self-esteem scores than nonabused respondents but did not differ significantly on measures of depression and attributional style. Respondents experiencing both physical and psychological abuse, however, exhibited higher levels of depression than nonabused college students or college students with a history of only one type of abuse. Regression analysis also revealed that psychological abuse was a more powerful predictor of depression, self-esteem, and attributional style (attributing outcomes for events to external, unstable, or specific causes) than was physical abuse. Other studies have confirmed the presence of low self-esteem, anxiety, depression, dissociation, and interpersonal sensitivity in adults with a history of psychological maltreatment as well as the central role of psychological maltreatment in predicting the effects of child maltreatment (e.g., Briere & Runtz, 1988, 1990; Downs & Miller, 1998; Hoglund & Nicholas, 1995; Kent & Waller, 1998).

SECTION SUMMARY

Authors have described psychological maltreatment as the most difficult form of child maltreatment to define. Disagreement originates in determining what is meant by the term *psychological.* Some experts emphasize *nonphysical behaviors on the part of adults,* such as failing to respond to a child's needs for nurturance and attention, terrorizing a child, or insulting or swearing at a child. Others focus on the *nonphysical consequences to the child victim* (e.g., "mental injury"), including a variety of emotional and cognitive symptoms such as anxiety and fear. Still other experts define psychological maltreatment broadly, including a combination of physical (e.g., physical neglect or sexual abuse) and nonphysical parental actions that result in negative psychological consequences. Although researchers have devised *numerous subtypes* of psychological maltreatment, significant variability in definitions continues to exist in the field, with little consensus regarding the most appropriate definition.

The *true rate* of psychological maltreatment is difficult to determine and largely unknown. Official estimates derived from reporting agencies indicate that between 4% and 28% of reported cases of child maltreatment are for psychological maltreatment, distinguishing psychological maltreatment as the least reported form of child maltreatment. Some evidence, however, suggests that psychological maltreatment is *underreported.* Self-report surveys also suggest that parents frequently engage in negative behaviors consistent with psychological maltreatment. Researchers have used official reports to study risk factors, with early findings showing no age correlation to psychological maltreatment and few gender differences, yet a significant race, ethnicity, and family income link. The frequency, intensity, duration, and context of maltreating and neglecting behaviors need additional study.

Results from studies evaluating the negative effect of psychological maltreatment should be considered tentative at best. This is an emerging research area, and many of the same methodological problems already discussed (e.g., lack of standardized definitions) apply here also. To date, studies have indicated that psychological maltreatment may result in a variety of problems for the victim that may extend into adulthood.

Negative effects associated with psychological maltreatment in children include difficulties in interpersonal, intellectual, and affective and behavioral realms of functioning. For example, these children demonstrate more problems (e.g., aggression, delinquency, self-abuse, anxiety, hostility, and anger) when compared with control children. Researchers have found similar problems in adults who report a childhood history of psychological maltreatment (e.g., low self-esteem, depression, and interpersonal sensitivity). Future research should attempt to examine the effect of development on the consequences of psychological maltreatment, the effects of psychological maltreatment alone or in combination with other forms of maltreatment, and the distinctive effects associated with various subtypes of psychological maltreatment.

EXPLAINING CHILD NEGLECT AND PSYCHOLOGICAL MALTREATMENT

Experts have applied many of the same theories proposed to explain the physical and sexual abuse of children in their attempts to specify the causes of child neglect and psychological maltreatment. Researchers, for example, have applied ecological, basic human needs, and transactional models (e.g., Belsky, 1980; Hart et al., 1996; Hickox & Furnell, 1989; Zigler & Hall, 1989; Zuravin, 1989) and social learning and intergenerational transmission theories (e.g., Crittenden, 1982; Hickox & Furnell, 1989; Ney, 1989) to child neglect and psychological maltreatment. Causal models have also incorporated characteristics of neglecting and psychologically maltreating parents, as well as parent-child relationships (e.g., Carlson, Cicchetti, Barnett, & Braumwald, 1989; Kneisl, 1991; Pearl, 1994). Because the fields of child neglect and psychological maltreatment are in the beginning stages of research inquiry, limited empirical evidence is available to support specific factors or causal models involved in producing neglectful or psychologically maltreating circumstances. To date, most research in this area has focused on parental characteristics of child neglecting and psychologically maltreating families.

Characteristics of Neglecting Parents

Studies evaluating the characteristics of neglecting parents have examined demographic as well as psychosocial characteristics. With regard to demographic characteristics, the majority of information has been obtained from official reporting statistics. The NIS-3 (Sedlak & Broadhurst, 1996) found that birth parents are the primary perpetrators of child neglect, accounting for 91% of reported cases. The mean age of neglecting parents is 31 years, and the gender distribution indicates that females are significantly more likely than males to be reported for neglect (AAPC, 1988; DHHS, 1996, 1998). The National Center on Child Abuse and Neglect found that females were reported as the perpetrator in 72% of cases (DHHS, 1998). The higher proportion of females reported for neglect may reflect social attitudes that mothers, rather than fathers, are responsible for meeting the needs of children.

Other researchers have examined the psychosocial characteristics of neglecting parents. Most research in this area has attempted to distinguish characteristics of neglectful parents compared with physically abusive parents and nonmaltreating parents. Several studies have evaluated social factors such as the mother's age, the number of children in the family, and educational achievement (e.g., Lujan, DeBruyn, May, & Bird, 1989; Zuravin, 1988b; Zuravin & DiBlasio, 1992). Studies conducted by Zuravin and her colleagues (e.g., Zuravin, 1988b; Zuravin & DiBlasio, 1992) have consistently found that lower educational achievement is associated with neglect. In addition, mothers who have a greater number of children during their teen years or who are younger at the birth of their first child are at increased risk for neglecting their children. Furthermore, teenage mothers whose first child was premature or had a low birth weight were more likely to neglect their children than older mothers whose infants were healthier (Zuravin & DiBlasio, 1992).

Other social factors, including the level of community integration and social support, may play a role in child neglect. Polansky, Ammons, and Gaudin (1985) found that compared with a control group, neglecting mothers were less involved in informal helping networks, exhibited less participation in social activities, and described themselves as more "lonely." Polansky, Gaudin, Ammons, and Davis (1985) investigated the level of social support for neglecting families by interviewing 152 neglecting and 154 nonneglecting families receiving AFDC. The investigators compared responses of families officially designated as neglecting, a control group of nonneglecting AFDC families, and a group of adults who were the next-door neighbors of the neglecting families. Results indicated that neglectful mothers viewed their neighborhood as less supportive than both controls and their next-door neighbors.

Researchers have also investigated the psychological characteristics of neglecting parents compared with abusive parents and nonabusive/nonneglectful parents. Neglectful parents exhibit poor problem-solving skills, intellectual deficits, limited parent-child interaction, and inappropriate developmental expectations for their children (Crittenden, 1988; Crittenden & Bonvillian, 1984; Hansen, Pallotta, Tishelman, Conaway, & MacMillan, 1989; Twentyman & Plotkin, 1982). For example, Twentyman and Plotkin found that neglectful parents' expectations of their children are either too high or too low compared with their nonneglectful counterparts. Additional studies comparing neglecting mothers with controls indicate that neglecting mothers report more depressive symptoms and levels of parental stress (Culp et al., 1989; Ethier et al., 1995; Pianta, Egeland, & Erickson, 1989).

Other studies have investigated the hypothesis that neglecting parents are neglectful because during their childhood they themselves received inadequate parenting. Several studies have reported a childhood history of both neglect and abuse in adults who neglect their children (e.g., C. S. Widom, 1989). It is difficult to determine, however, which form of maltreatment is the likely contributor to the current neglecting behavior. Few studies have examined the intergenerational transmission hypothesis with subject groups who have experienced child neglect only. One exception is Ethier's (1991) study in which she compared the childhood histories of physically abusive mothers with neglectful mothers (cited in Ethier, Palacio-Quintin, & Jourdan-Ionescu, 1992). Results indicated that neglectful mothers were more likely to have been victims of neglect, both physical and emotional.

Characteristics of Psychologically Maltreating Parents

There is little research examining the characteristics of psychologically maltreating parents. As is true for neglecting parents, most of the available demographic information comes from studies evaluating official reporting statistics. The AAPC (1988) found that parents are the primary perpetrators of psychological maltreatment, accounting for 90% of reported cases. The average age of psychologically maltreating parents was 33 years. The gender distribution of reported cases indicates that females (57%) are slightly more likely to be reported for psychological maltreatment than males (43%; DHHS, 1998). With regard to race, the parents of psychologically maltreated children are more likely to be Caucasian than in other forms of child maltreatment (DHHS, 1998).

Studies have examined the psychological characteristics of psychologically maltreating parents. Such parents exhibit more psychosocial problems, more difficulty coping with stress, more difficulty building relationships, and more social isolation compared with nonabusive parents (Pemberton & Benady, 1973). Researchers found similar characteristics in a study evaluating a group of parents legally established as emotionally abusive (Hickox & Furnell, 1989). Hickox and Furnell, for example, found that emotionally abusive parents were characterized by more problem psychosocial and background factors compared with a matched comparison group of parents identified as needing assistance with child care and management. Emotionally abusive parents had more difficulty building relationships, exhibited poor coping skills, and displayed deficits in child management techniques. In addition, emotionally abusive mothers demonstrated a lack of support networks (both personal and community) as well as greater levels of perceived stress, marital discord, and alcohol and drug use.

SECTION SUMMARY

Findings from official statistics that evaluate demographic and psychosocial characteristics of parents in neglecting and emotionally maltreating parents are preliminary and, as a result, should be viewed cautiously. The most consistent findings have been observed in *neglecting mothers,* who are characterized as having low educational achievement, increased levels of stress (e.g., greater numbers of children), inappropriate developmental expectations for their children, and low levels of community involvement and social support. Although fewer studies are available that evaluate psychologically maltreating parents, results suggest that *psychologically maltreating mothers* are more likely to be characterized by problems such as high levels of stress, psychosocial problems, social isolation, and deficits in child management skills. Future studies should attempt to replicate current findings while improving methodology and should also evaluate the characteristics of fathers in neglecting and psychologically maltreating families.

RESPONDING TO CHILD NEGLECT AND PSYCHOLOGICAL MALTREATMENT

Researchers and practitioners have proposed few interventions that are unique to child neglect and psychological maltreatment versus other forms of abuse (for reviews, see Becker et al., 1995; Kolko, 1998). Indeed, many of the interventions described previously (e.g., child protective services, out-of-home placement, economic assistance, therapeutic day care, and multiservice interventions) also apply to child neglect and psychological maltreatment. The paucity of unique research efforts directed at solutions and interventions is particularly true for the field of psychological maltreatment. Some experts have even questioned whether the addition of specific interventions for psychological maltreatment is feasible given the limited success of the already overwhelmed CPS system in meeting the needs of other maltreated groups (Claussen & Crittenden, 1991). As a result, research evaluating intervention approaches unique to psychological maltreatment is nearly nonexistent.

Multiservice intervention approaches are recommended to help psychologically maltreating and neglecting families.

Research directed at interventions specifically for neglected children and their families is less limited, although available studies suffer from a variety of methodological limitations, including single-subject research designs, exceedingly small sample sizes, nonstandardized assessment methods, and biased samples (Gaudin, 1993). In addition, most intervention programs directed at neglect include services for parents, with few direct services for children (Cohn & Daro, 1987; Kolko, 1998). The interventions for children that are available primarily focus on improving social interaction and skills (e.g., Davis & Fantuzzo, 1989; Fantuzzo, Stovall, Schachtel, Goins, & Hall, 1987). There appears to be general consensus among researchers and clinicians in the field that currently available interventions for addressing child neglect are ineffective (Daro, 1988; Gaudin, 1993).

One form of intervention that has shown promise with neglecting families is the parent-directed approach that takes advantage of behavioral techniques to teach neglecting parents specific skills. Lutzker, Lutzker, Braunling-McMorrow, and Eddleman (1987), for example, investigated the use of simple prompts to increase the appropriate affective responses by mothers during parent-child interactions. Mothers who received prompts to increase affective responses demonstrated more affective responses with their children than mothers who received no prompting. Other studies have demonstrated skills improvements in neglecting mothers, including problem-solving skills (Dawson, DeArmas, McGrath, & Kelly, 1986), personal hygiene skills (Lutzker, Campbell, & Watson-Perczel, 1984; Rosenfield-Schlichter, Sarber, Bueno, Greene, & Lutzker, 1983), nutrition skills (Sarber, Halasz, Messmer, Bickett, & Lutzker, 1983), and infant stimulation skills (Lutzker, Megson, Dachman, & Webb, 1985). Neglecting mothers have also learned to reduce the number of hazards in their home (Barone, Greene, & Lutzker, 1986).

Another form of intervention for neglecting families that has proven effective are programs that promote social support (see DePanfilis, 1996, for a review). Although research examining treatment effectiveness is limited, a variety of approaches to enhance the social connections of neglecting families appear promising. Interventions range from programs that teach parents how to establish and maintain their own social support systems to those that provide individual social support in the form of personal parent aides (e.g., DiLeonardi, 1993; Witt & Sheinwald, 1992). Crittenden (1996) has recommended that the limited social competencies of neglectful parents suggest that such services should be delivered by as few individuals as possible for an extended period.

Experts have also recommended multiservice intervention approaches for both psychologically maltreating and neglecting families because they are designed to target the multiproblem nature of such families (Daro, 1988; Fortin & Chamberland, 1995; Lujan et al., 1989). Multiservice interventions typically include the delivery of a broad range of services including combinations of the following: individual, family, and group counseling; social support services; behavioral skills training to eliminate problematic behavior; and parenting education. An example of this type of program is Project SafeCare, which provides a variety of services to families such as safety and accident prevention and the promotion of healthy parent-child interactions (cited in Kolko, 1998).

Evaluation studies of such programs have demonstrated some positive results. The National Center on Child Abuse and Neglect has recently funded a series of multiservice projects directed at chronically neglectful families. Evaluations of these projects have indicated that a combination of parenting groups, intensive in-home counseling, and supportive interventions (e.g., paraprofessional aides) has been effective in improving neglectful parenting practices (Landsman, Nelson, Allen, & Tyler, 1992). Other researchers have found family-focused, multiservice projects to be effective interventions for neglecting families (e.g., Daro, 1988; Lutzker, 1990a; Wesch & Lutzker, 1991). Two recent studies suggest, however, that outcomes for neglecting families are less positive than for abusive families or families of delinquents (Berry, 1991; Yuan & Struckman-Johnson, 1991).

SUMMARY

Child neglect and psychological maltreatment are the two most elusive forms of maltreatment and, as a result, have received less attention. The vague nature of these forms of maltreatment is evident by the observation that a significant proportion of the research directed toward them focuses on definitional issues. At the present, no single definition of child neglect or psychological maltreatment is universally accepted. Although experts generally agree on conceptual definitions of child neglect (i.e., deficits in the provision of a child's basic needs), little consensus exists regarding operational definitions. Establishing the parameters of psychological maltreatment has proved even more difficult and confusing. Researchers disagree about whether definitions should be broad or narrow and about the relative importance of parental behaviors (e.g., swearing at or denigrating a child) versus child outcomes (e.g., mental injury).

Given these definitional complexities, the true incidence of child neglect and psychological maltreatment is largely undetermined, as are the victim characteristics associated with these forms of child maltreatment. Researchers have obtained much of the information about rates and correlates of child neglect and psychological maltreatment from official reports made to CPS. Although such reports are limited (e.g., lack of definitional consensus among researchers), it is clear that hundreds of thousands of children are reported for child neglect and psychological maltreatment each year. Child neglect is the most frequently reported form of child maltreatment, accounting for approximately 52% to 55% of reported cases. Least commonly reported is psychological maltreatment, which accounts for 4% to 28% of reported cases. The majority of child neglect victims are under age 5, with the risk for neglect declining as children become older. Available research does not support an association between age and psychological maltreatment, suggesting that all children are equally vulnerable to this form of maltreatment. Child neglect and psychological maltreatment are similar in that both genders appear to be at equal risk, as are children who come from families experiencing a variety of financial stressors (e.g., low income and unemployment).

Studies examining the negative effects associated with child neglect and psychological maltreatment are limited in both number and quality, making the interpretations of findings difficult. Available research has consistently uncovered a variety of associated problems that are similar for both child neglect and psychological maltreatment. Child victims often demonstrate social difficulties, intellectual deficits, and emotional and behavioral problems. Although many experts believe that the negative effects of child neglect and psychological maltreatment extend into adulthood, more research is needed to establish the relationship between a childhood history of neglect and psychological maltreatment and adjustment problems in adulthood.

In attempting to establish the causes of child neglect and psychological maltreatment, researchers have often applied many of the same theories proposed to explain the physical and sexual abuse of children (e.g., environmental factors, parent-child interaction, and intergenerational transmission). Several studies are appearing that distinguish maltreating from nonmaltreating parents on various characteristics. For both forms of maltreatment, the parent-child interactions are disturbed and parents have increased levels of stress, with few social supports and limited integration into the community. Neglecting parents are also characterized by low educational achievement and tend to become parents at a young age. Further research is needed to determine additional contributing factors given that not all parents with these characteristics maltreat their children.

Few interventions are available to address the unique aspects of child neglect and psychological maltreatment, and as a result, research evaluating the effectiveness of therapy, protective services, and community interventions for victims of these forms of maltreatment is limited. Preliminary efforts directed at neglecting parents have been effective in teaching such parents specific skills such as increasing positive parent-child interactions, improving problem-solving abilities, and enhancing personal hygiene and nutrition skills. Although few direct services are implemented for children, available programs have been successful in improving social interaction and developmental skills. Multiservice intervention approaches designed to target the multiproblem nature of these families are also appearing and demonstrate some effectiveness.

6

Other Forms of Child Maltreatment

CHAPTER OUTLINE

AN INTERVIEW WITH DAVID WOLFE

"While we need to maintain family privacy, we also need to get out the message about the prevalence of abuse in particular neighborhoods and to offer support to parents."

David Wolfe, one of North America's foremost researchers on children exposed to marital violence, is Professor of Psychology and Psychiatry at the University of Western Ontario. He is a diplomate in clinical psychology certified by the American Board of Professional Psychology. He serves on the boards of several organizations, such as the Child Witness Preparation Program. He authored a significant book titled *Child Abuse: Implications for Child Development and Psychopathology.* Along with P. Jaffe and S. Wilson, he coauthored a best-selling family violence book titled *Children of Battered Women.* With C. Wekerle and K. Scott, he coauthored *Alternatives to Violence: Empowering Youth to Develop Healthy Relationships.* He is a member of the editorial boards of several journals, such as *Child Abuse & Neglect, Journal of Family Violence, Journal of Consulting and Clinical Psychology,* and *Journal of Interpersonal Violence.* He is also Past-President of the Division of Child, Youth, and Family of the American Psychological Association. He received his B.A. in psychology from the University of Rochester and his Ph.D. in clinical psychology (with an emphasis in child psychology) from the University of South Florida.

Q: What shaped your approach to the field of children exposed to marital violence?

A: In 1980, I met Peter Jaffe and became active in prevention of child abuse. With grant money, we designed group education and abuse prevention programs for children of battered women. We were interested in the similarities between children who witness violence and those who are abused themselves.

Q: What are your future personal goals?

A: For the next 10 years, at 6-month intervals, I would like to follow the progress of the adolescents we have been treating. We need to evaluate the effectiveness of the education and treatment we have given them. We would then be in a position to specify what changes are needed in education programs to prevent adolescents from becoming the next generation of abusive parents or partners.

Another interest I have is in prenatal education. The roots of child abuse and neglect are often visible before having children. We need to use prenatal screening as a method for identifying parents at high risk for child abuse. We then need to apply a public health model by adopting a referral system to help these at-risk parents obtain medical services and abuse prevention education. Screening could be the first step in starting the referral service.

Q: How can society diminish family violence?

A: We need to focus on cultural values. Family privacy is such a strongly held value that society fails to intervene sufficiently. Abuse is hidden behind closed doors. While we need to maintain family privacy, we also need to get out the message about the prevalence of abuse in particular neighborhoods and to offer support to parents.

Communities need to establish abuse prevention panels made up of volunteer citizens. These groups could establish community centers to assist violent families and recruit volunteers who are willing to go out and talk with their neighbors about abuse. Frequently, women's groups spearhead campaigns to raise community awareness. The media can contribute by providing information about abuse and the locations of agencies where families can get help. The approach needs to be inclusionary, rather than punitive. Isolation of parents and lack of support for parents play key roles in allowing child abuse to continue. Citizen support networks play a crucial role in preventing child abuse by offering a helping hand to abusive parents.

Q: Why can't we as a society seem to eliminate child abuse?

A: It would cost a lot of money, and all our money is tied up in responding to casualties. We spend millions of dollars on the crises caused by abuse—on crime and health costs. It would take a concerted effort to reach and educate those who will repeat the cycle across generations. As a society, we need to begin the prevention process by educating adolescents. A proactive approach to abuse prevention would be very costly initially but very cost-effective in the long run.

Q: How have governmental policies failed to prevent abuse?

A: The outdated views of politicians are one of the biggest stumbling blocks to action. The existing political paradigm can be summed up as, "If it ain't broke, don't fix it." Politicians work in a crisis mode. They allocate funds only for disasters. Politicians do not take the lead in long-range planning.

Since Kempe's initial "discovery" in 1962 that some parents physically abuse their children, awareness of the extent and nature of child maltreatment has been overwhelming. It seems that the more we learn about child maltreatment, the more we realize how complex the issues are and how little we truly understand about this social problem. Up to this point, we have focused on the major forms of child maltreatment that are recognized by most professionals and the general public. The increased awareness in society about physical and sexual abuse, child neglect, and psychological maltreatment has been accompanied by increased concern for children and their well-being more generally. The last 40 years of research have taught us that more children are maltreated than we expected and that this maltreatment takes a variety of forms. The concept of child maltreatment and exploitation has been extended to include a number of circumstances that are considered unhealthy or less than optimal for a child's development. In this chapter, we focus on several of those circumstances.

CHILDREN WHO OBSERVE VIOLENCE

Children suffer not only from abuse and neglect experienced directly but also from violence that they are exposed to indirectly. A growing literature focuses on forms of child maltreatment that center on experiencing violence indirectly through either exposure to the violence that occurs between family members (primarily parents) or exposure to violence that occurs within the community. These experiences are of concern, in part, because of the potential negative effects they have on children. Consider the following excerpt from a paper we received from one of our college students:

> The topic of marital violence and its effects on children who observe that violence is of exceptional interest to me. I chose this topic because I desire a better understanding of the problem, primarily because of my younger siblings who live in a home where violence, both physical and verbal, are far from uncommon. This scenario does not reflect the common situation of marital violence in which the male abuses the female; rather the abuser is my stepmother. For reasons that could constitute an entire paper on its own, my stepmother relieves her frustration through physical violence directed at my father. I can't count how many times I have seen her become angry and hit or throw things at my father. She even uses various objects to hit him.
>
> Initially, I was worried about my dad's safety, however, I realized he is a big man and would be all right. After they had my brother, Jordan, now 7, however, I began to worry about what effects the abuse would have on him. I wondered if he would learn to believe this kind of behavior is acceptable. My wondering has sadly proven correct. Jordan is an aggressive boy and is often in trouble for his problem behavior.
>
> Two years after Jordan's birth, my parents had another child, Max, who is now 5. Max has watched the violence between my parents continue during his childhood. In contrast to Jordan, though, Max's interaction with family and friends portrays a picture of a little boy who is self-conscious, has low self-esteem, and lacks confidence. I love him so much and it breaks my heart to see him develop this sort of low self-image. He is a loving, generous, and sweet child and in spite of the "little brother abuse" he receives, he still looks up to his big brother, Jordan.
>
> My parents have recently had a third child, my sister, Amy. I now wonder, what will happen to my beautiful baby sister? I want to know more about the topic of children who are exposed to marital violence so that I can provide my father with empirical proof of the repercussions of such a situation. Hopefully, he will do something about the violence in his home and my little brothers and sisters will benefit. (our notes)

The student who wrote these words has an interest in child maltreatment because his personal experience tells him what it is like to observe parental violence. Unfortunately, we know less about the nature, extent, and repercussions associated with exposure to various forms of violence, relative to more direct forms of child maltreatment. Most research in this area has focused on estimates of these forms of child maltreatment as well as the potential consequences that befall children who observe violence in their homes or the community.

Children Exposed to Marital Violence

The phrase "exposed to marital violence" is used to describe all the ways children observe violence between their parents. Some children, for example, may directly *observe* a violent act, whereas others *overhear* some form of violent behavior or *see the results* of the assaults (e.g., bruises). As noted in Chapter 5, exposure to marital violence is often conceptualized as a specific form of psychological maltreatment. Some experts classify exposure to marital violence as psychological neglect (e.g., Sedlak & Broadhurst, 1996), whereas others consider it a form of psychological abuse (e.g., Hart et al., 1996). Regardless of the classification, children exposed to marital violence experience multiple threats. Children in these violent homes fear for themselves as well as for the parent who is the direct recipient of violence. In addition, these children are likely to experience direct forms of abuse and neglect (e.g., Appel, Angelelli, & Holden, in press; Gibson & Gutierrez, 1991; McCloskey, Figueredo, & Koss, 1995).

> Children exposed to marital violence fear for themselves and for the parent who is assaulted.

Recognition that children exposed to interparental abuse, as a group, are in need of services grew from the work of advocates, clinicians, and researchers in the late 1970s. Before this time, the public and the scientific community seemed to ignore the possibility that marital violence might have an effect on children (Rossman, 1994). Although children exposed to marital violence have received more recognition in the intervening years, many factions within society continue to fail to acknowledge this form of violence as problematic for children. The American Bar Association states, for example, that despite its obligation to protect children living in violent households, the law has generally failed to even recognize their exposure as a problem (Davidson, 1994). Indeed, children in maritally violent homes have been described as the family violence victims "called the 'forgotten,' 'unacknowledged,' 'hidden,' 'unintended,' and 'silent' victims" (Holden, 1998, p. 1).

Since the late 1970s, children of marital violence have been increasingly recognized as an additional group of child maltreatment victims, and the amount of research focusing on the special needs of these children is growing. Given the relative historical indifference to this problem, it is not surprising that the research on children exposed to marital violence lags behind most other areas of child maltreatment research. Research in the field of children exposed to marital violence is exceptionally challenging. Reliance on maternal reports as the major source of data; near exclusive employment of small, shelter samples; failure to ascertain adequately exposure to marital violence; and insufficient use of comparison groups are the most obvious problems. Despite these limitations, research designs have steadily improved through the years and have yielded illuminating findings. Most of this research has focused on determining the magnitude of the problem regarding the number of children exposed to marital violence and the negative effects associated with such exposure. Research is also appearing that addresses potential methods of intervention for children who are exposed to marital violence.

Estimates of the Problem

Published estimates of the number of children in the United States exposed to marital violence range from 3.3 million to nearly 10 million (Carlson, 1984;

Straus, 1991a). The disparity in these estimates reflects the fact that the number of children exposed to marital violence is largely unknown and depends on the method of data collection and on the definition of marital violence that is used.

Some studies have used a retrospective design and questioned adults about their childhood memories of violence between their parents. On the basis of data from the 1985 National Family Violence Survey, Straus (1992) estimated that more than 10 million American children witness a physical assault between their parents. In this study, exposure to marital violence was measured (using the CTS) by asking adult respondents whether they recalled one or both parents hitting the other during their teenage years. Nearly 13% of adults in this survey recalled observing at least one incident of marital violence between their parents. Straus (1992) believes these figures underestimate the true amount of such experiences because most parents try to avoid physical fights when their children are present and because these figures represent only the violence that was observed between parents during the respondents' teenage years. Indeed, when the adults in the 1985 National Family Violence Survey were asked about interparental violence in their own relationships, 16% reported such violence within the past year, whereas 30% reported violence with their spouse at some time during their marriage (Gelles & Straus, 1988; Straus et al., 1980).

Retrospective studies of college students using the CTS have yielded similar results. Gelles (1980) found that 16% of college students reported exposure to at least one incident during the past year in which one of their parents had physically abused the other. Silvern, Karyl, Waelde, et al. (1995) also surveyed college students and found that 37% of the 550 undergraduates reported exposure to some form of marital violence while growing up. The most common type of violence reported in this study included throwing an object at a partner, pushing, shoving, or slapping.

Other studies have questioned parents involved in marital violence, primarily women residing in shelters, and found variable results. In a national survey of battered women, for example, fewer than 25% thought their children had *directly observed* the marital violence within their home (Tomkins et al., 1994). In contrast, other inquiries of battered women suggest that two thirds or more of children living in violent homes were exposed to the violence by directly observing the violence *or* its aftermath (Hilton, 1992; Holden & Ritchie, 1991). These results suggest that estimates vary, depending on the definitions used by researchers. In addition, estimates obtained from parents in violent relationships have been questioned on the grounds that parents involved in violent relationships may underestimate their children's exposure, perhaps from shame or guilt, stress or trauma, or a lack of awareness that their children were present (Elbow, 1982; Hilton, 1992). A recent study based on data from multiple informants (both parents and children), for example, found that mothers' reports of children's exposure agreed with fathers' fairly well. Parents' and children's reports, however, agreed much less closely (O'Brien, John, Margolin, & Erel, 1994).

Given the problems in collecting data from parents involved in violent relationships, researchers have also directly questioned children from community samples regarding their experiences with interparental violence. O'Brien et al.

(1994) interviewed 8- to 11-year-old children about whether they had witnessed physical aggression between their parents. Approximately one fourth of the children reported witnessing both husband-to-wife aggression and wife-to-husband aggression. Using a more narrow definition of violence, McCloskey et al. (1995) reported that 20% of the children in their community sample had seen their father slap their mother within the past year. These data are limited, however, to specific age groups of child victims as well as nonrandom samples of children (Margolin, 1998).

Consequences Associated With Exposure to Marital Violence

Since the late 1970s, researchers have made progress in documenting a number of profoundly negative psychosocial and physical problems in children exposed to marital violence (Jaffe, Hastings, & Reitzel, 1992; Kolbo, Blakely, & Engleman, 1996; Mertin, 1992). A summary of research findings on the effects associated with exposure to marital violence reveals that such children are prone to suffer problems in five general areas: (a) emotional functioning, (b) behavior problems, (c) social competence, (d) cognitive ability, and (e) physical health. Table 6.1 displays the effects associated with observing interparental violence for children.

Children exposed to marital violence tend to exhibit more behavior problems than nonexposed children and often display multiple problems (Gleason, 1995). In addition, the extent of children's problems is often at a level that warrants clinical intervention. Across studies, approximately 35% to 45% of shelter children receive scores within the clinically significant range (see Hughes, 1992; O'Keefe, 1994a; Sternberg et al., 1993; Wildin, Williamson, & Wilson, 1991). Researchers have also identified, however, a subgroup of children exposed to marital violence who appear to be well adjusted despite their violent home environments (Hughes & Luke, 1998). Several factors might mediate the psychological and developmental outcomes for children exposed to marital violence, such as the nature of the violence (e.g., severity and duration), age, gender, ethnicity, the level of stress experienced by the mother, the quality of mothering, availability of social support, whether the child had been exposed to other forms of violence (e.g., verbal or physical abuse), and child characteristics such as temperament and self-esteem (Jaffe et al., 1990; Jouriles & Norwood, 1995; O'Keefe, 1994a; Spaccarelli, Sandler, & Roosa, 1994). To date, however, research findings are inconsistent and call for additional studies to clarify which factors might increase or decrease the problems experienced by children exposed to interparental violence (see Fantuzzo et al., 1991; Holden & Ritchie, 1991; O'Keefe, 1994a).

Children exposed to marital violence also continue to demonstrate psychological difficulties as adults. Several studies have examined problems in college students or national samples of adults that are correlated with a history of childhood exposure to parental abuse. Long-term effects associated with a history

TABLE 6.1 Possible Effects for Children Associated With Observing Interparental Violence

Effect	Studies
Emotional functioning	
Anxiety/difficult temperament	Holden & Ritchie (1991) Hughes (1988) McKay (1987, 1994) Randolf & Conkle (1993)
Low self-esteem	Elbow (1982) Hughes (1988) McKay (1987, 1994)
Depression and suicide	Christopoulos et al. (1987) Hershorn & Rosenbaum (1985) Hughes (1986) O'Keefe (1994a) Koski (1987)
Trauma/stress reactions	Jaffe, Wolfe, & Wilson (1990) Kilpatrick & Williams (in press) Rossman et al. (1993) Silvern & Kaersvang (1989) Terr (1991)
Negative emotions (feelings of loss, anger, sadness, self-blame, etc.)	Alessi & Hearn (1984) Carlson (1984) Cassady et al. (1987) Ericksen & Henderson (1992) Jaffe et al. (1990) Layzer, Goodson, & DeLange (1986)
Behavior problems	
Aggression	Copping (1996) Holden & Ritchie (1991) O'Keefe (1994a) Randolf & Conkle (1993) Rutter & Giller (1983) Sternberg et al. (1993) Straus et al. (1980) Westra & Martin (1981)
Delinquency	Fagan & Wexler (1987) K. S. Widom (1989)
Alcohol/drug use	Dembo, Williams, Wothke, Schmeidler, & Brown (1992) Fantuzzo & Lindquist (1989) Keronac, Taggart, Lescop, & Fortin (1986) Layzer et al. (1986)
High levels of physical activity	Copping (1996) Gleason (1995)
Social competence	
Shyness/withdrawal	Hershorn & Rosenbaum (1985) Hughes (1986)

TABLE 6.1 Continued

Social incompetence	Hughes (1988) Layzer et al. (1986) Rossman et al. (1993) Wolfe, Zak, Wilson, & Jaffe (1986)
Low empathy	Hinchey & Gavelek (1982) M. S. Rosenberg (1987)
Cognitive ability	
School problems	Hilberman & Munson (1978) Layzer et al. (1986) Pfouts, Schopler, & Henley (1982) Westra & Martin (1981) Wildin, Williamson, & Wilson (1991)
Poor problem-solving and conflict resolution skills	Grossier (1986) Jaffe et al. (1990) Moore, Pepler, Mae, & Kates (1989) M. S. Rosenberg (1987) Straus et al. (1980)
Cognitive deficits	Hart & Brassard (1990) Westra & Martin (1981)
Negative perceptions	Sternberg et al. (1994)
Deficits in adaptive behavior	Gleason (1995)
Physical health	
Physical symptoms/ailments	Fantuzzo & Lindquist (1989) Mertin (1992) Stagg, Wills, & Howell (1989)
Somatic complaints	Copping (1996) Gleason (1995)

TABLE 6.2

of observing marital violence during childhood include depression, trauma-related symptoms (e.g., anxiety and sleep disturbance), low self-esteem, alcohol and drug use, poor social adjustment, general psychological distress, and ineffective conflict resolution strategies (Choice, Lamke, & Pittman, 1995; Henning, Leitenberg, Coffey, Turner, & Bennett, 1996; Silvern, Karyl, Waelde, et al., 1995; Straus, 1992). Other possible long-term effects noted in adults reporting a childhood history of interparental violence include verbal and physical violence against one's own spouse, verbal and physical abuse of one's own children, and participation in violence outside the family (e.g., arrests for criminal assault; Straus, 1992). There is also some evidence that the outcome for young adults who were exposed to parental violence as children depends on whether the violence was initiated by their mothers or fathers, with father-initiated violence associated with greater risk for psychological problems (Fergusson & Horwood, 1998).

Studies examining the negative effects associated with marital violence should be interpreted cautiously. First, measurement of children's actual exposure is rarely obtained. Some researchers have assumed, for example, that a child has been exposed to marital violence prima facie, if they reside with maritally violent parents. In addition, when the presence of exposure has been documented, researchers may not have considered the parameters of exposure such as the frequency of exposure, the severity of the violence observed, and the duration of exposure, all of which might potentially influence a child's functional outcome.

Another methodological problem is that most studies use small, nonrepresentative samples. The majority of studies, for example, include mothers and children temporarily residing in battered women's shelters. Such samples vary greatly from general population samples in many ways. These studies also rely on maternal reports of child difficulties, reports that may be biased or inaccurate. In one study, for example, mothers' reports of the degree of their children's behavioral difficulties varied, depending on whether the mothers were victims of spouse abuse (Sternberg et al., 1993). In this study, mothers whose children were exposed to marital violence alone or in addition to being physically abused demonstrated significantly more behavior problems relative to a nonabused control group. A group of physically abused children who had not been exposed to marital violence, however, did not differ from the control group, which may suggest that mothers report higher levels of problem behavior in their children when they themselves are victims. In addition, recent research indicates that maternal accounts of their children's difficulties are often inconsistent with fathers' descriptions as well as those of professionals (Christensen, Margolin, & Sullaway, 1992; Sternberg et al., 1993). Mothers in shelters are likely to be in a crisis situation brought on by factors such as injuries, insufficient funds, departure from their homes, depression, and posttraumatic stress disorder that may impair their objectivity (see Saunders, 1994; Walker, 1977).

Studies in this area often lack comparison groups and include samples of children who have observed marital violence *in addition* to experiencing either direct physical or sexual abuse (Appel et al., in press; McCloskey et al., 1995; O'Keefe, 1995; Peled & Davis, 1995; Straus, 1992). It is therefore difficult to ascertain precisely which factors contribute to the difficulties children experience. These research designs preclude the possibility, for example, of separating the effects of *observing* marital violence from the effects of *experiencing other forms* of maltreatment. In addition, children living in maritally violent homes often experience additional risk factors including marital conflict, parental alcoholism, low income, stress, and maternal impairment (Hughes, Parkinson, & Vargo, 1989). Without appropriate comparison groups (i.e., comparison groups of children who have been exposed to parental alcoholism, low income, and stress, for example, but have *not* been exposed to marital violence), it is impossible to determine which of these many factors, in addition to interparental violence, contribute to the negative outcomes observed in children. Although one study found that observation of marital violence contributed to child outcome above and beyond such factors, these factors can also serve as mediators of child outcome (e.g., Holden & Ritchie, 1991; O'Keefe, 1994a, 1994b).

A final criticism of research examining the effects associated with exposure to marital violence is the lack of theory-driven research and inattention to the processes that lead to behavioral problems in children (Holden, 1998). A new wave of research, however, is addressing both theoretical and conceptual issues within the field and attempts to link research with implications for intervention and social policy (Holden, Geffner, & Jouriles, 1998).

Interventions

Although involvement of professional groups in helping children exposed to marital violence should be beneficial, most groups have been slow to respond. The difficulties of these children are often overlooked because children exposed to marital violence are not themselves direct victims of physical or sexual abuse. Children who experience various forms of abuse directly are those who become the concern of child welfare and mental health professionals (Elbow, 1982). A variety of new services for children of battered women, however, have come into fruition recently, including individual treatment, group therapy, home visitations, and multiple component programs (see Peled & Davis, 1995; Peled, Jaffe, & Edleson, 1994; Silvern, Karyl, & Landis, 1995). Given the variability in children's responses to parental violence, it is evident that no single intervention is likely to effectively address every need of every child (Jouriles et al., 1998).

One of the most typical treatments for children exposed to marital violence is group counseling (Jaffe et al., 1990; Peled et al., 1994; Suderman & Jaffe, 1997). The goals of group treatment have been summarized by others and include the following: (a) labeling feelings, (b) dealing with anger, (c) developing safety skills, (d) obtaining social support, (e) developing social competence and a good self-concept, (f) recognizing one's lack of responsibility for a parent or for the violence, (g) understanding family violence, and (h) specifying personal wishes about family relationships (Hughes, 1992; Jaffe et al., 1990). Data about the effectiveness of group counseling for children exposed to marital violence are limited but appear promising. Several studies have demonstrated positive treatment effects including improved social skills, increased self-esteem, and decreased problematic behaviors and symptoms (e.g., Cassady, Allen, Lyon, & McGeehan, 1987; Peled & Edleson, 1992; Wagar & Rodway, 1995).

Other interventions incorporate multiservice components. Jouriles and colleagues (1998) described a program they developed for mothers and their children seeking refuge at a battered women's shelter. The program includes weekly in-home intervention sessions during an 8-month period that focus on providing mothers with social support, parent training (including child management and nurturing skills), and training in problem-solving and decision-making skills. The home-based interventions also include social support for the children of the battered women whereby child mentors are assigned to each mother-child dyad and serve as "big brothers" or "big sisters" by engaging the children in fun activities and providing positive attention and affection. Preliminary outcome evaluation using a randomized control group design suggests that families receiving the program demonstrate significant benefits, including reduced child antisocial behavior, enhanced child management and nurturance skills, and decreased parental psychological distress (Jouriles et al., 1998).

Children Who Witness Community Violence

Children experience violence not only within their homes but also within the community at large. Anyone watching the news on television or reading the newspaper can glimpse the regular violence occurring within American communities. Rates of violence are high in the United States with the homicide rate exceeding by several times the rate in any other Western industrialized country (Maguire & Pastore, 1994; Siegel, 1995).

Because of the significant amount of violence within American communities, many experts have expressed concern about the effects of such violence on children (Horn & Trickett, 1998; Osofsky, 1997, 1998; Wallen & Rubin, 1997). Given the knowledge that a child's exposure to violence within the family (e.g., spouse abuse) is associated with several negative developmental outcomes, it stands to reason that exposure to violence within the community might also be detrimental to children's development. Discussion of exposure to community violence is relevant to the topic of child maltreatment because *family* violence and *community* violence are interrelated. In one of the few studies to directly examine the relationship between community and domestic violence, Osofsky, Wewers, Hann, and Fick (1993) interviewed 53 African American mothers of children ages 9 to 12 living in a low-income neighborhood. Findings indicated that levels of violence within the home, as measured by the CTS, were significantly related to children's reported exposure to community violence.

It is clear that children are exposed to violence not only within the family but also within the larger communities in which their families reside. How often are children exposed to this violence—to shootings, stabbings, and other violent acts that occur in their neighborhoods? Are there negative effects associated with viewing such violence, and if so, what can be done to protect children from the negative influence of living in a violent community?

Estimates of the Problem

Although no official estimates of exposure to community violence exist, recent survey data indicate that children are exposed to violence at high rates, particularly in many inner-city neighborhoods. In a survey of 6th, 8th, and 10th graders in Connecticut in 1992, 40% reported witnessing at least one violent crime in the past year (Marans & Cohen, 1993). Richters and Martinez (1993b) found that in an elementary school in southeast Washington, D.C., 72% of 5th and 6th graders and 61% of 1st and 2nd graders reported witnessing at least one act of community violence.

The type of violence to which children are exposed varies and can include relatively minor acts of violence such as purse snatching as well as severe violence, including murder. Shakoor and Chalmers (1991) found that nearly three fourths of a sample of 1,000 African American elementary and high school students reported witnessing at least one robbery, stabbing, shooting, or murder. In a study of 2nd-, 4th-, 6th-, and 8th-grade African American children living in a Chicago neighborhood, one in four had witnessed a stabbing, and close to one third reported that they had seen a shooting. In an older group of 10- to 19-year-olds, 35% had witnessed a stabbing and 39% had witnessed a shooting. Nearly one fourth of the group of older children reported witnessing a killing (Bell & Jenkins, 1991, 1993).

Although some children may witness such extreme violence on only one occasion, there is some evidence that the nature of violence exposure in many communities is chronic and repeated. Studies of youth witnessing violence, for example, have found that nearly three fourths of youth witnessing a shooting had witnessed not just one but multiple shootings (Jenkins & Bell, 1994; Richters & Martinez, 1993a). In addition, in neighborhoods in which violence occurs, the percentage of children who report witnessing violence increases as the average age of the children increases, suggesting that the longer children reside in such neighborhoods, the more likely it is that they will be repeatedly exposed to violence (Horn & Trickett, 1998).

Effects Associated With Witnessing Community Violence

It is difficult to isolate the effects of witnessing community violence because children who witness community violence are also more likely to be poor, have a single parent, and experience violence within the home. Several recent studies, however, have examined some of the correlates of exposure to community violence (for reviews, see Horn & Trickett, 1998; Wallen & Rubin, 1997). Although the number of studies evaluating the effects of community violence exposure is limited, results of available studies suggest that children exposed to such incidents display a variety of psychological symptoms including PTSD symptoms (e.g., difficulty sleeping, repetitive dreams, and pessimism about the future), depression, aggression, and low self-esteem (Attar, Guerra, & Tolan, 1994; Fitzpatrick, 1993; Fitzpatrick & Boldizar, 1993; Freeman, Mokros, & Poznanski, 1993; Martinez & Richters, 1993; Pynoos, Frederick, Nader, & Arroyo, 1987; Terr, 1983).

Research has also determined that the greater a child's exposure to violence (e.g., nearness to the event or frequency of exposure to different types of violence), the greater the degree of difficulties experienced (Martinez & Richters, 1993; Pynoos et al., 1987). Martinez and Richters studied 165 African American children aged 6 to 10 years of age attending first, second, fifth, or sixth grades at a school located in southeast Washington, D.C. Exposure to community violence was assessed using the Survey of Children's Exposure to Community Violence, an interview that evaluates the frequency of a child's exposure to 20 types of violence such as shootings, muggings, and stabbings (Richters & Saltzman, 1990). Both the fifth- and sixth-grade children and all mothers provided estimates of the degree of exposure to community violence by responding to the survey. The first- and second-grade children provided estimates of exposure by completing a similar but more developmentally appropriate interview called Things I Have Seen and Heard (Richters & Martinez, 1990). Psychological difficulties were assessed using parent-report measures of stress and behavior problems as well as child-report measures of distress. Results indicated significant correlations between child-report measures of distress and exposure to community violence. Parents' estimates of their children's distress and exposure to violence, however, were not related to children's estimates of their own distress. These seemingly contradictory findings suggest a tendency for parents to underestimate the extent to which their children are exposed to violence as well as the extent to which their children display symptoms of distress.

There has also been interest in examining children who have lived through the experience of war (for a review, see Garmezy & Rutter, 1985). In their review of studies examining the effects associated with wartime violence, Garmezy and Rutter concluded that children exposed to such violence might develop serious difficulties including anxiety and fear, depression, psychosomatic complaints, and PTSD symptoms such as difficulty concentrating and sleep disturbances. The degree of psychological disturbance experienced by children, however, varied from one child to another. Researchers were not able to determine the extent to which the children's difficulties were the result of their actual exposure to violence or other stressful conditions associated with war (e.g., loss of a parent, poor nutrition, and inadequate sleeping conditions).

Research examining the effects associated with exposure to community violence is just beginning, and, as a result, findings should be interpreted cautiously. The most significant problem with the research to date is that all the studies are correlational in nature. In addition, most of the studies fail to distinguish between exposure to community violence and other potentially significant factors such as poverty, neglect, and violence within the home. As a result, the specific adverse effects of exposure to community violence, apart from these and other factors, are unclear. Studies have focused on how community violence exposure may affect children differently from exposure to domestic violence (Bell & Jenkins, 1993; Garbarino, 1992; Osofsky, 1995). Initial studies suggest that exposure to domestic violence may be more traumatic for children because of its chronic, frequent, and personal nature (Groves & Zuckerman, 1997; Horn & Trickett, 1998). Several studies suggest that violence committed in the home or by someone known to the child is more likely to evoke stress symptoms than violence occurring outside the home or by a stranger (Martinez & Richters, 1993; Osofsky et al., 1993; Richters & Martinez, 1993a).

Interventions

Given the negative effects associated with exposure to community violence, some type of intervention for children witnessing extreme trauma is warranted. Understandably, police and other professionals often focus on the needs of the perpetrators and direct victims of community violence and, unfortunately, often neglect the indirect victims. Children who witness community violence, for example, often encounter both delays in receiving treatment referrals and a lack of preventive intervention programs within their communities (Osofsky, 1998).

Several communities have developed intervention programs aimed at police responses.

In response to these problems, several communities have developed intervention programs, particularly those aimed at police responses to children exposed to community violence (see Groves & Zuckerman, 1997; Marans & Cohen, 1993; Osofsky, 1997). Osofsky (1998) described the Violence Intervention Project that she initiated in New Orleans in 1993. The project includes an educational program that provides information to police trainees and officers on the effects of violence on children. The program also includes a 24-hour hotline providing consultation for police or families who are concerned about children exposed to community violence.

Another program, the Child Witness to Violence Project, was founded in 1992 at Boston City Hospital (Groves & Zuckerman, 1997). This program provides therapeutic interventions for children who witness violence in their communities by including therapeutic and support services that focus on the child, his or her family, and additional community professionals involved with the family (e.g., schoolteachers). The program represents a multiservice intervention approach that focuses not only on providing therapeutic intervention for individual children but also on mobilizing the support that parents and other community caregivers can provide for these children.

Others have recommended public policy initiatives directed at alleviating some of the difficulties faced by children and families living in violent communities (American Psychological Association, 1993; Hawkins, 1995; Osofsky, 1995, 1997). Osofsky (1997) recently described the following public policy recommendations that she believes are necessary to focus attention on youth exposed to community violence and to guide program development to solve this problem:

1. A national campaign to change the social image of violence from acceptable to unacceptable
2. Education for parents, educators, criminal justice professionals, law enforcement officials, and medical and mental health professionals about the effects of violence on children and the methods to protect children from such violence

3. Development of community prevention and intervention programs to prevent violence and to address the negative consequences of such violence
4. Development and enforcement of gun laws that limit access of guns to children and adolescents
5. Provision of resources to enable the development of child and family intervention programs

SECTION SUMMARY

Although it is clear that significant numbers of children are exposed to the violence occurring between their parents, precise estimates of the incidence and prevalence of this problem are lacking. Published estimates range between approximately 3 and 10 million children. Despite difficulties in determining the extent of exposure to marital violence, studies demonstrate that such an experience is related to *negative psychological difficulties* that affect children's *emotional, behavioral, social, cognitive,* and *physical functioning.* Interpreting studies evaluating the negative effects associated with interparental violence is difficult, however, because of the large number of variables simultaneously influencing children's behavior (e.g., parental alcoholism, low income, and maternal impairment) and the *methodological problems* inherent in the studies conducted to date. *Intervention programs* designed to assist children and their families include *group therapies* for children as well as *multiservice component programs.*

Children are exposed to violence not only within their homes but also within their communities. Although no official estimates of this problem are available, survey data suggest that large numbers of youth living in inner-city neighborhoods are exposed to some type of violence within their communities. The type of violence varies but ranges from relatively *minor acts* (e.g., purse snatching) to more *severe forms* of violence (e.g., stabbings, shootings, and murder), and the violence is often *chronic* and *repeated.* Exposure to community violence has been associated with a variety of *negative effects,* but the most common outcomes include PTSD symptoms, depression, low self-esteem, and aggression. Research evaluating the effects associated with exposure to community violence should be interpreted cautiously, however, because of the difficulty in ferreting out the specific effects of observing community violence apart from other potentially significant factors (e.g., poverty, neglect, and violence within the home). Although *interventions* for children and families residing in violent communities are limited, efforts designed to address the issue are appearing including programs to enhance *police responses* to children exposed to violence, *multiservice approaches,* and *public policy initiatives.*

SIBLING ABUSE

Claims-makers are continually negotiating the specific boundaries of child maltreatment. Some professionals in the field have argued that conceptualizations of child maltreatment should be broadened to include other negative circumstances that are detrimental to children's development. Some professionals have argued that even heavy exposure to televised violence should be considered a form of child maltreatment (Eron & Huesmann, 1987). Others have suggested that ecological factors such as racism, sexism, and war zone environments should be considered child abuse (Hart et al., 1987; Jones & Jones, 1987). These claims-makers are not, of course, in agreement on the issue of just which circumstances constitute abuse and deserve the label *child maltreatment.* During the early 1980s, a new form of child maltreatment emerged: sibling abuse.

> I can't remember a time when my brother didn't taunt me, usually trying to get me to respond so he would be justified in hitting me. Usually he would be saying I was a crybaby or a sissy or stupid or ugly and that no one would like me, want to be around me, or whatever. Sometimes he would accuse me of doing something, and if I denied it, he would call me a liar. I usually felt overwhelmingly helpless because nothing I said or did would stop him. If no one else was around, he would start beating on me, after which he would stop and go away. (Wiehe, 1997, p. 34)

Most individuals who have a brother or sister can undoubtedly remember a time when they engaged in some altercation with their sibling: pulling hair, name-calling, pinching, pushing, and so on. Because such behaviors are so common, they are rarely defined as family violence (Gelles & Cornell, 1990; Wiehe, 1990). Should such interactions be labeled *abusive* and recognized as an additional form of child maltreatment? The answer to this question is a matter of some debate. Emery and Laumann-Billings (1998) have argued that although such behaviors may be inappropriate, because these behaviors are so common and largely involve relatively minor physical acts that result in little or no measurable harm, they should not be considered a form of *family violence.* Others argue that *because* negative interactions between siblings *are so common,* they should be recognized as one of the most serious forms of family violence and deserve more attention (Finkelhor & Dziuba-Leatherman, 1994; Wiehe, 1997). These individuals might argue that such interactions are often rationalized as sibling rivalry and considered a normal part of development between siblings. In the following paragraphs, we will attempt to distinguish between normative sibling interactions and sibling abuse. We will also examine research investigating the various types and frequency of negative encounters that occur between siblings and studies attempting to determine whether such interactions are harmful.

What Is Sibling Abuse?

Most, if not all, siblings hit, slap, and punch each other. Siblings often call each other names. Rivalry, jealousy, and anger commonly exist between siblings who realize that they cannot have the sole attention of their parents. Many of these behaviors, however, are described as "normal" sibling rivalry. Siblings also sometimes engage in mutual sexual behaviors, many of which are considered a normal part of exploratory play. Where should we draw the line between normal sibling aggression and exploratory sex play and those behaviors that are damaging and abusive?

> Where should we draw the line between normal sibling aggression and abusive behavior?

As we have noted in previous chapters, child maltreatment is difficult to define. One starting point is to define what should be considered normal sibling interaction. *Normal* behavior is often defined by a statistical standard that relies on the normal bell curve to define deviance, whereby approximately 66% of individual behavior falls within one standard deviation of the mean. Abusive behavior could be defined as those behaviors falling at the outer extreme of the distribution, indicating that the behavior is exceedingly severe or occurred excessively frequently. This definition of abusive sibling interaction is in stark contrast to definitional conceptualizations of sibling abuse that are so inclusive that the number of children experiencing sibling abuse exceeds 80% of the child population.

Many claims-makers prefer a broad definition of sibling abuse, arguing that the time has come to redefine what society views as normal sibling behavior. From this perspective, even a common behavior (e.g., siblings hitting or pushing one another) might be considered wrong and, as a result, recognized as problematic. It is true that in times past, many adult-child sexual relations were considered commonplace, as we noted in Chapter 1. Adult-child sexual interactions were not labeled as *abusive* until much later in history. Similarly, much of what we label as physical abuse today was viewed as merely stern discipline or punishment 25 years ago. How many of the interactions between siblings that we are aware of today are rationalized as legitimate behavior simply because they occur frequently?

Others have argued that overly inclusive definitions may be ineffective for discerning appropriate interventions and, ultimately, for understanding the problem of child maltreatment (Emery & Laumann-Billings, 1998). Consider, for example, an 8-year-old boy who frequently pushes his 4-year-old sister. His behavior is inappropriate and should be addressed, but it may not be helpful to label the behavior abusive. To label this behavior abusive seems to us to diminish the significance of the term. In response to these concerns, a more tempered approach is to delineate specific criteria against which to judge sibling interactions to determine whether a given interaction deserves the label of maltreatment or abuse. Several scholars have proposed specific factors that might distinguish between sibling abuse and normal sibling rivalry and sex play (e.g., DeJong, 1989; Wiehe, 1997). Criteria that might be helpful in distinguishing sibling abuse are displayed in Table 6.2. In some cases, it may be necessary for the sibling interaction to meet only one criterion to be established as abusive. Sexual intercourse between siblings, for example, is never considered develop-

Criteria to Consider in Distinguishing Sibling Abuse From Nonabusive Sibling Interactions

Power disparity between siblings	Negative sibling interactions that involve a significant difference in the distribution of power in age, physical size or strength, or social status
Frequency and duration of the interaction	Negative sibling interactions that occur for many months or years and that include multiple incidents
Element of pressure or secrecy	Negative sibling interactions that involve coercive pressure for involvement or that are carried out in a secretive way
Outcome of the interaction	Negative sibling interactions that result in some type of harm to the child who is the recipient of the behavior; harm can include physical as well as psychological injury
Developmental appropriateness	Negative sibling interactions that fall outside the realm of typical sibling rivalry or normal sex play exploration
Lack of appropriate parental intervention	Negative sibling interactions that occur without appropriate intervention from parents or guardians; inappropriate parental reactions/intervention include no response, indifference to the victim's suffering, and blame directed at the victim

mentally appropriate. In other cases, however, evaluation of a number of criteria may be necessary.

The first potential criterion is a *power disparity between siblings.* The interaction should be evaluated relative to power differences that could reflect an age discrepancy, physical power differential, or both. In our family, our 4-year-old daughter actually displays more violent behavior (e.g., kicking and hitting) than our 8-year-old son. Because she is younger and physically weaker than her brother, however, by definition her behaviors directed at her brother would not be considered abusive. Her behavior is inappropriate, and we try to respond to her aggression, but her behavior should not be labeled as abuse. Studies examining sexual interactions between siblings have consistently shown a significant age difference between siblings (e.g., Adler & Schutz, 1995). Some have also argued that the power differential criterion should additionally include differences based on societal stereotypes involving gender, whereby males dominate females regardless of age differences (Laviola, 1992). Another criterion to consider is the *frequency and duration of the interaction.* Most cases of severely negative sibling interactions involve multiple incidents occurring during several months or years (Adler & Schutz, 1995; Wiehe, 1997).

A third criterion to consider when distinguishing sibling abuse from other types of sibling interactions is the presence of an *element of pressure or secrecy.*

Adults who report experiencing significantly negative sibling interactions as children often describe themselves as nonconsenting and unwilling participants who were pressured into the interaction (Adler & Schütz, 1995; Canavan, Meyer, & Higgs, 1992). The abusive behavior also often has an element of misrepresentation or trickery (DeJong, 1989; Wiehe, 1997). The *outcome of the interaction* is another factor that should be considered. In most sibling interactions defined as abusive, there is an aspect of victimization whereby the recipient of the behavior is "hurt or injured by the action or actions of another" (Wiehe, 1997, p. 167). The hurt or injury might take a physical form such as bruises or cuts or might be more psychological in nature including feelings of anger, fear, or sadness (DeJong, 1989).

One of the most significant criterion to consider is the *developmental appropriateness of the behavior* occurring between siblings. Developmental research can provide a great deal of information about appropriate sexual interactions between siblings as well as typical forms of sibling rivalry (e.g., McHale & Pawletko, 1992; Quittner & Opipari, 1994; Rosenfeld et al., 1986). Kolodny (1980), for example, found that parents of children aged 6 to 7 years reported that 83% of their sons and 76% of their daughters had participated in sex play with siblings or friends of the same sex (cited in Rice, 1998). Exploratory behavior typically involves mutual genital display, touch, and fondling. Intercourse or attempted penetration, however, is not typical of sexual exploratory behavior in childhood (Anderson, 1979; Rosenfeld et al., 1986).

A final key feature of sibling abuse appears to be a *lack of appropriate parental intervention.* Adler and Schutz (1995) found that for the sibling incest cases they examined, 58% of siblings exposed to abuse experienced continued abuse because of ineffective parental intervention. Others have found that parents who discover inappropriate interactions between siblings fail to protect the victims, deny any suffering on the part of the victims, or respond negatively toward the victim with blame or disbelief (Laviola, 1992; Wiehe, 1997).

Forms of Negative Sibling Interaction

Although the majority of research has investigated physical violence between siblings, negative sibling interactions can also be characterized by inappropriate sexual behavior and verbal aggression. The various forms of physical violence, inappropriate sexual behavior, and verbal aggression that can occur between siblings are similar to the range of behaviors discussed throughout this book in describing various forms of child maltreatment between adults and children. *Physical violence* between siblings, for example, has occurred in a variety of forms. Consider the following example:

> I was 3 or 4 years old. My family went camping often. We were out at a little lake. I was walking with my two brothers . . . my brother pushed me into the water. I couldn't swim! They just stood on the dock and laughed at me. I was gasping for air. . . . Then the next thing I remember is someone

> pulling me out. It was a farmer driving by on his tractor. . . . He took us all back to camp. . . . I told my parents that my brothers had "pushed" me and they said I "fell" in. (Wiehe, 1997, p. 24)

This case example focuses on a relatively severe form of physical violence. Other forms of physical violence between siblings may include serious acts such as smothering, choking, and beating or stabbing with an object and less serious forms such as hitting, biting, slapping, shoving, and punching (Wiehe, 1997).

Inappropriate sexual behaviors between siblings have also been documented and range from fondling and genital touching to oral contact to penetration (Canavan et al., 1992; Wiehe, 1997). The most common sexual behavior among siblings appears to be genital fondling (Finkelhor, 1980; Wiehe, 1997). Finally, *negative verbal exchanges* also occur between siblings and can take the form of verbally aggressive behavior such as name-calling and verbal threats or comments intended to ridicule or degrade the sibling. Additional behaviors defined as psychological maltreatment in Chapter 5 have also been documented in sibling relationships, such as terrorizing acts (Wiehe, 1997). Wiehe, for example, described the case of a 37-year-old man whose brother had stabbed his pet frog to death in front of him when he was a child.

Estimates of the Problem

Most research attempting to evaluate the extent to which sibling abuse occurs has focused on physical violence between siblings. On the basis of research from the first National Family Violence Survey, Straus and his colleagues (1980) found that 82% of American children with siblings between the ages of 3 and 17 engaged in at least one violent act toward a sibling during a 1-year period. Violence was measured using the CTS and included minor acts as well as severe forms of violence. In addition, Steinmetz (1982) found that between 63% and 68% of adolescent siblings in the families she studied used physical violence to resolve conflicts with brothers or sisters. Roscoe, Goodwin, and Kennedy (1987) studied 244 junior high students who completed an anonymous questionnaire examining negative verbal and physical interactions and conflict resolution strategies between siblings. Results indicated that 88% of males and 94% of females reported that they were victims of sibling violence some time in the past year. Likewise, 85% of males and 96% of females admitted they were the perpetrators of sibling violence.

Critics have often argued the obvious: that children are immature and impulsive and most, if not all, siblings engage in aggressive interactions. All the research cited above, for example, suggests that the majority of violence between siblings involves minor forms of violence and does not meet the criteria for abuse outlined previously. Considerable research, however, suggests that more severe violence between siblings is not uncommon. Straus et al. (1980) found that 42% of parents reported kicking, biting, and punching between siblings; 40% reported hitting or attempted hitting with an object; and 16% reported siblings "beating up" one another. Roscoe et al. (1987) found similar results in their sample of junior high students: 46% reported being kicked, 38% reported being hit with an object, and 37% reported being hit with a fist.

Other studies have attempted to evaluate the extent to which siblings engage in sexual behavior with one another. Finkelhor (1980) surveyed 796 undergraduates at six New England colleges and found that 15% of the females and 10% of the males reported some type of sexual experience involving a sibling (Finkelhor, 1980). Bevc and Silverman (1993) also surveyed a college student sample but included only those who had been raised with opposite-sex siblings. Of the 367 students surveyed, 29% reported engaging in some type of sexual activity with a sibling. Males and females were nearly equally likely to report such an experience. Russell (1983), reporting on a community sample of 930 women residing in San Francisco, found that 2.5% of women reported experiencing some type of "exploitive sexual contact" with a sibling (5 or more years older) before their 18th birthday. The variability in these estimates is no doubt due to differences in the samples studied and in the definitions of abuse that were employed.

Studies examining sexual interactions between siblings have uncovered a range of behaviors that vary in their severity. Bevc and Silverman (1993) categorized descriptions of incestuous behavior between opposite-sex siblings into consummatory and nonconsummatory sexual activities. Consummatory acts consisted of some form of penetration or attempted penetration and usually culminated in ejaculation (e.g., attempted or completed genital intercourse and oral or anal intercourse). Nonconsummatory acts consisted of less intrusive forms of sexual contact such as sexual kissing or hugging, exhibiting or fondling sex organs or private body areas, and simulated intercourse. Of the college students who reported a history of sexual activity with a sibling, the majority (76%) reported engaging in the less severe forms of nonconsummatory sexual activity. Genital penetration, considered one of the most severe forms of sexual abuse, was reported by only 2% of the opposite-sex sibling pairs.

Not surprisingly, clinical populations are more likely to report experiencing severe forms of sexual abuse between siblings. Adler and Schutz (1995) found that although fondling was the most common type of sexual behavior between siblings, up to 42% experienced some form of penetration, either vaginal or anal. In addition, O'Brien (1991) found that 46% of his sample included penile penetration, whereas 89% of DeJong's (1989) sample included attempted and/or actual vaginal penetration.

Consequences Associated With Negative Sibling Interaction

A commonly held view is that violence or sexual activity between siblings is generally benign and within the context of normal play or exploration. Some authors maintain that even sexual interactions, particularly between children close in age, may be relatively innocuous (Finkelhor, 1980; Pittman, 1987; Steele & Alexander, 1981). Others contend that such interactions between siblings are always harmful (Brickman, 1984; Canavan et al., 1992). Unfortunately, little sound research has been conducted to address this question. In our review of the literature on sibling abuse, for example, we could uncover virtually no controlled studies. Most research relies on a small number of clinical case studies of women seeking therapy, and most studies fail to include a control group or the use of standardized assessment instruments. As a result, the research evaluating the effects of violence and sexual activity between siblings is inconclusive.

Although lacking in methodological rigor, available studies do demonstrate some consistency in the types of difficulties experienced by individuals who have engaged in negative sibling interactions. Table 6.3 displays the problems most frequently reported by adults with a childhood history characterized by negative sibling interactions. The problems experienced by individuals reporting a history of sibling abuse are similar to those reported by victims of other forms of child maltreatment and include low self-esteem, negative emotions, interpersonal problems, revictimization, and PTSD symptoms. In general, these problems have been noted in sibling abuse victims regardless of whether the type of experience included violence, sexual behavior, or verbal aggression. One exception is sexual dysfunction, which is associated primarily with sexual interactions between siblings.

Characteristics of Siblings Who Inflict Harm

Research evaluating gender characteristics has found that males and females engage in violence or sexual behavior directed at siblings to a nearly equal degree (Roscoe et al., 1987; Straus et al., 1980; Worling, 1995). With regard to age, however, differences have been noted suggesting that as children grow older, sibling violence becomes less common (Steinmetz, 1982; Straus et al., 1980). Sexual interactions between siblings also occur at a younger age, compared with other types of sexual offenses (Worling, 1995).

Researchers have evaluated additional risk factors associated with negative sibling interactions. Most research has relied on a small number of clinical cases and investigated characteristics of both children and adolescents who engage in physical violence or sexual behavior with their siblings. Perpetrators of sibling violence share several characteristic experiences including a history of physical child abuse and neglect, a chaotic family environment, excessive caretaking responsibilities for other family members, and parental absence or deprivation (Green, 1984; Rosenthal & Doherty, 1984).

The results of clinical studies of sibling sexual offenders are similar and suggest that these families are characterized by many forms of family dysfunction such as parental absence or rejection (Becker et al., 1986; DeJong, 1989; Smith & Israel, 1987), childhood physical and sexual abuse (Adler & Schutz, 1995; Becker et al., 1986; O'Brien, 1991; Smith, 1988; Smith & Israel, 1987), poor parental sexual boundaries (Canavan et al., 1992; Smith & Israel, 1987), family secrets (Canavan et al., 1992; Smith & Israel, 1987), lack of parental supervision (Smith & Israel, 1987), family stress and dysfunction (Adler & Schutz, 1995;

TABLE 6.3 Problems Associated With Negative Sibling Interactions

Difficulty with relationships
Mistrust
Suspiciousness
Fearfulness
Hateful feelings
Problems relating
Inability to form intimate relationships
Troubled parent-child relationships
Poor peer relationships
Aversion to nonsexual physical contact
Revictimization in subsequent relationships
Negative emotions
Self-blame
Depression
Anxiety
Anger
Low self-esteem
Sexual dysfunction
Avoidance of sexual contact
Sexual compulsiveness
Promiscuity
Sexual response difficulties
Posttraumatic stress symptoms
Intrusive thoughts
Flashbacks

SOURCE: Canavan, Meyer, & Higgs (1992); Daie, Witztum, & Eleff (1989); Laviola (1992); Wiehe (1997).

Canavan et al., 1992), and a history of maternal sexual or physical victimization (Adler & Schutz, 1995; Kaplan, Becker, & Martinez, 1990). More methodologically sound studies that use comparison groups and well-established reliable and valid questionnaires confirm these findings. Worling (1995), for example, compared 32 male sex offenders who assaulted younger siblings with 28 males who offended against nonsibling children. Results of this study were largely consistent with clinical studies in finding that adolescent sibling-incest offenders reported significantly more marital discord among parents, feelings of parental rejection, histories of childhood sexual victimization, parental physical discipline, a negative and argumentative family atmosphere, and general dissatisfaction with family relationships.

The families of siblings who engage in violent or sexually inappropriate behaviors appear to have several features in common. One possible explanation linking these characteristics with a pattern of abuse is that children who live with abusive and rejecting parents may turn to each other for comfort, nurturance, and support through sexual interactions (Dunn & McGuire, 1992). Conversely, sibling offenders may be pursuing some form of retribution within their families for the abuse and rejection that they have suffered (Schetky & Green, 1988). A social learning theory might also apply in that the heightened degree of marital discord, childhood sexual abuse, physical discipline, and negative communication patterns may serve as a source of modeling and may facilitate the attitude that family members are appropriate recipients of violence (Davis & Leitenberg, 1987; Worling, 1995).

SECTION SUMMARY

The past several years have seen a *conceptual broadening* of the circumstances that might be worthy of the child maltreatment label. One proposed form of child maltreatment, which some believe should be recognized as the most common form of family violence, is *sibling abuse*. Critics argue, however, that the majority of negative interactions that occur between siblings consist of minor forms of behavior that should be labeled as *normal sibling rivalry* or *exploratory sex play* rather than as child maltreatment. Criteria helpful in distinguishing sibling abuse from nonabusive sibling interactions include a *power disparity* between siblings, the *frequency and duration* of the interaction, an element of *pressure or secrecy*, the *outcome* of the interaction, the *developmental appropriateness* of the behavior, and a *lack of appropriate parental intervention*.

Because of the challenges and ambiguity in defining *abusive* behavior between siblings, the extent of sibling abuse has been difficult to determine. Research examining the *psychological sequelae* associated with negative sibling interactions is also limited, although available studies indicate that the problems reported by siblings are similar to those reported by victims of other forms of child maltreatment. The *families* who engage in violent or sexually inappropriate behavior share several common features including a *history of child abuse and neglect, a chaotic family environment, excessive caretaking responsibilities for other family members, a lack of parental supervision*, and *parental absence or rejection*.

CHILD MALTREATMENT OUTSIDE THE FAMILY

As we have noted throughout this book, the overwhelming majority of child maltreatment occurs *intrafamilially* and involves physical aggression, neglect, sexual abuse, and psychological maltreatment perpetrated primarily by parents or other caretakers responsible for the welfare of children. The concept of child maltreatment, as we have seen in this chapter, however, has been extended to include additional conditions and circumstances occurring both within the family (e.g., children exposed to marital violence) and outside the family (e.g., children exposed to community violence). In the following sections, we focus on additional forms of child maltreatment that primarily occur *extrafamilially,* such as abuse in institutions and day care settings, ritualistic abuse, sex rings, and the exploitation of children through pornography and prostitution. Despite the limited scientific knowledge about these forms of exploitation, their sensationalistic nature has made them popular in the media. Media and public attention focused on abuse in day care settings, ritualistic abuse, child pornography and prostitution, and sex rings has often contributed to the public's misperception about the extent of such child maltreatment. In general, these types of child exploitation occur less commonly than those discussed previously. Yet frequency of occurrence, alone, should not determine social concern about a problem. The negative impact on children's lives resulting from such experiences can be just as significant as other forms of child maltreatment.

Institutional Abuse

Institutional abuse can occur in various settings including, but not limited to, foster homes, group homes, residential treatment centers, and licensed child care facilities. In 1984, the issue of child abuse perpetrated by institutional personnel was dramatically brought into public view through the attention focused on the McMartin Preschool case in Manhattan Beach, California (see boxed insert in Chapter 4: "Do Children Fabricate Reports of Child Sexual Abuse?"). Although there were no convictions, the publicity surrounding this case brought institutional abuse into public focus and left many with the impression that children are at increased risk of abuse in child care settings.

Studies evaluating the extent of abuse and neglect in institutional settings suggest that child maltreatment in these out-of-home settings is less common than other forms of child maltreatment. Wang and Daro (1998) reported on data from the Annual Fifty State Survey and found that only 3% of confirmed abuse cases in 1997 occurred in day care centers, foster care, or other institutional care settings. Wang and Daro further asserted that this pattern has remained consistent during the past 11 years. Finkelhor et al. (1988) recently conducted a national survey of day care sexual abuse cases and estimated that the rate of sexual abuse in child care centers was 5.5 per 10,000 children, compared with 8.9 per 10,000 children in private households. These researchers concluded that children are at greater risk of being sexually abused at home than in child care centers and that child care centers are not a particularly high risk child maltreatment situation for children.

Although less common than other forms of child maltreatment, many children suffer sexual and physical abuse at the hands of individuals licensed to provide quality care for children. The majority of published research addressing child abuse and neglect in institutional settings has focused on physical and sexual abuse in child care centers. The characteristics of child maltreatment occurring in child care facilities differ in significant ways from abuse perpetrated in other circumstances (Faller, 1988b; Finkelhor et al., 1988; Kelley, Brant, & Waterman, 1993; Waterman, Kelly, Oliveri, & McCord, 1993). The proportion of women involved as perpetrators in child care centers, for example, is higher than in other cases of child maltreatment (Faller, 1988b; Kelley et al., 1993). Findings on child care abuse also suggest that such children are more likely to be abused by multiple perpetrators (Faller, 1988b; Finkelhor et al., 1988).

The types of sexual activity that occur in day care settings are similar to activities in other settings (e.g., activities ranging from fondling to sexual intercourse), but fondling appears to be the most commonly reported form of abuse in day care settings (e.g., Bybee & Mowbray, 1993a; Finkelhor et al., 1988). Aspects of physical abuse have also been described, including hitting, physical restraint, and food deprivation (Kelley et al., 1993). Other forms of sexual abuse described in day care settings include group sex situations in which three or more people are involved, pornography (e.g., taking pictures of children or of children and adults in various sexual activities), and more controversial claims such as bestiality and ritualistic elements of abuse (Bybee & Mowbray, 1993a; Faller, 1988b; Finkelhor et al., 1988; Kelley et al., 1993).

Studies examining the psychological impact of abuse in child care centers suggest that children abused in child care settings exhibit symptoms similar to children abused within their homes. A comprehensive study of sexual abuse in preschool settings described in *Behind the Playground Walls: Sexual Abuse in Preschools* (Waterman et al., 1993), for example, found that children who reported experiencing sexual abuse in preschools exhibited more social incompetence, cognitive problems, emotional difficulties, sexualized behaviors, and total behavior problems than a control group of children attending preschool. There is also evidence that abuse circumstances involving multiple perpetrators, multiple victims, pornography, and ritualistic elements are associated with more psychological difficulties for victims (Finkelhor et al., 1988; Kelley, 1989; Waterman et al., 1993).

In response to concern about the problem of institutional abuse, a number of policy and legislative changes have been initiated. Recommendations have been made for changes and reforms in the provision of institutional care services, and requirements providing for independent investigations into institutional maltreatment and state definitions of abuse and neglect that include persons providing out-of-home care have been established (Rindfleisch & Nunno, 1992). In addition, the U.S. Congress enacted a law in 1984 that required states to provide for employment history, background, and criminal checks to be made on new out-of-home care employees.

Additional responses to institutional abuse have focused on improving community detection and prevention of institutional abuse as well as providing treatment for children and families victimized by this form of abuse. One obvious first step in preventing and detecting abuse in day care centers is to increase supervision and monitoring at day care facilities to ensure the quality of care being provided (American Humane Association, 1993; Bybee & Mowbray, 1993b). Bybee and Mowbray also recommend educational initiatives to improve prevention and early detection efforts such as prevention education programs for children, parents, and day care workers. Finally, treatment should be available to all child victims of institutional abuse as well as to their families, who are also often affected by the abuse (Finkelhor et al., 1988; Kiser, Pugh, McColgan, Pruitt, & Edwards, 1991; Waterman et al., 1993).

Ritualistic Abuse

Through the late 1980s and early 1990s, many social scientists became interested in a form of abuse that was reportedly quite insidious and shockingly common: *ritualistic abuse.* Ritualistic abuse has been defined as

> abuse that occurs in a context linked to some symbols or group activities that have a religious, magical, or supernatural connotation, and where the invocation of these symbols or activities are [*sic*] repeated over time, and used to frighten and intimidate the children. (Finkelhor et al., 1988, p. 59)

Debates about ritualistic abuse have produced some of the most heated exchanges seen within the field of child maltreatment. These debates have centered on questions about the actual existence of this form of abuse (Jones, 1991; Putnam, 1991). Some of the most controversial claims involve cases of sexual abuse that are associated with forced drug use; cannibalism; impregnation; witnessing and receiving physical abuse or torture (e.g., biting, burning, whipping, and animal mutilation); being buried alive; death threats; witnessing or forced participation in infant "sacrifice" and adult murder; "marriage" to Satan; and acts involving feces, urine, and blood. Many issues remain unresolved. Several experts have questioned the foundation on which ritualistic abuse research is based, namely, the claims of victims reporting such experiences (see Box 6.1, "Satanic Ritual Abuse").

Information about ritualistic abuse comes primarily from reports of children attending day care centers and from the memories of adults reporting a history of childhood abuse. Research studies investigating the parameters of ritualistic abuse have focused on the prevalence of reported cases, the impact of this form of abuse on victims, and the characteristics of victims and perpetrators (for a review, see Kelley, 1996). Estimates of ritualistic abuse are difficult to determine not only because of disagreement about definitional issues but also because child protection and law enforcement agencies do not uniformly recognize ritualistic abuse as a specific and separate form of child maltreatment. Most studies attempting to determine estimates of ritualistic abuse either examine samples of children in day care centers, collect clinical samples, or survey mental health professionals about the number of cases they have encountered (e.g., Bottoms, Shaver, & Goodman, 1996; Goodman, Bottoms, & Shaver, 1994; Kelley, 1989; Snow & Sorenson, 1990). Although some of these reports indicate that as many as 13% of sexual abuse cases include ritualistic elements, most report that ritualistic abuse is relatively infrequent (e.g., Bottoms et al., 1996; Finkelhor et al., 1988; Goodman et al., 1994). Bottoms and colleagues, for

(text continued on p. 227)

BOX 6.1 Satanic Ritual Abuse

Patti was 32, and her sister, Bonnie, was 45 when they began seeing Huntington Beach therapist Timothy Maas in 1988. Soon after the treatment began, both reached the conclusion that they suffered from an unusual and controversial form of mental disorder called multiple personality disorder. The multiple personalities, they concluded, allowed them to repress three decades of abuse by their mother, 78-year-old Ellen Roe. As their therapy progressed, they uncovered increasingly bizarre memories—black-robed satanists performing bloody rituals, animal mutilations, satanic orgies, and infant sacrifices (Weber, 1991). Eventually, the two sisters brought a civil suit against their mother. In a 10 to 2 compromise vote, the jury ruled that although the women may well have been abused by someone, at worst Ellen Roe was guilty of negligence. The sisters were awarded no money (Lachnit, 1991).

Recall from Chapter 1 that from a social constructionist perspective, a social problem is anything that has been successfully labeled as such by interest groups. A social condition becomes a social problem only after claims-makers successfully raise awareness about that condition. Because claims-making about a condition, rather than the condition itself, is the central component in the definitional process, it is possible, in principle at least, that something could be seen as a social problem even if the condition does not exist. These issues have contributed to the controversy surrounding satanic ritual abuse.

To fully understand the controversy surrounding ritualistic abuse, we must consider the historical context in which these claims have appeared. Beginning in the 1980s, more and more adults began reporting recovered satanic memories of devil worship, human and animal sacrifices, and sexual torment. Children also reported abuse that included ritualistic elements. The term *satanic ritual abuse* (SRA) was introduced to describe this "new" form of child abuse. Although the term *ritualistic abuse* appeared later, it is a broader term that includes SRA as one of several forms of ritualistic abuse and de-emphasizes the satanic aspects emphasized in early definitions. Proponents of the reality of SRA have argued that thousands of children each year are victimized in satanic rituals involving cannibalism, sexual torture, incest, and murder. Critics, however, are skeptical and wonder whether large numbers of satanists actually are preying on children, or whether the so-called satanism scare is merely rumor and mass hysteria.

Many trace interest in SRA to the book *Michelle Remembers,* by psychiatrist Lawrence Pazder and his patient (and later, wife), Michelle Smith (Smith & Pazder, 1980). Smith was being treated by Pazder when she suddenly began to remember being victimized by a satanic cult during the 1950s. Among the many claims made by Smith was that she witnessed numerous ritualistic murders by the satanists. Smith also claimed that she was force-fed the ashes of a cremated victim. On another occasion, she reported that a fetus was butchered in front of her and that the bloody remains were smeared across her body (Victor, 1993).

Michelle Smith's story attracted considerable attention. Pazder and Smith were featured in *People Weekly* and the *National Enquirer.* They made numerous television and radio appearances and became nationally known "experts" on SRA (Victor, 1993). It was Pazder who coined the term *satanic ritual abuse* in a presentation to the American Psychiatric Association in 1980. Despite the considerable attention the case received, there was never any evidence uncovered that corroborated Michelle's stories. Her family, including two sisters who were not mentioned in the book, claimed that none of the SRA occurred (Victor, 1993).

Another survivor story that attracted national attention was *Satan's Underground,* by Lauren Stratford (1988). Like Michelle Smith, Stratford appeared on many television shows and used notoriety from her book to launch a career as an SRA therapist. When three writers for the evangelical magazine *Cornerstone* decided to investigate her story, however, they concluded that it was a "gruesome fantasy" (Passantino, Passantino, & Trott, 1990). Perhaps the most outrageous claim made by Stratford was that she was impregnated by satanists on three separate occasions and that each of the children was taken from her and killed. Because Stratford claimed to have led a fairly normal public life, Passantino and his colleagues found her claims easy to investigate. The *Cornerstone* writers found several people who knew Stratford in high school and college (when she claims to have had the children), but each witness denied that she was ever pregnant. Stratford could produce no witness to her pregnancy. According to Passantino and his colleagues, no one from Harvest House (the publisher) ever bothered to check her story.

Those who have been charged with investigating the SRA threat have expressed skepticism. FBI agent Kenneth Lanning (1991), a well-respected authority on child abuse, offered the following conclusions about SRA:

> In 1983 when I first began to hear victims' stories of bizarre cults and human sacrifice, I tended to believe them. I had been dealing with bizarre, deviant behavior for many years and had long since realized that almost anything is possible. The idea that there are a few cunning, secretive individuals in positions of power somewhere in this country regularly killing a few people as part of some ritual or ceremony and getting away with it is certainly within the realm of possibility. But the number of alleged cases began to grow and grow. We now have hundreds of victims alleging that thousands of offenders are murdering tens of thousands of people, and there is little or no corroborative evidence.
>
> Until hard evidence is obtained and corroborated, the public should not be frightened into believing that babies are being bred and eaten, that 50,000 missing children are being murdered in human sacrifices, or that Satanists are taking over America's day care centers. (pp. 172, 173)

Today, the social hysteria that characterized the satanism scare of the 1980s appears to have subsided (Mulhern, 1994). Although some observers remain true believers, it seems that most probably agree with Susan Kelley (1996), who reached the following conclusion after reviewing the literature: "The existence of a large scale network of satanic cults whose primary interest is the sexual abuse of children is clearly *not* supported by empirical findings or law enforcement findings" (p. 97). At the same time, however, the sexual abuse of children involving some *ritualistic elements* has been documented. It seems clear that child maltreatment, at times, does include abuse by adults who claim some allegiance to Satan, use satanic symbols, or invoke the name of Satan as a terrorizing tactic (Kelley, 1996; Waterman et al., 1993).

Perhaps the most fascinating aspect of the entire SRA debate is this: If there is so little evidence confirming the existence of SRA, why do so many perceive the SRA threat as real? One reason is that many of the major daytime talk shows (e.g., *The Oprah Winfrey Show, Geraldo,* and *Donahue*) and some prime-time shows (e.g., *20/20*) have aired programs on satanism and SRA. The 1988 Geraldo Rivera special "Exposing Satan's Underground," which featured Lauren Stratford and her story, attracted one of the largest audiences for an NBC documentary in history. Unfortunately, it is hard to imagine that many of the 19.8 million people who saw Stratford on *Geraldo* in 1988 were aware of the *Cornerstone* investigation or would later know that the book's publisher, Harvest House, pulled the book from store shelves in 1990 (Richardson, Best, & Bromley, 1991; Victor, 1993).

Another reason for misperceptions about SRA is that many helping professionals also believe SRA is real. Therapists, police officers, and child protection authorities, who are often required to attend seminars on current developments in their field, are exposed to SRA "experts." Although advertised as training workshops, these seminars tend to employ proselytizing techniques characteristic of organizations seeking recruits (Mulhern, 1991). Many well-meaning helping professionals, who are generally motivated by the desire to help abused clients, become convinced of the existence of SRA through these seminars. These professionals, in turn, have influenced state and county governments to respond to the SRA problem. In Los Angeles County, for example, a Ritual Abuse Task Force was formed in 1988 to deal with the perceived increase in SRA. The task force received front-page attention in the *Los Angeles Times* in 1992 when many of its members claimed that satanists were attempting to silence them by pumping the pesticide Diazinon into the air-conditioning vents of their offices, homes, and cars. Although Diazinon poisoning is easy to detect, according to the epidemiologist assigned to the case, none of the 43 alleged victims of the poisoning could provide any evidence (Curtis, 1992).

These factors help explain why so much of the general public believes that the SRA threat is real. Can these factors also explain why so many people believe they were personally exposed to satanic abuse? Imagine an individual who is suffering in some way. That person might turn to a therapist to help alleviate this suffering. Therapists have been trained to suspect childhood histories of abuse in a large percentage of their clients. They are also trained to listen to, and support, victim accounts of abuse. Add to this situation a societal fascination with satanism, and distortions are possible, maybe even likely. In some situations, SRA may provide a therapist and client a believable explanatory framework for psychological symptoms and problems. This may be especially likely with highly disturbed clients, who may be more susceptible to explanations and interpretations offered by therapists who probe for SRA patterns.

Clients' (through the popular media) and therapists' (through training seminars) exposure to the same theories of SRA may also explain why survivor stories, although independently offered, are often similar in detail. Proponents often cite this pattern as evidence that SRA must exist. According to Frank W. Putnam of the National Institute of Mental Health (1991), however, such reasoning represents a "naive and simplistic model of contagion. . . . The child abuse community is particularly susceptible to such a rumor process as there are multiple, interconnected communication/educational networks shared by therapists and patients alike" (p. 177). Satanist experts, talk show hosts, movies, and news magazine shows all share the same stories. Given that both therapists and potential clients are exposed to the same SRA stories, it is not surprising that survivor accounts are often similar.

Those who accept claims of SRA often maintain that society is simply unwilling to believe the "unbelievable." Proponents accurately remind us that sometimes the unbelievable is real. Until relatively recently, "outrageous" stories of sexual abuse and incest were dismissed as fantasy. At the same time, however, there is danger in accepting at face value accounts provided by "cult survivors," no matter how credible the witnesses might appear. Plausibility is not evidence. Lots of things are possible. The more outrageous the claims, the more the burden of proof must lie with those who are making the claims. Skeptics continue to raise several questions for which there appears to be no answer (see Richardson et al., 1991; Victor, 1993). If the number of satanists is increasing, they ask, where are they all? Where are the defectors who could so easily expose the satanists? Where are the dead bodies the satanists have supposedly used for sacrifices? Where are the animal carcasses that have supposedly been used to threaten children into silence?

Understandably, therapists do not see their clinical responsibility as one of corroborating client accounts of abuse. The therapist's role is to help the client heal and to provide a supportive environment. Raising skeptical questions could well be counterproductive to the therapist's role. According to Bottoms and her colleagues (1996), many of the clinicians surveyed who reported on client victims of SRA indicated that they openly questioned some of their clients' stories. These therapists were quick to point out, however, that they were careful not to assume the detective role and that the "facts" of the case were essentially irrelevant. Bottoms and her colleagues acknowledge the merit of this approach but raise questions about the consequences:

> When thousands of ritual abuse reports ignite widespread public and professional fears about a national or international satanic cult conspiracy, resulting in specific accusations of sexual abuse against preschool operators, teachers, parents, and other family members, as well as changes in state laws, it definitely *does* matter whether the cults actually exist. (p. 32)

Indeed, it is important that therapists recognize that unfounded claims of SRA probably hurt the goals of child protection. There can be little question that fabricated SRA stories have fueled the fire for skeptics who believe that children are not really abused. Although many recovered memories may be real, for example, fabricated SRA memories feed those skeptics who question the validity of *all* repressed memories. Similarly, although most childhood disclosures of abuse are substantiated, in a few highly publicized cases children have told improbable stories, also feeding skepticism. Attention to SRA appears to be creating additional problems, rather than providing much-needed solutions to child maltreatment.

---

example, surveyed clinical members of the American Psychological Association about their experiences with ritualistic abuse. Of the 2,722 respondents, 803 indicated that they had encountered one or more ritualistic or religion-related cases.

Reports of ritualistic abuse indicate that these cases tend to involve male and female victims to an equal degree (Snow & Sorenson, 1990; Waterman et al., 1993). With regard to perpetrator characteristics, however, gender discrepancies have been observed. Compared with nonritualistic abuse cases, ritualistic abuse is more likely to involve female perpetrators, multiple perpetrators, and multiple victims (Finkelhor et al., 1988; Jonker & Jonker-Bakker, 1991; Kelley, 1989; Snow & Sorenson, 1990; Waterman et al., 1993). Initial studies on the psychological impact of ritualistic abuse have found symptoms similar to those observed in sexually abused children, although several studies suggest that ritualistic abuse victims exhibit a greater degree of symptomatology compared with sexually abused children (Kelley, 1989; Waterman et al., 1993).

Organized Exploitation

Of all the major forms of child maltreatment discussed in this book, child sexual abuse is most likely to occur between a child and an adult who is not a family member. Organized exploitation is one form of child sexual abuse that typically occurs outside the family, although recent reports suggest that some elements of organized exploitation also occur intrafamilially (Itzin, 1997). *Organized exploi-*

tation typically refers to the sexual maltreatment of groups of children for the sexual stimulation of one or more perpetrators, for commercial gain, or both. Although the research on organized sexual exploitation is limited, this form of child maltreatment includes these activities, which are often interrelated: sex rings, pornography, and prostitution.

Child Sex Rings

Child sex rings consist of a number of children sexually abused by one or more perpetrators. Sexual demands are required for acceptance into the group, and various modes of deception, enticement, and manipulation ensure the cooperation of the children (Burgess, Groth, & McCausland, 1981; Lanning & Burgess, 1984).

Burgess and her colleagues have distinguished between the following three types of sex rings (Burgess & Hartman, 1987; Burgess, Hartman, McCausland, & Powers, 1984):

1. *Solo rings* consist of single adults involved with small groups of children.
2. *Syndicated rings* consist of multiple adults who create a well-structured organization for the purpose of recruiting children, producing pornography, delivering direct sexual services, and establishing a network of customers.
3. *Transitional rings* can be described as functioning at an intermediary position between solo and syndicated rings. The transitional ring consists of one or more adults and several children but does not include an organizational aspect. This type of ring may eventually move toward an organizational status (e.g., photographs may be sold).

One core element of sex rings, as noted in the above descriptions, is the inclusion of pornographic activities. Pornography is sometimes used to stimulate and instruct children in the groups (e.g., Burgess et al., 1984). In addition, the sexual activities of children in the rings are often photographed or videotaped, and it is believed that such rings may be the first phase of an organization leading to child prostitution and pornography (Creighton, 1993; Hunt & Baird, 1990; Wild, 1989).

Child Pornography

Child pornography has been defined as "photographs, films, videotapes, magazines, and books that depict children of either gender in sexually explicit acts" (Burgess & Hartman, 1987, p. 248). According to our discussion of child sexual abuse in Chapter 4, child pornography, by definition, is a form of child maltreatment. Child pornography, however, was legal in most U.S. states until the late 1970s. In 1978, the Protection of Children Against Sexual Exploitation Act was enacted in the United States to halt the production and dissemination of pornographic materials involving children. Soon thereafter, several other countries adopted prohibitions against child pornography as well (Doek, 1985; Tyler & Stone, 1985). In addition, the Child Sexual Abuse and Pornography Act of 1986 provided for federal prosecution of individuals engaged in child pornography, including parents who permit their children to engage in such activities (Otto & Melton, 1990). Legislation within the United States has also been passed in several states mandating that commercial film and photo processors inform authorities about suspected child pornography that is discovered during the processing of film (Wurtele & Miller-Perrin, 1992).

Determining the number of children involved in child pornography is an extremely difficult task, given that the production, distribution, and sale of child pornography are often cloaked in secrecy because such activities are illegal. Government subcommittees investigating the problem of child pornography in America, however, determined that a significant number of children are sexually exploited, with an estimated 7% of the pornographic industry in the United States involving children in sexual activities (cited in Pierce, 1984). Youth who are runaways constitute the majority of children involved in child pornography (Pierce, 1984).

Child pornography not only is abusive in and of itself but also may contribute to the problem of child maltreatment by stimulating adult sexual interest in children (Rush, 1980; Russell, 1988). Results of studies evaluating the role of pornography in affecting a perpetrator's likelihood of offending a child are equivocal. Some studies have found that CSA perpetrators do use pornography more than comparison groups, whereas others have found no relationship between sexual perpetration and pornography (Carter, Prentky, Knight, Vanderveer, & Boucher, 1987; Howe, 1995; Malamuth & Briere, 1986). There is no doubt, however, that child pornography contributes to the exploitation of children by creating a market for the victimization of children and by serving as a tool for perpetrators to educate and stimulate victims or to blackmail victims into maintaining secrecy about abusive activities (Burgess & Hartman, 1987; Hunt & Baird, 1990; Tyler & Stone, 1985).

Little has been written about addressing the problem of child pornography outside the enactment of federal and state legislation that prohibits the use of minors in the production of pornographic material. Although such laws have been somewhat successful in curtailing the problem within the United States, worldwide prohibitions will be necessary to completely eliminate the problem of child pornography (Tyler & Stone, 1985). With the advent of the computer, the problem has become increasingly complex because access to and trading of child pornography have become a worldwide problem of considerable magnitude (Durkin & Bryant, 1995; Hughes, 1996; Ireland, 1993).

Child Prostitution

Of all the various forms of organized exploitation, child prostitution has received the greatest empirical attention. Official estimates of child prostitution are not currently available. Surveys of adult prostitutes, however, suggest that a significant number began work as prostitutes when they were children. Silbert and Pines (1983) found that 70% of the 200 San Francisco street prostitutes they surveyed reported that they were under 21 years of age at the time they began prostitution. Of these, 60% reported they were under age 16 when they started work as prostitutes. Other studies report on child prostitutes as young as 10 years of age, with a median age for entry into prostitution at age 14 (e.g., Nadon, Koverola, & Schludermann, 1998).

> Adolescent prostitutes characteristically have a history of childhood physical and sexual abuse.

A considerable number of investigations have explored possible antecedents to child prostitution. Characteristics of adolescent prostitutes that have been repeatedly documented in the literature include a history of childhood maltreatment including physical and sexual abuse and exposure to interparental violence, personal and parental alcohol or drug abuse, and poor family functioning (e.g., Bagley & Young, 1987; Bracey, 1979; Earls & David, 1990; Silbert, 1982). One of the most predictive factors in the backgrounds of adolescent prostitutes, however, is their runaway youth status because of death of a parent, being kicked out of the family home, or running away from home because of alcoholism or abuse in the home (Nadon et al., 1998).

Like child sex rings, child prostitution is also associated with child pornography. Silbert and Pines (1983) found that 38% of their sample of San Francisco adult prostitutes described the taking of sexually explicit photographs of themselves for commercial purposes when they were children. Ten percent described being used in pornographic films and magazines when they were children. Child pornography and prostitution have also been linked in reports of international trafficking of women and children, a trade sometimes referred to as *sex tourism.* Sex tourism involves the purchase of women or children as part of a package that includes sexual privileges (Itzin, 1997; Joseph, 1995). According to Muntarbhorn (1995), the United Nations recently concluded that child prostitution and pornography represent "a vast national and transnational problem" (cited in Itzin, 1997, p. 62).

SUMMARY

In addition to the various forms of child maltreatment discussed in previous chapters, conceptions of child maltreatment have broadened to include other circumstances that are associated with negative developmental outcomes for children. Some of these forms of child maltreatment, such as exposure to marital and community violence, are common and have been increasingly recognized as threats to the well-being of children. Other circumstances have been described in the literature with healthy debate (e.g., sibling abuse), whereas others have been surrounded by controversy (e.g., ritualistic abuse). Still other forms of child maltreatment are less common, but no less damaging, including the abuse of children in alternative care and the involvement of children in child sex rings, pornography, and prostitution.

Estimates of the number of children who experience child maltreatment indirectly, through exposure to violence within their homes and communities, are staggering. Conservative estimates suggest that at least 3.3 million children are exposed to marital violence annually. Although no official estimates of the number of children exposed to community violence are available, survey data suggest that 40% or more of inner-city youth are exposed to some type of violence within the community. Exposure to marital and community violence is an adverse situation that is frequently associated with negative emotional outcomes including posttraumatic stress symptoms, depression, aggression, and low self-esteem. Exposure to marital violence has also been associated with cognitive (e.g., school problems), behavioral (e.g., aggression), and health (e.g., somatic symptoms) problems. Observing physical violence between one's parents or within the community may have a direct negative effect on children or an indirect effect mediated by factors such as parental alcoholism, direct physical or sexual abuse, family stressors, level of exposure, and so forth. The large number of variables simultaneously influencing children's behavior and the methodological problems inherent in the studies conducted to date make ferreting out the effects attributable to only observation of violence a truly challenging research task. In reality, little is known with certainty about the effects of observing marital or community violence. Interventions are primarily directed at both the child and his or her family. Programs for children exposed to marital violence typically include group therapy for children as well as multiservice programs. Interventions for children exposed to community violence have focused on police responses to children and public policy initiatives.

Some debate has surrounded the issue of whether sibling abuse should be considered an additional form of child maltreatment. On the one hand, some children experience severe physical violence or inappropriate sexual behaviors at the hands of siblings. On the other hand, sibling abuse may not be as pervasive as some accounts suggest. As is true with any form of child maltreatment, the extent of the problem depends on the definitions used by researchers, clinicians, and other professionals. Many have used overly inclusive definitions of sibling abuse, for example, resulting in estimates that suggest that more than 80% of children are victims of sibling abuse. Before defining an interaction between siblings as abusive, a number of factors should be considered including the frequency and duration of negative behaviors, the degree of resulting harm, the power disparity between siblings, elements of pressure or secrecy, the developmental appropriateness of the behavior, and the type of parental intervention initiated. Before determining the magnitude of sibling abuse, more sound research needs to be undertaken. Additional research should focus on the parameters of sibling abuse including incidence and prevalence rates, associated psychological symptoms, and victim and perpetrator characteristics.

Forms of child maltreatment occurring outside the family have also been described, including abuse in day care centers, ritualistic abuse, abuse in child sex rings, and the exploitation of children through pornography and prostitution. Many of these forms of child maltreatment have been the subject of sensationalistic media accounts that have contributed to public misperception about these forms of child maltreatment. Institutional abuse, for example, includes abuse in out-of-home settings such as foster care, residential treatment centers, and licensed child care facilities. Child maltreatment in these institutional settings, however, is much less common than abuse occurring within the home. Official estimates suggest that only 3% of confirmed child maltreatment cases involve institutional abuse. Most research on institutional abuse has focused on abuse occurring in child care facilities and suggests that this form of abuse is more likely to involve multiple perpetrators who are female. Although research has appeared describing the parameters of ritualistic abuse such as prevalence rates, associated psychological symptoms, and victim and perpetrator characteristics, ritualistic abuse represents one of the most controversial topics within the field of child maltreatment.

> Children involved in prostitution and pornography are often runaways from a dysfunctional or abusive home environment.

Organized exploitation is another form of child maltreatment that involves groups of children who are abused for the sexual stimulation of one or more perpetrators and often for commercial gain. Although research investigating organized exploitation is limited, this form of child maltreatment involves three interrelated activities that include child sex rings, pornography, and prostitution. One core element of child sex rings is the inclusion of pornographic activities, and many believe that sex rings may be the first phase of organized exploitation leading to child prostitution and child pornography. Another similarity between the various types of organized exploitation is that children involved in prostitution and pornography are often runaway youth attempting to escape a dysfunctional or abusive home environment. Interventions aimed at alleviating the problem of institutional abuse and organized exploitation have focused primarily on policy initiatives and legislative changes designed to protect children from these activities. Although these approaches have met with some success, more efforts need to be directed at these less common, but no less detrimental, forms of child maltreatment.

7

Looking Toward the Future

CHAPTER OUTLINE

AN INTERVIEW WITH DEBORAH DARO

"Child abuse will be diminished when parents are provided adequate supports to help them care for their children and communities are structured to assist families in this task."

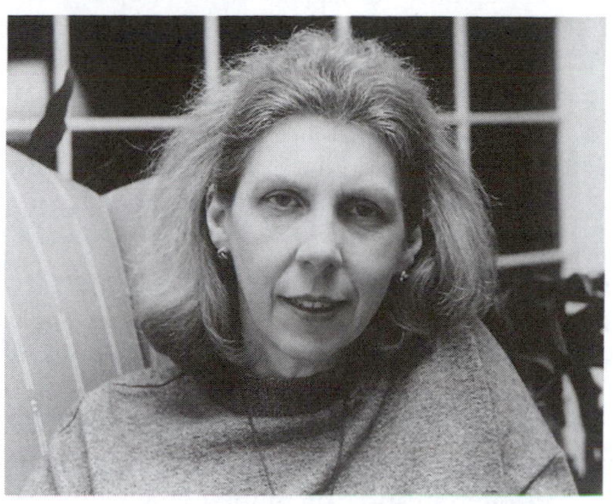

Deborah Daro serves as the Director of the National Center on Child Abuse Prevention Research, a program of the National Committee to Prevent Child Abuse. She brings to the center more than 20 years of experience in evaluating child abuse treatment and prevention programs. She has directed some of the largest multisite program evaluations completed in the field. All her program assessments have included a unique blend of quantitative and qualitative components, resulting in findings that have both statistical and program relevance. She has published and lectured widely. Her commentaries and findings are frequently cited in the rationale for numerous child abuse prevention and treatment reforms. She has served as President of the American Professional Society on the Abuse of Children and is presently on the Executive Council of the International Society for the Prevention of Child Abuse and Neglect. She holds a Ph.D. in social welfare and a master's degree in city and regional planning, both from the University of California at Berkeley.

Q: What sparked your interest in the area of child maltreatment?

A: Anne Cohn Donnelly introduced me to the issue in 1976. She was completing a comprehensive evaluation of the first wave of federally funded demonstration projects on the treatment of abuse and neglect. As a graduate student, I worked with her on this project and later went on to direct a similar evaluation of 19 clinical demonstration projects, each of which targeted families involved in a specific aspect of maltreatment (e.g., neglect, sexual abuse, adolescent maltreatment, and therapeutic services for abused children and parents involved in substance abuse and child abuse). The reason I got involved in this issue, and have remained involved for more than 20 years, is my belief that a society's treatment of its children reflects that society's values and priorities. Examining the issue of child maltreatment requires one to consider not only how individual parents treat their children but also how the systems put in place function to protect and nurture children.

Q: What are your current professional responsibilities?

A: I direct the National Center on Child Abuse Prevention Research, a program of the National Committee to Prevent Child Abuse. The center's dual goal is to enhance our understanding of how best to prevent child abuse and to serve as a link between research and practice. In this capacity, I am responsible for the design and implementation of a wide range of research projects and provide guidance to policy and program administrators on how to best use data in crafting effective prevention initiatives.

Q: What would you describe as your most influential contribution to the field of child maltreatment?

A: In cooperation with my NCPCA colleagues, we developed Healthy Families America (HFA), a national initiative to establish infrastructure necessary to sustain a universal support system for all new parents. Unlike prior prevention initiatives, HFA represents a new commitment to offering prevention at a scale and with the level of intensity necessary to effectively prevent child abuse for all parents willing to access assistance. The initiative is based on four principals: universal availability, differential service levels based on individual need, flexible replication within a quality framework, and dual emphasis on altering parental behaviors and community context.

Q: What is your current research focus?

A: As prevention seeks to go to scale, we need to understand more specifically why parents elect to engage or not engage in voluntary support services. Consequently, we are examining the participant, provider, program, and community characteristics that are associated with successful engagement and retention of families in prevention services. Also, we are examining the strategies that states are employing to transform isolated prevention *programs* targeting a specific group of parents into integrated prevention *systems* providing the institutional and normative support all parents require.

Q: What can be done to prevent child abuse?

A: Child abuse will be diminished when parents are provided adequate supports to help them care for their children and communities are structured to assist families in this task. Key to accomplishing this mission is providing a universal system of support for all new parents with service levels determined by a family's level of need. For families facing the greatest challenges in caring for their children (e.g., young, single, low-income parents), intensive home visitation services appear particularly promising in reducing maltreatment risk. As children grow, a variety of social services, health care, and educational opportunities need to be available for them and their parents. Equally important, however, is grounding these individual efforts in a normative and community context more supportive to all new parents. To succeed, prevention must produce communities that nurture stronger relationships and a sense of mutual reciprocity among all families.

Q: What is the biggest problem in trying to eliminate child maltreatment?

A: Child abuse will never be fully eliminated because society will continue to provide parents enormous latitude in how they care for their children. In a culture as diverse as the United States and which places a high value on freedom, family privacy, and individual liberties, excessive supervision or adherence to a single parental standard will be inappropriate and, in the long run, ineffective. That said, it is appropriate for a society to reach consensus on what it, in turn, expects from parents and what it is willing to offer parents in the way of continuing support. We will never be able to significantly reduce maltreatment levels if we do not find a better fit between our child protection rhetoric and our cultural norms and political actions.

Q: What types of policy recommendations are most needed in the field of child maltreatment?

A: Effectively combating child maltreatment will require policy reforms in a number of social institutions. Certainly, reform of the child welfare system is key. Emphasis needs to be placed on protecting children from harm, not simply punishing families after abuse occurs. Equally important to reforming child welfare practice, however, is creating a physical environment for families conducive to healthy development. Communities need to be safe, nurturing places for children and families where good health care, quality schools, sound housing, and safe open space are the rule rather than the exception. Further, as broad changes are recommended in welfare policy and health care delivery systems, care needs to be taken to document the spillover effects for children, particularly those living in poverty or in single-parent families.

Q: What type of advocacy interests do you have?

A: My advocacy interests lie not in promoting a given legislative agenda but rather in fostering a deep social commitment to child welfare across all economic groups. I want people to expect for all children what they expect for their own children—the opportunity to achieve their maximum potential. Too often, we seek to reduce only the worst types of abuse, rather than universally raising the safety bar for all children. Once the public realizes this message, they, not me, will advocate for the necessary legislative reforms.

Q: What do you think communities need to do to assist child victims of maltreatment?

A: The first thing communities have to do is reaffirm the child's right to be protected from further harm. Communities need to reaffirm the message to children that the abuse they have experienced is not their fault and that such behavior will be neither condoned nor tolerated. Although communities will have different standards regarding parental authority and family privacy, no community should condone abusive behavior. Second, communities need to have adequate services available to help children overcome the consequences of maltreatment. Finally, they need to provide directed assistance to parents willing to reexamine and change their behavior. If parents are unable or unwilling to accept responsibility for their actions, communities need to provide safe and stable alternatives for abused children.

We approach this final chapter with two primary goals in mind. First, we reexamine theoretical and methodological limitations that have hindered the accumulation of knowledge about child maltreatment (see Chapter 2). We also consider what some solutions might be. Second, we examine a variety of strategies designed to prevent child maltreatment. Because child maltreatment is one of the most enduring problems in all human history, it is hard to imagine a program or policy that will make it disappear. Many existing prevention efforts have been effective, however, and there is every reason to be optimistic that public and professional attention to the problem will produce increasingly positive results.

ADVANCING THE FIELD OF CHILD MALTREATMENT

Causes of Child Maltreatment

Examining Research Models

In discussions of the causes, experts have formulated a variety of models to identify correlates of child maltreatment. Some experts focus on the individual pathology of offenders and emphasize the deviant characteristics of child maltreatment perpetrators. In support of the individual pathology model, there is evidence that some offenders score high on measures of psychopathology (Williams & Finkelhor, 1990). Other evidence suggests that child maltreatment offenders exhibit specific cognitive distortions resulting in misperceptions about their victims. In sexual abuse, for example, perpetrators may hold misperceptions about children's consent and enjoyment related to the abuse (see Seidman et al., 1994). In physical child abuse, parents often have negative perceptions and hold unrealistic expectations of their children (Azar et al., 1988; Bauer & Twentyman, 1985).

Other models focus on social learning, which examines the role of childhood socialization in the development of violent and abusive offender behavior. Research on the intergenerational transmission of child maltreatment has consistently demonstrated a link between childhood abuse experiences and later adult perpetration (C. S. Widom, 1989). This cycle of abuse, however, is not a universal law, as many maltreated children do not become abusive adults, and many abusive adults did not grow up in abusive homes. These observations serve as a reminder that other factors, in addition to social learning principles, contribute to the occurrence of family violence.

Still other explanations focus on family and environmental stress factors. Structural factors within the family increase the likelihood of violence, such as spending a great amount of time with family members and the intensity of these interactions, power differentials that exist within the family, and the lack of public surveillance in families (e.g., Brinkerhoff & Lupri, 1988; Denzin, 1984; Gelles, 1993a). A social structural framework also implicates various forms of environmental stress as contributing to child maltreatment. Stress associated with unemployment, poverty, poor housing, family demands, and lack of social support (i.e., social isolation), for example, have been associated with all forms of child abuse (e.g., Whipple & Webster-Stratton, 1991).

Some experts have emphasized the role of sociocultural factors such as cultural acceptance of violence and parental dominance. Physical child abuse, for example, may reflect society's tolerance of lower levels of parent-to-child violence, including corporal punishment (Straus, 1994a).

Constructing Theories

In his well-known text on research methodology in the social sciences, Earl Babbie (1995) defines *theory* as "a systemic set of interrelated statements that intends to explain some aspect of social life" (p. 48). If one examines the models of child maltreatment described above in the context of Babbie's definition, it is clear that child maltreatment theory is lacking. There are empirical correlates, which focus on single-factor explanations, but this alone cannot fully explain child maltreatment. Only a few multidimensional models exist to describe the many factors and the interactional nature of these factors in the etiology of child maltreatment (e.g., Belsky, 1993).

Researchers within the field of child maltreatment need to direct more effort toward the development and integration of theory. Ideally, the scientific method, to which all social science students are exposed, begins with theory. Theory produces hypotheses, which lead to research, which produces findings, which are then used to modify theory. This *deductive* method of research is but one method, but it is the traditional and, arguably, the best method.

Methodological Issues

Identifying Research Limitations

We have discussed several methodological issues that historically have made child maltreatment a difficult topic to study. These issues continue to limit child maltreatment research. Methodological limitations include definitional ambiguity, a lack of experimental and longitudinal studies, an overreliance on correlational research, small and nonrepresentative samples, and inappropriate comparison groups.

In part because of these methodological problems, many within and outside social science circles do not consider child maltreatment a rigorous research area of social *science.* At various times in our professional careers, we have heard comments from colleagues suggesting that child maltreatment research is an advocacy topic and that publications in the field do not carry professional clout (see also Chapter 2). The issues that plague child maltreatment research are real and need to be addressed.

Overcoming Methodological Problems

It is obvious that top-quality research includes the commitment to longitudinal and experimental designs, large representative samples, and appropriate comparison groups. Training and educational programs for professionals in the field also need to emphasize the scientific method so that professionals are prepared to conduct and evaluate top-quality research. Publishers of research on child maltreatment, furthermore, need to commit to holding authors to high standards.

An additional recommendation is for individuals in the field to commit to a value-free research perspective. Of course, given the nature of the subject matter, a true value-free approach is undoubtedly impossible and is probably not desirable. At the same time, we must be careful not to discard the scientific method in favor of an advocacy-driven approach to knowledge. Despite the significant role of advocates in the discovery of child maltreatment, their involvement has produced a tenuous union between claims-making and scientific research. As stated in Chapter 1, advocacy involves the use—and sometimes misuse—of "facts" and scientific rhetoric in an attempt to advance a moral or interest group agenda. It is questionable, however, whether some of these "facts" have always served the interests of the victims of child maltreatment or the field as a whole. Crusades, for example, are often characterized by extreme statements or exaggerations that many in society simply do not accept. This type of advocacy tone no doubt contributes to the perception that child maltreatment has abandoned the scientific method.

An example from the university where we teach illustrates the potential problem of advocacy research. During a recent graduation ceremony, Dennis Praeger, a well-known radio talk show host in the Los Angeles area, said this: "I have never once come across a study that contravened common sense. Studies either substantiate common sense, or they are wrong" (Commencement address, Pepperdine University, April 25, 1997). Because the comment was directed at recent graduates, who supposedly had spent the previous 4 years being challenged about their own commonsense understandings of the world, many people were angered. Those of us in the social sciences were especially insulted, because Praeger's comment had been directed primarily at social science "findings" that he suggested are more political than empirical. This attitude illustrates that if our research digresses into advocacy couched in the language of science, then it can easily be dismissed by those who do not share our passion for child protection. How can we expect these same people to take us seriously when we do produce legitimate research? We need Dennis Praeger, and others such as him, to view our research as credible. Such individuals are the ones who will be talking on the radio, speaking to groups, or voting to appropriate funds to help alleviate child maltreatment.

Another example of the problems associated with mixing advocacy and research is illustrated in the book *Sexual Mutilations: A Human Tragedy* (Denniston & Milos, 1997). In advertisements from the publisher, the claim is made that the book will reveal the harmful physical, social, and emotional side effects of an involuntary sexual mutilation that affects 13.2 million boys annually. And what is this insidious act of sexual mutilation that adversely affects so many young boys? The answer is circumcision.

Whether circumcision has the harmful effects its authors claim is irrelevant for our purposes. The book is illustrative of our point because of the clear advocacy stance of the authors. Their purpose as authors is stated clearly in the advertisement: the elimination of the culturally accepted practice of circumcision. Adopting this advocacy tone, however, may be counterproductive to their cause because the book may be dismissed by many as claims-making couched in the language of science. Indeed, claims that circumcision is an emotionally damaging form of "sexual mutilation" are likely to be seen as outrageous by many Americans, a large percentage of whom are circumcised and may not feel emotionally scarred by the experience.

Debates About Definitions

A related issue concerns debates about definitions of child maltreatment. Terms such as *maltreatment, abuse,* and *neglect* are not objectively defined. Because the specific meanings of these terms are socially constructed, they vary dramatically from one culture to the next, one state to the next, and one person to the next. There is, for example, no federal definition of child maltreatment. Definitions vary, depending on their purpose; a social worker, therapist, researcher, or police officer may each mean something different when referring to child maltreatment. Such problems are inevitable because different definitions serve different purposes. The only solution, therefore, is to clearly define and operationalize all terms we use and not to assume that everyone is using the same definition.

One reason for definitional controversy is the confusion about research versus advocacy. The book *Sexual Mutilations: A Human Tragedy* once again serves as an effective illustration. These authors clearly attempt to influence a definition through claims-making and have employed a technique not uncommon in advocacy claims. They have taken a common practice (circumcision), given it a gruesome-sounding name (sexual mutilation), and defined it as a "human tragedy." "Sexual mutilation," they say, is clearly "child abuse"—therefore, circumcision is child abuse. If the authors are successful in their claims, they will have forever changed the concept of sexual mutilation. With each new "discovery" of a new form of abuse, however, the term becomes broader and broader, creating the danger that the label could essentially become useless.

Emery and Laumann-Billings (1998), in their review of current knowledge on child maltreatment, argue that there is an ever-increasing need to distinguish between less severe cases of harm or endangerment and the most serious forms of physical violence, emotional trauma, and sexual abuse. We agree and argue that it is probably inappropriate to use the same terms to describe severe abuse and less uniformly condemned forms of aggressive normative behavior (e.g., certain forms of sibling aggression and corporal punishment). According to Emery and Laumann-Billings, the literature on sibling violence serves as an ideal example. Experts estimate that 80% of children are pushed, hit, or grabbed by a sibling (Finkelhor & Dziuba-Leatherman, 1994). With exceptions, this type of behavior between siblings, especially younger ones, "surely is seen as normal if inappropriate behavior rather than violence by most parents and professionals" (Emery & Laumann-Billings, 1998, p. 123). The problem is that if we take this figure to its extreme and argue that 80% of the population is abused and victimized, then the terms *abuse* and *victimization* largely lose their meaning. Please do not misunderstand our point here. We agree with most of our colleagues that *all* family aggression, no matter how common, is inappropriate and should not be condoned by society. Our point is that we should be careful to not equate these different forms of aggression because they have differing causes and differing outcomes and typically require different intervention strategies.

> Less severe cases of harm should be distinguished from the most serious forms of violence and abuse.

Working With One Another

Hindering our progress in understanding child maltreatment are the many controversies that exist within the field. Some have noted a fair amount of antagonism and hostility between people who are presumably on the same team but cannot agree on the problem (Gelles & Loseke, 1993). All too often, child maltreatment experts see themselves as competitors for public attention and public support. One child protection expert, for example, might argue that parents spank too much, whereas another might claim that parents do not spank enough. One clinician might argue that repressed memories are common, whereas another might claim that they do not exist. Disagreement between competing claims-makers can sometimes become quite heated. In the long run, however, extreme disagreements do not serve the best interests of children. We encourage individuals within the field to use a reasonable level of restraint when engaged in such debates. Often, the battles are seemingly more divisive than they need to be. In the concluding chapter of *Current Controversies on Family Violence* (1993), editors Richard Gelles and Donileen Loseke admit to their contributing authors that they felt it necessary to "sanitize" many of the manuscripts, "stripping them of caustic, scathing, libelous, sarcastic, and personalistic criticisms" (p. 362). This type of antagonism within the family violence community, although perhaps predictable, is not in the best interests of children or the field. Gelles and Loseke argue, and we concur, that it is more fruitful to recognize the many similar perspectives various professionals bring to the issue. All child maltreatment professionals denounce violence and are concerned about victims who experience such violence. The belief we share is particularly obvious when one compares the antiviolence interests of the field with a society that implicitly condones, or at least tolerates, many forms of child maltreatment. We are, therefore, well served to remember that we are really all members of the same team.

> Despite disagreements, child maltreatment professionals are really all members of the same team.

PREVENTING CHILD MALTREATMENT

When one considers the scope of human history, it is shocking to see how societies have ignored children. Prior to the mid-1800s, for example, there is little historical reference to organized child protection. The Society for the Prevention of Cruelty to Children was not founded until 1875, 9 years *after* the formation of the Society for the Prevention of Cruelty to *Animals* (Emery & Laumann-Billings, 1998). Throughout most of human history, the dominance and authority of parents have been unquestioned, with children often becoming the victims as a result.

Although child maltreatment has been identified as a social problem only recently, the changing societal response to the problem during the past hundred years has been dramatic. Consider the following childhood memory of the first author:

> I remember my parents discussing with our neighbors a boy at my school whose back was lacerated from the beating he had received from his father. His injuries were discovered when our teacher noticed the markings after the boy's shirt flew up during a dodgeball game. Although I was only about age 10 or so at the time, I remember that many of the adults involved in the

> discussion seemed to believe that the boy's parents had "the right" to discipline their child as they saw fit.

It is doubtful that the adults involved in this discussion would express the same opinion today. Parents and professionals alike have become increasingly aware of the limitations placed on parental behaviors and the measures enacted to enhance the protection of children. Every state and district in the United States has enacted mandatory reporting laws for suspected child abuse (Schene, 1996). In addition, two thirds of children now report involvement in victimization prevention programs (Finkelhor & Dziuba-Leatherman, 1994), and television commercials regularly advertise the tragedy of child maltreatment. Given the historical record that demonstrates the tremendous degree of maltreatment that children have endured (deMause, 1974; Pleck, 1987), it is reasonable to conclude that children are probably more protected today than at any other time in history. This pattern of improvement, however, should not dampen our resolve for greater change. For the millions of victims of child maltreatment worldwide, the optimism of increasing community concern about child maltreatment provides little consolation. We must persevere in our attempts to address and alleviate their victimization.

In discussing the problems in the child protection system, Melton and Barry (1994) have written that "the system responds to allegations, not needs" (p. 5). Their argument, which seems generally true, is that CPS focuses on reporting and investigation to the exclusion of prevention and treatment. Many advocates also maintain that more efforts need to be directed at preventing violence before it occurs.

We thus turn our attention to a discussion of prevention efforts. We have divided these efforts into three categories that although not exhaustive of the many prevention programs that could be implemented, illustrate prevention strategies currently receiving the most attention. First, we discuss strategies that try to equip children to protect themselves. In general, these programs focus on sexual abuse. Second, we examine the many programs that identify at-risk parents, promote parental competency, and attempt to reduce the amount of stress experienced by families. Finally, we present a variety of societal measures that have the potential to reduce the amount of child victimization in society.

Targeting Potential Victims

School-Based Programs for Children

During the 1980s, school-based empowerment programs to help children avoid and report victimizations became popular (Finkelhor & Dziuba-Leatherman, 1994). These programs generally teach children knowledge and skills believed to be important in protecting themselves from a variety of dangerous situations. Most have focused on sexual abuse and emphasized two goals: *primary prevention* (keeping the abuse from occurring) and *detection* (encouraging children to report past and current abuse; Reppucci, Land, & Haugaard, 1998). Empowerment programs have obvious appeal because they are an inexpensive way to affect many school-age children, who, for the most part, are eager to learn (Daro & McCurdy, 1994). A 1990 survey of elementary school districts conducted by Breen, Daro, and Romano (1991) revealed that 85% of districts offered education programs, with 65% of those education programs mandated (cited in Finkelhor, Asdigian, & Dziuba-Leatherman, 1995). Finkelhor et al. conducted the National Youth Victimization Intervention Study, a telephone survey of 2,000 children and their caretakers, and found that 67% of children reported being exposed to victimization prevention programs, with 37% of the children reporting participation within the last year.

Research evaluations of school-based programs suggest that in general, exposure to victimization programs increases knowledge and protection skills (Daro & McCurdy, 1994; Wurtele & Miller-Perrin, 1992). The National Youth Victimization Prevention Study, for example, found that children who were exposed to comprehensive school-based prevention programs were more knowledgeable about the dangers of sexual abuse and more effectively equipped with protection strategies in comparison with children who had not been exposed or who were only minimally exposed. Unfortunately, no research has demonstrated a decline in the actual number of victimizations associated with prevention programs (Finkelhor et al., 1995; Reppucci et al., 1998). There is speculation that these programs might lead to increased disclosures by victimized children, although this hypothesis has not been sufficiently examined (Daro & McCurdy, 1994; Wurtele & Miller-Perrin, 1992).

Critics of sexual abuse prevention programs question whether the "relatively exclusive focus on children as their own protectors is appropriate" (Reppucci et al., 1998, p. 332). Many children may not be developmentally ready to protect themselves, and an overreliance on these types of programs may give parents and society a false sense of security. At the same time, we agree that

> children and adolescents have a right to be enlightened about sexuality and sexual abuse and to know about their right to live free from such abuse. The more pertinent question is not *whether* to educate children about sexual abuse but rather *how* to do so in an effective, sensitive manner. (Wurtele & Miller-Perrin, 1992, p. 89)

The Parental Role in Child Empowerment

Parents, of course, play an important role in empowering their own children to protect themselves. Because parents are the most likely offenders for most forms of child maltreatment, efforts that include parents primarily focus on sexual abuse, the form of child maltreatment most often perpetrated by a nonparent.

Various prevention formats designed for parents include audiovisual materials, books, and educational workshops (see Wurtele & Miller-Perrin, 1992). The Child Assault Prevention Project helps parents empower their children (Porch & Petretic-Jackson, 1986) in an educational workshop focusing on sexual abuse in general. It also informs parents about specific responses children can make to prevent abuse (e.g., saying "no" or screaming when confronted by a potentially abusive encounter). Studies indicate that parents not only want to be involved but also are effective in teaching their children about sexual abuse and appropriate protective skills (Wurtele, 1993; Wurtele, Kast, & Melzer, 1994; Wurtele, Kvaternick, & Franklin, 1992).

In addition, parents can play other roles in child maltreatment prevention. For example, they might interrupt abuse by learning to identify behaviors in a child that signal the child is being abused (Wurtele & Miller-Perrin, 1992). Wurtele and Miller-Perrin also describe the important role parents play in responding appropriately to the abuse disclosures of child victims, thereby reducing a child's feelings of self-blame, isolation, and anger.

Megan's Law (1996), the controversial sex-offender registry and community notification law, has stimulated considerable discussion about the need for parents to talk to their children about self-protection (see Box 7.1, "Megan's Law"). Critics of the law argue that one of the potential problems with community notification laws is that they might illicit a false sense of security. That is, parents might be left to assume that the state will let them know when dangerous predators are living close by and that once the parents are armed with this information, they will be able to protect their children from victimization. In reality, of course, Megan's Law cannot possibly provide these protections because most potentially dangerous people are not listed in the directory. Police departments are well aware of the limitations of community notification and have taken an active role in reminding parents of their responsibility. For example, on its web page announcing access to sex offender information through the Sex Offender Identification Line and Megan's Law CD-ROM, the Sacramento Police Department offers some sound advice to parents (see Box 7.2, "Child Protection Advice for Parents").

Targeting At-Risk Families

Emmanuelle, an 18-year-old high school senior, was desperate. The father of her child had abandoned her, she was unable to support herself and her child with her waitressing job, and her family was unwilling to help. With nowhere to turn, she left her two-and-one-half-year-old child at a Brooklyn hospital with a note:

To Whom It May Concern:

I am an 18-year-old student and I also work. I can't handle the pressure. I sometimes take it out on her. I love her and would not like to hurt her. Please find her a good home where she'll get the love she desires.

The next day Emmanuelle realized she had made a mistake and called the hospital to ask for her baby back. When she arrived, she was arrested and charged with child abandonment. (Fontana & Moohnan, 1994, pp. 227-228)

(text continued on p. 249)

BOX 7.1 Megan's Law

Richard and Maureen Kanka will remember the day July 29, 1994, forever. That is the day their 7-year-old daughter, Megan, was found raped and murdered in a grassy field close to their home. The murder suspect, Jesse Timmendequas, was a twice-convicted sex offender who was living across the street from the Kankas. In May 1997, Timmendequas was convicted of first-degree murder and later sentenced to death. During the trial, detectives testified that Timmendequas had confessed to touching the young girl, strangling her with a belt, tying a plastic bag over her head, and carrying the body out of his house in a toy chest and dumping it in a nearby park ("Man Found Guilty," 1997).

The Kanka family was understandably shocked and angered by Megan's murder. Why hadn't they been informed that a child molester was living across the street? Unknown to the Kanka family at the time, Timmendequas had actually been sharing the home with two other convicted sex offenders. Didn't the Kankas and others living in the community have a right to know? Maureen Kanka was determined that Megan's death would lead to something positive, and she began to speak out publicly about the need for community notification. Her campaign was successful, and many states implemented community notification policies. Then on May 17, 1996, less than 2 years after Megan's death, President Clinton signed a federal version of "Megan's Law." The law requires all states to track the whereabouts of sex offenders and to make the information available to the general public.

Because states have been left to decide for themselves how they will carry out the mandates of Megan's Law, specific policies vary. In New Jersey, where Megan Kanka was killed, the law calls for mandatory notification of schools, day care centers, and youth organizations when a moderate-risk offender is released. For high-risk offenders, police are *required* to go door-to-door and inform individuals that a sex offender resides in their community. In California, on the other hand, Megan's Law *permits* police to publicize the whereabouts of convicted sex offenders but does not *require* them to do so (Vellinga, 1997). People who want to know if there is a sex felon living nearby can either call a "900" number (The Sex Offender Identification Line, 1-900-463-0400) or consult Megan's Law CD-ROM, which is available for public viewing at police stations and provides the name, aliases, photograph, physical description, and residential ZIP code for 64,000 convicted sex offenders (see http://sacpd.org/megans.html for information about Megan's Law CD-ROM and http://sacpd.org/child-mol.html for information about the Sex Offender Identification Line). Several other states have made their registry available on the Internet (Bunn, 1998).

From a social constructionist standpoint, the rapid legislative response has been fascinating to observe. The horrifying murders of children such as Polly Klaas in California and Megan Kanka in New Jersey received national press and increased public fears of child predators. Advocates concerned about child protection, including relatives of the slain children, took their concerns to the public and to politicians. As is often the case with claims-makers, the rhetoric of risk became an important tool. Advocates often exaggerate the "high recidivism" rate[1] of sex offenders, the "high risk" to unsuspecting children,[2] and the potential benefit of a registry and notification system.[3] With public concerns heightened, politicians and lawmakers have had every reason to move quickly.

Despite overwhelming public and political support, however, Megan's Law has been widely criticized. Much of the criticism centers on constitutional issues. Many maintain that the law violates the *ex post facto* clause of the Constitution, which states that a new law cannot be retroactively imposed on someone convicted before the new law was enacted. Others question whether Megan's Law violates the *double jeopardy* clause of the Fifth

Amendment, which makes it illegal to impose a second punishment for the same offense. Supporters, however, have won most of the legal battles to date, arguing that the publication of information on sex offenders does not infringe on these constitutional rights because the notification itself is not punishment and does not itself restrict the person's freedom. The community may ostracize the criminal, but this is not due to any governmental action (Fein, 1995).

Of course, from a social scientific point of view, that community notification does not meet legal criteria of punishment is essentially irrelevant. Discrimination, ostracism, and scorn are costly punishments, even if they are not imposed directly by the state. Released offenders may also be the victims of harassment or vigilantism. Police departments are well aware of the potential for violence and often remind the public that harassment is illegal and probably counterproductive.[4] Despite the warnings, however, there have been isolated cases of vigilantism around the country.[5]

Given that a certain amount of ostracism, harassment, and violence is inevitable, it is important to consider what the potential consequences might be. We know that the best way to reduce recidivism is to reintegrate the individual into society. When a released prisoner finds a job, makes friends, reestablishes relationships with family, and becomes an accepted part of the community, he or she has an increased stake in conformity and a reduced probability of reoffense. With the words *Sex Offender* stamped across the forehead, however, such a reintegration seems unlikely. Is it possible that this type of ostracism might eventually lead to the behavior that we are trying to prevent?

Perhaps the most scathing critiques of Megan's Law come from those who see it as a "haphazard," "reactionary," "knee-jerk" overreaction, which serves more political interests than child protection interests.

> The key to what is wrong with Megan's Law is found in its very title. We ought to be suspicious whenever politicians make haste to pass a crime bill in the name of a particular crime victim or in the wake of a personal tragedy, ostensibly to ensure that it will not occur again. . . . It seems that whenever a criminal case makes national news, it becomes instant political capital for elected officials. (Semel, 1997, p. 21)

Although this criticism may or may not be true, it seems apparent that the registries are not likely to offer children much protection. They are filled with errors, omissions, and old addresses. The majority of people included in the registries have been convicted of molesting their own children and are relatively unlikely to reoffend, especially against nonfamily members. Critics maintain that publicizing offenders' names may hurt their own children more than anyone else (Vellinga, 1997). Some registries also include offenders who were convicted of sex crimes as many as 40 years ago, gay men convicted of sodomy, and underaged youth engaged in consensual sex (Bunn, 1998; Semel, 1997). Perhaps most problematic of all is that Megan's Law creates the mistaken illusion that the "real problem" with sexual abuse is the guy down the street. Research suggests that the majority of sex offenses against children are committed by parents or parent substitutes (DHHS, 1996). Likewise, children are much more likely to be killed by a family member or an acquaintance than by a stranger. In 1994, only 15% of child homicide victims were killed by a stranger, compared with 30% by a family member and 20% by an acquaintance (the offender was unknown in the remaining cases). For children under the age of 10, the percentage of family and acquaintance homicide is even higher (Greenfield, 1996).

The debate surrounding community notification and sex offender registries is far from over and represents a controversy with no easy answers. Although the arguments surrounding constitutionality, fairness, and political motivation are compelling to us as social scientists, as parents the desire to protect our children is strong. Laws and policies that contribute to only the *appearance* of protection, however, may do more harm than good.

Notes

1. Discussions of Megan's Law typically presuppose high recidivism rates, with advocate estimates ranging from 50% to 90%. Recidivism rates are difficult to calculate, however, and any simplistic statement on "the" recidivism rate is inevitably flawed. Recidivism estimates will vary dramatically, for example, depending on whether the offender victimized family members (lower rates) or nonfamily members (higher rates). Some studies examine recidivism after 2 years (lower rates), and some after 25 years (higher rates). As a result of these methodological complications, actual recidivism studies suggest rates varying from 8% to 50% (see Bunn, 1998; Sheppard, 1997), rates significantly lower than those often claimed by advocates.

2. Stranger abductions and murders, although especially tragic and horrifying, are extremely rare, at least compared with other forms of child victimization. For advocacy groups, politicians, and the media to suggest otherwise is somewhat misleading. Says journalism professor Steven Gorelick, who specializes in media coverage of crime and violence,

> I'm mostly concerned about the illusion of safety that is created by public crackdowns of these kinds of crimes. It's so easy. They're horrific, and they represent a quintessential kind of evil. But the press presents this information absent of the context of how infrequently these things occur. An educated person would conclude, if he's an avid newspaper reader or television watcher, that these kinds of infrequent crimes are the things to be concerned about. (quoted in Sheppard, 1997, p. 40)

3. Many critics argue that registries do little more than create the illusion of safety. They are filled with errors and old addresses. Sex offenders may be required to report address changes, but few actually do so. According to Sandra Baker, executive director of Sacramento's Child and Family Institute, offenders consider the registries a joke and do not feel the least bit compelled by their requirements.

4. In California, for example, authorities try to prevent harassment by requiring that those who want to view Megan's Law CD-ROM read the following notice (http://sacpd.org/child-mol.html):

> The release of this information to the public is a means of assuring public protection and not to punish the offender. The information may not be used to harass the offender or commit any crime against the offender. Public safety is best served when offenders are not concealing their location to avoid harassment.

5. Although most evidence suggests that vigilantism and harassment are somewhat unusual, several stories have appeared in newspapers across the country in the last few years. Here are a few examples: In New York, a man fired five bullets into the home of a convicted rapist who had been publicly identified by police (Hanley, 1998). In New Jersey, two people broke into the house of a released sex offender and beat up a man lying on the living room couch, only to discover later that the man was not the sex offender (Sheppard, 1997). In Washington State, a man's house was burned after his name was publicized (Sheppard, 1997). In Placentia, California, after police distributed fliers identifying a "serious sex offender" and child molester, neighbors picketed his house, harassed him with blow horns, and called 911 every time he left his house. When the *Los Angeles Times* ran a story and published a picture of the man, he lost his job. "I did a wrong thing, and I paid for it," he later told the *Times*. "Now I am trying to start over and I can't. Some people want me to put a gun to my head." (quoted in Sheppard, 1997, p. 38)

For Fontana and Moohnan (1994), the case of Emmanuelle illustrates the need for societal intervention rather than punishment. Emmanuelle was a young mother with no support. When her cries for help were not heard, she chose to abandon her baby. When she realized she had made a mistake, she was arrested.

BOX 7.2 Child Protection Advice for Parents

(The parental advice offered below comes from the Sacramento Police Department, Sacramento, California, on its web page announcing programs and services connected with California's version of Megan's Law [1996]. We include it here for two reasons. First, this information illustrates how police are taking advantage of the publicity surrounding Megan's Law to help educate parents. Second, these reminders are sound advice for all of us.)

Teach your children to avoid situations that put them in danger of abuse, molestation, or abduction. Help protect your child by establishing a home environment where your child feels safe to tell you anything, without fear of shame, ridicule, or punishment.

A safe and supportive home environment, combined with clear instructions about what behavior is acceptable and what is not, will guide your child's actions and encourage your child to tell you if something improper happens.

Many parents warn their children not to talk to strangers. But more often than not, an abuser or abductor is known to the child. He or she can be a school bus driver, teacher, relative, neighbor, or family friend.

It is best to teach your child to avoid certain situations or actions. Children should know from an early age that some behavior isn't acceptable, and that they have the right to tell an adult to leave them alone.

Here are some specific rules you can teach your child:

- Stay away from people who call you near their car, even if they offer to take you somewhere exciting.
- If someone tries to take you away, yell, "This person is not my father (or mother)" and scream.
- If you get lost in a store, find another mom with children or go to the checkout counter. Don't wander around on your own.
- You don't have to keep secrets from your parents. No one can hurt your parents or pets if you tell what happened.
- No one should touch you in the parts covered by your bathing suit, and you should not be asked to touch anyone there.
- Don't let anyone take your picture without permission from your parents or teacher.

SOURCE: Reprinted from Sacramento Police Department (1998, October 20). *Protecting Yourself and Your Family* [On-line]. Available: http://sacpd.org/dojmegan.html

They argue that with help, she might have been able to care for her child, whereas prosecuting her merely put "one more young woman in jail and another child in the city's already overstretched foster care system" (p. 229). In addition, Emmanuelle's situation sent a message to other needy parents: "Don't dare come out and ask for help, because you'll be thrown into prison and your baby will be taken away! Stay in your closet and beat up your kid or get rid of her. You'll be safer that way!" (p. 229).

According to Wekerle and Wolfe (1998), in recent years there has been a shift away from sickness or evil models that emphasize legal punishments toward a contextual approach that emphasizes parental competence and relieving parental stress. From this perspective, the best way to prevent child maltreatment is to meet the needs of at-risk families. Many abusive and neglectful parents, for example, may not know how to be good parents or may be experiencing pressures that make effective parenting difficult. They may be young and immature, have economic pressures, and be socially isolated. They or their child may have physical problems. Or, their child may have an especially difficult temperament. Programs that teach high-risk parents how to be effective parents should help reduce child maltreatment. There could be some less obvious indirect benefits of these programs as well. According to attachment theory (see Chapter 2), child maltreatment is more common when the parent-child relationship is weak and unrewarding (Wekerle & Wolfe, 1998). The vast majority of child maltreatment victims are insecurely attached to a parent (i.e., the mother is not a responsive, nurturant, and sensitive caregiver), and any program that enhances parenting effectiveness in general should indirectly improve the attachment bond between a parent and child, leading to lower rates of abuse.

Parental Competency: Identifying High-Risk Parents

Parental competency programs typically connect parents with a mentor who can provide social support, parenting suggestions, and help with life decisions (e.g., assisting with educational or occupational attainment and encouraging reduced family size). Although the specifics of parental education and support efforts will vary from program to program, the National Clearinghouse on Child Abuse and Neglect Information (1998b, p. 4) has identified several general goals:

- Increasing parent knowledge about general child development, child management techniques, and positive family functioning
- Improving overall child-rearing skills
- Increasing empathy for and awareness of others' needs
- Improving the positive self-concept and self-esteem of all family members
- Improving family and parent-child communication
- Building family support and cohesion
- Increasing parental knowledge about the triggers of abuse
- Increasing parents' use of nonviolent approaches to child discipline

Many of these programs attempt to identify high-risk parents (i.e., young, low-income, and single) and intervene before the first child is born (Daro & McCurdy, 1994). Other programs are school based and focus on the needs of teen mothers (National Clearinghouse on Child Abuse and Neglect Information, 1998b). In addition to offering parenting education, these programs provide life skills training and educational support for young mothers trying to complete school. Still other parental competency programs provide support through parent-to-parent volunteer mentoring programs.

Parental competency programs, especially those that incorporate *early intervention* and *home visitation,* are gaining considerable support. The U.S. Advisory

Board on Child Abuse and Neglect cited home visitation of at-risk parents as the one policy the government could implement right now to make a difference in reducing rates of child maltreatment (Krugman, 1995). More than half of the nation's states have parent support initiatives under way. Not only have these programs received considerable state and federal support, but several important private foundations, including the Carnegie Corporation of New York, the Commonwealth Fund, and the Ronald McDonald's House Charities, have actively supported early intervention programs (Daro, 1998).

One such effort, the Hawaii Healthy Start Program, began in 1985. Initially created by the Hawaii Family Stress Center in Honolulu, the Healthy Start Program has since expanded across the state and now serves 50% to 55% of the state's population (Daro, McCurdy, & Harding, 1998). The program offers a variety of voluntary services to high-risk parents, as identified by a list of 15 demographic and socioeconomic factors (e.g., marital status, education, family support, limited prenatal care, and history of substance abuse). Trained paraprofessionals visit families weekly, with visits tapering off as families accomplish certain required goals.

In a carefully controlled evaluation of the Healthy Start Program, Daro et al. (1998) randomly assigned families who had qualified into one of two groups. Those families whose children had been born on even days were offered Healthy Start Services, and children born on odd days were offered no services. Data collected 12 months after birth indicate that when compared with controls, Healthy Start mothers were more involved and sensitive to their children's needs, and the children were more responsive to their mothers. Healthy Start children were also at less risk of physical abuse. A second component of the study examined the long-term effects by comparing the family functioning of former Healthy Start clients with established norms. Healthy Start families scored average to above average on measures of parental functioning, positive parent-child interaction, and social support. In addition, Daro et al. identified several less quantifiable results, including emotional and social support from the paraprofessional visitor, increased access to medical and child care services, and information about child development and parenting. Only half of the parents reported using corporal punishment, for example, and those who did spank tended to use mild forms (e.g., a slap on the hand). Some parents reported that others in their household (e.g., grandparents, partners, and friends) were critical that they did not use more corporal punishment.

Hawaii's Healthy Start is part of a series of programs known as the Healthy Families of America (HFA), a joint effort of the National Committee to Prevent Child Abuse and the Ronald McDonald Children's Charities (Daro, 1998). HFA has a lofty goal: "to offer all new parents nation-wide support around the time their first baby is born" (p. 6). As of fall 1998, HFA programs are in two thirds of states and more than 300 communities (Daro, 1998). Although the specifics of the programs vary, in general programs begin before birth, are intensive (at least once a week), and provide social support for parents as well as instruction on parenting and child development (Daro et al., 1998; "Healthy Families America," 1994).

Another well-known parental competency program began in the mid-1970s and centers on pairing young single mothers with a public health nurse (Olds, Henderson, Tatelbaum, & Chamberlain, 1986). This project, known as the Prenatal Early Infancy Project, is highly regarded as an important success story in child maltreatment prevention (Wekerle & Wolfe, 1998). Research suggests that poor, young, single parents are less likely to have healthy children and are less likely to be capable caregivers. The project provides prenatal and early childhood services in an attempt to help young mothers understand child health and development and to help strengthen confidence in themselves and confidence in their capacity for change. Specifically, the program is designed to (a) improve the health of the infant, (b) improve parental caregiving, and (c) provide life course development support (e.g., educational, occupational, and pregnancy planning; Olds, 1997). In the original study, conducted in Elmira, New York, nurses visited parents an average of 9 times during the pregnancy and 23 times during the first 2 years of the child's life (Olds, 1997).

Research evaluating the effectiveness of parental competency programs leads to the conclusion that such programs are generally effective in meeting many of their goals. Follow-up evaluations of the Prenatal Early Infancy Project, for example, revealed that the mothers in the study spent more quality time with their children, were less likely to abuse their children, had fewer children, waited longer to have another child, spent less time on welfare, and had fewer arrests than parents in the control group (Emery & Laumann-Billings, 1998; Olds et al., 1986). Research on other home visitation programs has found that parents who were contacted as few as four times by a volunteer nurse had more parenting knowledge when compared with parents who had not been visited. Other positive outcomes include enhanced parenting knowledge and skills, fewer injuries to children, and less use of corporal punishment (for reviews, see Daro & McCurdy, 1994; Wekerle & Wolfe, 1993).

Parental Competency: Identifying Parents With High-Risk Children

Also relevant, but far less common, are programs that identify child temperament as a risk factor. All other things being equal, a child who is demanding, aggressive, or intense or who cries a lot is more likely to be a victim of maltreatment (Wekerle & Wolfe, 1998). As we discussed in Chapter 3, these difficult child behaviors interact with parent characteristics and can lead to negative parent-child interactions. In working with parents with irritable children, Dutch researcher van den Boom (1994, 1995) observed that parents often approached the child during fussy times and ignored the child when the fussiness stopped. Through time, the parent-child interactions became increasingly negative. To test his observations, van den Boom randomly assigned parents of irritable children into two groups. Parents in the experimental group attended information sessions and received home visitation designed to promote attachment and to teach parents how to appropriately respond to their children. Evaluations after 12 months (van den Boom, 1994) and 18 months (van den Boom, 1995) indicated that mothers in the experimental group were more responsive and attentive, and their children were more securely attached, compared with mothers and children in the control group (cited in Wekerle & Wolfe, 1998).

Targeting Society

Societal-level solutions are often the most difficult to articulate and to implement. It is commonly argued, for example, that child maltreatment solutions must begin with an emphasis on the various social ills that directly or indirectly influence child maltreatment (e.g., poverty, unemployment, inadequate housing, and teen pregnancy; Gelles & Straus, 1988). It is reasonable to assume that a societal commitment to eliminating these problems would be, at least indirectly, a commitment to eliminating child maltreatment (Pearl, 1994; Willis & Silovsky, 1998).

These enduring and complicated social problems are well beyond the scope of this book. Instead, we focus in this section on several significant societal-level changes that are relatively feasible and attainable. There is disagreement, of course, about which of these programs would actually make a difference. Furthermore, some of the solutions suggested below essentially compete with one another. A societal commitment made to support services for at-risk families, for example, is seemingly inconsistent with calls to increase offender costs. Regardless of inherent difficulties, it is important to consider societal changes and how they might alleviate child maltreatment.

Public Awareness of Child Maltreatment

One logical approach to prevention is publicizing positive parenting techniques, the potential problems with parental aggression, and the atrocities of child maltreatment. A review of nine community-based child maltreatment projects around the country illustrates several public awareness techniques that can be implemented (National Clearinghouse on Child Abuse and Neglect Information, 1998b). All the projects made staff available to the local media, and most regularly distributed press releases. Two of the nine wrote articles for the local papers. Two of the programs produced television and radio campaigns using the slogans "Only you can prevent child abuse" and "Put yourself in their place." One project produced a series of public service announcements that included a toll-free phone number for information on parenting. Another program publicized its services with an interactive "town meeting" format. Five projects sponsored community forums, conferences, and festivals (National Clearinghouse on Child Abuse and Neglect Information, 1998b).

Although there was no carefully controlled evaluation research of these public awareness efforts, each of the projects did use focus groups and interviews to help provide some information about effectiveness. Researchers concluded that the most effective programs were those that actively encouraged interaction between child abuse professionals and community residents, including town meetings, conferences, and call-in programs (National Clearinghouse on Child Abuse and Neglect Information, 1998b).

Condemning Culturally Accepted Violence

Children observe "accepted" forms of violence all around them. They are exposed to violence when they watch television, when their parents hit each other, when siblings are violent toward one another, and when they are themselves hit. Although there is considerable debate about the precise effects of these various forms of violence on children, there is every reason to be concerned.

One could certainly make the case that exposing children to much of this violence is morally wrong. Children should not have to see violence in their neighborhoods and homes, and they certainly should not have to be physically victimized by adults. Even beyond this moral argument, however, there is a compelling case to be made that exposure to violence, even acceptable societal violence, has a detrimental effect on the child and, therefore, society. There appears to be considerable agreement, at least on a theoretical level, that "violence begets violence." That is, societal acceptance and glorification of violence, the victimization of children, and marital violence all contribute to the overall level of violence in society (see Eron et al., 1987).

Despite general agreement, at least at some level, that violence begets violence, there is less agreement on how best to break this cycle of violence. One hotly debated and controversial topic during the 1990s has been how much of the responsibility for child maltreatment should be placed on the shoulders of the media. On the one hand, explanations of child maltreatment that reduce the problem to violence in the media clearly oversimplify a complex issue. As research on the relationship between television and violence increases, however, the potential causal significance of the media becomes more difficult to ignore. According to Comstock and Strasburger (1990), for example, the "now-sizable literature—over 1,000 articles, including reviews—gives considerable empirical support to the hypothesis that exposure to TV violence increases the likelihood of subsequent aggressive or antisocial behavior" (p. 32). This conclusion has gained considerable support, and today it is commonplace to hear many professionals inculpate media violence.

Another hotly debated issue is *corporal punishment.* Corporal punishment is so commonly practiced and accepted that it remains largely unnoticed. In one survey of 679 college students, the overwhelming majority of the respondents had been spanked (93%), believed spanking works (69%), believed parents should have the right to spank (85%), and planned to spank their own children

(83%; Graziano & Namaste, 1990). Currently, more than 90% of parents use corporal punishment on toddlers (Straus et al., 1997). Despite this overwhelming societal acceptance, there is an increasing willingness among social scientists and advocates to condemn its use (see Finkelhor & Dziuba-Leatherman, 1994; Graziano, 1994; Straus, 1994a).

Currently, more than 90% of parents use corporal punishment on toddlers.

Experts point to several specific problems with spanking (see Box 7.3, "Ten Myths That Perpetuate Corporal Punishment"). For some, there is an inherent contradiction between the ideal of the loving parent and the purposeful violence of corporal punishment (Graziano, 1994; Straus, 1994a). In addition, corporal punishment can and often does become abuse when parents are especially angry or stressed. The distinction between a spanking and a beating is far from clear, and this definitional vagueness provides parents considerable latitude that some maintain contributes to abuse (Graziano, 1994). Perhaps most significant of all, corporal punishment is correlated with a variety of behavioral problems, including aggression, delinquency, low self-esteem, depression, and emotional and behavioral problems (see Straus, 1994a for a review).

In a recent study published in the *Archives of Pediatric and Adolescent Medicine,* Straus et al. (1997) interviewed more than 800 mothers of 6- to 9-year-old children and found that the greater the use of corporal punishment in the week prior to the interview, the higher the level of antisocial behavior 2 years later (e.g., "cheats or tells lies," "is cruel or mean to others," "is disobedient at school"). The relationships persisted even when appropriate statistical controls were added to the analysis, including the child's tendency toward antisocial behavior, the family's SES, and emotional warmth and cognitive stimulation provided by the parents.

There are signs that the general public is listening to these criticisms because the trend is for fewer and fewer parents to spank their children (Straus et al., 1998). In addition, most states have banned corporal punishment in the public schools, and it is criminalized in some Scandinavian countries (Finkelhor & Dziuba-Leatherman, 1994). We are, of course, nowhere near criminalization in North America, but the logic of corporal punishment is increasingly questioned. The chances are good that your grandparents were spanked more than your parents and that your parents were spanked more than you. What about your children? Perhaps they will not be spanked at all.

Reevaluating Mandatory Reporting

Recall that during the child abuse prevention movement of the 1960s, all states adopted mandatory reporting laws. These laws, which have typically been heralded as a major victory for child protection, have in recent years come under

BOX 7.3 Ten Myths That Perpetuate Corporal Punishment

In his book *Beating the Devil Out of Them: Corporal Punishment in American Families,* Murray Straus (1994a) offers the most comprehensive statement to date on the problems of spanking as a discipline technique. One of the chapters of the book, "Ten Myths That Perpetuate Corporal Punishment," is summarized below:

Myth 1: Spanking Works Better. According to Straus, there is no evidence that spanking works better than other forms of discipline. What little evidence has been conducted suggests that spanking may be less effective than nonviolent forms of discipline (e.g., a time-out or a lost privilege).

Myth 2: Spanking Is Needed As a Last Resort. If one accepts the argument that spanking is no better than other forms of discipline, then it stands to reason that there are no situations when spanking is necessary. Straus argues that much of the time when parents resort to hitting, they are doing so from their own frustration. Essentially, they are sending a message to the child that if one is angry, hitting is justified.

Myth 3: Spanking Is Harmless. According to Straus, hitting is so firmly entrenched in our culture that it is difficult for us to admit that it is wrong. To do so would be to admit that our parents were wrong or we were wrong. The evidence suggests, however, that on average, spanking does more harm than good. Certainly, most people who were spanked "turn out fine," but this does not disprove the general pattern. That most smokers do not die of lung cancer does not disprove the evidence on the harmful effects of smoking.

Myth 4: One or Two Times Won't Cause Any Damage. It is true that the evidence suggests that spanking is most harmful when it is frequent and severe. If spanking is harmful in large quantities, however, how can it be good in small quantities?

Myth 5: Parents Can't Stop Without Training. Eliminating spanking would be easy, Straus maintains, if society would embrace the belief that a child should never be hit. Parent educators and social scientists are reluctant to take this stand, however, because of the belief that parents cannot be expected to stop unless they are presented with alternative parenting techniques. Straus maintains, however, that parents do not need training in alternative parenting techniques—they simply need to embrace the belief that spanking is wrong. Everyone agrees, for example, that demeaning or insulting language (i.e., psychological abuse) is wrong, and no one argues that parents cannot be expected to change without training. "Rather than arguing that parents need to learn certain skills before they can stop using corporal punishment," Straus (1994a) argues, "I believe that parents are more likely to use and cultivate those skills if they decide or are required to stop spanking" (p. 156).

Myth 6: If You Don't Spank, Your Children Will Be Spoiled or Run Wild. It is true that some children who are not spanked run wild, but it is equally true that some children who are spanked run wild. The key to having well-behaved children is being a consistent disciplinarian, not a physical disciplinarian.

Myth 7: Parents Spank Rarely or Only for Serious Problems. It is true that many parents perceive that they reserve spanking for serious problems, but Straus maintains that parents simply do not realize how often they hit their children. This is especially true for parents who use spanking as their primary discipline technique.

Myth 8: By the Time a Child Is a Teenager, Parents Have Stopped. The national child maltreatment surveys indicate that more than one half of parents of 13- and 14-year-olds had hit their child in the previous 12 months. With teenagers, the punishment is more likely to be a slap to the face than to the bottom.

Myth 9: If Parents Don't Spank, They Will Verbally Abuse Their Child. Parents who spank frequently are actually more likely to be verbally abusive.

Myth 10: It Is Unrealistic to Expect Parents to Never Spank. Straus (1994a) is clearly frustrated by the level of acceptance of corporal punishment. Is it unrealistic to expect husbands not to hit their wives, he asks? Why is violence unacceptable among strangers but acceptable between a parent and child? Criminalizing spanking is probably not feasible, but progress can be made "by showing parents that spanking is dangerous, that their children will be easier to bring up if they do not spank, and by clearly saying that a child should never, under any circumstances, be spanked" (p. 162).

---

increasing criticism. The problem begins with the well-documented observation that professionals fail to report approximately 50% of the suspected cases they encounter (Sedlak, 1990). There are a number of reasons mandated professionals might fail to report, including a lack of understanding about the reporting laws, concern for the parents, hesitancy to break the client-therapist confidentiality code, and a general reluctance to get involved (Wurtele & Miller-Perrin, 1992).

An additional difficulty with mandatory reporting laws is that CPS, which is charged with the task of coordinating social services for needy families, has become overwhelmed by the responsibility to investigate abuse allegations and to coordinate placement of those children who need to be removed from the home (Emery & Laumann-Billings, 1998; Schene, 1996). Mandated professionals are well aware of this reality, and it puts them in a difficult position when they encounter a case of suspected child maltreatment. Imagine, for example, the nature of the relationship that could develop between a clinical social worker and a troubled mother. After working together for several months, the mother, who has come to trust the social worker, confesses that she sometimes engages in behavior that the social worker would define as abusive. By law, the social worker is required to report the case to CPS. Experience tells her, however, that given the ambiguity of abuse definitions and the limited physical evidence in this particular case, it is unlikely that the abuse allegation would be substantiated. Even if it were substantiated, this is not, in the opinion of the social worker, an especially severe case of abuse that suggests removal of the children. The family needs help and wants help, and the social worker knows that she is in the best position to provide that help. If the social worker reports the case, she violates the trust she has painstakingly built. In addition, if this were the case, the most likely outcome would be "no provision of services, no legal action, and eventually, encouraging the family to seek treatment—exactly where they began the long, expensive, and intrusive process" (Emery & Laumann-Billings, 1998, p. 130).

In general, the consensus among legal scholars and others involved in child protection has been that mandatory reporting laws are essential to child protection (Wurtele & Miller-Perrin, 1992). Given the concerns about CPS and the corresponding reluctance to report cases, however, more and more experts are calling for a modification in mandatory reporting laws. One possible solution is to rewrite mandatory reporting laws to include only severe cases of child maltreatment. This would remove the reporting obligation from mental health professionals who encounter minor cases of abuse and might put them in a better position to help needy parents (Emery & Laumann-Billings, 1998).

More experts are calling for a modification in mandatory reporting laws.

Increasing Offender Costs

As noted throughout the book, there have been few legal and social costs to child maltreatment throughout history. For much of human history, adults physically and sexually abused children with state endorsement. Even today, many researchers and advocates argue that the social and legal costs of offender violence are too low and that parents sometimes abuse their children "because they can" (Gelles & Straus, 1988).

When approached from a deterrence perspective, the way to reduce the *crime* of child maltreatment is to punish the *criminal.* A father who beats his son is guilty of assault, and he should be treated as other assault offenders are treated. In more serious cases, the father should go to jail, the child should be removed from the home, or both. As society increasingly condemns violence in the family and increasingly censures violent family offenders, the cumulative effect should be less violence in the family (Williams, 1992).

Of course, the call for increasing offender costs seemingly contradicts the call for a societal commitment to support and services. Should violent parents be *helped,* or should they be *punished?* Many advocates maintain that both are achievable goals. The key, they argue, is working harder to distinguish between different levels of abuse. Although acknowledging that it is difficult to do so, Emery and Laumann-Billings (1998) argue that definitional differences between less serious and more serious forms of abuse should be clearly articulated in the law. In less serious cases of abuse, where parents are poor, young, stressed, and needy, family reunification should be the goal, and supportive intervention should be the means to achieving that goal. The goal of reunification can be successfully accomplished, however, only if intervention programs are in place to help these needy families and if the progress of reunified families is monitored. One such program is the Children's Safety Centers Network, Inc., in St. Paul, Minnesota (Hewitt, 1998). The centers pair families with volunteers and professionals who observe and monitor the progress of family interactions and provide suggestions for improving family relationships.

Most experts agree that in more serious cases, the goal of family reunification should be questioned. When the state does terminate parental rights, early adoption should be considered as an alternative to foster care (Emery & Laumann-Billings, 1998). In 1997, President Clinton signed into law the Adoption and Safe Families Act, legislation that represents a move toward these perspectives. The act unequivocally establishes the goals of safety of the child in making decisions about removal and reunification. In doing so, the law clarifies the states' responsibility to the child, explicitly noting that children should never be left in or returned to dangerous living situations. The law also provides incentives for adoption and other permanency options (Children's Defense Fund, 1997; National Clearinghouse on Child Abuse and Neglect Information, 1998a; see Box 7.4, "The Adoption and Safe Families Act of 1997").

Ultimately, distinguishing between different levels of abuse, the nature of the abuse, and the causes of the abuse should help settle controversy between supportive versus coercive intervention and between family reunification and termination. The ideal of termination of parental rights, or jail time for the offender, is "far more threatening when our definitions of abuse include relatively minor acts, as they currently do" (Emery & Laumann-Billings, 1998, p. 131). Distinguishing between different levels of abuse would "be a first step toward the broader goal of refocusing the child protection system on supporting ratherthan policing families under stress, while simultaneously pursuing more vigorous, coercive interventions with cases of serious child maltreatment" (p. 131).

Reevaluating Public Policy Commitment to Child Protection

It is commonly argued that the powerlessness of children contributes to violence because children lack the "resources to inflict costs on their attackers" (Gelles, 1983, p. 159). Because children lack the resources to protect themselves, they must turn to society (e.g., government, churches, and synagogues). In general, the more a society values its children, the less it will tolerate their victimization, and the more actively it will seek to protect them (Wurtele & Miller-Perrin, 1992).

> The more a society values its children, the less it will tolerate their victimization.

The issue of public support and funding for social services for children is, of course, politically charged and hotly debated. Regardless of these disagreements, however, most experts agree that in the current system, there are few social services available for children. Patricia Schene (1996), who for 17 years served as director of the Children's Division of the American Humane Association, sums up the problem like this:

> There are relatively few resources available for improving family functioning, treating the multiple service needs of abused and neglected children, and providing concrete assistance with housing, medical care, food, and other necessities, and there is almost no way for public social services to provide preventative or early intervention services to strengthen families before abuse or neglect takes hold. (p. 395)

BOX 7.4 The Adoption and Safe Families Act of 1997

The Adoption and Safe Families Act of 1997, signed into law by President Clinton on November 19, 1997, is one of the strongest statements every produced in this country on child protection. The law establishes child protection as a national goal and specifies procedures for ensuring that protection. In reviewing the law, and in considering the monumental task of implementation, the National Clearinghouse on Child Abuse and Neglect Information highlights a number of key principles that must be considered. These important insights from the clearinghouse are included below:

- *The safety of children is the paramount concern that must guide all child welfare services.* The new law requires that child safety be the paramount concern when making service provision, placement, and permanency planning decisions. The law reaffirms the importance of making reasonable efforts to preserve and reunify families, but also it now exemplifies when states are not required to make efforts to keep children with their parents, when doing so places a child's safety in jeopardy.
- *Foster care is a temporary setting and not a place for children to grow up.* To ensure that the system respects a child's developmental needs and sense of time, the law includes provisions that shorten the time frame for making permanency planning decisions and that establish a time frame for initiating proceedings to terminate parental rights. The law also strongly promotes the timely adoption of children who cannot return safely to their own homes.
- *Permanency planning efforts for children should begin as soon as a child enters foster care and should be expedited by the provision of services to families.* The enactment of a legal framework requiring permanency decisions to be made more promptly heightens the importance of providing quality services as quickly as possible to enable families in crisis to address problems. Only when timely and intensive services are provided to families can agencies and courts make informed decisions about parents' ability to protect and care for their children.
- *The child welfare system must focus on results and accountability.* The law makes it clear that it is no longer enough to ensure that procedural safeguards are met. It is critical that child welfare services lead to positive results. The law requires numerous tools for focusing attention on results, including an annual report on state performance, the creation of an adoption incentive payment for states designed to support the president's goal of doubling the annual number of children who are adopted or permanently placed by the year 2002, and a requirement for the department [DHHS] to study and make recommendations regarding additional performance-based financial initiatives in child welfare.
- *Innovative approaches are needed to achieve the goals of safety, permanency, and well-being.* The law recognizes that we do not yet have all of the solutions to achieve our goals. By expanding the authority for child welfare demonstration waivers, the law provides a mechanism to allow states greater flexibility to develop innovative strategies to achieve positive results for children and families.

SOURCE: Reprinted from National Clearinghouse on Child Abuse and Neglect Information (1998a, February 19). "Administration for Children and Families: Principles for Implementing the Adoption and Safe Families Act of 1997" [Online]. Available: http://www.calib.com/nccanch/asfa.html

As a society, we have tended to assume that the task of child protection should fall on the shoulders of CPS. In recent years, however, the ability of CPS to protect children *and* provide services for families has been increasingly questioned (see Chapter 3). Given the complications of child protection and the competing mandates with which CPS must deal (e.g., child protection *and* family reunification), the problems that the organization has experienced are hardly surprising. Increasing demand for services, insufficient staff, and excessive caseloads have transformed CPS into an investigation, rather than a social service, agency, one that responds primarily to cases of "imminent danger" (Hewitt, 1998; Thomas, 1998). The primary "service" provided by CPS is foster care for children who need to be temporarily removed from the home.

From 1994 to 1997, Harvard University convened a group of child welfare professionals to consider models for redesigning the child protection system in the United States. They concluded that CPS cannot by itself be expected to protect children *and* provide services for families. These dual goals can be accomplished only with the help of a variety of community partners, which must assume an active role in implementing programs to strengthen families and prevent child abuse (Thomas, 1998).

Perhaps the most troubling part of the neglect of social services for families is that with the success of programs such as the Prenatal and Early Infancy Project (e.g., Olds, 1997) and Hawaii's Healthy Start Program (Daro et al., 1998), there is every reason to believe social service programs can work. Bringing these programs to the hundreds of thousands of at-risk families in this country, however, is a huge task and will require a commitment to family protection that is unprecedented in the history of this country.

SUMMARY

Child maltreatment research is accompanied by many challenges. Theory in this field is not well developed and often relies on overly simplistic single-factor models. After more than 30 years of research, no single-factor model can fully explain child maltreatment. Future research should be devoted to discovering the multiple interacting risk factors that contribute to child maltreatment. There are also significant methodological complications that hamper research. Because of the complicated subject matter, many of these problems seem unavoidable. Others could be avoided, however, if researchers would recommit themselves to top-quality research. If we abandon the scientific method in favor of an advocacy-driven approach to knowledge, it is unlikely we can effectively serve the interest of children because our "findings" can be easily dismissed by those less sympathetic to our cause. We must also carefully define child maltreatment. If we dilute the term *abuse* too much (i.e., to include normative aggression in the family), the term may lose its meaning.

Preventing child maltreatment begins with social awareness, plus the recognition that expertise, energy, and money are needed to alleviate the conditions that produce child maltreatment. Many experts maintain, however, that these commitments have not yet been sufficiently demonstrated. Most community resources are tied up in responding to, rather than preventing, child maltreatment. Referring specifically to child abuse, for example, Wekerle and Wolfe (1993) argue that "current laws and priorities across North America are such that protection agencies have fewer and fewer resources to assist those families who have not, as yet, been identified as being in violation of any community standards" (p. 502). If we hope to dramatically alleviate the child maltreatment problem, our priorities must be changed.

Commitment to the prevention of child maltreatment is growing, as evidenced by the many prevention interventions that are beginning to appear, and several strategies seem especially promising. School-based education for children (e.g., elementary and junior high programs on physical and sexual abuse) is appealing because it has the potential to reach a large number of young people. Parental competency programs target at-risk parents (poor, young, single) and at-risk children with the goal of providing training and social support before any abuse can occur. Although evaluations are limited, available research indicates that these programs have tremendous potential for making a positive impact.

Another indication of the growing commitment to child protection is the work of the United Nations Convention on the Rights of the Child (U.N. General Assembly, 1989), a worldwide effort to define children's rights (Murphy-Berman, Levesque, & Berman, 1996). The findings of the convention raise awareness about the continuing vulnerability of children and articulate inherent childhood rights of *protection* (e.g., protection from abuse, torture, and exploitation), *enhancement* (e.g., rights to adequate standard of living and education), and *autonomous participation* (e.g., freedom of religion and privacy; Krugman, 1995; Murphy-Berman et al., 1996).

In the United States, the U.S. Advisory Board on Child Abuse and Neglect was created in 1988 to monitor progress toward fulfilling the mandates of the 1974 Child Abuse Prevention and Treatment Act. The board is active in evaluating protective services for children and suggesting future strategies. In its reports, the board has emphatically emphasized the need for all members of society to embrace children and the need to protect them:

> Child abuse is wrong. Not only is child abuse wrong, but the nation's lack of an effective response is also wrong. Neither can be tolerated. Together they constitute a moral disaster. . . . Tolerating child abuse denies the worth of children as human beings and makes a mockery of the American principle of respect for the rights and needs of each citizen.
>
> Child neglect is also wrong. Children must be given the basic necessities of life—food, shelter, clothing, health care, education, emotional nurturance—so that they do not suffer needless pain. . . . When those who have assumed the responsibility for providing the necessary resources for children (usually parents) fail to do so, it is wrong. When parents and other caretakers have the psychological capacity to care for their children adequately but lack economic resources to do so, society itself is derelict when it fails to provide such assistance. (U.S. Advisory Board on Child Abuse and Neglect, 1990, pp. 3-4, emphasis in original)

Few people disagree with these statements. But have we as individuals or as a society fully embraced the sentiments advocated here? It is one thing to support by belief or word, but it is quite another to support by actions. The vision of the U.S. Advisory Board on Child Abuse and Neglect (1993) for a "caring community" that values children and resolves to "know, watch, and support their neighbors' children and to offer help when needed in their neighbors' families" *is* an achievable goal (p. 82). Ultimately, child protection is in our hands. Given the history of child maltreatment, where family victimization has been allowed to flourish "behind closed doors," such a community commitment is not only desirable but necessary. It is our wish that the students reading this book will become part of the community dedicated to ending child maltreatment.

Appendix A

Resources Concerned With Child Maltreatment

Listed on the following pages are names and descriptions of resources that are concerned with issues associated with various forms of child maltreatment. These resources provide information, services, or both for victims of child maltreatment, perpetrators of child maltreatment, professionals working in the field, and other individuals interested in the topic of child maltreatment. Please note that although the addresses and telephone numbers listed for each organization were current at the time of publication, such information is subject to change. For additional information and resources related to child maltreatment, visit *http://www.childabuse.org/resources.html*

CHILD ABUSE ORGANIZATIONS

American Humane Association: American Association for Protecting Children (AAPC)

63 Inverness Dr. East
Englewood, CO 80112-5117
800-227-4645
Fax: 303-792-5333

The AAPC promotes child protection services through training, education, and consultation. It provides national statistics on child abuse issues and publishes books, working papers, fact sheets, and a quarterly magazine. It operates the National Resource Center on Child Abuse and Neglect (a federal agency).

American Professional Society on the Abuse of Children (APSAC)

332 S. Michigan Ave., Suite 1600
Chicago, IL 60604
312-554-0166
Fax: 312-554-0919

APSAC is an organization for professionals who work within the field of child maltreatment. The organization is committed to improving the coordination of services in the areas of prevention, treatment, and research. APSAC sponsors professional conferences and publishes a newsletter and journal.

Child Welfare League of America (CWLA)
440 First St. NW, Suite 310
Washington, DC 20001-2085
202-638-2952

CWLA publishes a variety of books, pamphlets, videos, and bibliographies for professionals, parents, and others concerned with the welfare of children. CWLA also publishes a magazine (*Children's Voice*) as well as the journal *Child Welfare.*

International Society for Prevention of Child Abuse and Neglect (ISPCAN)
401 N. Michigan Ave., Suite 2200
Chicago, IL 60611
312-644-6610 ext. 3273 & ext. 4713

ISPCAN is a membership organization that provides a forum for the exchange of information on child abuse and neglect globally. Benefits include the monthly *Child Abuse and Neglect: The International Journal,* a newsletter, and the biennial international congress on child abuse and neglect.

National Center on Child Abuse and Neglect (NCCAN)
U.S. Department of Health and Human Services
P.O. Box 1182
Washington, DC 20013
703-385-7565 or 800-394-3366

NCCAN publishes manuals for professionals involved in the child protection system to enhance community collaboration and the quality of services provided to children and families. NCCAN conducts research, collects information, and provides assistance to states and communities on child abuse issues.

National Committee to Prevent Child Abuse (NCPCA)
332 S. Michigan Ave., Suite 1600
Chicago, IL 60604
312-663-3520

The NCPCA provides many resources (e.g., educational pamphlets) and publishes a variety of materials on child abuse, child abuse prevention, and parenting. The NCPCA also publishes *Current Trends in Child Abuse Reporting and Fatalities: An Annual Fifty State Survey.* For a free catalog describing publications, contact NCPCA, Publications Dept. P.O. Box 2866, Chicago, IL 60690, (800) 55-NCPCA.

The United Way sponsors some local counseling programs for physically and sexually abusive parents and others involved in family violence (e.g., Parents Anonymous).

DOMESTIC VIOLENCE ORGANIZATIONS

Center for the Prevention of Sexual and Domestic Violence
936 N. 34th St., Suite 200
Seattle, WA 98013
206-634-1903
Fax: 206-634-0115

This educational resource center addresses issues of sexual abuse and domestic violence. The center offers workshops concerning clergy misconduct, spouse abuse, child sexual abuse, rape, and pornography. The center also distributes various materials associated with sexual and domestic violence.

Domestic Abuse Intervention Project (DAIP)
206 W. Fourth St., Room 201
Duluth, MN 55806
218-722-2781 or 218-722-4134
Fax: 218-722-1545

The DAIP is an educational resource center that provides a number of programs aimed at the problem of domestic violence. One program focuses on the provision of nonviolence classes for court-ordered individuals arrested for domestic assault. Another program offers a visitation center that is used for the safe exchange of children and/or supervised visits with noncustodial parents. The center also provides training and technical assistance to domestic violence programs around the world.

Family Violence Prevention Fund

383 Rhode Island St., Suite 304
San Francisco, CA 94103
415-252-8900
Fax: 415-252-8991
Publication orders: 415-252-8089

This fund is a nonprofit organization concerned with domestic violence education, prevention, advocacy, and public policy reform. This organization publishes public health education materials and produces training and education materials.

National Coalition Against Domestic Violence

Membership information:
P.O. Box 34103
Washington, DC 20043-4103
202-638-6388

To order publications:
P.O. Box 18749
Denver, CO 80218-0749
303-839-1852

The coalition works to end domestic violence against children and women. It provides technical assistance, newsletters, and publications.

OTHER ORGANIZATIONS

Father Flanagan's Boys Home (Boys Town)

14100 Crawford St.
Boys Town, NE 68010
402-498-1301

Boys Town operates a variety of services for children and families including a residential treatment center, residential services, emergency shelter, family preservation, treatment foster care, and parenting classes in 13 states. The Boys Town National Training Center offers training to other child care professionals, school districts, mental health facilities, and other organizations.

Illusion Theatre

528 Hennepin Ave., Suite 704
Minneapolis, MN 55403
612-339-4944
Fax: 612-337-8042

Illusion Theatre attempts to prevent child sexual abuse through the distribution of theatrical productions addressing sexual abuse, interpersonal violence, and AIDS. The organization publishes sexual abuse prevention materials, a newsletter, and a video program.

PACER Center

4826 Chicago Ave. South
Minneapolis, MN 55417
612-827-2966

The center offers the Let's Prevent Abuse project featuring three puppet shows for children (grades K-4) on abuse and training for professionals who work with children (birth-12) with and without disabilities. The project also offers workshops and written materials to groups and parent organizations about child maltreatment and the increased vulnerability for children with disabilities.

VOICES in Action, Inc. (Victims of Incest Can Emerge Survivors)

P.O. Box 148309
Chicago, IL 60614
773-327-1500

VOICES in Action is an international nonprofit organization working to support and empower victims of childhood sexual abuse and to educate the public about the prevalence of incest. VOICES holds annual conferences, publishes a bimonthly newsletter, and provides referrals to self-help and therapy resources. The organization also has a web site (*http://www.voices-action.org*).

Young Women's Christian Association (YWCA)
624 9th St. NW
Washington, DC 20001
202-626-0700

Local organizations offer a variety of services such as exercise, fitness, infant care, children's programs, food banks, and abuse counseling. Telephone the local YWCA in your area only.

LEGAL SERVICES

American Bar Association Center on Children and the Law
740 15th St. NW
Washington, DC 20005
202-662-1720

This group provides training and technical assistance to prosecutors handling child abuse cases. State statutes, case law, and other resources are available. Advances in law and public policy to improve the circumstances of children are a goal of this group. Publications are available.

American Bar Association IOLTA Clearinghouse
541 N. Fairbanks Court
Chicago, IL 60611-3314
312-988-5748

This group collects funds and distributes them for programs and for support of legal personnel in special projects.

American Civil Liberties Union (ACLU): Children's Rights Project
132 W. 43rd St.
New York, NY 10036
212-229-0540
Fax: 212-229-0749

The Children's Rights Project is a national program of litigation, advocacy, and education to ensure that when government child welfare systems must intervene in the lives of troubled families and children, they do so according to constitutional and statutory standards of fairness and due process and in accordance with reasonable professional standards.

National Association of Counsel for Children (NACC)
1205 Oneida St.
Denver, CO 80220
303-322-2260

The NACC is a professional organization for lawyers and other practitioners who represent children in court. The association publishes a variety of materials relating to children's legal rights and sponsors child abuse training.

National Center for Prosecution of Child Abuse: American Prosecutors Research Institute
99 Canal Center Plaza, Suite 510
Alexandria, VA 22314
703-739-0321

The institute has on-staff attorneys who offer technical assistance to attorneys and other professionals working in the field of child abuse. They also provide training and publications.

National Center on Women and Family Law, Inc.
275 7th Ave., Suite 1206
New York, NY 10001
212-741-9480

This organization publishes a newsletter and serves as a clearinghouse on legal issues related to family violence.

National Council of Juvenile and Family Court Judges
P.O. Box 8970
Reno, NV 89507
702-784-6012

The council represents America's 9,000-plus judges who exercise jurisdiction over delinquency, abuse and neglect, divorce, custody, support, domestic violence, and similar cases throughout the country. This past year, the national council conducted or assisted in conducting 142 training programs at its headquarters' training facility, the National College of Juvenile and Family Law.

Resource Center on Domestic Violence: Child Protection and Custody, National Council of Juvenile and Family Court Judges

Family Violence Project
P.O. Box 8970
Reno, NV 89507
702-784-6012 or 800-527-3223
Fax: 702-784-6160

This organization provides information and technical assistance on topics such as child abuse and neglect, the foster care system, and child custody disputes. The organization distributes a number of publications (e.g., model codes and court programs) to assist judges and others on family violence.

MEDICAL RESOURCES

American Academy of Pediatrics, Department C

P.O. Box 927, SW
Elk Grove Village, IL 60009-2188
708-228-5005

The academy publishes information on issues such as child sexual abuse, identification, and effects on victims.

American Medical Association

Department of Mental Health
515 N. State St.
Chicago, IL 60610
312-464-5066

This association of doctors provides referrals and brochures containing help for doctors treating family violence victims.

Domestic Violence Project of the American Academy of Facial Plastic and Reconstructive Surgery

1110 Vermont Ave. NW, Suite 220
Washington, DC 20005
800-842-4546

This group, along with the National Coalition Against Domestic Violence (202-638-6388), provides some free facial and reconstructive and plastic surgery for victims of family violence.

Health Resource Center and Domestic Violence, Family Violence Prevention Fund

383 Rhode Island St., Suite 304
San Francisco, CA 94103-5133
415-252-8900 or 888-792-2873

This organization attempts to strengthen the health care response to domestic violence. It provides publications and technical assistance.

RESOURCE CENTERS AND CLEARINGHOUSES (PUBLICATIONS)

Boulder County Safehouse

P.O. Box 4157
Boulder, CO 80306
303-449-8623

This group publishes books in English and Spanish on children and family violence. These books are especially useful to parents, teachers, and health care workers.

Family Resource Coalition

200 S. Michigan Ave., 16th Floor
Chicago, IL 60604
312-341-0900

This group attempts to strengthen families through prevention. The coalition is also a clearinghouse and provides technical assistance.

Family Violence and Sexual Assault Institute
1310 Clinic Dr.
Tyler, TX 75701
903-595-6799
Fax: 903-595-6799

The institute is a nonprofit organization committed to education, networking, and the dissemination of information to reduce and prevent domestic violence and sexual assault. A large number of unpublished articles (e.g., convention papers) and references to published articles are available. The organization prepares special bibliographies and treatment manuals and publishes a quarterly newsletter that reviews books and media and announces conferences.

Higher Education Center Against Violence and Abuse
386 McNeal Hall
1985 Buford Ave.
St. Paul, MN 55108-6142
612-624-0721
800-646-2282 (within Minnesota)
Fax: 612-625-4288
E-mail: mincava@umn.edu

This Minnesota-based organization provides training for professionals in higher education. The group provides technical assistance, plans conferences, and helps fund pilot projects. It provides an electronic clearinghouse for colleges, universities, and career schools.

Kempe National Center for the Prevention and Treatment of Child Abuse and Neglect
1205 Oneida St.
Denver, CO 80220
303-321-3963

The Kempe National Center is a resource center for research in all forms of child maltreatment that is committed to multidisciplinary approaches to the treatment, recognition, and prevention of child maltreatment. The center offers a catalog of books, pamphlets, and articles.

National Center for Missing and Exploited Children
2101 Wilson Blvd., Suite 550
Arlington, VA 22201
703-235-3900 or 800-843-5678

The center is a clearinghouse and resource center funded by the federal Office of Juvenile Justice and Delinquency Prevention. It provides a number of useful publications.

National Clearinghouse on Child Abuse and Neglect Information
P.O. Box 1182
Washington, DC 20012
703-385-7565 or 800-394-3366

This clearinghouse offers annotated bibliographies and can provide statistics.

National Clearinghouse on Families and Youth
P.O. Box 13505
Silver Spring, MD 20911-3505
301-608-8098

This clearinghouse individualizes research, provides networking, and supplies updates on youth initiatives.

National Institute of Justice
U.S. Department of Justice
National Criminal Justice
Reference Service
P.O. Box 6000

Rockville, MD 20849-6000
301-251-5500 or 800-851-3420
E-mail: askncjrs@ncjrs.aspensys.com

The National Institute of Justice develops research and collects information about crime. Part of the U.S. Department of Justice, it provides the largest clearinghouse of criminal justice information in the world and many related services. The National Criminal Justice Reference Service will provide electronic versions of many documents.

National Resource Center on Domestic Violence
6400 Flank Dr., Suite 1300
Harrisburg, PA 17112-2778
800-537-2238
Fax: 717-545-9456

This center furnishes information and resources to advocates and policymakers.

National Self-Help Clearinghouse
Graduate School of City
University of New York
25 W. 43rd St., Room 620
New York, NY 10036
212-354-8525
212-642-2944

This organization lists self-help groups and makes referrals to national self-help groups for those needing assistance.

Youth Services Clearinghouse
Contact Center, Inc.
P.O. Box 81826
Lincoln, NE 68501
402-464-0602
Fax: 402-464-5931

The clearinghouse provides information and referrals to programs that serve youth. Topics include alcohol and drug abuse, runaways, youth employment, education, dropouts, and literacy.

CULTURE-SPECIFIC RESOURCES

United States

American Indian Institute (AII)
College of Continuing Education and Public Service
The University of Oklahoma
555 Constitution St., Suite 237
Norman, OK 73072-7820
405-325-4127
Fax: 405-325-7757
E-mail: aii@cce.occe.ou.edu

The institute serves North American Indian tribes and bands through workshops, seminars, and consultation and technical assistance on a state, regional, national, and international basis. The AII also cosponsors annually the National American Indian Conference on Child Abuse and Neglect.

COSSMHO
1501 16th St. NW
Washington, DC 20036
202-387-5000
Fax: 202-797-4353

COSSMHO is a national nonprofit coalition of Hispanic organizations serving the Mexican American, Puerto Rican, Cuban, and Latino communities in health and human services, substance abuse prevention, and family strengthening. Coalition affiliates include 220 local agencies in 32 states, the District of Columbia, and Puerto Rico.

National Black Child Development Institute, Inc.
1023 15th St. NW, Suite 600
Washington, DC 20005
202-387-1281
Fax: 202-234-1738

The institute, together with its 42 affiliates composed of volunteers, works to improve the quality of life for African American children and youth through public education and services in child care, education, child welfare, and health. Publications on issues in the above areas also are available.

People of Color Leadership Institute (POCLI)

714 G St. SE
Washington, DC 20003
202-544-3144
Fax: 202-547-3601

POCLI's mission is to increase knowledge skills as well as competency in ethnic and cultural issues among child and family welfare professionals and agencies and to promote leadership among professionals of color in the fields of child and family welfare, juvenile justice, mental health, and preventive services. POCLI has developed an agency self-assessment tool, which allows agencies to assess their level of cultural competence, and a staff training curriculum guide. Both are available at cost. POCLI staff also provide training in the fields of child abuse and neglect, attitude competency, domestic violence, substance abuse, and family support preservation.

Canada

London Family Court Clinic

254 Pall Mall St., Suite 200
London, Ontario N6A 5P6
Canada
519-679-7250

This clinic provides educational pamphlets on violence prevention for schoolchildren and teenagers.

Metro Action Committee on Public Violence Against Women and Children (METRAC)

158 Spadina Road
Toronto, Ontario M5R 2T8
Canada
416-392-3135
Fax: 416-392-3136

METRAC attempts to prevent violence against women and children by promoting research on violence, services for survivors, and legal system reform. The organization publishes informational packets as well as books.

National Clearinghouse on Family Violence

Family Violence Prevention Division
in Health Canada
Social Services Programs,
Health Canada
1st Floor, Finance Bldg.
Tunney's Pasture
Ottawa, Ontario K1A 1B5
Canada
613-952-6396
800-267-1291 (Canada)

The clearinghouse is a national resource center for all Canadians seeking information about violence within the family and new resources being used to address it. The clearinghouse offers publications on family violence, bibliographies, and a referral service.

HOTLINES

Father Flanagan's Boys Home (dial toll-free 800-448-3000)

Boys Town operates a national toll-free hotline for youth problems.

National Child Abuse Hotline (dial toll-free 800-422-4453 or 800-4-A-Child)

The hotline provides crisis counseling, child abuse reporting information, and information and referrals for every county in the United States and the District of Columbia. The hotline is staffed 24 hours a day, 7 days a week, by mental health professionals.

National Directory of Hotlines and Crisis Intervention Centers (dial toll-free 800-999-9999 or 800-999-9915)

The directory is a 24-hour nationwide hotline for runaways and troubled youth and their families. The hotline offers referrals to services in a caller's local area.

To locate additional hotlines, look in the nonbusiness section of a telephone directory under "Social Service Agencies," "Shelters," and "Women's Organizations."

GENERAL CRIME VICTIM ORGANIZATIONS

National Organizations for Victim Assistance
1757 Park Rd. NW
Washington, DC 20010
202-232-6682

This group runs public education programs, provides direct services to victims, and develops public policy and training programs for policymakers and health care providers.

National Victim Center
555 Madison Ave., Suite 2001
New York, NY 10022
800-FYI-CALL

This organization provides research, education, training, advocacy, and resources for those working with crime victims. It networks through an INFOLINK line. It has some publications (e.g., on stalking).

National Victims Resource Center
Box 6000
Rockville, MD 20850
800-627-6872

The center represents the primary source of information on U.S. crime victims. The organization is responsible for distributing all publications of Office of Justice Programs on victim-related issues, including domestic violence victims.

RELIGIOUS INFORMATION

California Professional Society on Abuse of Children (CAPSAC)
Orange, CA
619-773-1649

Phone to obtain CAPSAC's *Anthology of Sermons* (1996).

Center for the Prevention of Sexual and Domestic Violence
936 N. 34th St., Suite 200
Seattle, WA 98193
206-634-1903

This center provides educational materials for religious organizations preparing sermons for clergy and lessons for Sunday school classes. It educates clergy about child abuse and inappropriate behaviors of clergy.

Promise Keepers
10200 W. 44th Ave.
Wheatridge, CO 80033
303-964-7600 or 800-501-0211

This interfaith Christian group (for men only) has a number of local organizations that hold conventions. The purpose of the organization is to encourage male bonding and to provide sermons about the commitments of men to their families.

RELEVANT DIRECTORIES

National Directory of Children, Youth and Families Services

To order:
National Directory of Children, Youth and Families Services
14 Inverness Drive East, Suite D-144
Englewood, CO 80112
800-343-6681

The directory is produced annually and lists more than 30,000 agencies, including Human/ Social Services, Health, Mental Health/ Substance Abuse, Juvenile Justice, Treatment Centers, and Specialized Hospitals.

National Directory of Domestic Violence Programs

To order:
National Coalition Against Domestic Violence
P.O. Box 18749
Denver, CO 80218
303-839-1852

The directory is a guide to community shelter, safe home, and service programs concerned with domestic violence. The directory also contains a list of national information and resource centers as well as military programs.

The 1994 North American Directory of Programs for Runaways, Homeless Youth and Missing Children

To order:
American Youth Work Center
1200 17th St. NW, 4th Floor
Washington, DC 20036
202-785-0764

This directory lists 500 programs designed to protect street children from potentially abusive and exploitative situations.

TREATMENT RESOURCES

Adults Molested As Children United (AMACU)

P.O. Box 952
San Jose, CA 95108
408-453-7616

AMACU is a self-help program for adults who were sexually abused as children. The program attempts to help resolve the problems experienced by the victims of child sexual abuse. The program was developed by Parents United. To find a local AMACU group, or for referrals to local sexual abuse treatment specialists, contact the office listed above.

Children of Alcoholics Foundation

P.O. Box 4185
Grand Central Station
New York, NY 10163-4185
212-754-0656 or 800-359-2623

The foundation seeks to promote public and professional awareness of the problems of children of alcoholics and disseminates new research findings to break the vicious cycle of family alcoholism. The foundation operates a help line, which provides referrals to national and local self-help and counseling groups and treatment agencies.

Incest Survivors Anonymous (ISA)

P.O. Box 17245
Long Beach, CA 90807-7245
310-428-5599

ISA provides information on self-help meetings that are Twelve-Step and Twelve-Tradition or spiritually oriented for survivors of incest. Check local listings or check local social service agencies for information about meetings in your area.

National Adolescent Perpetrator Network
1205 Oneida St.
Denver, CO 80220
303-321-3963

This network of people involved in identification, intervention, and treatment of sexually abusive youth facilitates communication, referrals, training, and research. The network is a program of the C. Henry Kempe National Center for the Treatment and Prevention of Child Abuse and Neglect.

Parents Anonymous
National Parents Anonymous
675 W. Foothill Blvd, Suite 220
Claremont, CA 91711
909-621-6184

Parents Anonymous has 2,100 local groups across the United States, and many of these have groups for adult survivors of child abuse. To locate a group in your area, look in the white pages of your telephone directory under Parents Anonymous or contact the national office listed above.

Shield Abuse & Trauma Project
39-09 214th Place
Bayside, NY 11361
718-229-5757 ext. 216
Fax: 718-225-3159

The Shield Abuse & Trauma Project provides a unique program of services to individuals with developmental disabilities who have experienced abuse or other traumatic experiences resulting in emotional, behavioral, or interpersonal difficulties. The project provides individual and group treatment services in addition to organizational training and consulting services. Organizational training and consulting are geared to help agencies understand the impact of abuse and/or trauma on these individuals and to assist in creating more effective intervention in all settings.

Appendix B

Related Readings for Victims, Professionals, and Others

The following references vary in their appropriateness for different readers. Some focus on different victim groups, and others address more tangential issues. Some address issues of importance to practitioners, and others address research concerns. Individuals involved in family violence are best served in making reading selections by consulting with a mental health professional familiar with their situation.

Ammerman, R. T., & Hersen, M. (1992). *Assessment of family violence: A clinical and legal sourcebook.* New York: John Wiley.

Araji, S. K. (1997). *Sexually aggressive children: Coming to understand them.* Thousand Oaks, CA: Sage.

Bachman, R. (1992). *Death and violence on the reservation: Homicide, family violence, and suicide in American Indian populations.* New York: Auburn House.

Barnett, O. W., Miller-Perrin, C. L., & Perrin, R. D. (1997). *Family violence across the lifespan.* Thousand Oaks, CA: Sage.

Bergen, R. K. (Ed.). (1998). *Issues in intimate violence.* Thousand Oaks, CA: Sage.

Berry, D. B. (1995). *The domestic violence sourcebook.* Los Angeles: Lowell House.

Bottoms, B. L., & Goodman, G. S. (1996). *International perspectives on child abuse and children's testimony: Psychological research and law.* Thousand Oaks, CA: Sage.

Boulder County Safehouse. (1990). *We can't play at my house: Children and domestic violence* (Handbook for teachers, Bk. 2). Boulder, CO: Author.

Briere, J. (1992). *Child abuse trauma.* Newbury Park, CA: Sage.

Briere, J., Berliner, L., Bulkley, J. A., Jenny, C., & Reid, T. (1996). *The APSAC handbook on child maltreatment.* Thousand Oaks, CA: Sage.

Brohl, K. (1996). *Working with traumatized children: A handbook for healing.* Washington, DC: Child Welfare League of America.

Burton, J. E., Rasmussen, L. A., Bradshaw, J., Christopherson, B. J., & Huke, S. C. (1998). *Treating children with sexually abusive behavior problems.* Binghamton, NY: Haworth.

Caffaro, J. V., & Conn-Caffaro, A. (1998). *Sibling abuse trauma: Assessment and intervention strategies for children, families, and adult survivors.* Binghamton, NY: Haworth.

California Professional Society on Abuse of Children (CAPSAC). (1996). *Anthology of sermons.* Orange: Author. (Available by calling 619-773-1649)

Campbell, J. C. (1995). *Assessing dangerousness: Violence by sexual offenders, batterers, and child abusers.* Thousand Oaks, CA: Sage.

Campbell, J. C. (Ed.). (1998). *Empowering survivors of abuse: Health care, battered women, and their children.* Thousand Oaks, CA: Sage.

Ceci, S. J., & Hembrooke, H. (1998). *Expert witnesses in child abuse cases: What can and should be said in court.* Washington, DC: American Psychological Association.

Child Welfare League of America. (1998). *Children's legislative agenda 1998: Budget updates and issue briefs.* Washington, DC: Author.

Child Welfare League of America. (1998). *CWLA standards of excellence for services for abused or neglected children and their families.* Washington, DC: Author.

Davis, R. C., Lurigio, A. J., & Skogan, W. G. (Eds.). (1997). *Victims of crime.* Thousand Oaks, CA: Sage.

Day, P., Robison, S., & Sheikh, L. (1998). *Ours to keep: A guide for building a community assessment strategy for child protection.* Washington, DC: Child Welfare League of America.

Deblinger, E., & Heflin, A. H. (1996). *Treating sexually abused children and their nonoffending parents: A cognitive behavioral approach.* Thousand Oaks, CA: Sage.

DeWoody, M. (1994). *Health care reform and child welfare: Meeting the needs of abused and neglected children.* Washington, DC: Child Welfare League of America.

Dorman, R. L., Moore, D. J., Schaerfl-Murphy, C., & Spottsville, S. A. (1998). *Planning, funding, and implementing a child abuse prevention project.* Washington, DC: Child Welfare League of America.

Eldridge, H. (1997). *Maintaining change: Relapse prevention for adult male perpetrators of child sexual abuse.* Thousand Oaks, CA: Sage.

Evans, R. M. (1995). *Childhood hurts.* New York: Bantam.

Ewing, C. P. (1997). *Fatal families: The dynamics of intrafamilial homicide.* Thousand Oaks, CA: Sage.

Fairstein, L. A. (1993). *Sexual violence: Our war against rape.* New York: William Morrow.

Fedders, C., & Elliott, L. (1987). *Shattered dreams.* New York: Harper & Row.

Flannery, R. B., Jr. (1992). *Post trauma stress disorder.* New York: Crossword.

Fontes, L. A. (Ed.). (1995). *Sexual abuse in nine North American cultures: Treatment and prevention.* Thousand Oaks, CA: Sage.

Forward, S. D. (1989). *Toxic parents.* New York: Bantam.

Fredrickson, R. (1992). *Repressed memories.* New York: Fireside/Parkside.

Friedrich, W. (1990). *Psychotherapy of sexually abused children and their families.* New York: Norton.

Garbarino, J., Guttmann, E., & Seeley, J. W. (1986). *The psychologically battered child.* San Francisco: Jossey-Bass.

Geffner, R., Sorensen, S., & Lundberg-Love, P. (1997). *Violence and sexual abuse at home.* Binghamton, NY: Haworth.

Gelles, R. J. (1996). *The book of David: How preserving families can cost children's lives.* New York: Basic Books.

Gelles, R. J. (1997). *Intimate violence in families* (3rd ed.). Thousand Oaks, CA: Sage.

Gelles, R. J., & Cornell, C. P. (1990). *Intimate violence in families* (2nd ed.). Newbury Park, CA: Sage.

Gelles, R. J., & Loseke, D. R. (1993). *Current controversies on family violence.* Newbury Park, CA: Sage.

Giardino, A. P., Christian, C. W., & Giardino, E. R. (1997). *A practical guide to the evaluation of child physical abuse and neglect.* Thousand Oaks, CA: Sage.

Giardino, A. P., Finkel, M. A., Giardino, E. R., Seidl, T., & Ludwig, S. (1992). *A practical guide to the evaluation of sexual abuse in the prepubertal child.* Newbury Park, CA: Sage.

Gordon, B. N., & Schroeder, C. S. (1995). *Sexuality: A developmental approach to problems.* New York: Plenum.

Gould, J. W. (1998). *Conducting scientifically based child custody evaluations.* Thousand Oaks, CA: Sage.

Greenberg, K. E. (1994). *Family abuse: Why do people hurt each other?* New York: Twenty-First Century.

Hampton, R. L. (1991). *Black family violence: Current research and theory.* Lexington, MA: Lexington Books.

Hampton, R. L., Senatore, V., & Gullotta, T. P. (1998). *Substance abuse, family violence, and child welfare.* Thousand Oaks, CA: Sage.

Herman, J. L. (1992). *Trauma and recovering.* New York: HarperCollins.

Hewitt, S. K. (1998). *Small voices: Assessing allegations of sexual abuse in preschool children.* Thousand Oaks, CA: Sage.

Hoghughi, M. S., Bhat, S. R., & Graham, F. (1997). *Working with sexually abusive adolescents.* Thousand Oaks, CA: Sage.

Holden, G. W., Geffner, R., & Jouriles, E. N. (Eds.). (1998). *Children exposed to marital violence: Theory, research, and applied issues.* Washington, DC: American Psychological Association.

Horton, A. L., & Williamson, J. A. (1988). *Abuse and religion: When praying isn't enough.* Lexington, MA: Lexington Books.

Howing, P. T., Wodarski, J. S., Kurtz, P. D., & Gaudin, J. M. (1993). *Maltreatment and the school-age child.* Binghamton, NY: Haworth.

Hunter, N. (1991). *Abused boys.* New York: Fawcett.

Inciardi, J. A., Surratt, H. L., & Saum, C. A. (1997). *Cocaine-exposed infants: Social, legal, and public health issues.* Thousand Oaks, CA: Sage.

Jackson, H., & Nuttal, R. (1997). *Childhood abuse: Effects on clinicians' personal and professional lives.* Thousand Oaks, CA: Sage.

Jaffe, P. G., Wolfe, D. A., & Wolfe, S. K. (1990). *Children of battered women.* Newbury Park, CA: Sage.

Kalichman, S. C. (1993). *Mandated reporting of suspected child abuse: Ethics, law, and policy.* Washington, DC: American Psychological Association.

Karp, C. L., & Butler, T. L. (1996). *Treatment strategies for abused children: From victim to survivor.* Thousand Oaks, CA: Sage.

Karp, C. L., Butler, T. L., & Bergstrom, S. C. (1998). *Treatment strategies for abused adolescents.* Thousand Oaks, CA: Sage.

Kendig, B., & Lowry, C. (1998). *Cedar house: A model child abuse treatment program.* Binghamton, NY: Haworth.

Knapp, S. J., & VandeCreek, L. (1997). *Treating patients with memories of abuse: Legal risk management.* Washington, DC: American Psychological Association.

Leberg, E. (1997). *Understanding child molesters: Take charge.* Thousand Oaks, CA: Sage.

Lee, S. A. (1995). *The survivor's guide: For teenage girls surviving sexual abuse.* Thousand Oaks, CA: Sage.

Levy, B. (1992). *In love and danger: A teen's guide to breaking free of abusive relationships.* Seattle, WA: Seal.

Levy, T. M., & Orlans, M. (1998). *Attachment, trauma, and healing: Understanding and treating attachment disorder in children and families.* Washington, DC: Child Welfare League of America.

Loftus, E., & Ketcham, K. (1994). *The myth of repressed memory.* New York: St. Martin's.

Lutzker, J. R. (Ed.). (1997). *Handbook of child abuse research and treatment.* New York: Plenum.

MacFarlane, K., & Waterman, J. (Eds.). (1986). *Sexual abuse of young children.* New York: Guilford.

Marshall, W. L., Fernandez, Y. M., Hudson, S. M., & Ward, T. (1998). *Sourcebook of treatment programs for sexual offenders.* New York: Plenum.

Marwick, C. (1994). Health and justice professionals set goals to lessen domestic violence. *Journal of the American Medical Association, 271,* 1147-1148.

McCroskey, J., & Meezan, W. (1997). *Family preservation and family functioning.* Washington, DC: Child Welfare League of America.

Mones, P. (1991). *When a child kills: Abused children who kill their parents.* New York: Pocket Books.

Mitchell, J., & Morse, J. (1998). *From victims to survivors: Reclaimed voices of women sexually abused in childhood by females.* Washington, DC: Accelerated Development.

Morgan, M. (1995). *How to interview sexual abuse victims.* Thousand Oaks, CA: Sage.

Munson, L., & Riskin, K. (1995). *In their own words: A sexual abuse workbook for teenage girls.*

Washington, DC: Child Welfare League of America.

Myers, J. E. B. (1997). *A mother's nightmare: Incest.* Thousand Oaks, CA: Sage.

Myers, J. E. B. (1998). *Legal issues in child abuse and neglect.* Thousand Oaks, CA: Sage.

Newell, B. (1993, Winter). Children's rights [Special issue]. *NCADV Voice.*

Orleman, J. (1998). *Telling secrets: An artist's journey through childhood trauma.* Washington, DC: Child Welfare League of America.

Osmond, M., Durham, D., Leggett, A., & Keating, J. (1998). *Treating the aftermath of sexual abuse: A handbook for working with children in care.* Washington, DC: Child Welfare League of America.

Osofsky, J. D. (Ed.). (1997). *Children in a violent society.* New York: Guilford.

Parker, B. (1993). Abuse of adolescents: What can we learn from pregnant teenagers? *AWHONN's Clinical Issues, 4,* 363-370.

Parnell, T. F., & Day, D. O. (1997). *Munchausen by proxy syndrome.* Thousand Oaks, CA: Sage.

Paymar, M. (1993). *Violent no more: Helping men end domestic abuse.* Alameda, CA: Hunter House.

Pearce, J. W., & Pezzot-Pearce, T. D. (1997). *Psychotherapy of abused and neglected children.* New York: Guilford.

Petit, M. R., & Curtis, P. A. (1997). *Child abuse and neglect: A look at the states.* Washington, DC: Child Welfare League of America.

Poole, D. A., & Lamb, M. E. (1998). *Investigative interviews of children.* Washington, DC: American Psychological Association.

Pope, K. S., & Brown, L. S. (1996). *Recovered memories of abuse: Assessment, therapy, forensics.* Washington, DC: American Psychological Association.

Porett, J., & Lipczenko, D. (1993). *When I was little like you.* Washington, DC: Child Welfare League of America.

Quinsey, V. L., Harris, G. T., Rice, M. E., & Cormier, C. A. (1998). *Violent offenders: Appraising and managing risk.* Washington, DC: American Psychological Association.

Read, J. D., & Lindsay, D. S. (1997). *Recollections of trauma: Scientific evidence and clinical practice.* New York: Plenum.

Richards, K. N. (1998). *Tender mercies: Inside the world of a child abuse investigator.* Washington, DC: Child Welfare League of America.

Robinson, B. E., & Rhoden, J. L. (1998). *Working with children of alcoholics: The practitioner's handbook.* Thousand Oaks, CA: Sage.

Rossman, B. B. R., & Rosenberg, M. S. (1998). *Multiple victimization of children: Conceptual, developmental, research, and treatment issues.* Binghamton, NY: Haworth.

Roy, M. (1988). *Children in crossfire.* Deerfield Beach, FL: Health Communications.

Russell, M. N. (1995). *Confronting abusive beliefs.* Thousand Oaks, CA: Sage.

Ryan, G., & Lane, S. (Eds.). (1997). *Juvenile sexual offending: Causes, consequences, and correction.* San Francisco: Jossey-Bass.

Salter, A. C. (1995). *Transforming trauma.* Thousand Oaks, CA: Sage.

Sanders, T. L. (1991). *Male survivors.* Freedom, CA: Crossing Press.

Saradjian, J. (1996). *Women who sexually abuse children: From research to clinical practice.* Chichester, UK: Wiley.

Schaefer, K. (1993). *What only a mother can tell you about child sexual abuse.* Washington, DC: Child Welfare League of America.

Spanos, N. P. (1996). *Multiple identities and false memories: A sociocognitive perspective.* Washington, DC: American Psychological Association.

Stahl, P. M. (1994). *Conducting child custody evaluations: A comprehensive guide.* Thousand Oaks, CA: Sage.

Stern, P., & Saunders, B. E. (1997). *Preparing and presenting expert testimony in child abuse litigation: A guide for expert witnesses and attorneys.* Thousand Oaks, CA: Sage.

Thompson, R. A. (1995). *Preventing child maltreatment through social support.* Thousand Oaks, CA: Sage.

Tomkins, A. J., Steinman, M., Kenning, M. K., Somaia, M., & Afrank, J. (1992). Children who witness woman battering. *Law & Policy, 14*(2/3), 169-181.

Trickett, P. K., & Schellenbach, C. J. (Eds.). (1998). *Violence against children in the family and the community.* Washington, DC: American Psychological Association.

Truscott, D. (1992). Intergenerational transmission of violent behavior in adolescent males. *Aggressive Behavior, 18,* 327-335.

Wallace, H. (1996). *Family violence: Legal, medical, and social perspectives.* Boston: Allyn & Bacon.

Whitaker, L. C., & Pollard, J. W. (1996). *Campus violence: Kinds, causes, and cures.* New York: Haworth.

Wiehe, V. R. (1996). *Working with child abuse and neglect: A primer.* Thousand Oaks, CA: Sage.

Wiehe, V. R. (1997). *Sibling abuse: Hidden physical, emotional, and sexual trauma.* Thousand Oaks, CA: Sage.

Wiehe, V. R. (1998). *Understanding family violence.* Thousand Oaks, CA: Sage.

Wieland, S. (1997). *Hearing the internal trauma: Working with children and adolescents who have been sexually abused.* Thousand Oaks, CA: Sage.

Wiklund, P. (1995). *Sleeping with a stranger: How I survived marriage to a child molester.* Holbrook, MA: Adams Media.

Wolfe, D. A. (1996). *The youth relationships manual.* Thousand Oaks, CA: Sage.

Wolfe, D. A., McMahon, R. J., & Peters, R. D. (1997). *Child abuse: New directions in prevention and treatment across the lifespan.* Thousand Oaks, CA: Sage.

Wolfe, D. A., Wekerle, C., & Scott, K. (1997). *Alternatives to violence: Empowering youth to develop healthy relationships.* Thousand Oaks, CA: Sage.

References

Abel, G. G., Becker, J. V., & Cunningham-Rathner, J. (1984). Complications, consent, and cognitions in sex between children and adults. *International Journal of Law and Psychiatry, 7,* 89-103.

Abel, G. G., Becker, J. V., & Skinner, L. J. (1986). Behavioral approaches to treatment of the violent sex offender. In L. H. Roth (Ed.), *Clinical treatment of the violent person* (pp. 100-123). New York: Guilford.

Abel, G. G., Gore, D. K., Holland, C. L., Camp, N., Becker, J. V., & Rathner, J. (1989). The measurement of the cognitive distortions of child molesters. *Annals of Sex Research, 2,* 135-153.

Abel, G. G., & Rouleau, J. L. (1990). The nature and extent of sexual assault. In W. L. Marshall, D. R. Laws, & H. E. Barbaree (Eds.), *Handbook of sexual assault: Issues, theories, and treatment of the offender* (pp. 9-21). New York: Plenum.

Achenbach, T. M., & Edelbrock, C. S. (1983). *Manual for the Child Behavior Checklist and Revised Child Behavior Profile.* Burlington: University of Vermont Press.

Acton, R. G., & During, S. M. (1992). Preliminary results of aggression management training for aggressive parents. *Journal of Interpersonal Violence, 7,* 410-417.

Adler, J., Carroll, G., Smith, V., & Rogers, P. (1994, November 14). Innocents lost. *Newsweek, 124,* 26-30.

Adler, N., & Schutz, J. (1995). Sibling incest offenders. *Child Abuse & Neglect, 19,* 811-819.

Adoption and Safe Families Act. (1997). H.R. 876.ENR, 105th Cong. [Online]. Available: http://thomas.loc.gov/egl-bin/query

Ainsworth, M. D. S. (1973). The development of infant-mother attachment. In B. Caldwell & H. Ricciuti (Eds.), *Review of child development research* (Vol. 3, pp. 1-94). Chicago: University of Chicago Press.

Ainsworth, M. D. S., & Bowlby, J. (1991). An ethological approach to personality development. *American Psychologist, 46,* 331-341.

Alessandri, S. M. (1991). Play and social behavior in maltreated pre-schoolers. *Development and Psychopathology, 3,* 191-205.

Alessi, J. J., & Hearn, K. (1984). Group treatment of children in shelters for battered women. In A. R. Roberts (Ed.), *Battered women and their families* (pp. 49-61). New York: Springer.

Alexander, P. C., & Lupfer, S. L. (1987). Family characteristics and long-term consequences associated with sexual abuse. *Archives of Sexual Behavior, 16,* 235-245.

Alexander, P. C., Neimeyer, R. A., & Follette, V. M. (1991). Group therapy for women sexually abused as children: A controlled study and investigation of individual differences. *Journal of Interpersonal Violence, 6,* 218-231.

Alfaro, J. D. (1981). Report on the relationship between child abuse and neglect and later socially deviant behavior. In R. J. Hunter & Y. E. Walker (Eds.), *Exploring the relationship between child abuse and delinquency* (pp. 175-219). Montclair, NJ: Allanheld, Osmun.

Allen, D. M., & Tarnowski, K. J. (1989). Depressive characteristics of physically abused children. *Journal of Abnormal Child Psychology, 17,* 1-11.

American Association for Protecting Children. (1985). *Highlights of official child neglect and abuse reporting, 1983.* Denver, CO: American Humane Association.

American Association for Protecting Children. (1988). *Highlights of official child neglect and abuse reporting, 1986.* Denver, CO: American Humane Association.

American Association for Protecting Children. (1989). *Highlights of official child neglect and abuse reporting, 1987.* Denver, CO: American Humane Association.

American Humane Association. (1981). *Annual report, 1980: National analysis of official child neglect and abuse reporting.* Denver, CO: Author.

American Humane Association. (1984). *Highlights of official child abuse and neglect reporting: 1982.* Denver, CO: Author.

American Humane Association. (1993). *Child abuse and day care* (Fact Sheet No. 11). (Available from the American Humane Association, 63 Inverness Drive East, Englewood, CO 80112-5117)

American Psychiatric Association. (1994). *Diagnostic and statistical manual of mental disorders* (4th ed.). Washington, DC: Author.

American Psychological Association, Commission on Violence and Youth. (1993). *Violence and youth: Psychology's response* (Vol. 1). Washington, DC: Author.

Ammerman, R. T. (1991). The role of the child in physical abuse: A reappraisal. *Violence and Victims, 6,* 87-101.

Ammerman, R. T., Van Hasselt, V. B., Hersen, M., McGonigle, J. J., & Lubetsky, M. J. (1989). Abuse and neglect in psychiatrically hospitalized multihandicapped children. *Child Abuse & Neglect, 13,* 335-343.

Amundson, M. J. (1989). Family crisis care: A home-based intervention program for child abuse. *Issues in Mental Health Nursing, 10,* 285-296.

Anderson, D. (1979). Touching: When is it caring and nurturing or when is it exploitative and damaging. *Child Abuse & Neglect, 3,* 793-794.

Appel, A. E., Angelelli, M. J., & Holden, G. W. (in press). The co-occurrence of spouse and physical child abuse: A review and appraisal. *Journal of Family Psychology.*

Asbury, J. (1993). Violence in families of color in the United States. In R. L. Hampton, T. P. Gullotta, G. R. Adams, E. H. Potter, III, & R. P. Weissberg (Eds.), *Family violence: Prevention and treatment* (pp. 159-178). Newbury Park, CA: Sage.

Attar, B. K., Guerra, N. G., & Tolan, P. H. (1994). Neighborhood disadvantage, stressful life events, and adjustment in urban elementary-school children. *Journal of Clinical Psychology, 23,* 391-400.

Ayoub, C. C., & Milner, J. S. (1985). Failure to thrive: Parental indicators, types, and outcomes. *Child Abuse & Neglect, 9,* 491-499.

Azar, S. T. (1988). Methodological considerations in treatment outcome research. In G. T. Hotaling, D. Finkelhor, J. T. Kirkpatrick, & M. A. Straus (Eds.), *Coping with family violence* (pp. 288-298). Newbury Park, CA: Sage.

Azar, S. T. (1997). A cognitive behavioral approach to understanding and treating parents who physically abuse their children. In D. A. Wolfe, R. J. McMahon, & R. D. Peters (Eds.), *Child abuse: New directions in prevention and treatment across the lifespan* (pp. 79-101). Thousand Oaks, CA: Sage.

Azar, S. T., Barnes, K. T., & Twentyman, C. T. (1988). Developmental outcomes in abused children: Consequences of parental abuse or a more general breakdown in caregiver behavior? *Behavior Therapist, 11,* 27-32.

Azar, S. T., Ferraro, M. H., & Breton, S. J. (1998). Intrafamilial child maltreatment. In T. H. Ollendick & M. Hersen (Eds.), *Handbook of child psychopathology* (pp. 483-504). New York: Plenum.

Azar, S. T., & Siegel, B. R. (1990). Behavioral treatment of child abuse: A developmental perspective. *Behavior Modification, 14,* 279-300.

Babbie, E. (1995). *The practice of social research.* Belmont, CA: Wadsworth.

Bachman, R., & Saltzman, L. E. (1996). *Violence against women: Estimates from the redesigned survey* (NCJ No. 154348). Rockville, MD: U.S. Department of Justice, Bureau of Justice Statistics.

Bagley, C. (1990). Is the prevalence of child sexual abuse decreasing? Evidence from a random sample of 750 young adult women. *Psychological Reports, 66,* 1037-1038.

Bagley, C. (1991). The prevalence and mental health sequels of child abuse in a community sample of women aged 18-27. *Canadian Journal of Community Mental Health, 10*(1), 103-116.

Bagley, C., & Ramsay, R. (1986). Sexual abuse in childhood: Psychological outcomes and implications for social work practice. *Journal of Social Work and Human Sexuality, 4,* 33-47.

Bagley, C., Wood, M., & Young, L. (1994). Victim to abuser: Mental health and behavioral sequels of child sexual abuse in a community survey of young adult males. *Child Abuse & Neglect, 18,* 683-697.

Bagley, C., & Young, L. (1987). Juvenile prostitution and child sexual abuse: A controlled study. *Journal of Community Mental Health, 6,* 5-26.

Baily, T. F., & Baily, W. H. (1986). *Operational definitions of child emotional maltreatment: Final report* (National Center on Child Abuse and Neglect, DHHS Publication No. 90-CA-0956). Washington, DC: Government Printing Office.

Bakan, D. (1971). *Slaughter of the innocents: A study of the battered child phenomenon.* San Francisco: Jossey-Bass.

Bakwin, H. (1949). Emotional deprivation in infants. *Journal of Pediatrics, 35,* 512-521.

Bandura, A. (1971). *Social learning theory.* Morristown, NJ: General Learning.

Bandura, A., Ross, D., & Ross, S. A. (1961). Transmission of aggression through imitation of aggressive models. *Journal of Abnormal and Social Psychology, 67,* 575-582.

Barbaree, H., Marshall, W., & Hudson, S. (Eds.). (1993). *The juvenile sex offender.* New York: Guilford.

Barone, V. J., Greene, B. F., & Lutzker, J. R. (1986). Home safety with families being treated for child abuse and neglect. *Behavioral Modification, 14,* 230-254.

Bartley, N. (1998, April 10). Ex-teacher pleads guilty to child rape. *Seattle Times* [Online]. Available: http://www.seattletimes.com

Barton, K., & Baglio, C. (1993). The nature of stress in child-abusing families: A factor analytic study. *Psychological Reports, 73,* 1047-1055.

Bass, E., & Davis, L. (1988). *The courage to heal.* New York: Harper & Row.

Bath, H. I., & Haapala, D. A. (1993). Intensive family preservation services with abused and neglected children: An examination of group differences. *Child Abuse & Neglect, 17,* 213-225.

Bauer, W. D., & Twentyman, C. T. (1985). Abusing, neglectful, and comparison mothers' responses to child-related and non-child-related stressors. *Journal of Consulting and Clinical Psychology, 53,* 335-343.

Baumeister, R. F., Stillwell, A., & Wotman, S. R. (1990). Victim and perpetrator accounts of interpersonal conflict: Autobiographical narratives about anger. *Journal of Personality and Social Psychology, 59,* 994-1005.

Bays, J. (1990). Substance abuse and child abuse: Impact of addiction on the child. *Pediatric Clinics of North America, 37,* 881.

Bays, J., & Chadwick, D. (1993). Medical diagnosis of the sexually abused child. *Child Abuse & Neglect, 17,* 91-110.

Becker, H. W. (1963). *Outsiders.* New York: Free Press.

Becker, J. V. (1994). Offenders: Characteristics and treatment. *Future of Children, 4,* 176-197.

Becker, J. V., Alpert, J. L., BigFoot, D. S., Bonner, B. L., Geddie, L. F., Henggeler, S. W., Kaufman, K. L., & Walker, C. E. (1995). Empirical research on child abuse treatment: Report by the Child Abuse and Neglect Treatment Working Group, American Psychological Association. *Journal of Clinical Child Psychology, 24,* 23-46.

Becker, J. V., Kaplan, M. S., Cunningham-Rathner, J., & Kavoussi, R. (1986). Characteristics of adolescent sexual perpetrators: Preliminary findings. *Journal of Family Violence, 1,* 85-87.

Begley, S. (1997, September 22). The nursery's littlest victims. *Newsweek, 130,* 72-73.

Beitchman, J. H., Zucker, K. J., Hood, J. E., daCosta, G. A., & Akman, D. (1991). A review of the short-term effects of child sexual abuse. *Child Abuse & Neglect, 15,* 537-556.

Beitchman, J. H., Zucker, K. J., Hood, J. E., daCosta, G. A., Akman, D., & Cassavia, E. (1992). A review of the long-term effects of child sexual abuse. *Child Abuse & Neglect, 16,* 101-118.

Bell, C., & Jenkins, E. J. (1991). Traumatic stress and children. *Journal of Health Care for the Poor and Underserved, 2,* 175-185.

Bell, C., & Jenkins, E. J. (1993). Community violence and children on Chicago's South-Side. *Psychiatry, 56,* 46-54.

Bell, R. Q., & Chapman, M. (1986). Child effects in studies using experimental or brief longitudinal approaches to socialization. *Developmental Psychology, 22,* 595-603.

Belsky, J. (1980). Child maltreatment: An ecological integration. *American Psychologist, 35,* 320-335.

Belsky, J. (1993). Etiology of child maltreatment: A developmental-ecological analysis. *Psychological Bulletin, 114,* 413-434.

Benatar, P., Geraldo, N., & Capps, R. (1981). *Hell is for children* [Record]. Los Angeles: Rare Blue Music, Inc./Neil Geraldo (ASCAP), Red Admiral Music Inc./Big Tooth Music Co. (BMI), Rare Blue Music Inc./Muscletone Music (ASCAP). (1980)

Benedict, M., White, R., Wulff, L., & Hall, B. (1990). Reported maltreatment in children with multiple disabilities. *Child Abuse & Neglect, 14,* 207-217.

Berger, A. (1985). Characteristics of abusing families. In L. L'Abate (Ed.), *The handbook of family psychology and therapy* (pp. 900-936). Homewood, IL: Dorsey.

Bergman, A. B. (1997, January). Wrong turns in sudden infant death syndrome research. *Pediatrics* [Online], *99*(1), 119-121. Available: http://proquest.umi.com

Berlin, F. S., & Meinecke, C. F. (1981). Treatment of sex offenders with anti-androgenic medication: Conceptualization, review of treatment modalities and preliminary findings. *American Journal of Psychiatry, 138,* 601-607.

Berliner, L. (1991). Clinical work with sexually abused children. In C. R. Hollin & K. Howells (Eds.), *Clinical approaches to sex offenders and their victims* (pp. 209-228). New York: John Wiley.

Berliner, L. (1994). The problem with neglect. *Journal of Interpersonal Violence, 9,* 556.

Berliner, L., & Conte, J. R. (1990). The process of victimization: The victim's perspective. *Child Abuse & Neglect, 14,* 29-40.

Berliner, L., & Elliott, D. M. (1996). Sexual abuse of children. In J. Briere, L. Berliner, J. A. Bulkley, C. Jenny, & T. Reid (Eds.), *The APSAC handbook on child maltreatment* (pp. 51-71). Thousand Oaks, CA: Sage.

Berman, P. (1990). Group therapy techniques for sexually abused preteen girls. *Child Welfare, 69,* 239-252.

Berry, M. (1991). The assessment of imminence of risk of placement: Lessons from a family preservation program. *Children and Youth Services Review, 13,* 239-256.

Berson, N., & Herman-Giddens, M. (1994). Recognizing invasive genital care practices: A form of child sexual abuse. *The APSAC Advisor, 7*(1), 13-14.

Besharov, D. (1985). "Doing something" about child abuse: The need to narrow the grounds for state intervention. *Harvard Journal of Law and Public Policy, 3,* 539-589.

Besharov, D. (1990). *Recognizing child abuse.* New York: Free Press.

Besharov, D. (1991). Reducing unfounded reports. *Journal of Interpersonal Violence, 6,* 112-115.

Besharov, D. (1996, December 1). When home is hell: We are too reluctant to take children from bad parents. *Washington Post,* pp. C1, C5-C6.

Best, J. (Ed.). (1989). *Images of issues: Typifying contemporary social problems.* New York: Aldine de Gruyter.

Beutler, L. E., Williams, R. E., & Zetzer, H. A. (1994). Efficacy of treatment for victims of child sexual abuse. *Future of Children, 4*(2), 156-175.

Bevc, I., & Silverman, I. (1993). Early proximity and intimacy between siblings and incestuous behavior: A test of the Westermarck theory. *Ethology and Sociobiology, 14,* 171-181.

Biringen, Z., & Robinson, J. (1991). Emotional availability in mother-child interactions: A reconceptualization for research. *American Journal of Orthopsychiatry, 61*(2), 258-271.

Birns, B., & Meyer, S. L. (1993). Mothers' role in incest: Dysfunctional women or dysfunctional theories? *Journal of Child Sexual Abuse, 2*(3), 127-135.

Black, M., Schuler, M., & Nair, P. (1993). Prenatal drug exposure: Neurodevelopmental outcome and parenting environment. *Journal of Pediatric Psychology, 18,* 605-620.

Blake-White, J., & Kline, C. M. (1985). Treating the dissociative process in adult victims of childhood incest. *Social Casework, 66,* 394-402.

Blankenhorn, D. (1994, December 19). Not orphanages or prisons, but responsible fathers. *Los Angeles Times,* p. B7.

Boney-McCoy, S., & Finkelhor, D. (1995). The psychosocial sequelae of violent victimization in a national youth sample. *Journal of Consulting and Clinical Psychology, 63,* 726-736.

Bools, C., Neale, B., & Meadow, R. (1994). Munchausen syndrome by proxy: A study of psychopathology. *Child Abuse & Neglect, 18,* 773-788.

Bottoms, B. L., & Goodman, G. S. (Eds.). (1996). *International perspectives on child abuse and children's testimony: Psychological research and law.* Thousand Oaks, CA: Sage.

Bottoms, B. L., Shaver, P. R., & Goodman, G. S. (1996). An analysis of ritualistic and religion-related child abuse allegations. *Law and Human Behavior, 20*(1), 1-34.

Bousha, D. M., & Twentyman, C. T. (1984). Mother-child interactional style in abuse, neglect, and control groups: Naturalistic observations in the home. *Journal of Abnormal Psychology, 93,* 106-114.

Bower, B. (1993a). Sudden recall: Adult memories of child abuse spark heated debate. *Science News, 144,* 177-192.

Bower, B. (1993b). The survivor syndrome. *Science News, 144,* 202-204.

Bowlby, J. (1980). *Attachment and loss: Loss* (Vol. 3). London: Hogarth.

Boyd, C., Guthrie, B., Pohl, J., Whitmarsh, J., & Henderson, D. (1994). African-American women who smoke crack cocaine: Sexual trauma and the mother-daughter relationship. *Journal of Psychoactive Drugs, 26,* 243-247.

Bracey, D. (1979). *Baby pros: Preliminary profiles of juvenile prostitutes.* New York: John Jay Press.

Bradford, J. (1990). The antiandrogen and hormonal treatment of sex offenders. In W. L. Marshall, D. R. Laws, & H. E. Barbaree (Eds.), *Handbook of sexual assault: Issues, theories, and treatment of the offender* (pp. 297-327). New York: Plenum.

Brassard, M. R., Germain, R., & Hart, S. N. (1987). *Psychological maltreatment of children and youth.* New York: Pergamon.

Brassard, M. R., Hart, S. N., & Hardy, D. (1991). Psychological and emotional abuse of children. In R. T. Ammerman & M. Hersen (Eds.), *Case studies in family violence* (pp. 255-270). New York: Plenum.

Brassard, M. R., Hart, S. N., & Hardy, D. (1993). The psychological maltreatment rating scales. *Child Abuse & Neglect, 17,* 715-729.

Braun, S., & Pasternak, J. (1994, September 2). Life of violence catches up to suspected murderer, 11. *Los Angeles Times,* pp. A1, A18.

Breen, M., Daro, D., & Romano, N. (1991). Prevention services and child abuse: A comparison of services availability in the nation and Michigan. Chicago: National Committee for Prevention of Child Abuse.

Bremner, R. H. (1971). *Children and youth in America: A documentary history: Vol. 2. 1866-1932.* Cambridge, MA: Harvard University Press.

Bresee, P., Stearns, G. B., Bess, B. H., & Packer, L. S. (1986). Allegations of child sexual abuse in child custody disputes: A therapeutic assessment model. *American Journal of Orthopsychiatry, 56,* 560-569.

Brickman, J. (1984). Feminist, nonsexist, and traditional models of therapy: Implications for working with incest. *Women & Therapy, 3,* 49-67.

Briere, J. (1992a). *Child abuse trauma: Theory and treatment of the lasting effects.* Newbury Park, CA: Sage.

Briere, J. (1992b). Methodological issues in the study of sexual abuse effects. *Journal of Consulting and Clinical Psychology, 60,* 196-203.

Briere, J., & Conte, J. (1993). Self-reported amnesia for abuse in adults molested as children. *Journal of Traumatic Stress, 6,* 21-31.

Briere, J., & Elliott, D. M. (1994). Immediate and long-term impacts of child sexual abuse. *Future of Children, 4*(2), 54-69.

Briere, J., & Runtz, M. (1987). Post sexual abuse trauma: Data and implications for clinical practice. *Journal of Interpersonal Violence, 2,* 367-379.

Briere, J., & Runtz, M. (1988). Multivariate correlates of childhood psychological and physical maltreatment among university women. *Child Abuse & Neglect, 12,* 331-341.

Briere, J., & Runtz, M. (1989). The Trauma Symptoms Checklist (TSC-33): Early data on a new scale. *Journal of Interpersonal Violence, 4,* 151-163.

Briere, J., & Runtz, M. (1990). Differential adult symptomatology associated with three types of child abuse histories. *Child Abuse & Neglect, 14,* 357-364.

Brinkerhoff, M. B., & Lupri, E. (1988). Interpersonal violence. *Canadian Journal of Sociology, 13,* 407-434.

Brown, J., Cohen, P., Johnson, J. G., & Salzinger, S. (1998). A longitudinal analysis of risk factors for child maltreatment: Findings of a 17-year prospective study of officially recorded and self-reported child abuse and neglect. *Child Abuse & Neglect, 22,* 1065-1078.

Browne, A., & Finkelhor, D. (1986). Impact of child sexual abuse: A review of the research. *Psychological Bulletin, 99,* 66-77.

Bruce, D. A., & Zimmerman, R. A. (1989). Shaken impact syndrome. *Pediatric Annals, 18,* 482-494.

Brunk, M., Henggeler, S. W., & Whelan, J. P. (1987). Comparison of multi-systemic therapy and parent training in the brief treatment of child abuse and neglect. *Journal of Consulting and Clinical Psychology, 55,* 171-178.

Bryan, J. W., & Freed, F. W. (1982). Corporal punishment: Normative data and sociological and psychological correlates in a community population. *Journal of Youth and Adolescence, 11,* 77-87.

Bryer, J. B., Nelson, B. A., Miller, J. B., & Krol, P. A. (1987). Childhood sexual and physical abuse as factors in adult psychiatric illness. *American Journal of Psychiatry, 144,* 1426-1430.

Budin, L. E., & Johnson, C. F. (1989). Sex abuse prevention programs: Offenders' attitudes about their efficacy. *Child Abuse & Neglect, 13,* 77-87.

Bunn, A. (1998, April 21). Digitizing Megan's law. *The Village Voice* [Online], *43*(16), 31. Available: http://proquest.umi.com

Burgess, A. W., Groth, A. N., & McCausland, M. (1981). Child sex initiation rings. *American Journal of Orthopsychiatry, 51,* 110-119.

Burgess, A. W., & Hartman, C. R. (1987). Child abuse aspects of child pornography. *Psychiatric Annals, 17,* 248-253.

Burgess, A. W., Hartman, C. R., McCausland, M. P., & Powers, P. (1984). Response patterns in children and adolescents exploited through sex rings and pornography. *American Journal of Psychiatry, 141*(5), 656-662.

Burke, P. J., Stets, J. E., & Pirog-Good, M. A. (1989). Gender identity, self-esteem, and physical and sexual abuse in dating relationships. In M. A. Pirog-Good & J. E. Stets (Eds.), *Violence in dating relationships: Emerging social issues* (pp. 72-93). New York: Praeger.

Burkett, L. P. (1991). Parenting behaviors of women who were sexually abused as children in their families of origin. *Family Process, 30,* 421-434.

Burnam, M. A., Stein, J. A., Golding, J. M., Siegel, J. M., Sorenson, S. B., Forsythe, A. B., & Telles, C. A. (1988). Sexual assault and mental disorders in a community population. *Journal of Consulting and Clinical Psychology, 56,* 843-850.

Butler, K. (1994, June 26). Clashing memories, mixed messages. *Los Angeles Times Magazine,* 12.

Bybee, D., & Mowbray, C. T. (1993a). An analysis of allegations of sexual abuse in a multi-victim day-care center case. *Child Abuse & Neglect, 17,* 767-783.

Bybee, D., & Mowbray, C. T. (1993b). Community response to child sexual abuse in day-care settings. *Families in Society: The Journal of Contemporary Human Services, 74*(5), 268-281.

Cabrino, J. (1978). The elusive crime of emotional abuse. *Child Abuse & Neglect, 2,* 89-99.

Cahill, C., Llewelyn, S. P., & Pearson, C. (1991). Treatment of sexual abuse which occurred in childhood: A review. *British Journal of Clinical Psychology, 30,* 1-12.

Caliso, J. A., & Milner, J. S. (1994). Childhood physical abuse, childhood social support, and adult child abuse potential. *Journal of Interpersonal Violence, 9,* 27-44.

Canavan, M. M., Meyer, W. J., & Higgs, D. C. (1992). The female experience of sibling incest. *Journal of Marital and Family Therapy, 18*(2), 129-142.

Cappell, C., & Heiner, R. B. (1990). The intergenerational transmission of family aggression. *Journal of Family Violence, 5,* 135-152.

Carlson, B. E. (1984). Children's observations of interparental violence. In A. R. Roberts (Ed.), *Battered women and their families* (pp. 147-167). New York: Springer.

Carlson, V., Cicchetti, D., Barnett, D., & Braumwald, K. (1989). Disorganized/disoriented attachment relationships in maltreated infants. *Developmental Psychology, 25,* 525-531.

Carroll, C. A., & Haase, C. C. (1987). The function of protective services in child abuse and neglect. In R. Helfer & R. Kempe (Eds.), *The battered child* (4th ed., pp. 137-151). Chicago: University of Chicago Press.

Carter, D. L., Prentky, R. A., Knight, R. A., Vanderveer, P. L., & Boucher, R. J. (1987). Use of pornography in the criminal and developmental histories of sexual offenders. *Journal of Interpersonal Violence, 2,* 196-211.

Casanova, G. M., Domanic, J., McCanne, T. R., & Milner, J. S. (1992). Physiological responses to non-child-related stressors in mothers at risk for child abuse. *Child Abuse & Neglect, 16,* 31-44.

Cassady, L., Allen, B., Lyon, E., & McGeehan, D. (1987, July). *The child-focused intervention program: Treatment and program evaluation for children in a battered women's shelter.* Paper presented at the Third National Family Violence Research Conference, Durham, NH.

Cavaiola, A. A., & Schiff, M. (1988). Behavioral sequelae of physical and/or sexual abuse in adolescents. *Child Abuse & Neglect, 12,* 181-188.

Cavaliere, F. (1995, February). Parents killing kids: A nation's shame. *APA Monitor, 26*(2), p. 34.

Ceci, S., & Bruck, M. (1993). Suggestibility of the child witness: A historical review and synthesis. *Psychological Bulletin, 113,* 403-439.

Celano, M. P. (1990). Activities and games for group psychotherapy with sexually abused children. *International Journal of Group Psychotherapy, 40,* 419-429.

Cerezo, M. A. (1997). Abusive family interaction: A review. *Aggression and Violent Behavior, 2*(3), 215-240.

Chaffin, M. (1994). Research in action: Assessment and treatment of child sexual abusers. *Journal of Interpersonal Violence, 9,* 224-237.

Chan, Y. C. (1994). Parenting stress and social support of mothers who physically abuse their children in Hong Kong. *Child Abuse & Neglect, 18,* 261-269.

Chapman, J., & Smith, B. (1987). *Child sexual abuse: An analysis of case processing.* Washington, DC: American Bar Association.

Child Abuse Prevention and Treatment Act of 1974, Pub. L. No. 93-247.

Child Sexual Abuse and Pornography Act of 1986, Pub. L. No. 99-628.

Child Welfare League of America. (1986). *Too young to run: The status of child abuse in America.* New York: Author.

Children's Bureau. (1997, July 30). *Foster care and adoption statistics current reports.* Administration for Children and Families, U.S. Department of Health and Human Services [Online]. Available: http://www.acf.dhhs.gov/programs/cb/stats/afcars/index.htm

Children's Defense Fund (1997, November 20). *New law furthers safety and permanence for chil*dren [Online]. Available: http://www.childrensdefense.org/safestart_pass1.html

Chiriboga, C. A. (1993). Fetal effects. *Neurologic Clinics, 3,* 707-728.

Choice, P., Lamke, L. K., & Pittman, J. F. (1995). Conflict resolution strategies and marital distress as mediating factors in the link between witnessing interparental violence and wife battering. *Violence and Victims, 10,* 107-119.

Christensen, A., Margolin, G., & Sullaway, M. (1992). Interparental agreement on child behavior problems. *Psychological Assessment, 4,* 419-425.

Christensen, M. J., Brayden, R. M., Dietrich, M. S., McLaughlin, F. J., Sherrod, K. B., & Altemeier, W. A. (1994). The prospective assessment of self-concept in neglectful and physically abusive low income mothers. *Child Abuse & Neglect, 18,* 225-232.

Christopoulos, C., Bonvillian, J. D., & Crittenden, P. M. (1988). Maternal language input and child maltreatment. *Infant Mental Health Journal, 9,* 272-286.

Christopoulos, C., Cohn, A. D., Shaw, D. S., Joyce, S., Sullivan-Hanson, J., Kraft, S. P., & Emery, R. E. (1987). Children of abused women: I. Adjustment at time of shelter residence. *Journal of Marriage and the Family, 49,* 611-619.

Chu, J. A., & Dill, D. L. (1990). Dissociative symptoms in relation to childhood physical and sexual abuse. *American Journal of Psychiatry, 147,* 887-892.

Cicchetti, D., & Barnett, D. (1991). Toward the development of a scientific nosology of child maltreatment. In D. Cicchetti & W. Grove (Eds.), *Thinking clearly about psychology: Essays in honor of Paul E. Meehl* (pp. 346-377). Minneapolis: University of Minnesota Press.

Cicchetti, D., & Rizley, R. (1981). Developmental perspectives on the etiology, intergenerational transmission, and sequelae of child maltreatment. In D. Cicchetti & R. Rizley (Eds.), *New directions for child development: Developmental perspectives on child maltreatment* (pp. 31-55). San Francisco: Jossey-Bass.

Cicchetti, D., & Toth, S. (1995). A developmental psychopathology perspective on child abuse and neglect. *Journal of the American Academy of Child and Adolescent Psychiatry, 34,* 541-565.

Cicchetti, D., Toth, S., & Bush, M. (1988). Developmental psychopathology and incompetence in childhood: Suggestions for intervention. In B. Lahey & A. Kazdin (Eds.), *Advances in clinical child psychology* (pp. 1-71). New York: Plenum.

Claussen, A. H., & Crittenden, P. M. (1991). Physical and psychological maltreatment: Relations among types of maltreatment. *Child Abuse & Neglect, 15,* 5-18.

Cloud, J. (1998, May 4). A matter of hearts. *Seattle Times,* pp. 60-64.

Cohen, J. A., & Mannarino, A. P. (1993). A treatment model for sexually abused preschoolers. *Journal of Interpersonal Violence, 8,* 115-131.

Cohn, A. H., & Daro, D. (1987). Is treatment too late: What ten years of evaluation research tell us. *Child Abuse & Neglect, 11,* 433-442.

Cole, P. M., Woolger, C., Power, T. G., & Smith, K. D. (1992). Parenting difficulties among adult survivors of father-daughter incest. *Child Abuse & Neglect, 16,* 239-249.

Comstock, G., & Strasburger, V. C. (1990). Deceptive appearances: Television violence and aggressive behavior. *Journal of Adolescent Health Care, 11,* 31-44.

Conaway, L. P., & Hansen, D. J. (1989). Social behavior of physically abused and neglected children: A critical review. *Clinical Psychology Review, 9,* 627-652.

Conger, R. D., Burgess, R., & Barrett, C. (1979). Child abuse related to life change and perceptions of illness: Some preliminary findings. *Family Coordinator, 28,* 73-78.

Connelly, C. D., & Straus, M. A. (1992). Mother's age and risk for physical abuse. *Child Abuse & Neglect, 16,* 709-718.

Conte, J. R. (1993). Sexual abuse of children. In R. L. Hampton, T. P. Gullotta, G. R. Adams, E. H. Potter, III, & R. P. Weissberg (Eds.), *Family violence: Prevention and treatment* (pp. 56-85). Newbury Park, CA: Sage.

Conte, J. R., & Schuerman, J. R. (1987). Factors associated with an increased impact of child sexual abuse. *Child Abuse & Neglect, 11,* 201-211.

Conte, J. R., Wolf, S., & Smith, T. (1989). What sexual offenders tell us about prevention strategies. *Child Abuse & Neglect, 13,* 293-301.

Copping, V. E. (1996). Beyond over- and under-control: Behavioral observations of shelter children. *Journal of Family Violence, 11*(1), 41-57.

Corder, B. F., Haizlip, T., & DeBoer, P. A. (1990). A pilot study for a structured, time-limited therapy group for sexually abused pre-adolescent children. *Child Abuse & Neglect, 14,* 243-251.

Corse, S., Schmid, K., & Trickett, P. K. (1990). Social network characteristics of mothers in abusing and nonabusing families and their relationships to parenting beliefs. *Journal of Community Psychology, 18,* 44-59.

Courtois, C., & Watts, C. (1982). Counseling adult women who experienced incest in childhood or adolescence. *Personnel and Guidance Journal, 60,* 275-279.

Creighton, S. J. (1993, December). Organized abuse: NSPCC experience. *Child Abuse Review, 2,* 232-243.

Crittenden, P. M. (1982). Abusing, neglecting, problematic, and adequate dyads: Differentiating patterns of interaction. *Merrill-Palmer Quarterly, 27,* 201-218.

Crittenden, P. M. (1984). Sibling interaction: Evidence of a generational effect in maltreating infants. *Child Abuse & Neglect, 8,* 433-438.

Crittenden, P. M. (1988). Distorted patterns of relationship in maltreating families: The role of internal representation models. *Journal of Reproductive and Infant Psychology, 6,* 183-199.

Crittenden, P. M. (1990). Internal representational models of attachment relationships. *Infant Mental Health Journal, 11,* 259-277.

Crittenden, P. M. (1992). Children's strategies for coping with adverse home environments: An interpretation using attachment theory. *Child Abuse & Neglect, 16,* 329-343.

Crittenden, P. M. (1996). Research on maltreating families: Implications for intervention. In J. Briere, L. Berliner, J. A. Bulkley, C. Jenny, & T. Reid (Eds.), *The APSAC handbook on child maltreatment* (pp. 158-174). Thousand Oaks, CA: Sage.

Crittenden, P. M. (1998). Dangerous behavior and dangerous contexts: A 35-year perspective on research on the developmental effects of child physical abuse. In P. K. Trickett & C. J. Schellenbach (Eds.), *Violence against children in the family and the community* (pp. 11-38). Washington, DC: American Psychological Association.

Crittenden, P. M., & Ainsworth, M. (1989). Child maltreatment and attachment theory. In D. Cicchetti & V. Carlson (Eds.), *Child maltreatment: Theory and research on the causes and consequences of child abuse and neglect* (pp. 432-463). New York: Cambridge University Press.

Crittenden, P. M., & Bonvillian, J. D. (1984). The effect of maternal risk status on maternal sensitivity to infant cues. *American Journal of Orthopsychiatry, 54,* 250-262.

Crittenden, P. M., Partridge, M. F., & Claussen, A. H. (1991). Family patterns of relationships in normative and dysfunctional families. *Development and Psychopathology, 3,* 491-512.

Crouch, J. L., & Milner, J. S. (1993). Effects of child neglect on children. *Criminal Justice and Behavior, 20,* 49-65.

Crowe, H. P., & Zeskind, P. S. (1992). Psychophysiological and perceptual responses to infant cries varying in pitch: Comparison of adults with low and high scores on the Child Abuse Potential Inventory. *Child Abuse & Neglect, 16,* 19-29.

Culp, R. E., Culp, A. M., Soulis, J., & Letts, D. (1989). Self-esteem and depression in abusive, neglecting, and nonmaltreating mothers. *Infant Mental Health Journal, 10,* 243-251.

Culp, R. E., Little, V., Letts, D., & Lawrence, H. (1991). Maltreated children's self-concept: Effects of a comprehensive treatment program. *American Journal of Orthopsychiatry, 61*(1), 114-121.

Curtis, A. (1992, December 1). Some on ritual abuse task force say satanists are poisoning them. *Los Angeles Times,* pp. B1, B4.

Dadds, M., Smith, M., Weber, Y., & Robinson, A. (1991). An exploration of family and individual profiles following father-daughter incest. *Child Abuse & Neglect, 15,* 575-586.

Daie, N., Witztum, E., & Eleff, M. (1989). Long term effects of sibling incest. *Journal of Clinical Psychiatry, 50*(11), 428-431.

Damon, L., Todd, J., & MacFarlane, K. (1987). Treatment issues with sexually abused young children. *Child Welfare, 116,* 125-137.

Daro, D. (1988). *Confronting child abuse: Research for effective program design.* New York: Free Press.

Daro, D. (1998). What is happening in the U.S. *The Link: The Official Newsletter of the International Society for Prevention of Child Abuse and Neglect (ISPCAN), 7,* 6-7.

Daro, D., & Alexander, R. (1994). Preventing child abuse fatalities: Moving forward. *The APSAC Advisor, 7*(4), 49-50.

Daro, D., & Gelles, R. J. (1992). Public attitudes and behaviors with respect to child abuse prevention. *Journal of Interpersonal Violence, 7,* 517-531.

Daro, D., & McCurdy, K. (1994). Preventing child abuse and neglect: Programmatic interventions. *Child Welfare, 73,* 405-430.

Daro, D., McCurdy, K., & Harding, K. (1998). *The role of home visiting in preventing child abuse: An evaluation of the Hawaii healthy start program.* Chicago: National Committee to Prevent Child Abuse, Center on Child Abuse Prevention Research.

Davidson, H. (1994). *The impact of domestic violence on children: A report to the president of the American Bar Association* (2nd rev. ed.; Report No. 549-0248). Chicago: American Bar Association.

Davis, G. E., & Leitenberg, H. (1987). Adolescent sex offenders. *Psychological Bulletin, 101,* 417-427.

Davis, J. A., & Smith, T. W. (1994). *General social surveys, 1972-1994: Cumulative codebook* (National Data Program for the Social Sciences Series, No. 14). Chicago: National Opinion Research Center.

Davis, L. (1991). Murdered memory. *Health, 5,* 79-84.

Davis, S. P., & Fantuzzo, J. W. (1989). The effects of adult and peer social initiations on the social behavior of withdrawn and aggressive maltreated preschool children. *Journal of Family Violence, 4,* 227-248.

Dawson, B., DeArmas, A., McGrath, M. L., & Kelly, J. A. (1986). Cognitive problem-solving training to improve the child-care judgment of child neglectful parents. *Journal of Family Violence, 1,* 209-221.

DeAngelis, T. (1993, November). APA panel is examining memories of child abuse. *APA Monitor, 24*(11), p. 44.

DeBellis, M. D., Burke, L., Trickett, P. K., & Putnam, F. W. (1996). Antinuclear antibodies and thyroid function in sexually abused girls. *Journal of Traumatic Stress, 9,* 369-378.

DeBellis, M. D., Chrousos, G. P., Dorn, L. D., Burke, L., Helmers, K., Kling, M. A., Trickett, P. K., & Putnam, F. W. (1994). Hypothalamic-pituitary-adrenal axis dysregulation in sexually abused girls. *Journal of Clinical Endocrinology and Metabolism, 78,* 249-255.

DeBellis, M. D., Lefter, L., Trickett, P. K., & Putnam, F. W. (1994). Urinary catecholamine excretion in sexually abused girls. *Journal of the American Academy of Child and Adolescent Psychiatry, 33,* 320-327.

DeJong, A. R. (1989). Sexual interactions among siblings and cousins: Experimentation or exploitation? *Child Abuse & Neglect, 13,* 271-279.

deMause, L. (1974). *A history of childhood.* New York: Psychotherapy Press.

Dembo, R., Williams, L., Wothke, W., Schmeidler, J., & Brown, C. H. (1992). The role of family factors, physical abuse, and sexual victimization experiences in high-risk youths' alcohol and other drug use and delinquency: A longitudinal model. *Violence and Victims, 7,* 245-266.

Denham, S. A., Renwick, S. M., & Holt, R. W. (1991). Working and playing together: Prediction of preschool social-emotional competence from mother-child interaction. *Child Development, 62,* 242-249.

Denniston, G. C., & Milos, M. F. (Eds.). (1997). *Sexual mutilations: A human tragedy.* New York: Plenum.

Denzin, N. K. (1984). Toward a phenomenology of domestic, family violence. *American Journal of Sociology, 90,* 483-513.

DePanfilis, D. (1996). Social isolation of neglectful families: A review of social support assessment and intervention models. *Child Maltreatment, 1*(1), 37-52.

Department of Health and Human Services. (1981). *Study findings: National study of the incidence and severity of child abuse and neglect* (DHHS Publication No. OHDS 81-30325). Washington, DC: Government Printing Office.

Department of Health and Human Services. (1988). *Study findings: Study of national incidence and prevalence of child abuse and neglect* (DHHS Publication No. ADM 20-01099). Washington, DC: Government Printing Office.

Department of Health and Human Services. (1993). *A report on the maltreatment of children with disabilities* (DHHS Publication No. 105-89-1630). Washington, DC: Government Printing Office.

Department of Health and Human Services. (1994). *Child maltreatment 1992: Reports from the states to the National Center on Child Abuse and Neglect.* Washington, DC: Government Printing Office.

Department of Health and Human Services, Children's Bureau. (1996). *Child maltreatment 1994: Reports from the states to the National Child Abuse and Neglect Data System.* Washington, DC: Government Printing Office.

Department of Health and Human Services, Children's Bureau. (1998). *Child maltreatment 1996: Reports from the states to the National Child Abuse and Neglect Data System.* Washington, DC: Government Printing Office.

de Paul, J., & Arruabarrena, M. I. (1995). Behavior problems in school-aged physically abused and neglected children in Spain. *Child Abuse & Neglect, 19,* 409-418.

DiLeonardi, J. W. (1993). Families in poverty and chronic neglect of children. *Families in Society, 74,* 557-562.

Disbrow, M. A., Doerr, H., & Caulfield, C. (1977). Measuring the components of parents' potential for child abuse and neglect. *Child Abuse & Neglect, 1,* 279-296.

Dodge, K. A., Bates, J. E., & Pettit, G. S. (1990). Mechanisms in the cycle of violence. *Science, 250,* 1678-1682.

Doek, J. E. (1985). Child pornography and legislation in the Netherlands. *Child Abuse & Neglect, 9,* 411-412.

Doll, L., Joy, D., & Bartholow, B. (1992). Self-reported childhood and adolescent sexual abuse among homosexual and bisexual men. *Child Abuse & Neglect, 16,* 855-864.

Dollard, J., Doob, L. W., Miller, N. E., & Sears, R. R. (1939). *Frustration and aggression.* New Haven, CT: Yale University Press.

Dore, M. M., Doris, J., & Wright, P. (1995). Identifying substance abuse in maltreating families: A child welfare challenge. *Child Abuse & Neglect, 19,* 531-543.

Dowdney, L., & Pickles, A. R. (1991). Expression of negative affect within disciplinary encounters: Is there dyadic reciprocity? *Developmental Psychology, 27,* 606-617.

Downs, W. R., & Miller, B. A. (1998). Relationships between experiences of parental violence during childhood and women's psychiatric symptomatology. *Journal of Interpersonal Violence, 13*(4), 438-455.

Drake, B., & Zuravin, S. (1998). Bias in child maltreatment reporting: Revisiting the myth of classlessness. *American Journal of Orthopsychiatry, 68*(2), 295-304.

Drotar, D., Eckerle, D., Satola, J., Pallotta, J., & Wyatt, B. (1990). Maternal interactional behavior with nonorganic failure-to-thrive infants: A case comparison study. *Child Abuse & Neglect, 14,* 41-51.

Dubowitz, H. (1994). Neglecting the neglect of neglect. *Journal of Interpersonal Violence, 9,* 556-560.

Dubowitz, H., Black, M., Harrington, D., & Verschoore, A. (1993). A follow-up study of behavior problems associated with child sexual abuse. *Child Abuse & Neglect, 17,* 743-754.

Dubowitz, H., Black, M., Starr, R., & Zuravin, S. (1993). A conceptual definition of child neglect. *Criminal Justice and Behavior, 20,* 8-26.

Dubowitz, H., Hampton, R. L., Bithoney, W. G., & Newberger, E. H. (1987). Inflicted and noninflicted injuries: Differences in child and familial characteristics. *American Journal of Orthopsychiatry, 57,* 525-535.

Dunn, J., & McGuire, S. (1992). Sibling and peer relationships in childhood. *Journal of Child Psychology and Psychiatry, 33,* 67-105.

Durfee, M. (1994). History and status of child death review teams. *The APSAC Advisor, 7*(4), 4-5.

Durkin, K. F., & Bryant, C. D. (1995). "Log on to sex": Some notes on the carnal computer and erotic cyberspace as an emerging research frontier. *Deviant Behavior: An Interdisciplinary Journal, 16,* 179-200.

Earls, C. M., & David, H. (1990, December). Early family and sexual experiences of male and female prostitutes. *Canada's Mental Health,* 7-11.

Eckenrode, J., Laird, M., & Doris, J. (1993). School performance and disciplinary problems among abused and neglected children. *Developmental Psychology, 29,* 53-63.

Egan, K. (1983). Stress management with abusive parents. *Journal of Clinical Child Psychology, 12,* 292-299.

Egeland, B. (1991). From data to definition. *Development and Psychopathology, 3,* 37-43.

Egeland, B. (1993). A history of abuse is a major risk factor for abusing the next generation. In R. J. Gelles & D. R. Loseke (Eds.), *Current controversies on family violence* (pp. 197-208). Newbury Park, CA: Sage.

Egeland, B., Jacobvitz, D., & Sroufe, A. (1988). Breaking the cycle of child abuse. *Child Development, 59,* 1080-1088.

Egeland, B., & Sroufe, A. (1981). Developmental sequelae of maltreatment in infancy. *New Directions for Child Development, 11,* 77-92.

Egeland, B., Sroufe, L. A., & Erickson, M. F. (1983). The developmental consequences of different patterns of maltreatment. *Child Abuse & Neglect, 7,* 459-469.

Elbow, M. (1982). Children of violent marriages: The forgotten victims. *Social Casework: The Journal of Contemporary Social Work, 63,* 465-471.

Ellerstein, N. S., & Canavan, W. (1980). Sexual abuse of boys. *American Journal of Diseases of Children, 134,* 255-257.

Elliott, D. M., & Briere, J. (1994). Forensic sexual abuse evaluations: Disclosures and symptomatology. *Behavioral Sciences and the Law, 12,* 261-277.

Elliott, F. A. (1988). Neurological factors. In V. B. Van Hasselt, R. L. Morison, A. S. Bellack, & M. Hersen (Eds.), *Handbook of family violence* (pp. 359-382). New York: Plenum.

Elliott, M. (1993). *Female sexual abuse of children.* New York: Guilford.

Elliott, M. (1994). Impaired object relations in professional women molested as children. *Psychotherapy, 31,* 79-86.

Elliott, M., & Briere, J. (1992). Sexual abuse trauma among professional women: Validating the Trauma Symptom Checklist-40 (TSC-40). *Child Abuse & Neglect, 16,* 391-398.

Elliott, M., Browne, K., & Kilcoyne, J. (1995). Child sexual abuse prevention: What offenders tell us. *Child Abuse & Neglect, 19,* 579-594.

Elwell, M. E., & Ephross, P. H. (1987). Initial reactions of sexually abused children. *Social Casework, 68,* 109-116.

Emans, R. L. (1988). Psychology's responsibility in false accusations of child abuse. *Journal of Clinical Psychology, 44,* 1000-1004.

Emery, R. E. (1989). Family violence. *American Psychologist, 44,* 321-328.

Emery, R. E., & Laumann-Billings, L. (1998, February). An overview of the nature, causes, and consequences of abusive family relationships: Toward differentiating maltreatment and violence. *American Psychologist* 53(2), 121-135.

Empey, L. T., & Stafford, M. C. (1991). *American delinquency: Its meaning and construction.* Belmont, CA: Wadsworth.

Ericksen, J. R., & Henderson, A. D. (1992). Witnessing family violence: The children's experience. *Journal of Advanced Nursing, 17,* 1200-1209.

Erickson, M. F., & Egeland, B. (1987). A developmental view of the psychological consequences of maltreatment. *School Psychology Review, 16,* 156-168.

Erickson, M. F., & Egeland, B. (1996). Child neglect. In J. Briere, L. Berliner, J. A. Bulkley, C. Jenny, & T. Reid (Eds.), *The APSAC handbook on child maltreatment* (pp. 4-20). Thousand Oaks, CA: Sage.

Erickson, M. F., Egeland, B., & Pianta, R. (1989). The effects of maltreatment on the development of young children. In D. Cicchetti & V. Carlson (Eds.), *Child maltreatment: Theory and research on the causes and consequences of child abuse and neglect* (pp. 647-684). New York: Cambridge University Press.

Eron, L. D., & Huesmann, L. R. (1987). Television as a source of maltreatment of children. *School Psychology Review, 16*(2), 195-202.

Eron, L. D., Huesmann, L. R., Lefkowitz, M. M., & Walder, L. O. (1987). How learning conditions in early childhood—including mass media—relate to aggression in later adolescence. *Psychological Reports, 9,* 291-334.

Ethier, L. S., Lacharite, C., & Couture, G. (1995). Childhood adversity, parental stress and depression of negligent mothers. *Child Abuse & Neglect, 19,* 619-632.

Ethier, L. S., Palacio-Quintin, E., & Jourdan-Ionescu, C. (1992, June). Abuse and neglect:

Two distinct forms of maltreatment. *Canada's Mental Health,* 13-19.

Everson, M. D., & Boat, B. W. (1989). False allegations of sexual abuse by children and adolescents. *American Academy of Child and Adolescent Psychiatry, 28,* 230-235.

Everson, M. D., & Boat, B. W. (1990). Sexualized doll play among young children: Implications for the use of anatomical dolls in sexual abuse evaluations. *Journal of the American Academy of Child and Adolescent Psychiatry, 29,* 736-742.

Everson, M. D., Hunter, W. M., Runyon, D., & Edelson, G. A. (1990). Maternal support following disclosure of incest. *Annual Progress in Child Psychiatry and Child Development, 9,* 292-306.

Ewigman, B., Kivlahan, C., & Land, G. (1993). The Missouri Child Fatalities Study: Underreporting of maltreatment fatalities among children younger than five years of age, 1983 through 1986. *Pediatrics, 91,* 330-337.

Ezzo, G. (1998). Commentary on spanking articles by Larzelere and Lowe. *Marriage & Family: A Christian Journal, 1*(2), 208-211.

Fagan, J., & Wexler, S. (1987). Families of violent delinquents. *Criminology, 25,* 643-669.

Faller, K. C. (1988a). *Child sexual abuse: An interdisciplinary manual for diagnosis, case management, and treatment.* New York: Columbia University Press.

Faller, K. C. (1988b). The spectrum of sexual abuse in daycare: An exploratory study. *Journal of Family Violence, 3*(4), 283-298.

Faller, K. C. (1989). Why sexual abuse? An exploration of the intergenerational hypothesis. *Child Abuse & Neglect, 13,* 543-548.

Faller, K. C. (1993). Research on false allegations of sexual abuse in divorce. *The APSAC Advisor, 6*(1), 7-10.

Fantuzzo, J. W. (1990). Behavioral treatment of the victims of child abuse and neglect. *Behavior Modification, 14,* 316-339.

Fantuzzo, J. W., DePaola, L. M., Lambert, L., Martino, T., Anderson, G., & Sutton, S. (1991). Effects of interparental violence on the psychological adjustment and competencies of young children. *Journal of Consulting and Clinical Psychology, 59,* 258-265.

Fantuzzo, J. W., & Lindquist, C. U. (1989). The effects of observing conjugal violence on children: A review and analysis of research methodology. *Journal of Family Violence, 4,* 77-94.

Fantuzzo, J. W., Stovall, A., Schachtel, D., Goins, C., & Hall, R. (1987). The effects of peer social initiations on social behavior of withdrawn maltreated preschool children. *Journal of Behavior Therapy and Experiential Psychiatry, 18,* 357-363.

Fantuzzo, J. W., Sutton-Smith, B., Atkins, M., Meyers, R., Stevenson, H., Coolahan, K., Weiss, A., & Manz, P. (1996). Community-based resilient peer treatment of withdrawn maltreated preschool children. *Journal of Consulting and Clinical Psychology, 64,* 1377-1386.

Farrington, K. M. (1980). Stress and family violence. In M. A. Straus & G. T. Hotaling (Eds.), *The social causes of husband-to-wife violence* (pp. 94-114). Minneapolis: University of Minnesota Press.

Fein, B. (1995). Megan's law. *ABA Journal, 81,* 38-42.

Feinauer, L. L. (1989). Comparison of long-term effects of child abuse by type of abuse and by relationship of the offender to the victim. *American Journal of Family Therapy, 17,* 48-56.

Feldman, W., Feldman, E., Goodman, J. T., McGrath, P. J., Pless, R. P., Corsini, L., & Bennett, S. (1991). Is childhood sexual abuse really increasing in prevalence? An analysis of the evidence. *Pediatrics, 88*(1), 29-33.

Feldman-Summers, S., & Pope, K. S. (1994). The experience of forgetting childhood abuse: A national survey of psychologists. *Journal of Consulting and Clinical Psychology, 62,* 636-639.

Felson, R. (1996). Mass media effect on violent behavior. *Annual Review of Sociology, 22,* 103-126.

Fergusson, D. M., & Horwood, L. J. (1998). Exposure to interparental violence in childhood and psychosocial adjustment in young adulthood. *Child Abuse & Neglect, 22,* 339-357.

Finkelhor, D. (1979). *Sexually victimized children.* New York: Free Press.

Finkelhor, D. (1980). Sex among siblings: A survey of prevalence, variety, and effects. *Archives of Sexual Behavior, 9,* 171-193.

Finkelhor, D. (1981). The sexual abuse of boys. *Victimology: An International Journal, 6,* 76-84.

Finkelhor, D. (1984). *Child sexual abuse: New theory and research.* New York: Free Press.

Finkelhor, D. (1990). Is child abuse overreported? The data rebut arguments for less intervention. *Public Welfare, 48,* 23-29.

Finkelhor, D. (1993). Epidemiological factors in the clinical identification of child sexual abuse. *Child Abuse & Neglect, 17,* 67-70.

Finkelhor, D. (1994a). Current information on the scope and nature of child sexual abuse. *Future of Children, 4*(2), 31-53.

Finkelhor, D. (1994b). The international epidemiology of child sexual abuse. *Child Abuse & Neglect, 18,* 409-417.

Finkelhor, D. (1996). Introduction. In J. Briere, L. Berliner, J. A. Bulkley, C. Jenny, & T. Reid (Eds.), *The APSAC handbook on child maltreatment* (pp. ix-xiii). Thousand Oaks, CA: Sage.

Finkelhor, D., Asdigian, N., & Dziuba-Leatherman, J. (1995). The effectiveness of victimization prevention instruction: An evaluation of children's responses to actual threats and assaults. *Child Abuse & Neglect, 19,* 141-153.

Finkelhor, D., & Berliner, L. (1995). Research on the treatment of sexually abused children: A review and recommendations. *Journal of the American Academy of Child and Adolescent Psychiatry, 34,* 1408-1423.

Finkelhor, D., & Dziuba-Leatherman, J. (1994). Victimization of children. *American Psychologist, 49,* 173-183.

Finkelhor, D., & Dziuba-Leatherman, J. (1995). Victimization prevention programs: A national survey of children's exposure and reactions. *Child Abuse & Neglect, 19,* 129-139.

Finkelhor, D., Hotaling, G., Lewis, I. A., & Smith, C. (1990). Sexual abuse in a national survey of adult men and women: Prevalence, characteristics, and risk factors. *Child Abuse & Neglect, 14,* 19-28.

Finkelhor, D., & Lewis, I. A. (1988). An epidemiologic approach to the study of child molestation. *Annals of the New York Academy of Sciences, 528,* 64-78.

Finkelhor, D., Moore, D., Hamby, S. L., & Straus, M. A. (1997). Sexually abused children in a national survey of parents: Methodological issues. *Child Abuse & Neglect, 21,* 1-9.

Finkelhor, D., Williams, L., & Burns, N. (1988). *Nursery crimes: Sexual abuse in daycare.* London: Sage.

Firstman, R., & Talan, J. (1997). *The death of innocents: A true story of murder, medicine, and high-stakes science.* New York: Bantam.

Fitten, R. K. (1997, July 25). Burien teacher's sex with a young student shatters the boy's family, and hers. *Seattle Times* [Online]. Available: http://www.seattletimes.com

Fitzpatrick, K. M. (1993). Exposure to violence and presence of depression among low-income, African American youth. *Journal of Consulting and Clinical Psychology, 61,* 528-531.

Fitzpatrick, K. M., & Boldizar, J. P. (1993). The prevalence and consequences of exposure to violence among African American youth. *Journal of the American Academy of Child and Adolescent Psychiatry, 32,* 424-430.

Fleisher, L. D. (1987). Wrongful birth: When is there liability for prenatal injury? *American Journal of Diseases in Children, 141,* 1260.

Follette, V. M., Alexander, P. C., & Follette, W. C. (1991). Individual predictors of outcome in group treatment for incest survivors. *Journal of Consulting and Clinical Psychology, 59,* 150-155.

Fontana, V., & Alfaro, J. (1987). *High risk factors associated with child maltreatment fatalities.* New York: Mayor's Task Force on Child Abuse and Neglect.

Fontana, V. J., & Moohnan, V. (1994). Establish more crisis intervention centers. In D. Bender & B. Leone (Eds.), *Child abuse: Opposing viewpoints* (pp. 227-234). San Diego, CA: Greenhaven.

Fornek, S., & O'Donnell, M. (1994, December 19). State addresses orphanage idea. *Chicago Sun-Times.*

Fortin, A., & Chamberland, C. (1995). Preventing the psychological maltreatment of children. *Journal of Interpersonal Violence, 10,* 275-295.

Fowler, W. E., & Wagner, W. G. (1993). Preference for and comfort with male versus female counselors among sexually abused girls in individual treatment. *Journal of Counseling Psychology, 40,* 65-72.

Frankel, K. A., & Bates, J. E. (1990). Mother-toddler problem solving: Antecedents in attachment, home behavior, and temperament. *Child Development, 61,* 810-819.

Freeman, L. N., Mokros, H., & Poznanski, E. O. (1993). Violent events reported by normal urban school-aged children: Characteristics and depression correlates. *Journal of the American Academy of Child and Adolescent Psychiatry, 32*(2), 419-423.

Freund, K., & Langevin, R. (1976). Bisexuality in homosexual pedophilia. *Archives of Sexual Behavior, 5,* 415-423.

Freund, K., McKnight, C. K., Langevin, R., & Cibiri, S. (1972). The female child as a surrogate object. *Archives of Sexual Behavior, 2,* 119-133.

Friedrich, W. N. (1990). *Psychotherapy of sexually abused children and their families.* New York: Norton.

Friedrich, W. N. (1993). Sexual victimization and sexual behavior in children: A review of recent literature. *Child Abuse & Neglect, 17,* 59-66.

Friedrich, W. N., Berliner, L., Urquiza, A. J., & Beilke, R. L. (1988). Brief diagnostic group treatment of sexually abused boys. *Journal of Interpersonal Violence, 3,* 331-343.

Friedrich, W. N., & Boriskin, J. A. (1976). The role of the child in abuse: A review of the literature. *American Journal of Orthopsychiatry, 46*(4), 580-590.

Friedrich, W. N., Enbender, A. J., & Luecke, W. J. (1983). Cognitive and behavioral characteristics of physically abused children. *Journal of Consulting and Clinical Psychology, 51,* 313-314.

Friedrich, W. N., Grambsch, P., Broughton, D., Kuiper, J., & Beilke, R. L. (1991). Normative sexual behavior in children. *Pediatrics, 88,* 456-464.

Friedrich, W. N., Grambsch, P., & Damon, L. (1992). The Child Sexual Behavior Inventory: Normative and clinical findings. *Journal of Consulting and Clinical Psychology, 60,* 303-311.

Friedrich, W. N., Luecke, W. M., Beilke, R. L., & Place, V. (1992). Psychotherapy outcome of sexually abused boys. *Journal of Interpersonal Violence, 7,* 396-409.

Friedrich, W. N., Urquiza, A. J., & Beilke, R. (1986). Behavioral problems in sexually abused young children. *Journal of Pediatric Psychology, 11,* 47-57.

Frodi, A., & Lamb, M. (1980). Child abusers' responses to infant smiles and cries. *Child Development, 51,* 238-241.

Fromuth, M. E. (1986). The relationship of child sexual abuse with later psychological adjustment in a sample of college women. *Child Abuse & Neglect, 10,* 5-15.

Gagan, R. J., Cupoli, J. M., & Watkins, A. H. (1984). The families of children who fail to thrive: Preliminary investigations of parental deprivation among organic and nonorganic cases. *Child Abuse & Neglect, 8,* 93-103.

Ganaway, G. K. (1989). Historical versus narrative truth: Clarifying the role of exogenous trauma in the etiology of MPD and its variants. *Dissociation, 2,* 205-220.

Garbarino, J. (1992). *Children in danger: Coping with the consequences of community violence.* San Francisco: Jossey-Bass.

Garbarino, J., & Crouter, A. (1978). Defining the community context for parent-child relations: The correlates of child maltreatment. *Child Development, 49,* 604-616.

Garbarino, J., & Gilliam, G. (1980). *Understanding abusive families.* Lexington, MA: Lexington Books.

Garbarino, J., Guttman, E., & Seely, J. (1986). *The psychologically battered child.* San Francisco: Jossey-Bass.

Garbarino, J., & Kostelny, K. (1992). Child maltreatment as a community problem. *Child Abuse and Neglect, 16,* 455-464.

Garmezy, N., & Rutter, M. (1985). Acute reactions to stress. In M. Rutter & L. Hersov (Eds.), *Child and adolescent psychiatry: Modern approaches* (2nd ed., pp. 152-176). Oxford, UK: Blackwell Scientific.

Garrity-Rokous, F. E. (1994). Punitive legal approaches to the problem of prenatal drug exposure. *Infant Mental Health Journal, 15,* 218-237.

Gates, D. (1994, December 12). History of the orphanage. *Newsweek, 124,* 33.

Gaudin, J. M. (1993). Effective intervention with neglectful families. *Criminal Justice and Behavior, 20,* 66-89.

Gaudin, J. M., Jr., Wodarski, J. S., Arkinson, M. K., & Avery, L. S. (1990). Remedying child neglect: Effectiveness of social network interventions. *Journal of Applied Social Sciences, 15,* 97-123.

Gelles, R. (1973). Child abuse as psychopathology: A sociological critique and reformulation. *American Journal of Orthopsychiatry, 43,* 611-621.

Gelles, R., & Hargreaves, E. (1981). Maternal employment and violence towards children. *Journal of Family Issues, 2,* 509-530.

Gelles, R. J. (1980). A profile of violence toward children in the United States. In G. Gerbner, C. J. Ross, & E. Zigler (Eds.), *Child abuse: An agenda for action* (pp. 82-105). New York: Oxford University Press.

Gelles, R. J. (1983). An exchange/social control theory. In D. Finkelhor, R. J. Gelles, G. T. Hotaling, & M. A. Straus (Eds.), *The dark side of families: Current family violence research* (pp. 151-165). Beverly Hills, CA: Sage.

Gelles, R. J. (1989). Child abuse and violence in single-parent families: Parent absence and economic deprivation. *American Journal of Orthopsychiatry, 59*(4), 492-501.

Gelles, R. J. (1993a). Constraints against family violence: How well do they work? *American Behavioral Scientist, 36,* 575-586.

Gelles, R. J. (1993b). The doctrine of family reunification: Child protection or risk? *The APSAC Advisor, 6*(2), 9-10.

Gelles, R. J., & Cornell, C. P. (1990). *Intimate violence in families* (2nd. ed.). Newbury Park, CA: Sage.

Gelles, R. J., & Harrop, J. (1989). *The risk of abusive violence among children with non-biological parents.* Paper presented at the annual meeting of the National Council on Family Relations, New Orleans, LA.

Gelles, R. J., & Loseke, D. R. (1993). Conclusions: Social problems, social policy, and controversies on family violence. In R. J. Gelles & D. R. Loseke (Eds.), *Current controversies on family violence* (pp. 357-366). Newbury Park, CA: Sage.

Gelles, R. J., & Straus, M. A. (1979). Determinants of violence in the family: Toward a theoretical integration. In W. R. Burr, R. Hill, F. I. Nye, & I. Reiss (Eds.), *Contemporary theories about the family* (pp. 549-581). New York: Free Press.

Gelles, R. J., & Straus, M. A. (1987). Is violence toward children increasing? A comparison of 1975 and 1985 national survey rates. *Journal of Interpersonal Violence, 2,* 212-222.

Gelles, R. J., & Straus, M. A. (1988). *Intimate violence.* New York: Simon & Schuster.

George, R., Wulczyn, F., & Fanshel, D. (1994). A foster care research agenda for the 90s. *Child Welfare, 73,* 525-549.

Giarretto, H. (1982). A comprehensive child sexual abuse treatment program. *Child Abuse & Neglect, 6,* 263-278.

Gibbs, J. (1975). *Crime, punishment, and deterrence.* New York: Elsevier.

Gibbs, N. (1993, January 18). 'Til death do us part. *Time, 141,* 38, 40-45.

Gibson, J. W., & Gutierrez, L. (1991). A service program for safe-home children [Special issue: Family violence]. *Families in Society, 72,* 554-562.

Gil, D. G. (1970). *Violence against children: Physical child abuse in the United States.* Cambridge, MA: Harvard University Press.

Gil, E., & Johnson, T. C. (1993). *Sexualized children: Assessment and treatment of sexualized children and children who molest.* Rockville, MD: Launch.

Ginsburg, H., Wright, L. S., Harrell, P. M., & Hill, D. W. (1989). Childhood victimization: Desensitization effects in the later lifespan. *Child Psychiatry and Human Development, 20,* 59-71.

Gleason, W. J. (1995). Children of battered women: Developmental delays and behavioral dysfunction. *Violence and Victims, 10,* 153-160.

Gold, C. A. (1993). Long-term consequences of childhood physical and sexual abuse. *Archives of Psychiatric Nursing, 7*(3), 163-173.

Gomes-Schwartz, B., Horowitz, J. M., & Cardarelli, A. P. (1990). *Child sexual abuse: The initial effects.* Newbury Park, CA: Sage.

Goodman, G., Bottoms, B., Schwartz-Kenney, B., & Rudy, L. (1991). Children's memory of a stressful event: Improving children's reports. *Journal of Narrative Life History, 1,* 69-99.

Goodman, G. S., Bottoms, B. L., & Shaver, P. R. (1994). *Characteristics and sources of allegations of ritualistic child abuse* (Executive Summary of the final report to the National Center on Child Abuse and Neglect [Grant No. 90CA1405]). Washington, DC: National Center on Child Abuse and Neglect.

Goodman, G. S., Taub, E. P., Jones, D. P. H., England, T., Port, L. K., Rudy, L., & Prado, L. (1992). Testifying in criminal court. *Monograph of the Society for Research in Child Development, 57*(5), 1-141.

Gray, E. (1993). *Unequal justice: The prosecution of child sexual abuse.* New York: Free Press.

Graziano, A. M. (1994). Why we should study subabusive violence against children. *Journal of Interpersonal Violence, 9,* 412-419.

Graziano, A. M., & Mills, J. (1992). Treatment for abused children: When is a partial solution acceptable? *Child Abuse & Neglect, 16,* 217-228.

Graziano, A. M., & Namaste, K. A. (1990). Parental use of physical force in child discipline: A survey of 679 college students. *Journal of Interpersonal Violence, 5,* 449-463.

Green, A. H. (1984). Child abuse by siblings. *Child Abuse & Neglect, 8,* 311-317.

Greenfield, L. A. (1996, March). *Child victimizers: Violent offenders and their victims* (NCJ No. 153258). Washington, DC: U.S. Department of Justice, Bureau of Justice Statistics.

Groff, M. G., & Hubble, L. M. (1984). A comparison of father-daughter and stepfather-daughter incest. *Criminal Justice and Behavior, 11,* 461-475.

Gross, A. B., & Keller, H. R. (1992). Long-term consequences of childhood physical and psychological maltreatment. *Aggressive Behavior, 18,* 171-185.

Grossier, D. (1986). *Child witness to family violence: Social problem-solving skills and behavior adjustment.* Unpublished doctoral dissertation, University of Denver, Denver, CO.

Groth, A. N. (1979). Sexual trauma in the life histories of rapists and child molesters. *Victimology: An International Journal, 4,* 10-16.

Groth, A. N., Hobson, W. F., & Gary, T. S. (1982). The child molester: Clinical observations. In J. Conte & D. A. Shorte (Eds.), *Social work and child sexual abuse* (pp. 129-144). New York: Haworth.

Groves, B., & Zuckerman, B. (1997). Interventions with parents and community caregivers. In J. D. Osofsky (Ed.), *Children in a violent society* (pp. 183-201). New York: Guilford.

Gruber, K. J., & Jones, R. J. (1983). Identifying determinants of risk of sexual victimization of youth: A multivariate approach. *Child Abuse & Neglect, 7,* 17-24.

Hadeed, A. J., & Siegel, S. R. (1989). Maternal cocaine use during pregnancy: Effect on the newborn infant. *Pediatrics, 84,* 205.

Hamberger, L. K. (1994). Introduction: Domestic partner abuse: Expanding paradigms for understanding and intervention. *Violence and Victims, 9,* 91-94.

Hanley, R. (1998, July 1). Neighbor accused of firing at house of paroled rapist. *New York Times* [Online], p. B6. Available: http://proquest.umi.com

Hansen, D. J., Pallotta, G. M., Tishelman, A. C., Conaway, L. P., & MacMillan, V. M. (1989). Parental problem-solving skills and child behavior problems: A comparison of physically abusive, neglectful, clinic, and community families. *Journal of Family Violence, 4,* 353-368.

Harry, J. (1989). Parental physical abuse and sexual orientation in males. *Archives of Sexual Behavior, 18*(3), 251-261.

Hart, S. N., & Brassard, M. R. (1989). *Developing and validating operationally defined measures of emotional maltreatment: A multimodal study of the relationships between caretaker behaviors and child characteristics across three developmental levels* (Grant No. DHHS 90CA1216). Washington, DC: Department of Health and Human Services and National Center on Child Abuse and Neglect.

Hart, S. N., & Brassard, M. R. (1990). Psychological maltreatment of children. In R. T. Ammerman & M. Hersen (Eds.), *Treatment of family vio-*

lence: A sourcebook (pp. 77-112). New York: John Wiley.

Hart, S. N., & Brassard, M. R. (1991). Psychological maltreatment: Progress achieved. *Development and Psychopathology, 3,* 61-70.

Hart, S. N., & Brassard, M. R. (1993). Psychological maltreatment. *Violence Update, 3*(7), 4, 6-7, 11.

Hart, S. N., Brassard, M. R., & Karlson, H. C. (1996). Psychological maltreatment. In J. Briere, L. Berliner, J. A. Bulkley, C. Jenny, & T. Reid (Eds.), *The APSAC handbook on child maltreatment* (pp. 72-89). Thousand Oaks, CA: Sage.

Hart, S. N., Germain, R., & Brassard, M. R. (1987). The challenge: To better understand and combat psychological maltreatment of children and youth. In M. R. Brassard, R. Germain, & S. N. Hart (Eds.), *Psychological maltreatment of children and youth* (pp. 3-24). New York: Pergamon.

Hartman, C. R., & Burgess, A. W. (1988). Information processing of trauma. *Journal of Interpersonal Violence, 3,* 443-457.

Haskett, M. (1990). Social problem-solving skills of young physically abused children. *Child Psychiatry and Human Development, 21,* 109-118.

Hathaway, P. (1989, May). Failure to thrive: Knowledge for social workers. *Health and Social Work,* 122-126.

Haugaard, J. J., & Reppucci, N. D. (1988). *The sexual abuse of children.* San Francisco: Jossey-Bass.

Hawkins, J. D. (1995). Controlling crime before it happens: Risk-focused prevention. *National Institute of Justice, 229,* 10-18.

Hay, T., & Jones, L. (1994). Societal interventions to prevent child abuse and neglect. *Child Welfare, 73,* 379-403.

Hayashino, D. S., Wurtele, S. K., & Klebe, K. J. (1995). Child molesters: An examination of cognitive factors. *Journal of Interpersonal Violence, 10,* 106-116.

Haynes, C., Cutler, C., Gray, J., O'Keefe, K., & Kempe, R. (1983). Nonorganic failure to thrive: Decision for placement and videotaped evaluations. *Child Abuse & Neglect, 7,* 309-319.

Hazzard, A. (1993). Trauma-related beliefs as mediators of sexual abuse impact in adult women survivors: A pilot study. *Journal of Child Sexual Abuse, 2,* 55-69.

Healthy Families America. (1994, October). *Violence Update, 5*(2), 1-4.

Heath, L., Kruttschnitt, C., & Ward, D. A. (1986). Family violence, television viewing habits, and other adolescent experiences related to violence criminal behavior. *Criminology, 24,* 235-267.

Hechler, D. (1988). *The battle and the backlash: The child sexual abuse war.* Lexington, MA: Lexington Books.

Hegar, R. L., & Yungman, J. J. (1989). Toward a causal typology of child neglect. *Child Youth Services Review, 11,* 203-220.

Hegar, R. L., Zuravin, S. J., & Orme, J. G. (1994). Factors predicting severity of physical child abuse injury. *Journal of Interpersonal Violence, 9,* 170-183.

Heim, N., & Hursch, C. J. (1979). Castration for sex offenders: A review and critique of recent European literature. *Archives of Sexual Behavior, 8,* 281-304.

Helfer, R. E. (1990, June). The neglect of our children. *The World & I,* 531-541.

Henning, K., Leitenberg, H., Coffey, P., Turner, T., & Bennett, R. T. (1996). Long-term psychological and social impact of witnessing physical conflict between parents. *Journal of Interpersonal Violence, 11,* 35-51.

Hensey, O. J., Williams, J. K., & Rosenbloom, L. (1983). Intervention in child abuse: Experiences in Liverpool. *Developmental Medicine and Neurology, 25,* 606-611.

Herdt, G. (1987). *The Sambia: Ritual and gender in New Guinea.* New York: Holt, Rinehart & Winston.

Herman, J. L. (1992). *Trauma and recovery.* New York: Basic Books.

Herman, J. L., & Schatzow, E. (1987). Recovery and verification of memories of childhood sexual trauma. *Psychoanalytic Psychology, 4,* 1-14.

Herrenkohl, E. C., Herrenkohl, R. C., Rupert, L. J., Egolf, B. P., & Lutz, J. G. (1995). Risk factors for behavioral dysfunction: The relative impact of maltreatment, SES, physical health problems, cognitive ability, and quality of parent-child interaction. *Child Abuse & Neglect, 19,* 191-203.

Herrenkohl, R. C., Herrenkohl, E. C., & Egolf, B. P. (1983). Circumstances surrounding the occurrence of child maltreatment. *Journal of Consulting and Clinical Psychology, 51,* 424-431.

Herrenkohl, R. C., Herrenkohl, E. C., Egolf, B. P., & Wu, P. (1991). The developmental consequences of abuse: The Lehigh longitudinal study. In R. H. Starr & D. A. Wolfe (Eds.), *The effects of child abuse and neglect: Issues and research* (pp. 57-85). New York: Guilford.

Hershorn, M., & Rosenbaum, A. (1985). Children of marital violence: A closer look at the unintended victims. *American Journal of Orthopsychiatry, 55,* 260-266.

Hewitt, S. K. (1998). *Small voices: Assessing allegations of sexual abuse in preschool children.* Thousand Oaks, CA: Sage.

Hickox, A., & Furnell, J. R. G. (1989). Psychosocial and background factors in emotional abuse of children. *Child: Care, Health and Development, 15,* 227-240.

Hilberman, E., & Munson, K. (1978). Sixty battered women. *Victimology: An International Journal, 2,* 460-470.

Hillson, J. M. C., & Kupier, N. A. (1994). A stress and coping model of child maltreatment. *Clinical Psychology Review, 14,* 261-285.

Hilton, Z. N. (1992). Battered women's concerns about their children witnessing wife assault. *Journal of Interpersonal Violence, 7,* 77-86.

Hinchey, F. S., & Gavelek, J. R. (1982). Empathic responding in children of battered mothers. *Child Abuse & Neglect, 6,* 395-401.

Hirschi, T. (1969). *Causes of delinquency.* Berkeley: University of California Press.

Ho, P. (1959). *Studies on the population of China, 1368-1953.* Cambridge, MA: Harvard University Press.

Ho, T. P., & Kwok, W. M. (1991). Child sexual abuse in Hong Kong. *Child Abuse & Neglect, 15,* 597-600.

Hoffman-Plotkin, D., & Twentyman, C. T. (1984). A multimodal assessment of behavioral and cognitive deficits in abused and neglected preschoolers. *Child Development, 55,* 794-802.

Hoglund, C. L., & Nicholas, K. B. (1995). Shame, guilt, and anger in college students exposed to abusive family environments. *Journal of Family Violence, 10*(2), 141-157.

Holden, G. W. (1998). Introduction: The development of research into another consequence of family violence. In G. W. Holden, R. Geffner, & E. N. Jouriles (Eds.), *Children exposed to marital violence* (pp. 1-18). Washington, DC: American Psychological Association.

Holden, G. W., Geffner, R., & Jouriles, E. N. (Eds.). (1998). *Children exposed to marital violence.* Washington, DC: American Psychological Association.

Holden, G. W., & Ritchie, K. L. (1991). Linking extreme marital discord, child rearing, and child behavior problems: Evidence from battered women. *Child Development, 62,* 311-327.

Horn, J. L., & Trickett, P. K. (1998). Community violence and child development: A review of research. In P. K. Trickett & C. J. Schellenbach (Eds.), *Violence against children in the family and the community* (pp. 103-138). Washington, DC: American Psychological Association.

Hotaling, G. T., Straus, M. A., & Lincoln, A. J. (1990). Intrafamily violence and crime and violence outside the family. In M. A. Straus & R. J. Gelles (Eds.), *Physical violence in American families: Risk factors and adaptations to violence in 8,145 families* (pp. 431-470). New Brunswick, NJ: Transaction Books.

Hotaling, G. T., & Sugarman, D. B. (1986). An analysis of risk markers in husband to wife violence: The current state of knowledge. *Violence and Victims, 1,* 101-124.

Howe, D. (1995). Pornography and the paedophile: Is it criminogenic? *British Journal of Medical Psychology, 68*(1), 15-27.

Howes, C., & Eldredge, R. (1985). Responses of abused, neglected, and non-maltreated children to the behaviors of their peers. *Journal of Applied Developmental Psychology, 6,* 261-270.

Hughes, D. (1996). Sex tours via the Internet. *Agenda: Empowering Women for Equality, 28,* 71-76.

Hughes, H. M. (1986). Research with children in shelters: Implications for clinical services. *Children Today, 15*(2), 21-25.

Hughes, H. M. (1988). Psychology and behavior correlates of family violence in child witnesses and victims. *American Journal of Orthopsychiatry, 58,* 77-90.

Hughes, H. M. (1992). Impact of spouse abuse on children of battered women: Implications for practice. *Violence Update, 2*(17), 1, 9-11.

Hughes, H. M., & Luke, D. A. (1998). Heterogeneity in adjustment among children of battered women. In G. W. Holden, R. Geffner, & E. N. Jouriles (Eds.), *Children exposed to marital violence* (pp. 185-221). Washington, DC: American Psychological Association.

Hughes, H. M., Parkinson, D., & Vargo, M. (1989). Witnessing spouse abuse and experiencing physical abuse: A "double whammy"? *Journal of Family Violence, 4,* 197-209.

Hunt, P., & Baird, M. (1990). Children of sex rings. *Child Welfare, 69,* 195-207.

Hunter, J. A., Childers, S. E., Gerald, R., & Esmaili, H. (1990). An examination of variables differentiating clinical subtypes of incestuous child molesters. *International Journal of Offender Therapy and Comparative Criminology, 34,* 95-104.

Hunter, J. A., Goodwin, D. W., & Becker, J. V. (1994). The relationship between phallometrically measured deviant sexual arousal and clinical characteristics in juvenile sexual offenders. *Behavior Research and Therapy, 32,* 533-538.

Hunter, R., & Kilstrom, N. (1979). Breaking the cycle in abusive families. *American Journal of Psychiatry, 136,* 1320-1322.

Hunter, R. S., Kilstrom, N., Kraybill, E. N., & Loda, F. (1978). Antecedents of child abuse and neglect in premature infants: A prospective study in a newborn intensive care unit. *Pediatrics, 61,* 629-635.

Ireland, K. (1993). Sexual exploitation of children and international travel tourism. *Child Abuse Review, 2,* 263-271.

Itzin, C. (1997). Pornography and the organization of intra- and extrafamilial child sexual abuse. In G. K. Kantor & J. L. Jasinski (Eds.), *Out of the darkness: Contemporary perspectives on family violence* (pp. 58-79). Thousand Oaks, CA: Sage.

Jackson, J., Calhoun, K., Amick, A., Maddever, H., & Habif, V. (1990). Young adult women who report childhood intrafamilial sexual abuse: Subsequent adjustment. *Archives of Sexual Behavior, 19,* 211-221.

Jaffe, P. G., Hastings, E., & Reitzel, D. (1992). Child witnesses of woman abuse: How can schools respond? *Response, 79*(2), 12-15.

Jaffe, P. G., Wolfe, D. A., & Wilson, S. K. (1990). *Children of battered women.* Newbury Park, CA: Sage.

Jehu, D., Klassen, C., & Gazan, M. (1986). Cognitive restructuring of distorted beliefs associated with childhood sexual abuse. *Journal of Social Work and Human Sexuality, 4,* 49-69.

Jenkins, E. J., & Bell, C. C. (1994). Violence exposure, psychological distress, and high risk behaviors among inner-city high school students. In S. Friedman (Ed.), *Anxiety disorders in African-Americans* (pp. 76-88). New York: Springer.

Johnson, B. K., & Kenkel, M. B. (1991). Stress, coping and adjustment in female adolescent incest victims. *Child Abuse & Neglect, 15,* 293-305.

Johnson, R., & Morse, H. (1968). *The battered child: A study of children with inflicted injuries.* Denver, CO: Denver Department of Welfare.

Johnson, T. C. (1989). Female child perpetrators: Children who molest other children. *Child Abuse & Neglect, 13,* 571-585.

Jones, D. P. H. (1986). Individual psychotherapy for the sexually abused child. *Child Abuse & Neglect, 10,* 377-385.

Jones, D. P. H. (1991). Ritualism and child sexual abuse. *Child Abuse & Neglect, 15,* 163-170.

Jones, D. P. H. (1994). Editorial: The syndrome of Munchausen by proxy. *Child Abuse & Neglect, 18,* 769-771.

Jones, D. P. H., & McGraw, J. M. (1987). Reliable and fictitious accounts of sexual abuse to children. *Journal of Interpersonal Violence, 2,* 27-45.

Jones, E. D., & McCurdy, K. (1992). The links between types of maltreatment and demographic characteristics of children. *Child Abuse & Neglect, 16,* 201-215.

Jones, J. E. (1992). State intervention in pregnancy: Comment. *Louisiana Law Review, 52,* 1159-1160.

Jones, R. L., & Jones, J. M. (1987). Racism as psychological maltreatment. In M. R. Brassard, R. Germain, & S. N. Hart (Eds.), *Psychological maltreatment of children and youth* (pp. 146-158). New York: Pergamon.

Jonker, F., & Jonker-Bakker, P. (1991). Experiences with ritualisitic child sexual abuse: A case study from the Netherlands. *Child Abuse & Neglect, 15,* 191-196.

Joseph, C. (1995). Scarlet wounding: Issues of child prostitution. *Journal of Psychohistory, 23*(1), 2-17.

Jouriles, E. N., McDonald, R., Stephens, N., Norwood, W., Spiller, L. C., & Ware, H. S. (1998). In G. W. Holden, R. Geffner, & E. N. Jouriles (Eds.), *Children exposed to marital violence* (pp. 337-369). Washington, DC: American Psychological Association.

Jouriles, E. N., & Norwood, W. D. (1995). Physical aggression toward boys and girls in families characterized by the battering of women. *Journal of Family Violence, 9,* 69-78.

Justice, B., & Calvert, A. (1990). Family environment factors associated with child abuse. *Psychological Reports, 66,* 458.

Justice, B., & Justice, R. (1979). *The broken taboo.* New York: Human Sciences Press.

Kalichman, S. C., Craig, M. E., & Follingstad, D. R. (1989). Factors influencing the reporting of father-child sexual abuse: Study of licensed practicing psychologists. *Professional Psychology: Research and Practice, 20,* 84-89.

Kalmuss, D. S. (1984). The intergenerational transmission of marital aggression. *Journal of Marriage and the Family, 46,* 11-19.

Kaplan, M. S., Becker, J. V., & Martinez, D. F. (1990). A comparison of mothers of adolescent incest versus non-incest perpetrators. *Journal of Family Violence, 5,* 209-214.

Katz, R. C. (1990). Psychosocial adjustment in adolescent child molesters. *Child Abuse & Neglect, 14,* 567-575.

Kaufman, J., & Cicchetti, D. (1989). The effects of maltreatment on school-aged children's socioemotional development: Assessments in a day-camp setting. *Developmental Psychology, 25,* 516-524.

Kaufman, J., & Zigler, E. (1987). Do abused children become abusive parents? *American Journal of Orthopsychiatry, 57,* 186-192.

Kavanagh, C. (1982). Emotional abuse and mental injury. *Journal of the American Academy of Child Psychiatry, 21,* 171-177.

Kelleher, K., Chaffin, M., Hollenberg, J., & Fischer, E. (1994). Alcohol and drug disorders among physically abusive and neglectful parents in a community-based sample. *American Journal of Public Health, 84,* 1586-1590.

Kelley, S. J. (1989). Stress responses of children to sexual abuse and ritualistic abuse in day care centers. *Journal of Interpersonal Violence, 4,* 502-513.

Kelley, S. J. (1996). Ritualistic abuse of children. In J. Briere, L. Berliner, J. A. Bulkley, C. Jenny, & T. Reid (Eds.), *The APSAC handbook on child maltreatment* (pp. 90-99). Thousand Oaks, CA: Sage.

Kelley, S. J., Brant, R., & Waterman, J. (1993). Sexual abuse of children in day care centers. *Child Abuse & Neglect, 17,* 71-89.

Kempe, C., & Helfer, R. (1972). *Helping the battered child and his family.* Philadelphia: J. B. Lippincott.

Kempe, C. H., Silverman, F. N., Steele, B. F., Droegemueller, W., & Silver, H. K. (1962). The battered child syndrome. *Journal of the American Medical Association, 17,* 17-24.

Kempe, R. S., Cutler, C., & Dean, J. (1980). The infant with failure-to-thrive. In C. H. Kempe & R. E. Helfer (Eds.), *The battered child* (3rd ed., pp. 163-182). Chicago: University of Chicago Press.

Kempe, R. S., & Goldbloom, R. B. (1987). Malnutrition and growth retardation ("failure to thrive") in the context of child abuse and neglect. In R. E. Helfer & R. S. Kempe (Eds.), *The battered child* (4th ed., pp. 312-335). Chicago: University of Chicago Press.

Kendall-Tackett, K. A., Williams, L. M., & Finkelhor, D. (1993). Impact of sexual abuse on children: A review and synthesis of recent empirical studies. *Psychological Bulletin, 113,* 164-180.

Kent, A., & Waller, G. (1998). The impact of childhood emotional abuse: An extension of the child abuse and trauma scale. *Child Abuse & Neglect, 22,* 393-399.

Keronac, S., Taggart, M. E., Lescop, J., & Fortin, M. F. (1986). Dimensions of health in violent families. *Health Care for Women International, 7,* 413-426.

Kiersch, T. A. (1990). Treatment of sex offenders with Depo-Provera. *Bulletin of the American Academy of Psychiatry and Law, 6,* 239-255.

Kilpatrick, K. L., & Williams, L. M. (in press). Posttraumatic stress disorder in child witnesses to domestic violence. *American Journal of Orthopsychiatry.*

Kinard, E. M. (1982). Experiencing child abuse: Effects on emotional adjustment. *American Journal of Orthopsychiatry, 52,* 82-91.

Kirkham, M. A., Schinke, S. P., Schilling, R. F., Meltzer, N. J., & Norelius, K. L. (1986). Cognitive-behavioral skills, social supports, and child abuse potential among mothers of handicapped children. *Journal of Family Violence, 1,* 235-245.

Kiser, L. J., Pugh, R. L., McColgan, E. B., Pruitt, D. B., & Edwards, N. B. (1991). Treatment strategies for victims of extrafamilial child sexual abuse. *Journal of Family Psychotherapy,* 2(1), 27-39.

Kneisel, C. R. (1991). Healing the wounded, neglected inner child of the past. *Nursing Clinics of North America, 26,* 745-755.

Knopp, F., Freeman-Longo, R., & Stevenson, W. (1992). *Nationwide survey of juvenile and adult sex-offender treatment programs and model.* Orwell, VT: Safer Society Press.

Knutson, J. F. (1978). Child abuse as an area of aggression research. *Journal of Orthopsychiatry, 3,* 20-27.

Kolbo, J. R., Blakely, E. H., & Engleman, D. (1996). Children who witness domestic violence: A review of empirical literature. *Journal of Interpersonal Violence, 11*(2), 281-293.

Kolko, D. J. (1987). Treatment of child sexual abuse: Programs, progress, and prospects. *Journal of Family Violence, 2,* 303-318.

Kolko, D. J. (1992). Characteristics of child victims of physical violence. *Journal of Interpersonal Violence, 7,* 244-276.

Kolko, D. J. (1996a). Clinical monitoring of treatment course in child physical abuse: Child and parent reports. *Child Abuse & Neglect, 20,* 23-43.

Kolko, D. J. (1996b). Individual cognitive behavioral treatment and family therapy for physically abused children and their offending parents: A comparison of clinical outcomes. *Child Maltreatment, 1*(4), 322-342.

Kolko, D. J. (1998). Treatment and intervention for child victims of violence. In P. K. Trickett & C. J. Schellenbach (Eds.), *Violence against children in the family and the community* (pp. 213-249). Washington, DC: American Psychological Association.

Koski, P. (1987). Family violence and nonfamily deviance: Taking stock of the literature. *Marriage and Family Review, 12,* 23-46.

Kratcoski, P. C. (1984). Perspectives on intrafamily violence. *Human Relations, 37,* 443-453.

Kroll, P. D., Stock, D. F., & James, M. E. (1985). The behavior of adult alcoholic men abused as children. *Journal of Nervous and Mental Disease, 173,* 689-693.

Krugman, R. D. (1995). Future directions in preventing child abuse. *Child Abuse & Neglect, 19,* 272-279.

Krugman, S., Mata, L., & Krugman, R. (1992). Sexual abuse and corporal punishment during childhood: A pilot retrospective survey of university students in Costa Rica. *Pediatrics, 90,* 157-161.

Kruttschnitt, C., & Dornfeld, M. (1992). Will they tell? Assess preadolescents' reports of family violence. *Journal of Research on Crime and Delinquency, 29,* 136-147.

Kurtz, P. D., Gaudin, J. M., Howing, P. T., & Wodarski, J. S. (1993). The consequences of physical abuse and neglect on the school age child: Mediating factors. *Children and Youth Services Review, 15,* 85-104.

Kurtz, P. D., Gaudin, J. M., Wodarski, J. S., & Howing, P. T. (1993). Maltreatment and the school-aged child: School performance consequences. *Child Abuse & Neglect, 17,* 581-589.

Lacey, K. A., & Parkin, J. M. (1974). The normal short child. *Archives of Disabled Children, 49,* 417.

Lachenmeyer, J. R., & Davidovicz, H. (1987). Failure to thrive: A critical review. In B. B. Lahey & A. E. Kazdin (Eds.), *Advances in clinical psychology* (Vol. 10, pp. 335-359). New York: Plenum.

Lachnit, C. (1991, April 13). "Satan trial": Jurors rule for two sisters. *Orange County Register,* p. 26.

Lahey, B. B., Conger, R. D., Atkeson, B. M., & Treiber, F. A. (1984). Parenting behavior and emotional status of physically abusive mothers. *Journal of Consulting and Clinical Psychology, 52,* 1062-1071.

Landsman, M. J., Nelson, K., Allen, M., & Tyler, M. (1992). *The self-sufficiency project: Final re-*

port. Iowa City, IA: National Resource Center on Family Based Services.

Lang, R. A., Flor-Henry, P., & Frenzel, R. R. (1990). Sex hormone profiles in pedophilic and incestuous men. *Annals of Sex Research, 3,* 59-74.

Lang, R. A., & Frenzel, R. R. (1988). How sex offenders lure children. *Annals of Sex Research, 1,* 303-317.

Langan, P. A., & Harlow, C. W. (1994, June). *Child rape victims, 1992* (NCJ-147001). Washington, DC: U.S. Department of Justice, Bureau of Justice Statistics.

Langevin, R. (1993). A comparison of neuroendocrine and genetic factors in homosexuality and in pedophilia. *Annals of Sex Research, 6,* 67-76.

Langevin, R., Lang, R. A., & Curnoe, S. (1998). The prevalence of sex offenders with deviant fantasies. *Journal of Interpersonal Violence, 13*(3), 315-327.

Lanktree, C. B., Briere, J., & Zaidi, L. Y. (1991). Incidence and impacts of sexual abuse in a child outpatient sample: The role of direct inquiry. *Child Abuse & Neglect, 15,* 447-453.

Lanning, K. V. (1991). Ritual abuse: A law enforcement view or perspective. *Child Abuse & Neglect, 15,* 171-173.

Lanning, K. V., & Burgess, A. W. (1984, January). Child pornography and sex rings. *FBI Law Enforcement Bulletin,* 10-16.

Larrance, D. T., & Twentyman, C. T. (1983). Maternal attributions and child abuse. *Journal of Abnormal Psychology, 92,* 449-457.

Larson, C. S., Terman, D. L., Gomby, D. S., Quinn, L. S., & Behrman, R. E. (1994). Sexual abuse of children: Recommendations and analysis. *Future of Children, 4*(2), 4-30.

Laumann, E., Gagnon, J., Michael, R., & Michaels, S. (1994). *The social organization of sexuality: Sexual practices in the United States.* Chicago: University of Chicago Press.

Laviola, M. (1992). Effects of older brother-young sister incest: A study of the dynamics of 17 cases. *Child Abuse & Neglect, 16,* 409-421.

Laws, D. R., & Marshall, W. L. (1990). A conditioning theory of the etiology and maintenance of deviant sexual preferences and behavior. In W. L. Marshall, D. R. Laws, & H. E. Barbaree (Eds.), *Handbook of sexual assault: Issues, theories, and treatment of the offender* (pp. 209-229). New York: Plenum.

Lawson, C. (1993). Mother-son sexual abuse: Rare or underreported? A critique of the research. *Child Abuse & Neglect, 17,* 261-269.

Layzer, J. I., Goodson, B. D., & DeLange, C. (1986). Children in shelters. *Response, 9*(2), 2-5.

Limber, S. P., & Nation, M. A. (1998). Violence within the neighborhood and community. In P. K. Trickett & C. J. Schellenbach, (Eds.), *Violence against children in the family and the community* (pp. 171-193). Washington, DC: American Psychological Association.

Lindberg, M. (1991). An interactive approach to assessing the suggestibility and testimony of eyewitnesses. In J. Doris (Ed.), *The suggestibility of children's recollections: Implications for eyewitness testimony* (pp. 47-55). Washington, DC: American Psychological Association.

Lipovsky, J. A., & Elliott, A. N. (1993). Individual treatment of the sexually abused child. *The APSAC Advisor, 6*(3), 15-18.

Lloyd, J. C., & Sallee, A. L. (1994). The challenge and potential of family preservation services in the public child welfare system. *Protecting Children, 10*(3), 3-6.

Loftus, E., & Ketcham, K. (1991). *Witness for the defense.* New York: St. Martin's.

Loftus, E. F. (1993). The reality of repressed memories. *American Psychologist, 48,* 518-537.

Lopez, M. A., & Heffer, R. W. (1998). Self-concept and social competence of university student victims of childhood physical abuse. *Child Abuse & Neglect, 22,* 183-195.

Loring, M. T. (1994). *Emotional abuse.* New York: Lexington Books.

Lugavere, J. P. (1996, September 18). Molester castration measure signed. *Los Angeles Times,* p. A10.

Lujan, C., DeBruyn, L. M., May, P. A., & Bird, M. E. (1989). Profile of abused and neglected American Indian children in the Southwest. *Child Abuse & Neglect, 13,* 449-461.

Lutzker, J. R. (1990a). Behavioral treatment of child neglect. *Behavior Modification, 14,* 301-315.

Lutzker, J. R. (1990b). Project 12-Ways: Treating child abuse and neglect from an ecobehavioral perspective. In R. F. Dangel & R. F. Polster

(Eds.), *Parent training: Foundations of research and practice.* New York: Guilford.

Lutzker, J. R., Campbell, R. V., & Watson-Perczel, M. (1984). Using the case study method to treat several problems in a family indicated for child neglect. *Education and Treatment of Children, 7,* 315-333.

Lutzker, J. R., Frame, R., & Rice, J. (1982). Project 12-Ways: An ecobehavioral approach to the treatment and prevention of child abuse and neglect. *Education and Treatment of Children, 5,* 141-155.

Lutzker, J. R., Megson, D. A., Dachman, R. S., & Webb, M. E. (1985). Validating and training adult-child interaction skills to professionals and to parents indicated for child abuse and neglect. *Journal of Child and Adolescent Psychotherapy, 2,* 91-104.

Lutzker, J. R., & Rice, J. M. (1987). Using recidivism data to evaluate Project 12-Ways: An ecobehavioral approach to the treatment and prevention of child abuse and neglect. *Journal of Family Violence, 2,* 283-290.

Lutzker, S. Z., Lutzker, J. R., Braunling-McMorrow, D., & Eddleman, J. (1987). Prompting to increase mother-baby stimulation with single mothers. *Journal of Child and Adolescent Psychotherapy, 4,* 3-12.

Lynch, M. A., & Roberts, J. (1982). *Consequences of child abuse.* London: Academic Press.

Lyons, T. J., & Oates, R. K. (1993). Falling out of bed: A relatively benign occurrence. *Pediatrics, 92,* 125.

MacMillan, V. M., Olson, R. L., & Hansen, D. J. (1991). Low and high deviant analogue assessment of parent-training with physically abusive parents. *Journal of Family Violence, 6,* 279-301.

Madonna, P. G., Van Scoyk, S., & Jones, D. P. H. (1991). Family interactions within incest and non-incest families. *American Journal of Psychiatry, 148,* 46-49.

Maguire, K., & Pastore, A. L. (Eds.). (1994). *Sourcebook of criminal justice statistics: 1993.* Washington, DC: U.S. Department of Justice, Bureau of Justice Statistics.

Malamuth, N. M., & Briere, J. (1986). Sexual violence in the media: Indirect effects on aggression against women. *Journal of Social Issues, 42,* 75-92.

Malatack, J. J., Wiener, E. S., Gartner, J. C., Zitelli, B. J., & Brunetti, E. (1985). Munchausen by proxy: A new complication of central venous catheterization. *Pediatrics, 75,* 523-525.

Malinosky-Rummell, R., & Hansen, D. J. (1993). Long-term consequences of childhood physical abuse. *Psychological Bulletin, 114,* 68-79.

Man found guilty in Megan's killing. (1997, May 31). *Sacramento Bee* [Online]. Available: http://www.sacbee.com

Mannarino, A. P., Cohen, J. A., & Berman, S. R. (1994). The Children's Attributions and Perceptions Scale: A new measure of sexual abuse-related factors. *Journal of Clinical Child Psychology, 23,* 204-211.

Mannarino, A. P., Cohen, J. A., Smith, J. A., & Moore-Motily, S. (1991). Six- and twelve-month follow-up of sexually abused girls. *Journal of Interpersonal Violence, 6,* 494-511.

Marans, S., & Cohen, D. (1993). Children and inner-city violence: Strategies for intervention. In L. Leavitt & N. Fox (Eds.), *Psychological effects of war and violence on children* (pp. 281-302). Hillsdale, NJ: Lawrence Erlbaum.

Margolin, G. (1998). Effects of domestic violence on children. In P. K. Trickett & C. J. Schellenbach (Eds.), *Violence against children in the family and the community* (pp. 57-101). Washington, DC: American Psychological Association.

Margolin, L., & Craft, J. L. (1990). Child abuse by adolescent caregivers. *Child Abuse & Neglect, 14,* 365-373.

Marques, J., Nelson, C., West, M. A., & Day, D. M. (1994). The relationship between treatment goals and recidivism among child molesters. *Behavior Research and Therapy, 32,* 577-588.

Marshall, L. L., & Rose, P. (1990). Premarital violence: The impact of family of origin violence, stress, and reciprocity. *Violence and Victims, 5,* 51-64.

Marshall, W. L., & Barbaree, H. E. (1988). The long-term evaluation of a behavioral treatment program for child molesters. *Behavior Research and Therapy, 26,* 499-511.

Marshall, W. L., Barbaree, H. E., & Butt, J. (1988). Sexual offenders against male children: Sexual preferences. *Behavior Research and Therapy, 26,* 383-391.

Marshall, W. L., Barbaree, H. E., & Christophe, D. (1986). Sexual offenders against female children: Sexual preferences for age of victims and type of behavior. *Canadian Journal of Behavioral Science, 18,* 424-439.

Marshall, W. L., & Eccles, A. (1993). Pavlovian conditioning processes in adolescent sex offenders. In H. Barbaree, W. Marshall, & S. Hudson (Eds.), *The juvenile sex offender* (pp. 118-142). New York: Guilford.

Marshall, W. L., Jones, R., Ward, T., Johnston, P., & Barbaree, H. E. (1991). Treatment outcome with sex offenders. *Clinical Psychology Review, 11,* 465-485.

Marshall, W. L., & Pithers, W. (1994). A reconsideration of treatment outcome with sex offenders. *Criminal Justice and Behavior, 21,* 10-27.

Martin, J. A., & Elmer, E. (1992). Battered children grown-up: A follow-up study of individuals severely maltreated as children. *Child Abuse & Neglect, 16,* 75-87.

Martinez, P., & Richters, J. E. (1993). The NIMH Community Violence Project: Children's distress symptoms associated with violence exposure. In D. Reiss, J. E. Richters, M. Radke-Yarrow, & D. Scharff (Eds.), *Children and violence* (pp. 82-95). New York: Guilford.

Mash, E. J., Johnston, C., & Kovitz, K. (1983). A comparison of the mother-child interactions of physically abused and non-abused children during play and task situations. *Journal of Clinical Child Psychology, 12,* 337-346.

Mathews, J. K., Matthews, R., & Speltz, K. (1989). *Female sexual offenders: An exploratory study.* Orwell, VT: Safer Society Press.

McClain, P., Sacks, J., Froehlke, R., & Ewigman, D. (1993). Estimates of fatal child abuse and neglect, United States, 1979 through 1988. *Pediatrics, 91,* 338-343.

McCloskey, L. A., Figueredo, A. J., & Koss, M. P. (1995). The effects of systemic family violence on children's mental health. *Child Development, 66,* 1239-1261.

McClung, J. J., Murray, R., & Braden, N. J. (1988). Intentional ipecac poisoning in children. *American Journal of Diseases in Children, 142,* 637-639.

McCurdy, K., & Daro, D. (1993). *Current trends in child abuse reporting and fatalities: The results of the 1992 annual fifty state survey.* Chicago: National Center on Child Abuse Prevention Research.

McCurdy, K., & Daro, D. (1994a). Child maltreatment: A national survey of reports and fatalities. *Journal of Interpersonal Violence, 9,* 75-94.

McCurdy, K., & Daro, D. (1994b). *Current trends in child abuse reporting and fatalities: The results of the 1993 annual fifty state survey.* (Available from the National Committee to Prevent Child Abuse, 332 South Michigan Ave., Suite 1600, Chicago, IL 60604)

McDermott, T. (1997, November 16). Terry McDermott: LeTourneau and Billie: Similar cases but different outcomes. *Seattle Times* [Online]. Available: http://www.seattletimes.com

McGee, R. A., & Wolfe, D. A. (1991). Psychological maltreatment: Toward an operational definition. *Development and Psychopathology, 3,* 3-18.

McGuire, T., & Feldman, K. (1989). Psychological morbidity of children subjected to Munchausen syndrome by proxy. *Pediatrics, 83,* 289-292.

McHale, S. M., & Pawletko, T. M. (1992). Differential treatment of siblings in two family contexts. *Child Development, 63,* 68-91.

McKay, E. J. (1987, July). *Children of battered women.* Paper presented at the Third National Family Violence Research Conference, Durham, NH.

McKay, M. M. (1994). The link between domestic violence and child abuse: Assessment and treatment considerations. *Child Welfare, 73,* 29-39.

Meadow, R. (1977). Munchausen syndrome by proxy: The hinterland of child abuse. *Lancet, 2,* 343-345.

Meadow, R. (1990). Suffocation, recurrent apnea, and sudden infant death. *Journal of Pediatrics, 117,* 351-356.

Megan's Law, 1996, Pub. L. No. 104-145.

Meichenbaum, D. (1977). *Cognitive-behavior modification: An integrative approach.* New York: Plenum.

Melton, G. B., & Barry, F. D. (1994). Neighbors helping neighbors: The vision of the U.S. Advisory Board on Child Abuse and Neglect. In

G. B. Melton & F. D. Barry (Eds.), *Protecting children from abuse and neglect* (pp. 1-13). New York: Guilford.

Melton, G. B., Goodman, G. S., Kalichman, S. C., Levine, M., Saywitz, K., & Koocher, G. P. (1995). Empirical research on child maltreatment and the law. *Journal of Clinical Child Psychology, 24*(Suppl.), 47-77.

Mennen, F. E., & Meadow, D. (1994). A preliminary study of the factors related to trauma in childhood sexual abuse. *Journal of Family Violence, 9,* 125-142.

Mennen, F. E., & Meadow, D. (1995). The relationship of abuse characteristics to symptoms in sexually abused girls. *Journal of Interpersonal Violence, 10,* 259-274.

Mertin, P. G. (1992). An adaptation of the Conflict Tactics Scales. *Australian Journal of Marriage and the Family, 13,* 166-169.

Merton, R. K. (1938). Social structure and anomie. *American Sociological Review, 3,* 672-682.

Miller-Perrin, C. L. (1998). Sexually abused children's perceptions of sexual abuse: An exploratory analysis and comparison across ages. *Journal of Child Sexual Abuse, 7*(1), 1-22.

Milner, J. S. (1993). Social information processing and physical child abuse. *Clinical Psychology Review, 13,* 275-294.

Milner, J. S. (1998). Individual and family characteristics associated with intrafamilial child physical and sexual abuse. In P. K. Trickett & C. J. Schellenbach (Eds.), *Violence against children in the family and the community* (pp. 141-170). Washington, DC: American Psychological Association.

Milner, J. S., & Chilamkurti, C. (1991). Physical child abuse perpetrator characteristic: A review of the literature. *Journal of Interpersonal Violence, 6,* 336-344.

Milner, J. S., & Dopke, C. (1997). Child physical abuse: Review of offender characteristics. In D. A. Wolfe, R. J. McMahon, & R. D. Peters (Eds.), *Child abuse: New directions in prevention and treatment across the lifespan* (pp. 27-54). Thousand Oaks, CA: Sage.

Milner, J. S., Halsey, L. B., & Fultz, J. (1995). Empathic responsiveness and affective reactivity to infant stimuli in high- and low-risk for physical child abuse mothers. *Child Abuse & Neglect, 19,* 767-780.

Milner, J. S., & Robertson, K. R. (1990). Comparison of physical child abusers, intrafamilial sexual child abusers, and child neglecters. *Journal of Interpersonal Violence, 5,* 37-48.

Miner, M., Marques, J., Day, D., & Nelson, C. (1990). Impact of relapse prevention in treating sex offenders: Preliminary findings. *Annals of Sex Research, 3,* 165-185.

Mitchell, J., & Morse, J. (1998). *From victims to survivors: Reclaimed voices of women sexually abused in childhood by females.* Washington, DC: Accelerated Development.

Mollerstrom, W. W., Patchner, M. A., & Milner, J. S. (1992). Family functioning and child abuse potential. *Journal of Clinical Psychology, 48,* 445-454.

Montgomery, N. (1996, July 9). Sex charges against teachers still shock, but not so unusual. *Seattle Times* [Online]. Available: http://www.seattletimes.com

Montoya, J. (1993). Something not so funny happened on the way to conviction: The pretrial interrogation of child witnesses. *Arizona Law Review, 35,* 927.

Moore, T., Pepler, D., Mae, R., & Kates, M. (1989). Effects of family violence on children: New directions for research and intervention. In B. Pressman, G. Cameron, & M. Rothery (Eds.), *Intervening with assaulted women: Current theory, research, and practice.* Hillsdale, NJ: Lawrence Erlbaum.

Morency, N. L., & Krauss, R. M. (1982). The nonverbal encoding and decoding of affect in first and fifth graders. In R. S. Feldman (Ed.), *Development of nonverbal behavioral skill.* New York: Springer-Verlag.

Morganthau, T., Springen, K., Smith, V. E., Rosenberg, D., Beals, G., Bogert, C., Gegax, T. T., & Joseph, N. (1994, December 12). The orphanage. *Newsweek, 124,* 28-32.

Morrison, J. (1989). Childhood sexual histories of women with somatization disorder. *American Journal of Psychiatry, 146,* 239-241.

Morrow, K. B. (1991). Attributions of female adolescent incest victims regarding their molestation. *Child Abuse & Neglect, 15,* 477-482.

Mulhern, S. (1991). Satanism and psychotherapy: A rumor in search of an inquisition. In J. Richardson, J. Best, & D. Bromley (Eds.), *The satanism scare* (pp. 145-174). New York: Aldine de Gruyter.

Mulhern, S. (1994). Satanism, ritual abuse, and multiple personality disorder: A sociohistorical perspective. *International Journal of Clinical and Experimental Hypnosis, 42*(4), 265-288.

Munkel, W. I. (1994). Neglect and abandonment. In A. E. Brodeur & J. A. Monteleone (Eds.), *Child maltreatment: A clinical guide and reference* (pp. 241-257). St. Louis, MO: Medical Publishing.

Murphy-Berman, V., Levesque, H. L., & Berman, J. J. (1996). U.N. Convention on the Rights of the Child: A cross-cultural view. *American Psychologist, 51,* 1257-1261.

Murrin, M. R., & Laws, D. R. (1990). The influence of pornography on sexual crimes. In W. L. Marshall, D. R. Laws, & H. E. Barbaree (Eds.), *Handbook of sexual assault: Issues, theories, and treatment of the offender* (pp. 73-91). New York: Plenum.

Mydans, S. (1994, June 3). Prosecutors are rebuked on child sex abuse case. *New York Times,* p. A7.

Myers, J. E. B. (1992). *Evidence in child abuse and neglect cases.* New York: John Wiley.

Myers, J. E. B. (1993). Commentary: A call for forensically relevant research. *Child Abuse & Neglect, 17,* 573-579.

Myers, J. E. B. (1994). Adjudication of child sexual abuse cases. *Future of Children, 4*(2), 84-101.

Myers, J. E. B., & Peters, W. D. (1987). *Child abuse reporting and legislation in the 1980s.* Denver, CO: American Humane Association.

Nadon, S. M., Koverola, C., & Schludermann, E. H. (1998). Antecedents to prostitution: Childhood victimization. *Journal of Interpersonal Violence, 13*(2), 206-221.

Nasjleti, M. (1980). Suffering in silence: The male incest victim. *Child Welfare, 59,* 269-275.

National Center for Prosecution of Child Abuse. (1993). *Legislation requiring sex offenders to register with a government agency.* Alexandria, VA: Author.

National Center on Child Abuse and Neglect. (1978). *Child sexual abuse: Incest, assault, and sexual exploitation: A special report.* Washington, DC: Author.

National Center on Child Abuse and Neglect. (1993). *A report on the maltreatment of children with disabilities.* Washington, DC: Department of Health and Human Services.

National Child Protection Act of 1993, Pub. L. No. 103-209.

National Clearinghouse on Child Abuse and Neglect Information. (1992). *Reporting drug-exposed infants.* Fairfax, VA: Caliber Associates.

National Clearinghouse on Child Abuse and Neglect Information. (1998a, February 19). *Administration for Children and Families: Principles for implementing the Adoption and Safe Families Act of 1997* [Online]. Available: http://www.calib.com/nccanch/asfa.html

National Clearinghouse on Child Abuse and Neglect Information. (1998b, October 19). *NCCAN lessons learned: The experience of nine child abuse and neglect prevention programs* [Online]. Available: http://www.calib.com/nccancn/pubs/lessons/prevcomp.html

Nelson, K. (1994). Innovative service models in social services. *Journal of Clinical Child Psychology, 23,* 26-31.

Nelson, K., Saunders, E., & Landsman, M. J. (1990). *Chronic neglect in perspective: A study of chronically neglecting families in a large metropolitan county.* Oakdale: National Resource Center on Family Based Services, University of Iowa School of Social Work.

Neumann, D. A., Houskamp, B. M., Pollock, V. E., & Briere, J. (1996). The long-term sequelae of childhood sexual abuse in women: A meta-analytic review. *Child Maltreatment, 1*(1), 6-16.

Ney, P. G. (1989). Child mistreatment: Possible reasons for its transgenerational transmission. *Canadian Journal of Psychiatry, 34,* 594-601.

Ney, P. G., Fung, T., & Wickett, A. R. (1994). The worst combinations of child abuse and neglect. *Child Abuse & Neglect, 18,* 705-714.

Nuttall, R., & Jackson, H. (1994). Personal history of childhood abuse among clinicians. *Child Abuse & Neglect, 18,* 455-472.

Oates, R. K., & Bross, D. C. (1995). What have we learned about treating child physical abuse? A literature review of the last decade. *Child Abuse & Neglect, 19,* 463-474.

O'Brien, M. (1991). Taking sibling incest seriously. In M. Patton (Ed.), *Family sexual abuse: Frontline research and evaluation* (pp. 75-92). Newbury Park, CA: Sage.

O'Brien, M., John, R. S., Margolin, G., & Erel, O. (1994). Reliability and diagnostic efficacy of parents' reports regarding children's exposure to marital aggression. *Violence and Victims, 9,* 45-62.

Office of Juvenile Justice and Delinquency Prevention. (1995). *OJJDP fact sheet* (No. 21). Rockville, MD: Juvenile Justice Clearing House.

O'Hagan, K. (1993). *Emotional and psychological abuse of children.* Toronto, Ontario, Canada: University of Toronto Press.

O'Hagan, K. (1995). Emotional and psychological abuse: Problems of definition. *Child Abuse & Neglect, 19,* 449-461.

Ohlin, L., & Tonry, M. (1989). Family violence in perspective. In L. Ohlin & M. Tonry (Eds.), *Violence in marriage* (pp. 1-18). Chicago: University of Chicago Press.

O'Keefe, M. (1994a). Adjustment of children from maritally violent homes. *Families in Society, 75,* 403-415.

O'Keefe, M. (1994b). Linking marital violence, mother-child/father-child aggression, and child behavior problems. *Journal of Family Violence, 9,* 63-78.

O'Keefe, M. (1995). Predictors of child abuse in maritally violent families. *Journal of Interpersonal Violence, 10*(1), 3-25.

Olds, D. (1997). The prenatal early infancy project: Preventing child abuse and neglect in the context of promoting maternal and child health. In D. A. Wolfe, R. J. McMahon, & R. D. Peters (Eds.), *Child abuse: New directions in prevention and treatment across the lifespan* (pp. 130-154). Thousand Oaks, CA: Sage.

Olds, D. L., Henderson, C. R., Tatelbaum, R., & Chamberlain, R. (1986). Preventing child abuse and neglect: A randomized trial of nurse home visitation. *Pediatrics, 78,* 65-68.

Osmond, M., Durham, D., Leggett, A., & Keating, J. (1998). *Treating the aftermath of sexual abuse: A handbook for working with children in care.* Washington, DC: Child Welfare League of America.

Osofsky, J. D. (1995). The effects of violence exposure on young children. *American Psychologist, 50,* 782-788.

Osofsky, J. D. (1998). Children as invisible victims of domestic and community violence. In G. W. Holden, R. Geffner, & E. N. Jouriles (Eds.), *Children exposed to marital violence* (pp. 95-117). Washington, DC: American Psychological Association.

Osofsky, J. D., Wewers, S., Hann, D., & Fick, A. (1993). Chronic community violence: What is happening to our children? *Psychiatry, 56,* 36-45.

Osofsky, J. D. (Ed.). (1997). *Children in a violent society.* New York: Guilford.

Otto, R. K., & Melton, G. B. (1990). Trends in legislation and case law on child abuse and neglect. In R. T. Ammerman & M. Hersen (Eds.), *Children at risk: An evaluation of factors contributing to child abuse and neglect* (pp. 55-83). New York: Plenum.

Overholser, J. C., & Beck, S. J. (1989). The classification of rapists and child molesters. *Journal of Offender Counseling, Services & Rehabilitation, 13,* 15-25.

Pagelow, M. (1984). *Family violence.* New York: Praeger.

Paget, K. D., Philp, J. D., & Abramczyk, L. W. (1993). Recent developments in child neglect. In T. H. Ollendick & R. J. Prinz (Eds.), *Advances in clinical child psychology* (Vol. 15, pp. 121-174). New York: Plenum.

Parish, R. A., Myers, P. A., Brandner, A., & Templin, K. H. (1985). Developmental milestones in abused children, and their improvement with a family-oriented approach to the treatment of child abuse. *Child Abuse & Neglect, 9,* 245-250.

Parke, R. D., & Collmer, C. W. (1975). Child abuse: An interdisciplinary analysis. In E. M. Hetherington (Ed.), *Review of child development research* (Vol. 5, pp. 509-590). Chicago: University of Chicago Press.

Passantino, G., Passantino, B., & Trott, J. (1990). Satan's sideshow. *Cornerstone, 90,* 24-28.

Paveza, G. J. (1988). Risk factors in father-daughter child sexual abuse: A case-control study. *Journal of Interpersonal Violence, 3,* 290-306.

Pearl, P. S. (1994). Emotional abuse. In A. E. Brodeur & J. A. Monteleone (Eds.), *Child maltreatment: A clinical guide and reference* (pp. 259-283). St. Louis, MO: Medical Publishing.

Peled, E., & Davis, D. (1995). *Groupwork with children: A practitioner's manual.* Thousand Oaks, CA: Sage.

Peled, E., & Edleson, J. L. (1992). Multiple perspectives on groupwork with children of battered women. *Violence and Victims, 7,* 327-346.

Peled, E., Jaffe, P. J., & Edleson, J. L. (1994). *Ending the cycle of violence: Community response to children of battered women.* Thousand Oaks, CA: Sage.

Pelton, L. H. (1994). The role of material factors in child abuse and neglect. In G. B. Melton & F. D. Barry (Eds.), *Protecting children from abuse and neglect* (pp. 166-181). New York: Guilford.

Pemberton, D. A., & Benady, D. R. (1973). Consciously rejected children. *British Journal of Psychiatry, 123,* 575-578.

Pence, D., & Wilson, C. (1994). *Team investigation of child sexual abuse: Uneasy alliance.* Thousand Oaks, CA: Sage.

Perry, N., & McAuliff, B. (1993). The use of videotaped child testimony: Public policy implications. *Notre Dame Journal of Law, Ethics, and Public Policy, 7,* 387.

Perry, N. W. (1992). How children remember and why they forget. *The APSAC Advisor, 5,* 1-2, 13-16.

Peters, D., & Range, L. (1995). Childhood sexual abuse and current suicidality in college women and men. *Child Abuse & Neglect, 19,* 335-341.

Peters, J., Dinsmore, J., & Toth, P. (1989). Why prosecute child abuse? *South Dakota Law Review, 34,* 649-659.

Peters, J. M. (1989). Criminal prosecution of child abuse: Recent trends. *Pediatric Annals, 18,* 505-509.

Pfohl, S. J. (1977, February). The "discovery" of child abuse. *Social Problems, 24*(9), 310-323.

Pfouts, J. H., Schopler, J. H., & Henley, C. H. (1982). Forgotten victims of family violence. *Social Work, 27,* 367-368.

Pianta, R., Egeland, B., & Erickson, M. F. (1989). The antecedents of maltreatment: Results of the Mother-Child Interaction Research Project. In D. Cicchetti & V. Carlson (Eds.), *Child maltreatment: Theory and research on the causes and consequences of child abuse and neglect* (pp. 203-253). New York: Cambridge University Press.

Pierce, R. L. (1984). Child pornography: A hidden dimension of child abuse. *Child Abuse & Neglect, 8,* 483-493.

Piers, M. W. (1978). *Infanticide: Past and present.* New York: Norton.

Pithers, W., & Kafka, M. (1990). Relapse prevention with sex aggressors: A method for maintaining therapeutic gain and enhancing external supervision. In W. L. Marshall, D. R. Laws, & H. E. Barbaree (Eds.), *Handbook of sexual assault: Issues, theories, and treatment of the offender* (pp. 343-361). New York: Plenum.

Pittman, F. (1987). *Turning points: Treating families in transition and crisis.* New York: Norton.

Pleck, E. (1987). *Domestic tyranny: The making of American sound policy against family violence from colonial times to present.* New York: Oxford University Press.

Plotkin, R. C., Azar, C. S., Twentyman, C. T., & Perri, M. G. (1981). A critical evaluation of the research methodology employed in the investigation of causative factors of child abuse and neglect. *Child Abuse & Neglect, 5,* 449-455.

Polansky, N. A., Ammons, P. W., & Gaudin, J. M. (1985, January). Loneliness and isolation in child neglect. *Social Casework: The Journal of Contemporary Social Work, 66,* 38-47.

Polansky, N. A., Ammons, P. W., & Weathersby, B. L. (1983, September-October). Is there an American standard of child care? *Social Work, 28,* 341-346.

Polansky, N. A., Chalmers, M. A., & Williams, D. P. (1987). Assessing adequacy of rearing: An urban scale. *Child Welfare, 57,* 439-448.

Polansky, N. A., Gaudin, J. M., Ammons, P. W., & Davis, K. B. (1985). The psychological ecology of the neglectful mother. *Child Abuse & Neglect, 9,* 265-275.

Polansky, N. A., & Williams, D. P. (1978). Class orientation to child neglect. *Social Work, 23,* 397-401.

Porch, T. L., & Petretic-Jackson, P. A. (1986, August). Child sexual assault prevention: *Evaluating parent education workshops.* Paper presented at the convention of the American Psychological Association, Washington, DC.

Powers, J. L., & Eckenrode, J. (1988). The maltreatment of adolescents. *Child Abuse & Neglect, 12,* 189-199.

Powers, J. L., Eckenrode, J., & Jaklitsch, B. (1990). Maltreatment among runaway and homeless youth. *Child Abuse & Neglect, 14,* 87-98.

Prendergast, W. E. (1979). The sex offender: How to spot him before it is too late. *Sexology,* 46-51.

Prino, C. T., & Peyrot, M. (1994). The effect of child physical abuse and neglect on aggressive, withdrawn, and prosocial behavior. *Child Abuse & Neglect, 18,* 871-884.

Protection of Children Against Sexual Exploitation Act of 1978, Pub. L. No. 95-225.

Putnam, F. W. (1991). The satanic ritual abuse controversy. *Child Abuse & Neglect, 15,* 175-179.

Putnam, F. W., Helmers, K., & Trickett, P. K. (1993). Development, reliability, and validation of a child dissociation scale. *Child Abuse & Neglect, 17,* 731-740.

Pynoos, R. S., Frederick, C., Nader, K., & Arroyo, W. (1987). Life threat and posttraumatic stress in school-age children. *Archives of General Psychiatry, 44,* 1057-1063.

Quinsey, V. L., Chaplin, T. C., & Carrigan, W. F. (1979). Sexual preferences among incestuous and nonincestuous child molesters. *Behavior Therapy, 10,* 562-565.

Quinsey, V. L., Harris, G. T., Rice, M. E., & Lalumiere, M. L. (1993). Assessing treatment efficacy in outcome studies of sex offenders. *Journal of Interpersonal Violence, 8,* 512-523.

Quittner, A. L., & Opipari, L. C. (1994). Differential treatment of siblings: Interview and diary analyses comparing two family contexts. *Child Development, 65,* 800-814.

Rabb, J., & Rindfleisch, N. (1985). A study to define and assess severity of institutional abuse/neglect. *Child Abuse & Neglect, 9,* 285-294.

Rabinowitz, D. (1990, May). From the mouths of babes to a jail cell: Child abuse and the abuse of justice: A case study. *Harper's Magazine, 280,* 52-63.

Randolf, M. K., & Conkle, L. K. (1993). Behavioral and emotional characteristics of children who witness parental violence. *Family Violence and Sexual Assault Bulletin, 9*(2), 23-27.

Ray, K. C., Jackson, J. L., & Townsley, R. M. (1991). Family environments of victims of intrafamilial and extrafamilial child sexual abuse. *Journal of Family Violence, 6,* 365-374.

Regehr, C. (1990). Parental responses to extrafamilial child sexual assault. *Child Abuse & Neglect, 14,* 113-120.

Reno, J. (1994). Foreword. *The APSAC Advisor, 7*(4), 1.

Reppucci, N. D., Land, D., & Haugaard, J. J. (1998). Child sexual abuse prevention programs that target young children. In P. K. Trickett & C. J. Schellenbach (Eds.), *Violence against children in the family and the community* (pp. 317-337). Washington, DC: American Psychological Association.

Reuterman, N. A., & Burcky, W. D. (1989). Dating violence in high school: A profile of the victims. *Psychology: A Journal of Human Behavior, 26,* 1-9.

Rew, L., & Esparza, D. (1990). Barriers to disclosure among sexually abused male children. *Journal of Child and Adolescent Psychiatric and Mental Health Nursing, 3,* 120-127.

Rice, F. P. (1995). *Human development: A lifespan approach.* Englewood Cliffs, NJ: Prentice Hall.

Rice, F. P. (1998). *Human development: A lifespan approach* (3rd ed.). Upper Saddle River, NJ: Prentice Hall.

Richardson, J., Best, J., & Bromley, D. (Eds.). (1991). *The satanism scare.* New York: Aldine de Gruyter.

Richters, J. E., & Martinez, P. (1990). *Things I have seen and heard: A structured interview for assessing young children's violence exposure.* Rockville, MD: National Institute of Mental Health.

Richters, J. E., & Martinez, P. (1993a). The NIMH Community Violence Project: Children as victims and witnesses to violence. In D. Reiss, J. E. Richters, M. Radke-Yarrow, & D. Scharf (Eds.), *Children and violence* (pp. 7-21). New York: Guilford.

Richters, J. E., & Martinez, P. (1993b). Violent communities, family choices, and children's chances: An algorithm for improving the odds. *Development and Psychopathology, 5,* 609-627.

Richters, J. E., & Saltzman, W. (1990). *Survey of children's exposure to community violence: Parent report.* Rockville, MD: National Institute of Mental Health.

Riggs, D. S., O'Leary, K. D., & Breslin, F. C. (1990). Multiple correlates of physical aggression in dating couples. *Journal of Interpersonal Violence, 5,* 61-73.

Riley, N. E. (1996, February). China's "missing girls": Prospects and policy. *Population Today* [Online], 24(2), 4. Available: http://-proquest.umi.com

Rindfleisch, N., & Nunno, M. (1992). Progress and issues in the implementation of the 1984 out-of-home care protection amendment. *Child Abuse & Neglect, 16,* 693-708.

Roberts, R. N., Wasik, B. H., Casto, G., & Ramey, C. T. (1991). Family support in the home: Programs, policy, and social change. *American Psychologist, 46,* 131-137.

Rohrbeck, C. A., & Twentyman, C. T. (1986). Multimodal assessment of impulsiveness in abusing, neglecting, and nonmaltreating mothers and their preschool children. *Journal of Consulting and Clinical Psychology, 54,* 231-236.

Romer, S. (1990). Child sexual abuse in custody and visitation disputes: Problems, progress, and prospects. *Golden Gate University Law Review, 20,* 647-680.

Romero, J., & Williams, L. (1995). Recidivism among convicted sex offenders: A 10-year follow-up study. *Federal Probation, 49*(1), 58-64.

Roscoe, B., Goodwin, M. P., & Kennedy, D. (1987). Sibling violence and agonistic interactions experienced by early adolescents. *Journal of Family Violence, 2*(2), 121-137.

Rosenbaum, A. (1988). Methodological issues in marital violence research. *Journal of Family Violence, 3,* 91-104.

Rosenbaum, A., & O'Leary, K. D. (1981). Marital violence: Characteristics of abusive couples. *Journal of Consulting and Clinical Psychology, 49,* 63-76.

Rosenberg, D. A. (1987). Web of deceit: A literature review of Munchausen syndrome by proxy. *Child Abuse & Neglect, 11,* 547-563.

Rosenberg, M. S. (1987). Children of battered women: The effects of witnessing violence on their social problem-solving abilities. *Behavior Therapies, 10,* 85-89.

Rosenfeld, A. A., Bailey, R., Siegel, B., & Bailey, G. (1986). Determining incestuous contact between parent and child: Frequency of children touching parents' genitals in a nonclinical population. *Journal of the American Academy of Child Psychiatry, 25,* 481-484.

Rosenfeld, A. A., Siegel, B., & Bailey, R. (1987). Familial bathing patterns: Implications for cases of alleged molestation and for pediatric practice. *Pediatrics, 79,* 224-229.

Rosenfield-Schlichter, M. D., Sarber, R. E., Bueno, G., Greene, B. F., & Lutzker, J. R. (1983). Maintaining accountability for an ecobehavioral treatment for one aspect of child neglect: Personal cleanliness. *Education and Treatment of Children, 6,* 153-164.

Rosenthal, J. A., Motz, J. K., Edmonson, D. A., & Groze, V. (1991). A descriptive study of abuse and neglect in out-of-home placement. *Child Abuse & Neglect, 15,* 249-260.

Rosenthal, P. A., & Doherty, M. B. (1984). Serious sibling abuse by preschool children. *Journal of the American Academy of Child Psychiatry, 23*(2), 186-190.

Rossman, B. B. R. (1994). Children in violent families: Current diagnostic and treatment considerations. *Family Violence and Sexual Assault Bulletin, 10*(3-4), 29-34.

Rossman, B. B. R., Bingham, R. D., Cimbora, D. M., Dickerson, L. K., Dexter, R. M., Balog, S. A., & Mallah, K. (1993, August). *Relationships of trauma severity to trauma symptoms for child witnesses.* Paper presented at the annual meeting of the American Psychological Association, Toronto, Ontario, Canada.

Roth, S., & Newman, E. (1991). The process of coping with sexual trauma. *Journal of Traumatic Stress, 4,* 279-297.

Rudin, M. M., Zalewski, C., & Bodmer-Turner, J. (1995). Characteristics of child sexual abuse victims according to perpetrator gender. *Child Abuse & Neglect, 19,* 963-973.

Runyan, D. K., Hunter, W. M., & Everson, M. D. (1992). *Maternal support for child victims of sexual abuse: Determinants and implications* (Final report [Grant No. 90-CA-1368]). Washington, DC: National Center on Child Abuse and Neglect.

Rush, F. (1980). *The best kept secret: Sexual abuse of children.* Englewood Cliffs, NJ: Prentice Hall.

Russell, D. E. (1983). The incidence and prevalence of intrafamilial and extrafamilial sexual abuse of female children. *Child Abuse & Neglect, 7,* 133-146.

Russell, D. E. H. (1988). Pornography and rape: A causal model. *Political Psychology, 9,* 41-73.

Rust, J. O., & Troupe, P. A. (1991). Relationships of treatment of child sexual abuse with school achievement and self-concept. *Journal of Early Adolescence, 11,* 420-429.

Rutter, M., & Giller, H. (1983). *Juvenile delinquency: Trends and perspectives.* New York: McGraw-Hill.

Ryan, G., & Lane, S. (Eds.). (1991). *Juvenile sexual offending.* Lexington, MA: Lexington Books.

Sacramento Police Department, Sacramento, CA. (1998, October 20). *Protecting yourself and your family* [Online]. Available: http://sacpd.org/dojmegan.html

Salter, A. C. (1988). *Treating child sex offenders and victims: A practical guide.* Newbury Park, CA; Sage.

Salzinger, S., Feldman, R. S., Hammer, M., & Rosario, M. (1993). The effects of physical abuse on children's relationships. *Child Development, 64,* 169-187.

Salzinger, S., Kaplan, S., Pelcovitz, D., Samit, C., & Krieger, R. (1984). Parent and teacher assessment of children's behavior in child maltreating families. *Journal of the American Academy of Child Psychiatry, 23,* 459-464.

Santana, A. (1998, March 15). Imprisoned Letourneau is pregnant. *Seattle Times* [Online]. Available: http://www.seattletimes.com

Saradjian, J. (1996). *Women who sexually abuse children: From research to clinical practice.* Chichester, UK: Wiley.

Sarber, R. E., Halasz, M. M., Messmer, M. C., Bickett, A. D., & Lutzker, J. R. (1983). Teaching menu planning and grocery shopping to a mentally retarded mother. *Mental Retardation, 21,* 101-106.

Sariola, H., & Uutela, A. (1994). The prevalence and context of child sexual abuse in Finland. *Child Abuse & Neglect, 18,* 827-835.

Saunders, B. E., Villeponteaux, L. A., Lipovsky, J. A., & Kilpatrick, D. G. (1992). Child sexual assault as a risk factor for mental disorder among women: A community survey. *Journal of Interpersonal Violence, 7,* 189-204.

Saunders, D. G. (1994). Posttraumatic stress symptom profiles of battered women: A comparison of survivors in two settings. *Violence and Victims, 9,* 31-44.

Saywitz, K., Goodman, G. S., Nicholas, E., & Moan, S. F. (1991). Children's memories of a physical examination involving genital touch: Implications for reports of child sexual abuse. *Journal of Consulting and Clinical Psychology, 59,* 682-691.

Saywitz, K., & Nathanson, R. (1993). Children's testimony and their perceptions of stress in and out of the courtroom. *Child Abuse & Neglect, 17,* 613-622.

Saywitz, K., & Snyder, L. (1993). Improving children's testimony with preparation. In G. S. Goodman & B. L. Bottoms (Eds.), *Child victims, child witnesses: Understanding and improving testimony* (pp. 117-146). New York: Guilford.

Scavo, R. R. (1989, February). Female adolescent sex offenders: A neglected treatment group. *Social Casework: The Journal of Contemporary Social Work, 70,* 114-117.

Schellenbach, C. J. (1998). Child maltreatment: A critical review of research on treatment for physically abusive parents. In P. K. Trickett & C. J. Schellenbach (Eds.), *Violence against children in the family and the community* (pp. 251-268). Washington, DC: American Psychological Association.

Schene, P. (1996). Child abuse and neglect policy: History, models, and future directions. In J. Briere, L. Berliner, J. A. Bulkley, C. Jenny, & T. Reid (Eds.), *The APSAC handbook on child maltreatment* (pp. 385-397). Thousand Oaks, CA: Sage.

Schetky, D. H., & Green, A. H. (1988). *Child sexual abuse: A handbook for health care and legal professionals.* New York: Brunner/Mazel.

Schmitt, B. D. (1987). The child with nonaccidental trauma. In R. Helfer & R. Kempe (Eds.), *The battered child* (4th ed., pp. 178-196). Chicago: University of Chicago Press.

Schwartz, I. M., AuClaire, P., & Harris, L. J. (1991). Family preservation services as an alternative to out-of-home placement of adolescents. In K. Wells & D. E. Biegel (Eds.), *Family preservation services: Research and evaluation* (pp. 33-46). Newbury Park, CA: Sage.

Sedlak, A. J. (1990). *Technical amendment to the study findings: National incidence and prevalence of child abuse and neglect: 1988.* Rockville, MD: Westat.

Sedlak, A. J. (1991). *National incidence and prevalence of child abuse and neglect: 1988: Revised report.* Rockville, MD: Westat.

Sedlak, A. J., & Broadhurst, D. D. (1996). *Third national incidence study on child abuse and neglect.* Washington, DC: U.S. Department of Health and Human Services.

Segal, Z. V., & Stermac, L. E. (1990). The role of cognition in sexual assault. In W. L. Marshall, D. R. Laws, & H. E. Barbaree (Eds.), *Handbook of sexual assault: Issues, theories, and treatment of the offender* (pp. 161-174). New York: Plenum.

Seidman, B. T., Marshall, W. L., Hudson, S. M., & Robertson, P. J. (1994). An examination of intimacy and loneliness in sex offenders. *Journal of Interpersonal Violence, 9,* 518-534.

Semel, E. (1997, October). Counterpoint: Megan's law is a knee-jerk reaction to a senseless personal tragedy. *Corrections Today* [Online], *59*(6), 21. Available: http://proquest.umi.com

Sgroi, S. M. (1982). Family treatment of child sexual abuse. *Journal of Social Work and Human Sexuality, 1,* 109-128.

Shakeshaft, C., & Cohan, A. (1995, March). Sexual abuse of students by school personnel. *Phi Delta Kappan* [Online], *76*(7), 512. Available: *http://proquest.umi.com*

Shakoor, B. H., & Chalmers, D. (1991). Co-victimization of African American children who witness violence and the theoretical implications of its effects on their cognitive, emotional, and behavioral development. *Journal of the National Medical Association, 83,* 233-238.

Sheppard, J. (1997, November). Double punishment? *American Journalism Review* [Online], *19*(9), 36-41. Available: http://proquest. umi. com

Shields, N. M., McCall, G., & Hanneke, C. R. (1988). Patterns of family and nonfamily violence: Violent husbands and violent men. *Violence and Victims, 3,* 83-97.

Siegel, J. M., Sorenson, S. B., Golding, J. M., Burnam, M. A., & Stein, J. A. (1987). The prevalence of childhood sexual assault: The Los Angeles Epidemiologic Catchment Area Project. *American Journal of Epidemiology, 126,* 1141-1153.

Siegel, L. J. (1995). *Criminology.* St. Paul, MN: West.

Silbert, M. (1982). Prostitution and sexual assault: Summary of results. *International Journal for Biosocial Research, 3,* 69-71.

Silbert, M., & Pines, A. M. (1983). Early sexual exploitation as an influence in prostitution. *Social Work, 28,* 285-289.

Silvern, L., & Kaersvang, L. (1989). The traumatized children of violent marriages. *Child Welfare, 68,* 421-436.

Silvern, L., Karyl, J., & Landis, T. Y. (1995). Individual psychotherapy for the traumatized children of abused women. In E. Peled, P. G. Jaffe, & J. L. Edelson (Eds.), *Ending the cycle of violence: Community responses to children of battered women* (pp. 43-76). Thousand Oaks, CA: Sage.

Silvern, L., Karyl, J., Waelde, L., Hodges, W. F., Starek, J., Heidt, E., & Min, K. (1995). Retrospective reports of parental partner abuse: Relationships to depression, trauma symptoms and self-esteem among college students. *Journal of Family Violence, 10,* 177-202.

Simons, R. L., Whitbeck, L. B., Conger, R. D., & Chyi-In, W. (1991). Intergenerational transmission of harsh parenting. *Developmental Psychology, 27,* 159-171.

Sirles, E. A., & Franke, P. J. (1989). Factors influencing mothers' reactions to intrafamily sexual abuse. *Child Abuse & Neglect, 13,* 131-139.

Smith, B., Hillenbrand, S., & Govestsky, S. (1990). *The problem response to child sexual abuse offender: How is it working?* Chicago: American Bar Association.

Smith, H., & Israel, E. (1987). Sibling incest: A study of the dynamics of 25 cases. *Child Abuse & Neglect, 11,* 101-108.

Smith, M., & Pazder, L. (1980). *Michelle remembers.* New York: Crongdon & Lattes.

Smith, S. (1975). *The battered child syndrome.* London: Butterworths.

Smith, S. M., Hanson, R., & Noble, S. (1974). Social aspects of the battered baby syndrome. *British Journal of Psychiatry, 125,* 568-582.

Smith, W. L. (1994). Abusive head injury. *The APSAC Advisor, 7*(4), 16-19.

Smith, W. R. (1988). Delinquency and abuse among juvenile sexual offenders. *Journal of Interpersonal Violence, 3,* 400-413.

Smolowe, J. (1995, December 11). Making the tough calls. *Time, 146,* 40-44.

Snow, B., & Sorenson, T. (1990). Ritualistic child abuse in a neighborhood setting. *Journal of Interpersonal Violence, 5*(4), 474-487.

Sokol, R., & Clarren, S. K. (1989). Guidelines for use of terminology describing the impact of prenatal alcohol on the offspring. *Alcoholism: Clinical and Experimental Research, 13,* 597-598.

Sovinski, C. J. (1997). The criminalization of maternal substance abuse: A quick fix to a complex problem. *Pepperdine Law Review, 25*(1), 107-139.

Spaccarelli, S., Sandler, I. N., & Roosa, M. (1994). History of spouse violence against mother: Correlated risks and unique effects in child mental health. *Journal of Family Violence, 9,* 79-98.

Spector, M., & Kitsuse, J. I. (1977). *Constructing social problems.* Menlo Park, CA: Benjamin Cummings.

Spencer, J. W., & Knudsen, D. D. (1992). Out-of-home maltreatment: An analysis of risk in various settings for children. *Children and Youth Services Review, 14,* 485-492.

Spitz, R. A. (1945). Hospitalism. *Psychoanalytic Study of the Child, 1,* 53-74.

Springs, F. E., & Friedrich, W. N. (1992). Health risk behaviors and medical sequelae of childhood sexual abuse. *Mayo Clinic Proceedings, 67,* 527-532.

Stagg, V., Wills, G. D., & Howell, M. (1989). Psychopathology in early childhood witness of family violence. *Topics in Early Childhood Special Education, 9,* 73-87.

Starr, R. H., Jr. (1982). A research-based approach to the prediction of child abuse. In R. H. Starr, Jr. (Ed.), *Child abuse prediction: Policy implications* (pp. 105-134). Cambridge, MA: Ballinger.

State of Oregon Children's Services Division. (1991). *Mental injury: The hidden hurt* [Brochure]. Salem: Author.

Steele, B. F., & Alexander, H. (1981). Long-term effects of sexual abuse in childhood. In P. B. Mrazek & C. H. Kempe (Eds.), *Sexually abused children and their families* (pp. 223-233). New York: Pergamon.

Steele, B. J., & Pollock, C. (1968). A psychiatric study of parents who abuse infants and small children. In R. Helfer & C. H. Kempe (Eds.), *The battered child* (pp. 89-133). Chicago: University of Chicago Press.

Steiger, H., & Zanko, M. (1990). Sexual traumata among eating disordered, psychiatric, and normal female groups: Comparison of prevalence and defense styles. *Journal of Interpersonal Violence, 5,* 74-86.

Stein, T. J. (1993). Legal perspectives on family violence against children. In R. L. Hampton, T. P. Gullotta, G. R. Adams, E. H. Potter, III, & R. P. Weissberg (Eds.), *Family violence: Prevention and treatment* (pp. 179-197). Newbury Park, CA: Sage.

Steinmetz, S. K. (1982). A cross-cultural comparison of sibling violence. *International Journal of Family Psychiatry, 2,* 337-351.

Steinmetz, S. K. (1987). Family violence: Past, present, and future. In M. B. Sussman & S. K. Steinmetz (Eds.), *Handbook of marriage and the family* (pp. 725-765). New York: Plenum.

Stermac, L., Hall, K., & Henskens, M. (1989). Violence among child molesters. *Journal of Sex Research, 26,* 450-459.

Sternberg, K. J., Lamb, M. E., Greenbaum, C., Cicchetti, D., Dawud, S., Cortes, R. M., Krispin, O., & Lorey, F. (1993). Effects of domestic violence on children's behavior problems and depression. *Developmental Psychology, 29,* 44-52.

Sternberg, K. J., Lamb, M. E., Greenbaum, C., Dawud, S., & Cortes, R. M. (1994). The effects of domestic violence on children's perceptions of their perpetrating and non-perpetrating parents. *International Journal of Behavioral Development, 17*(4), 779-795.

Stouthamer-Loeber, M., van Kammen, W., & Loeber, R. (1992). Researchers' forum: The nuts and bolts of implementing large-scale longitudinal studies. *Violence and Victims, 7,* 63-78.

Stratford, L. (1988). *Satan's underground.* Eugene, OR: Harvest House.

Straus, M. A. (1977). Societal morphogenesis and intrafamily violence in cross-cultural perspective. *Annals of the New York Academy of Sciences, 285,* 717-730.

Straus, M. A. (1979). Measuring intrafamily conflict and aggression: The Conflict Tactics Scale (CT). *Journal of Marriage and the Family, 41,* 75-88.

Straus, M. A. (1980). Societal stress and marital violence in a national sample of American families. In F. Wright, C. Bahn, & R. W. Rieber (Eds.), *Annals of the New York Academy of Sciences: Vol. 347. Forensic psychology and psychiatry* (pp. 229-250). New York: New York Academy of Sciences.

Straus, M. A. (1983). Ordinary violence, child abuse, and wife beating: What do they have in common? In D. Finkelhor, R. J. Gelles, G. T. Hotaling, & M. A. Straus (Eds.), *The dark side of families* (pp. 213-234). Beverly Hills, CA: Sage.

Straus, M. A. (1991a, September). *Children as witness to marital violence: A risk factor for lifelong problems among a nationally representative sample of American men and women.* Paper presented at the Ross Roundtable on Children and Violence, Washington, DC.

Straus, M. A. (1991b). Conceptualization and measurement of battering: Implications for public policy. In M. Steinman (Ed.), *Woman battering: Policy responses* (pp. 19-47). Cincinnati, OH: Anderson.

Straus, M. A. (1991c). Discipline and deviance: Physical punishment of children and violence and other crime in adulthood. *Social Problems, 38,* 133-154.

Straus, M. A. (1992). Children as witnesses to marital violence: A risk factor for life-long problems among a nationally representative sample of American men and women. In *Children and violence: A report of the Twenty-Third Ross Roundtable on Initial Approaches to Common Paediatric Problems.* Columbus, OH: Ross Laboratories.

Straus, M. A. (1993). Physical assaults by wives: A major social problem. In R. J. Gelles & D. J. Loseke (Eds.), *Current controversies on family violence* (pp. 67-87). Newbury Park, CA: Sage.

Straus, M. A. (1994a). *Beating the devil out of them: Corporal punishment in American families.* New York: Lexington Books.

Straus, M. A. (1994b). Should the use of corporal punishment by parents be considered child abuse? In M. A. Mason & E. Gambrill (Eds.), *Debating children's lives: Current controversies on children and adolescents* (pp. 197-203). Thousand Oaks, CA: Sage.

Straus, M. A., Gelles, R. J., & Steinmetz, S. K. (1980). *Behind closed doors: Violence in the American family.* Garden City, NY: Doubleday.

Straus, M. A., & Hamby, S. L. (1997). Measuring physical and psychological maltreatment of children with the conflict tactics scales. In G. K. Kantor & J. L. Jasinski (Eds.), *Out of the darkness: Contemporary perspectives on family violence* (pp. 119-135). Thousand Oaks, CA: Sage.

Straus, M. A., Hamby, S. L., Finkelhor, D., Moore, D. W., & Runyan, D. (1998). Identification of child maltreatment with the parent-child conflict tactics scales: Development and psychometric data for a national sample of American parents. *Child Abuse and Neglect, 22,* 249-270.

Straus, M. A., & Mathur, A. K. (1996). Social change and the trends in approval of corporal punishment by parents from 1968 to 1994. In D. Frehsee, W. Horn, & K.-D. Bussmann (Eds.), *Family violence against children: A challenge for society* (pp. 91-105). New York: Walter de Gruyter.

Straus, M. A., & Mouradian, V. E. (in press). Impulsive corporal punishment by mothers and antisocial behavior and impulsiveness of children. *Behavioral Sciences and the Law.*

Straus, M. A., Sugarman, D. B., & Giles-Sims, J. (1997, August). Spanking by parents and subsequent antisocial behavior of children. *Ar-*

chives of Pediatric and Adolescent Medicine, 151, 761-767.

Studer, M. (1984). Wife-beating as a social problem: The process of definition. *International Journal of Women's Studies, 7,* 412-422.

Sturgeon, V. H., & Taylor, J. (1980). Report of a five year follow-up study of mentally disordered sex offenders released from Atascadero State Hospital in 1973. *Criminal Justice Journal, 4,* 41-63.

Suderman, M., & Jaffe, P. (1997). Children and youth who witness violence: New directions in intervention and prevention. In D. A. Wolfe, R. J. McMahon, & R. D. Peters (Eds.), *Child abuse: New directions in prevention and treatment across the lifespan* (pp. 55-78). Thousand Oaks, CA: Sage.

Sudia, C. (1986). Preventing out-of-home placement of children: The first steps to permanency planning. *Children Today, 15*(6), 4-5.

Swett, C., Surrey, J., & Cohen, C. (1990). Sexual and physical abuse histories and psychiatric symptoms among male psychiatric outpatients. *American Journal of Psychiatry, 147,* 632-636.

Terr, L. (1983). Chowchilla revisited: The effects of psychic trauma four years after a school-bus kidnapping. *American Journal of Psychiatry, 140,* 1543-1550.

Terr, L. (1991). Child traumas: An outline and overview. *American Journal of Psychiatry, 50,* 15-19.

Thigpen, S. M., & Bonner, B. L. (1994). Child death review teams in action. *The APSAC Advisor, 7*(4), 5-8.

Thomas, J. N. (1998). Community partnerships: A movement with a mission. *The APSAC Advisor, 11,* 2-3.

Thomas, W. I., & Thomas, D. S. (1928). *The child in America: Behavioral problems and programs.* New York: Knopf.

Timnick, L. (1985, August 25). 22% in survey were child abuse victims. *Los Angeles Times,* p. 1.

Tjaden, P., & Thoennes, N. (1992). Predictors of legal intervention in child maltreatment cases. *Child Abuse & Neglect, 16,* 807-821.

Tolan, P. H., & Guerra, N. (1998). Societal causes of violence against children. In P. K. Trickett & C. J. Schellenbach (Eds.), *Violence against children in the family and the community* (pp. 195-209). Washington DC: American Psychological Association.

Tomkins, A. J., Mohamed, S., Steinman, M., Macolini, R. M., Kenning, M. K., & Afrank, J. (1994). The plight of children who witness woman battering: Psychological knowledge and policy implications. *Law and Psychology Review, 18,* 137-187.

Toufexis, A. (1994, April 11). When is crib death a cover for murder? *TIME Domestic* [Online], *143*(15). Available: http://www.pathfinder.com

Travis, C. (1993, January). Beware the incest-survivor machine. *New York Times,* p. 1.

Trickett, P. K., Aber, J. L., Carlson, V., & Cicchetti, D. (1991). Relationship of socioeconomic status to the etiology and developmental sequelae of physical child abuse. *Developmental Psychology, 27,* 148-158.

Trickett, P. K., & Kuczynski, L. (1986). Children's misbehaviors and parental discipline strategies in abusive and nonabusive families. *Developmental Psychology, 22,* 115-123.

Trickett, P. K., McBride-Chang, C., & Putnam, F. W. (1994). The classroom performance and behavior of sexually abused females. *Development and Psychopathology, 6,* 183-194.

Trickett, P. K., & Putnam, F. W. (1998). Developmental consequences of child sexual abuse. In P. K. Trickett & C. J. Schellenbach (Eds.), *Violence against children in the family and the community* (pp. 39-56). Washington, DC: American Psychological Association.

Truesdell, D. L., McNeil, J. S., & Deschner, J. (1986, March-April). The incidence of wife abuse in incestuous families. *Social Work, 31,* 138-140.

Truscott, D. (1992). Intergenerational transmission of violent behavior in adolescent males. *Aggressive Behavior, 18,* 327-335.

Tuteur, J. M., Ewigman, B. E., Peterson, L., & Hosokawa, M. C. (1995). The maternal observation matrix and Mother-Child Interaction Scale: Brief observational screening instruments for physically abusive mothers. *Journal of Clinical Child Psychology, 24*(1), 55-62.

Twentyman, C. T., & Plotkin, R. C. (1982). Unrealistic expectations of parents who maltreat their children: An educational deficit that pertains to child development. *Journal of Clinical Psychology, 38,* 497-503.

Tyler, R. P., & Stone, L. E. (1985). Child pornography: Perpetuating the sexual victimization of children. *Child Abuse & Neglect, 9,* 313-318.

Underwood, A., & Begley, S. (1998, August 17). Death of the innocents. *Newsweek, 132,* 36.

Urquiza, A. J., & Goodlin-Jones, B. L. (1994). Child sexual abuse and adult revictimization with women of color. *Violence and Victims, 9,* 223-232.

U.N. General Assembly. (1989, November). *Adoption of a convention on the rights of the child* (U.N. Doc. A/Res/44/25). New York: Author.

U.S. Advisory Board on Child Abuse and Neglect. (1990). *First report of the U.S. Advisory Board on Child Abuse and Neglect.* Washington, DC: Department of Health and Human Services and National Council on Child Abuse and Neglect.

U.S. Advisory Board on Child Abuse and Neglect. (1993). *Neighbors helping neighbors: A new national strategy for the protection of children.* Washington, DC: Government Printing Office.

U.S. Bureau of the Census. (1997). *Statistical abstract of the United States* (117th ed.). Washington, DC: U.S. Department of Commerce.

Van Biema, D. (1995, December 11). Abandoned to her fate. *Time, 146*(24), 32-36.

van den Boom, D. C. (1994). The influence of temperament and mothering on attachment and exploration: An experimental manipulation of sensitive responsiveness among lower-class mothers with irritable infants. *Child Development, 65,* 1457-1477.

van den Boom, D. C. (1995). Do first-year intervention effects endure? Follow-up during toddlerhood of a sample of Dutch irritable infants. *Child Development, 66,* 1798-1816.

Vellinga, M. L. (1997, February 2). Crackdown on sex offenders raises tough questions. *Sacramento Bee* [Online]. Available: http://www.sacbee.com

Victor, J. S. (1993). *Satanic panic.* Chicago: Open Court.

Violence in families leads to delinquency, OJJDP study finds. (1995, February). *Criminal Justice Newsletter, 26*(3), 6-7.

Vissing, Y. M., Straus, M. A., Gelles, R. J., & Harrop, J. W. (1991). Verbal aggression by parents and psychosocial problems of children. *Child Abuse & Neglect, 15,* 223-238.

Vondra, J., Barnett, D., & Cicchetti, D. (1990). Self-concept, motivation, and competence among preschoolers from maltreating and comparison families. *Child Abuse & Neglect, 14,* 525-540.

Wagar, J. M., & Rodway, M. R. (1995). An evaluation of a group treatment approach for children who have witnessed wife abuse. *Journal of Family Violence, 10,* 295-306.

Walker, C. E., Bonner, B. L., & Kaufman, K. L. (1988). *The physically and sexually abused child.* New York: Pergamon.

Walker, E., Downey, G., & Bergman, A. (1989). The effects of parental psychopathology and maltreatment on child behavior: A test of the diathesis-stress model. *Child Development, 60,* 15-24.

Walker, L. E. (1977). Battered women and learned helplessness. *Victimology: An International Journal, 2,* 525-534.

Wallen, J., & Rubin, R. H. (1997). The role of the family in mediating the effects of community violence on children. *Aggression and Violent Behavior, 2*(1), 33-41.

Walton, E., Fraser, M. W., Lewis, R. E., & Pecora, P. (1993). In-home family-focused reunification: An experimental study. *Child Welfare, 72,* 473-487.

Wang, C. T., & Daro, D. (1996). *Current trends in child abuse reporting and fatalities: The results of the 1995 annual fifty state survey.* Chicago: National Committee to Prevent Child Abuse.

Wang, C. T., & Daro, D. (1997). *Current trends in child abuse reporting and fatalities: The results of the 1996 annual fifty state survey.* Chicago: National Center on Child Abuse Prevention Research.

Wang, C. T., & Daro, D. (1998). *Current trends in child abuse reporting and fatalities: The results of the 1997 annual fifty state survey.* Chicago: National Center on Child Abuse Prevention Research.

Wasik, B., & Roberts, R. N. (1994). Survey of home visiting programs for abused and neglected children and their families. *Child Abuse & Neglect, 18,* 271-283.

Waterman, J., Kelly, R. J., Oliveri, M. K., & McCord, J. (1993). *Behind the playground walls: Sexual abuse in preschools.* New York: Guilford.

Wauchope, B. A., & Straus, M. A. (1990). Physical punishment and physical abuse of American children: Incidence rates by age, gender, and occupational class. In M. A. Straus & R. J. Gelles (Eds.), *Physical violence in American families: Risk factors and adaptations to violence in 8,145 families* (pp. 133-148). New Brunswick, NJ: Transaction Books.

Weber, T. (1991, April 13). Tearful jurors say they'll never forget horrifying testimony. *Orange County Register,* p. 26.

Wecht, C. H. (1998, January 7). The death of innocents: A true story of murder, medicine, and high-stakes science. *Journal of the American Medical Association* [Online], *279*(1), 85-86. Available: http://proquest.umi.com

Weinberg, S. K. (1955). *Incest behavior.* New York: Citadel.

Weis, J. G. (1989). Family violence research methodology and design. In L. Ohlin & M. Tonry (Eds.), *Family violence* (pp. 117-162). Chicago: University of Chicago Press.

Wekerle, C., & Wolfe, D. A. (1993). Prevention of child abuse and neglect: Promising new directions. *Clinical Psychology Review, 13,* 501-540.

Wekerle, C., & Wolfe, D. A. (1998). Windows for preventing child and partner abuse: Early childhood and adolescence. In P. K. Trickett & C. J. Schellenbach (Eds.), *Violence against children in the family and the community* (pp. 339-369). Washington, DC: American Psychological Association.

Wells, R. D., McCann, J., Adams, J., Voris, J., & Ensign, J. (1995). Emotional, behavioral, and physical symptoms reported by parents of sexually abused, nonabused, and allegedly abused prepubescent females. *Child Abuse & Neglect, 19,* 155-163.

Wells, S. J. (1994a). Child protective services: Research for the future. *Child Welfare League of America, 123,* 431-447.

Wells, S. J. (1994b). The role of child protective services in responding to and preventing child deaths. *The APSAC Advisor, 7*(4), 31-34.

Wesch, D., & Lutzker, J. R. (1991). A comprehensive 5-year evaluation of Project 12-Ways: An ecobehavioral program for treating and preventing child abuse and neglect. *Journal of Family Violence, 6,* 17-35.

Westra, B., & Martin, H. P. (1981). Children of battered women. *Maternal Child Nursing, 10,* 41-54.

Whipple, E. E., & Webster-Stratton, C. (1991). The role of parental stress in physically abusive families. *Child Abuse & Neglect, 15,* 279-291.

Widom, C. S. (1989). Does violence beget violence? A critical examination of the literature. *Psychological Bulletin, 106,* 3-28.

Widom, C. S. (1995, March). Victims of childhood sexual abuse: Later criminal consequences. *National Institute of Justice,* 1-8.

Widom, K. S. (1989). Child abuse, neglect, and violent criminal behavior. *Criminology, 27,* 251-271.

Wiehe, V. R. (1990). *Sibling abuse: Hidden physical, emotional, and sexual trauma.* Lexington, MA: Lexington Books.

Wiehe, V. R. (1996). *Working with child abuse and neglect: A primer.* Thousand Oaks, CA: Sage.

Wiehe, V. R. (1997). *Sibling abuse* (2nd ed.). Thousand Oaks, CA: Sage.

Wiese, D., & Daro, D. (1995). *Current trends in child abuse reporting and fatalities: The results of the 1994 annual fifty state survey.* Chicago: National Committee to Prevent Child Abuse.

Wild, N. J. (1989). Prevalence of child sex rings. *Pediatrics, 83,* 553-558.

Wildin, S. R., Williamson, W., & Wilson, G. S. (1991). Children of battered women: Developmental and learning profile. *Clinical Pediatrics, 30,* 299-302.

Williams, K. R. (1992). Social sources of marital violence and deterrence: Testing an integrated theory of assaults between partners. *Journal of Marriage and the Family, 54,* 620-629.

Williams, K. R., & Hawkins, R. (1989). Controlling male aggression in intimate relationships. *Law and Society Review, 23,* 591-612.

Williams, L. M. (1994). Recall of childhood trauma: A prospective study of women's memories. *Journal of Consulting and Clinical Psychology, 62,* 1167-1176.

Williams, L. M., & Finkelhor, D. (1990). The characteristics of incestuous fathers: A review of recent studies. In W. L. Marshall, D. R. Laws, & H. E. Barbaree (Eds.), *Handbook of sexual assault: Issues, theories, and treatment of the offender* (pp. 231-255). New York: Plenum.

Williams, M. B. (1993). Assessing the traumatic impact of child sexual abuse: What makes it more severe? *Journal of Child Sexual Abuse, 2,* 41-59.

Williamson, J. M., Borduin, C. M., & Howe, B. A. (1991). The ecology of adolescent maltreatment: A multilevel examination of adolescent physical abuse, sexual abuse, and neglect. *Journal of Consulting and Clinical Psychology, 59,* 449-457.

Willis, D. J., & Silovsky, J. (1998). Prevention of violence at the societal level. In P. K. Trickett & C. J. Schellenbach (Eds.), *Violence against children in the family and the community* (pp. 401-416). Washington, DC: American Psychological Association.

Wincze, J. P., Bansal, S., & Malamud, M. (1986). Effects of medroxyproesterone acetate on subjective arousal, arousal to erotic stimulation and nocturnal penile tumescence in male sex offenders. *Archives of Sexual Behavior, 15,* 293-305.

Wind, T. W., & Silvern, L. (1992). Type and extent of child abuse as predictors of adult functioning. *Journal of Family Violence, 7,* 261-281.

Wind, T. W., & Silvern, L. (1994). Parenting and family stress as mediators of the long-term effects of child abuse. *Child Abuse & Neglect, 18,* 439-453.

Witt, D., & Sheinwald, J. (1992). *The family empowerment program: A social group work model of long-term, intensive, and innovative strategies to reduce the incidence of chronic neglect for at risk parents* (Project report from FY88 Grant No. 90CA1392, National Center on Child Abuse and Neglect). Pontiac, MI: Oakland Family Services.

Wodarski, J. S., Kurtz, P. D., Gaudin, J. M., & Howing, P. T. (1990). Maltreatment and the school age child: Major academic, socioemotional, and adaptive outcomes. *Social Work, 35,* 506-513.

Wolfe, D. A. (1987). *Child abuse: Implications for child development and psychopathology.* Newbury Park, CA: Sage.

Wolfe, D. A. (1991). *Preventing physical and emotional abuse of children.* New York: Guilford.

Wolfe, D. A., Edwards, B., Manion, I., & Koverola, C. (1988). Early intervention for parents at risk of child abuse and neglect: A preliminary investigation. *Journal of Consulting and Clinical Psychology, 56,* 40-47.

Wolfe, D. A., & Mosk, M. D. (1983). Behavioral comparisons of children from abusive and distressed families. *Journal of Consulting and Clinical Psychology, 51,* 702-708.

Wolfe, D. A., & Wekerle, C. (1993). Treatment strategies for child physical abuse and neglect: A critical progress report. *Clinical Psychology Review, 13,* 473-500.

Wolfe, D. A., Wolfe, V. V., & Best, C. L. (1988). Child victims of sexual abuse. In V. B. Van Hasselt, R. L. Morrison, A. S. Bellack, & M. Hersen (Eds.), *Handbook of family violence* (pp. 157-185). New York: Plenum.

Wolfe, D. A., Zak, L., Wilson, S. K., & Jaffe, P. G. (1986). Child witnesses to violence between parents: Critical issues in behavioral and social adjustment. *Journal of Abnormal Child Psychology, 14,* 95-104.

Wolfgang, M. E., & Ferracuti, F. (1972). *Delinquency in a birth cohort.* London: Tavistock.

Wolfner, G. D., & Gelles, R. J. (1993). A profile of violence toward children: A national study. *Child Abuse & Neglect, 17,* 197-212.

Wolock, T., & Horowitz, B. (1984). Child maltreatment as a social problem: The neglect of neglect. *American Journal of Orthopsychiatry, 54,* 530-542.

Worling, J. R. (1995). Adolescent sibling-incest offenders: Differences in family and individual functioning when compared to adolescent nonsibling sex offenders. *Child Abuse & Neglect, 19,* 633-643.

Wozencraft, T., Wagner, W., & Pellegrin, A. (1991). Depression and suicidal ideation in sexually abused children. *Child Abuse & Neglect, 15,* 505-511.

Wurtele, S. K. (1993). The role of maintaining telephone contact with parents during the teaching of a personal safety program. *Journal of Child Sexual Abuse, 2*(1), 65-82.

Wurtele, S. K., Kast, L. C., & Melzer, A. M. (1994). Sexual abuse prevention education for young children: A comparison of teachers and parents as instructors. *Child Abuse & Neglect, 16,* 865-876.

Wurtele, S. K., Kvaternick, M., & Franklin, C. F. (1992). Sexual abuse prevention for preschoolers: A survey of parents' behaviors, attitudes, and beliefs. *Journal of Child Sexual Abuse, 1,* 113-128.

Wurtele, S. K., & Miller-Perrin, C. L. (1992). *Preventing child sexual abuse: Sharing the responsibility.* Lincoln: University of Nebraska Press.

Wyatt, G. E. (1985). The sexual abuse of Afro-American and White-American women in childhood. *Child Abuse & Neglect, 9,* 507-519.

Wyatt, G. E. (1994). Sociocultural and epidemiological issues in the assessment of domestic violence. *Journal of Social Distress and the Homeless, 3,* 7-21.

Yanagida, E. H., & Ching, J. W. (1993). MMPI profiles of child abusers. *Journal of Clinical Psychology, 49,* 569-576.

Yesavage, J. A., & Widrow, L. (1985). Early parental discipline and adult self-destructive acts. *Journal of Nervous and Mental Disease, 17,* 74-77.

Yorukoglu, A., & Kemph, J. P. (1966). Children not severely damaged by incest with a parent. *Journal of American Academy of Child Psychiatry, 5,* 111-124.

Young, R. E., Bergandi, T. A., & Titus, T. G. (1994). Comparison of the effects of sexual abuse on male and female latency-aged children. *Journal of Interpersonal Violence, 9,* 291-306.

Youngblade, L. M., & Belsky, J. (1990). Social and emotional consequences of child maltreatment. In R. T. Ammerman & M. Hersen (Eds.), *Children at risk: An evaluation of factors contributing to child abuse and neglect* (pp. 109-140). New York: Plenum.

Yuan, Y. T., & Struckman-Johnson, D. L. (1991). Placement outcomes for neglected children with prior placements in family preservation programs. In K. Wells & D. E. Biegel (Eds.), *Family preservation services: Research and evaluation* (pp. 92-118). Newbury Park, CA: Sage.

Zigler, E., & Hall, N. W. (1989). Child abuse in America. In D. Cicchetti & V. Carlson (Eds.), *Child maltreatment: Theory and research on the causes and consequences of child abuse and neglect* (pp. 38-75). San Francisco: Jossey-Bass.

Zingraff, M. T., Leiter, J., Myers, K. A., & Johnsen, M. C. (1993). Child maltreatment and youthful problem behavior. *Criminology, 31*(2), 173-202.

Zuckerman, B., & Bresnahan, K. (1991). Developmental and behavioral consequences of prenatal drug and alcohol exposure. *Pediatric Clinics of North America, 38,* 1387-1406.

Zuravin, S. J. (1986). Residential density and urban child maltreatment: An aggregate analysis. *Journal of Family Violence, 1,* 307-322.

Zuravin, S. J. (1988a). Child abuse, child neglect, and maternal depression: Is there a connection? In National Center on Child Abuse and Neglect (Ed.), *Child neglect monograph: Proceedings from a symposium.* Washington, DC: Clearinghouse on Child Abuse and Neglect Information.

Zuravin, S. J. (1988b). Child maltreatment and teenage first births: A relationship mediated by chronic sociodemographic stress? *American Journal of Orthopsychiatry, 50,* 91-103.

Zuravin, S. J. (1989). The ecology of child abuse and neglect: Review of the literature and presentation of data. *Violence and Victims, 4*(2), 101-120.

Zuravin, S. J. (1991). Research definitions of child physical abuse and neglect: Current problems. In R. H. Starr, Jr. & D. A. Wolfe (Eds.), *The effects of child abuse and neglect: Research issues* (pp. 100-128). New York: Guilford.

Zuravin, S. J., & DiBlasio, F. A. (1992). Child-neglecting adolescent mothers: How do they differ from their nonmaltreating counterparts? *Journal of Interpersonal Violence, 7,* 471-487.

Zuravin, S. J., & Grief, G. L. (1989). Normative and child-maltreating AFDC mothers. *Social Casework: The Journal of Contemporary Social Work, 74,* 76-84.

Zuravin, S. J., & Taylor, R. (1987). *Family planning behaviors and child care adequacy: Final report.* Washington, DC: Department of Health and Human Services, Office of Population Affairs.

Author Index

Subject Index

About the Authors

Cindy L. Miller-Perrin is Associate Professor of Psychology at Pepperdine University in Malibu, California. After receiving her doctorate in clinical psychology from Washington State University, she completed a postdoctoral fellowship at the University of Washington, where she was involved in research and clinical work with developmentally delayed children. Her major research and publications are on child sexual abuse, and she has had a variety of experiences working with maltreated children and their families. She has coauthored two books including *Child Sexual Abuse: Sharing the Responsibility* (with S. Wurtele) and *Family Violence Across the Lifespan* (with O. Barnett and R. Perrin).

Robin D. Perrin is Associate Professor of Sociology at Pepperdine University in Malibu, California. He received his doctorate in sociology from Washington State University in 1989. Following his doctoral studies, he was Assistant Professor of Sociology at Seattle Pacific University in Seattle, Washington. His research interests and publications are in the area of deviant behavior and the sociology of religion. He has coauthored two books, *Deviance: Being, Behaving, and Branding* (with D. Ward and T. Carter) and *Family Violence Across the Lifespan* (with O. Barnett and C. Miller-Perrin). He has also served as Assistant Editor of the *Journal for the Scientific Study of Religion.*